WOODROW WILSON AND WORLD WAR I
1917–1921

The
New American Nation Series

EDITED BY

HENRY STEELE COMMAGER

AND

RICHARD B. MORRIS

WOODROW WILSON
AND
WORLD WAR I
1917 ★ 1921

ROBERT H. FERRELL

1817

HARPER & ROW, PUBLISHERS, New York
Cambridge, Philadelphia, San Francisco, London,
Mexico City, São Paulo, Singapore, Sydney

For PFC Ernest H. Ferrell, Sr., AEF
defensive sector, Oise-Aisne, Meuse-Argonne

Photo credits appear on page 346.

WOODROW WILSON AND WORLD WAR I, 1917–1921. Copyright © 1985 by Robert H.
Ferrell. All rights reserved. Printed in the United States of America. No part of this
book may be used or reproduced in any manner whatsoever without written permis-
sion except in the case of brief quotations embodied in critical articles and reviews.
For information address Harper & Row, Publishers, Inc., 10 East 53rd Street, New
York, N.Y. 10022. Published simultaneously in Canada by Fitzhenry & Whiteside
Limited, Toronto.

FIRST EDITION

Maps by John Hollingsworth

Library of Congress Cataloging in Publication Data
Ferrell, Robert H.
　Woodrow Wilson and World War I, 1917–1921.

　　Bibliography: p.
　　Includes index.
　　1. World War, 1914–1918—United States. 2. Wilson,
Woodrow, 1856–1924. 3. United States—Politics and
government—1913–1921. 4. United States—Foreign
relations—1913–1921.　I. Title.
D619.F34 1985　　　940.3′73　　　84-48160
ISBN 0-06-011229-8　　　　　85 86 87 88 89 HC 10 9 8 7 6 5 4 3 2 1
ISBN 0-06-091216-2 (pbk.)　　85 86 87 88 89 HC 10 9 8 7 6 5 4 3 2 1

Contents

Illustrations

MAPS

Editors' Introduction

THIRTY years ago Arthur S. Link, now editor of *The Papers of Woodrow Wilson*, introduced the New American Nation series with a volume on *Woodrow Wilson and the Progressive Era*. In our introduction to that authoritative work we promised that it would be "followed by a volume on the First World War and the collapse of Wilsonian idealism and internationalism." With the advantage of a longer perspective and a prodigious treasure of documents and monographs, Robert Ferrell has now redeemed that promise.

So different are the stories that Link and Ferrell have to tell that they seem, on the surface at least, almost to defy historical continuity. In the whole of the earlier history of the presidency only James Madison was confronted with a comparable shift in the currents of politics from placid to turbulent, and, since Wilson, only Franklin Roosevelt. Madison's talents were adapted to the pursuits of peace, not war, and his second administration was a failure. While Roosevelt displayed the same genius in war as in peace, it was Wilson's misfortune that, though his rhetoric was moving, his skills consummate, and his judgment sound in domestic affairs, all these failed him confronting the challenges of war and diplomacy, at home and abroad.

The special virtues of Ferrell's history are first, a style which felicitously combines lively narrative and pungent analysis and which gives the reader a sense of being a spectator in the world-shaking events which parade before him, and enables him to understand their complexity and their significance. On the battlefront he properly focuses on the impact of the American forces in the resolution of the world conflict. From Belleau Wood to Meuse-Argonne the agonies and triumphs of Pershing's AEF are graphically depicted, while the problems of separate command are viewed from both the American and the Allied perspectives. The mobilization of the home front and the problems of supply and logistics have seldom been examined in such rich detail, with credits and debits acutely distributed.

A second virtue of Ferrell's book is a judiciousness at once sympathetic and critical: sympathy with a stricken scholar-statesman who knew he was right—and was more often than not—but could not win either foreign statesmen or domestic politicians to his view; critical of a leader unable to bridge the gap between lofty ideals of democracy for the world at large and justice at home in the realm of civil liberties, the latter exemplified by the "Red scare" and the President's scant attention to the claims of the blacks who fought with the whites, but in segregated divisions, to "make the world safe for democracy."

For the historical philosopher, as for the dramatist and moralist, the second Wilson administration holds a special fascination. For President Wilson not only presided over the irrevocable end of isolation in his own country, but, together with Lloyd George, Clemenceau, and Lenin—and millions of unwitting victims—over one of the great climacterics of history. Wilson had embraced the first of Churchill's commandments: "In war, Resolution," but not the second, "In victory, Magnanimity."

HENRY STEELE COMMAGER
RICHARD B. MORRIS

Acknowledgments

NO one can write without the help of friends, and I am much indebted to Daniel R. Beaver, Martha E. Beier, Lenore Bradley, Edward H. Buehrig, John Garry Clifford, Edward M. Coffman, John Milton Cooper, Jr., Calvin D. Davis, James E. Hewes, Jr., Michael J. Hogan, Robert J. Maddox, Robert K. Murray, Forrest C. Pogue, Donald Smythe, Roland N. Stromberg, David F. Trask, Stephen L. Vaughn, John E. Wilz, Kurt Wimer. Emily Morison Beck opened the diary of her father, Samuel Eliot Morison. Russell H. Bostert lent his manuscript about his Williams College colleague, Richard A. Newhall. Brigadier General James L. Collins, Jr., allowed use of the diary and papers of his father who was General Pershing's aide. Eugene Davidson responded to an arcane query. I greatly benefited from conversation with John W. Davidson, and from his library of Peace Conference materials. Edward G. Duffy lent a manuscript biography of his father, Francis Joseph Duffy. Howard Gotlieb and Wilton B. Fowler helped with the Edward M. House diary, and I am especially indebted to Howard for a kindness that made my task much easier. Roger Hilsman shared a story that his father told about working for Pershing in the twenties. Philip C. Jessup permitted quotation from wartime letters to his parents. Jan Shipps lent a copy of a manuscript. Richard J. Sommer opened the World War I collection in the U.S. Army's Military History Institute at Carlisle Barracks. Nicolas Spulber explained the post-World War I recession. John Hollingsworth drew the maps.

The editor of The Papers of Woodrow Wilson, and dean of Wilson studies, Arthur S. Link, allowed use of materials in his office in the Firestone Library at Princeton, especially the diary of the President's White House physician, Cary T. Grayson, and the manuscript biography of the President by his brother-in-law, Stockton Axson. He also made it possible for me to read forthcoming wartime volumes of the Wilson Papers. And let me thank him, too, for a wonderfully close examination of the present manuscript, catching errors that somehow had gotten by. David W. Hirst, associate editor of the Wilson Papers, has been of assistance on many occasions over the years. And I do want to thank the other present members of the Wilson Papers project: John E. Little, Fredrick Aandahl, Manfred F. Boemeke, Phyllis Marchand, and Margaret D. Link.

The editors of the New American Nation series, Henry Steele Commager and Richard B. Morris, are no nominal editors, and have read drafts, not simply the book's final version. It is impossible to thank them enough.

Hugh Van Dusen and Janet Goldstein, and before them Corona Machemer and Liza Pulitzer, have been the best of editors at Harper & Row. And special thanks to William Monroe, also of Harper.

Lila and Carolyn, too, again.

CHAPTER 1

April 1917

ON the evening of April 2, 1917, a soft spring rain was falling in Washington, darkening the sky and setting the scene in somber splendor as President Woodrow Wilson, escorted by a troop of cavalry, drove up the hill to the Capitol to ask for war. The colonnaded building was aglow, illuminated by the floodlights that have made its white dome a part of the city's prospect at night. As the President passed by, soldiers and Marines stood at attention. Thousands of citizens watched and waved little flags. Pacifists gazed sadly toward the man who had gained reelection a few months before with such slogans as "He kept us out of war" and "War in the East, peace in the West, thank God for Wilson."

Once inside the Capitol the President made his way to the room reserved for him, where he paused to prepare for his ordeal. Alone except for Ellery Sedgwick, editor of the *Atlantic Monthly*, unaware of the latter's observing eye, he walked to a little fireplace over which hung a large mirror, and stared into it, distraught, chin shaking, face flushed. He placed his left elbow on the mantel and gazed steadily at himself, until he composed his features. Then he strode into the corridor and through the swinging doors of the House chamber.[1] The time was 8:32.

Speaker Champ Clark gaveled the audience to order: "Gentlemen, the President of the United States!"

Everyone rose, applauding, as Wilson made his way to the rostrum, where he nervously fingered the note cards of his address. As soon as people on the floor and in the galleries—members of the

House and Senate, Supreme Court, Cabinet, diplomatic corps, distinguished guests—resumed their seats and the hall quieted, he began, in a low and husky voice.

The war message, as it became known, proved the greatest address the President ever made, and in long retrospect stands as one of the finest speeches of the present century. Wilson was one of the principal orators of his generation in an era still reverent of the golden age of oratory that had opened with Webster and Hayne, Calhoun and Clay. At Princeton University in the nineties and after the turn of the century he had transfixed students and, for a while, faculty. In a bare two years, 1911–13, in fair part because of his oratory, he had become governor of New Jersey, President of the United States.

The nation's Chief Executive knew what he wanted. In his first term in Washington, until the year in which he spoke for war, he had championed economic, social, and political reform, and pushed his measures through Congress, revealing himself as a master of American politics. In his second term this intelligent, principled, intense —and to his critics, imperious—man had determined to marshal the might of his country to end the carnage of the World War by bringing victory to the Allied Powers—Great Britain, France, Russia, Italy. He believed the war was in its final stages. American belligerency would shorten it. He then would organize peace for Europe and the world.[2] International affairs, he told the hushed throng, allowed no double moral standard for individuals and nations. "We are at the beginning of an age in which it will be insisted that the same standards of conduct and of responsibility for wrong done shall be observed . . . " Halfway, almost casually, he spoke words his generation would not forget: the world, he said, must be made safe for democracy. Deaf old Senator John Sharp Williams of Mississippi, whose father had been killed in the Battle of Shiloh defending the Confederacy, faintly heard the ringing phrase, grasped its meaning, and began to clap. Floor and galleries broke into a roar of applause.

The President's voice rose and fell. Many times the audience applauded. Senators waved small silk flags—a senator had presented each of his colleagues with a flag.

At last came the peroration. To address Congress on so fearful a subject, Wilson began, was a distressing and oppressive duty. Months of fiery trial and sacrifice lay ahead. "But the right is more precious than peace, and we shall fight for the things which we have always carried nearest our hearts—for democracy, for the right of those who submit to authority to have a voice in their own governments, for the rights and liberties of small nations, for a universal dominion of right by such a concert of free peoples as shall bring peace and safety to all nations and make the world itself at last free." To such a task Americans could dedicate life and fortune, spend blood and might for the principles that gave the nation birth and happiness and peace. "God helping her, she can do no other!"[3]

The war resolution passed the Senate on April 4 by 82 yeas to 6 nays, and in the early morning of Good Friday, April 6, passed the House, 373 to 50. A clerk delivered the document to the White House shortly after one o'clock that day. Wilson was at lunch with his wife and his cousin, Helen Bones, but quickly rose, went into a small room next to the main lobby, and signed the resolution that would send 50,000 men to their deaths.

Americans never before had made the sacrifices their government now was calling for. Two and a half years the country had remained at peace, watching with horror the trench fighting in France that killed and maimed hundreds of thousands of young men. In 1916 a futile contest between German and French armies for Verdun cost 350,000 lives. That same year on a gray May afternoon off Jutland, rippling flashes and the boom of distant guns heralded an equally futile contest between British and German fleets, turning ships into sheets of flame and towering pillars of smoke. Now America's men would be asked to take up arms, face the degradation of war, stare death in the face, and die on foreign soil.

And yet Wilson felt confident of the outcome, for he knew he was appealing to a far different nation than in Lincoln's time a half century earlier. Born in 1856 in Staunton, Virginia, he remembered the election of 1860 when men ran past his father's gate shouting that Lincoln had been elected, warning that war was in the offing. But fratricidal enmities of the past had disappeared, and by April 1917 the President of the United States was leader of perhaps the greatest nation in the world. In size of population, in sheer economic strength, no other country compared to the United States of America.

Just two years before, in 1915, population had reached 100 million, up from 3 million in the eighteenth century at the time of the Revolution, and larger than any of the European great powers save

Russia with its polyglot empire of 170 million. The American multi-plication table, the American penchant for producing large families, had been the primary cause of the population growth. Through the nineteenth century, average family size was 5. In 1900 it slackened, but not much—in 1910 it stood at 4.5; it did not fall to below break-even, 4, until 1940. Meanwhile immigration helped push up the census returns—between 1865 and 1916, 27 million people passed through Ellis Island or otherwise entered the United States. The 1910 census showed 13.5 million Americans born abroad, 18.8 million native-born with one or both parents born abroad. Of for-eign-born, 6 million came from Central and Eastern Europe, 4.2 million from Northwestern Europe, 1.5 million from Southern Europe, 1.4 million from the Western Hemisphere.[4]

That a third of America's 100 million consisted of immigrants or citizens of immigrant parentage became worrisome once World War I began, because of fear that foreign nations might prey on their divided loyalties. Some of the excessive patriotism—the "100 per cent Americanism"—of the era undoubtedly stemmed from this fear. "Absolute and Unqualified Loyalty to Our Country" flashed the huge electric sign above the Preparedness parade on New York's Fifth Avenue in 1916.[5] President Wilson had headed the Preparedness parade in Washington that year. Mrs. Wilson long remembered how young and vital he looked as he walked along at good pace, wearing white flannel trousers, blue sack coat, white shoes, white straw hat, carrying a flag a yard and a half long—"What a picture, as the breeze caught and carried out the Stars and Stripes!"[6] Doubts about the patriotism of immigrants dissolved after entrance into war showed them groundless.

In another measure of national power, the economy, no one raised a question in April 1917. For several decades America's in-dustry and agriculture had led the world. The smoking blast fur-naces and rolling mills of Pennsylvania, Ohio, and Alabama turned out 45 million tons of steel ingots and castings in 1917, compared with 26 million in 1910. Britain in 1917 produced 9.5 million. Every industrial gauge—railroad engines and cars, cement, textiles—told the same story. Trade magazines proclaimed American wares the best in the world. As a necessary adjunct to industrialization, Ameri-can agriculture produced more than enough to feed the urban pop-ulation. Although farm land in the trans-Appalachian West was not especially productive, with yields per acre well below those of European countries except Russia and notably below the farms of Germany, American farms were large and there were many of them. American farms were becoming mechanized, and by 1917 farmers represented a diminishing segment of the population, making up a quarter of the national work force. Thus the United States did not have to face the same pressures from agricultural interests as European countries that had to protect farmers by tariffs. Britain made no effort at protection and allowed agriculture to decline. By World War I, Western European countries were importing grain from Russia and Rumania, the British Isles from the Argentine, Australia, and India.

America's foreign trade had increased for a generation before 1917. In 1910 exports stood at $1.7 billion, imports $1.5 billion, with a favorable balance of $188 million, far different from preceding years when the country imported more than it sent out and balanced with foreign investment, for which it paid interest. In 1914–16, trade with the Allies climbed from $754 million to $2.7 billion, trade with Germany dropped from $345 million to $2 million. In 1917, exports rose to $6.2 billion, imports to $3 billion, a favorable balance of $3.2 billion. Gold and sales of foreign investments injected $5 billion into the economy in 1915–17, a substantial part of the national income ($60.4 billion in 1917), and created a boom. Some of the gold was capital in flight, most of it payment for war orders. It was too much, for the economy had expanded to near capacity without any restraint on consumer income, and prices inflated by half. A fair amount of increase in trade from 1910 to 1917 indicated inflation. Trade nonetheless was markedly up. War hastened London's decline as the world's financial center, its place taken by New York. At war's end American foreign investments still were small, and did not grow during the twenties, one of the reasons for the Great Depression of the thirties. But they too showed the financial shift: in 1897 they stood at $700 million; by 1914, $3.5 billion; by 1919, $7 billion.[7]

American products, mainly agricultural but increasingly industrial, went abroad in foreign ships, the merchant marine never having recovered after the destruction by Confederate raiders during the Civil War. Tonnage appeared impressive, 8.8 million gross tons in 1917, but 6.3 million was coastal or on the Great Lakes or rivers.[8]

For the average American, on the farm or in a town of 2,500 or more inhabitants (as were half of all Americans in 1917), industrialization had not yet produced much that Americans as a whole could consume immediately and thereby raise their standard of living. In 1917, the average hourly wage was $.364. Average weekly hours in manufacturing were 54.6, in a six-day week—which helped generate income, although not a great deal. Low hourly pay for all industries, including farm labor, made an average annual income of $830. Highest paid were clerical employees, laborers in manufacturing, and workers on steam railroads, $1,477. Schoolteachers received $648. Farm labor was far down, $481. The mass of Americans had not yet crossed the threshold into a consumer-oriented economy. As late as 1920 almost no farmhouses, and only one city house in ten, had electricity, which greatly limited the number of potential customers for refrigerators, washing machines, vacuum cleaners, electric irons, fans. For every hundred people in cities, thirteen possessed bathtubs and six had telephones.[9]

A few individuals lived much better. Most of them had built their mansions at Newport and Saratoga and along Fifth Avenue or on fashionable avenues in other cities—Euclid, in Cleveland—before the war, but some still were going up. The steel magnate Charles M. Schwab, who died penniless a generation later, was building an estate, Loretto, near his plant in Bethlehem, Pennsylvania, which he completed in 1919—a forty-four-room mansion, seventeen out-buildings, seventy employees, a thousand acres.

Because of low per-capita incomes, the rising price level in 1917 sorely worried the average wage earner. Prices had shot up (if 1913 equaled 100, 1917 reached 147.8). In the latter year five pounds of flour cost $.35, bread $.09, round steak $.29 a pound, bacon $.41, butter $.48, milk (delivered) $.22 a quart, coffee $.30 a pound, five pounds of sugar $.46, ten pounds of potatoes $.43. Eggs, surprisingly, cost $.48 a dozen, because of poverty of the breeds—also the frenetic manner in which chickens scurried about the barnyard, tiring themselves out.[10]

Curiously, the deprivations of the average American in the time of Woodrow Wilson and World War I had not produced any large-scale hatred of the controllers of industrial America—industrial owners, corporate managers, trade associations. After the strikes and violence and agricultural turmoil of the nineties, caused by the economy's doldrums after the Panic of 1893—a depression that was worldwide—enmity largely disappeared. Growth of labor unions made skilled laborers less sensitive to the size of corporations, more assured of their own position in the industrial scene. Engineers' associations and new agrarian organizations stressed cooperation instead of class conflict. War in Europe beginning in 1914 brought slightly better incomes, and the improvement helped convince Americans they bought from companies, not octopuses, and worked for firms, not trusts.[11]

The movement of American economic life away from the isolation of rural America, toward the interconnections of city life, had changed the nation's political concerns in the nineties, turning them from the trinity of issues since the Civil War: Reconstruction, tariff, civil service reform. The first sign of new interests appeared on the local scene, in municipal and state government—attacks on city bosses and venal state officials. People also questioned the bona fides of U.S. senators, elected indirectly by state legislatures, for many senators were none other than businessmen who either believed they should bring their talents into politics or felt with equal unction they should protect their businesses by occupying the seats of national power. It seemed necessary to let the people speak through direct election of senators, initiative, referendum, recall, direct primary, short and secret ballot. Just before World War I reformers on the state level sensed that legislation did not regulate and only defined interstices within which malefactors of great wealth carried out their purposes, and the result was a rapid increase in administrative bodies and regulatory commissions. Meanwhile, on the national scene, Presidents Theodore Roosevelt, Taft, and Wilson all espoused these progressive causes, and T.R. and Wilson enjoyed remarkable legislative success and popular acclaim.

Then such domestic preoccupations came to a halt and Americans entered a war caused by forces and factors that reached far back in European history—the very history that they or their ancestors hoped to escape by coming to the New World. Causes of World War I were linked to the Napoleonic Wars and their aftermath, especially unification of Germany in the latter nineteenth century. Nationalism was the major source of trouble, to a lesser extent the alliances that joined the Germans (population 65 million) and Austro-Hungarians (30 million) in opposition to the Russians (170 million) and French (39 million). For a while the British (48 million) remained in isolation, and as late as midsummer 1914 were still indecisive regarding their position in the opposing alliances. This led the Germans to believe they could support the Austrians in a small war against

Serbia (where leading government figures had conspired in the murder of Archduke Francis Ferdinand) and to reason that even if the Russians and French fought against them, the British would not.

As Americans watched the dangerous politics of the Continent in the years before their involvement, they cherished the advice of Presidents Washington and Jefferson and took refuge in two antithetical views of international affairs that were to baffle Europeans. One was that force was entirely justified for solving insurmountable political problems. Americans accepted war because it had assisted national growth. And yet—the second of their views—they feared involvement in World War I. They believed that as a nation they would disgrace themselves by resort to force. The mission of America was to save the world, not destroy it. Beginning in the eighties they had supported Pan-American conferences, arbitration and conciliation treaties, the First and Second Hague Peace conferences (1899, 1907), and anticipated a third, which unhappily failed to meet because of World War I.[12] As late as April 1, 1917, probably a majority of Americans favored peace. They felt that while their government could perhaps have avoided the war, the war ought somehow to have avoided America. Senator Reed Smoot of Utah wrote on April 6, 1917: "This war is a very unpopular one. I believe a majority of the people are opposed to it. I am still receiving many protests from all parts of the country."[13]

Historians of American neutrality from August 1914 until April 1917 have often found it tempting to show how events changed policy: Germany's invasion of Belgium in 1914 contrary to the treaty of neutrality of 1837, destruction of the university library at Louvain and killing of civilians on the pretext that they were ununiformed snipers, execution of 5,000 hostages during the Belgian occupation, and a submarine policy that, unlike the equally illegal British blockade, killed people in torpedoings at sea; and all the while, the gradual infiltration of what a later generation described as British propaganda but in fact was the bond of a common language and heritage binding American to Briton.[14]

But for the nation to go to war a catalyst was necessary, and it proved none other than President Wilson, whom everyone had presumed to be as neutral as it was possible to be. Wilson, it now is clear, was unneutral from the beginning. He waited for sentiment to change so that forces and factors positioned themselves in such a way that a careful Chief Executive could reasonably make a move.

Madison had done this before the War of 1812 and referred to it in *Federalist* No. 10. As early as August 1914, Wilson told his brother-in-law, Stockton Axson, that a German victory would be a disaster to the world, for it would mean universal militarism. "The United States, itself, will have to become a military nation, for Germany will push her conquests into South America, if not actually into the United States." His personal sympathies, he said, were all with the Allies. He did not believe the German problem was the Kaiser, controlled by the military. The old system, diplomatic and military, was at fault. Germany had been on the verge of conquering the world commercially, but the General Staff saw a shortcut, a chance to dispose of opponents one by one—the British would not oppose Germany.[15] In December 1915 the President heard his minister to Belgium, Brand Whitlock, say that he, the minister, was heart and soul for the Allies. "So am I," was the response. "No decent man, knowing the situation and Germany, could be anything else. But that is only my own personal opinion and there are many others in this country who do not hold that opinion. In the West and Middle West frequently there is no opinion at all. I am not justified in forcing my opinion upon the people of the United States and bringing them into a war which they do not understand."[16]

Several years later, during the Paris Peace Conference, the President was lunching with Axson and said he never had liked German ways and was the only one of the principal Allied statesmen at Paris, the Big Four, who had been always and consistently anti-German. During graduate school days at Johns Hopkins in the eighties when friends were "hypnotized by German scholarship and German philosophy," he was "a lonely rebel." In all the work of reorganization and reformation at Princeton as president of the university from 1902 until 1910, he was out of sympathy with German principles of education. "I have never liked the way the German mind works, nor have I been sympathetic with the German character. So out of sympathy am I with things German that, as you know, I never visited Germany in my summer vacations when I used to go to England and sometimes to France."[17]

Publicly the President maintained he was against his country's entrance into war. He went to great lengths to display his neutrality, and was so explicit that one must believe he did it not to win reelection, or to side with the majority of his countrymen who hated entering the war, but because he wished to stand aside from the war spirit in Europe, rather than succumb to emotion. The President possessed an uncanny ability to prevent his emotions from affecting his policies. Sometimes, as in 1916, British practices of pressing neutral commerce, such as blacklisting American firms suspected of trading with the Central Powers, drove Wilson almost to real impartiality. In August 1914 he declared the war a natural raking-out of the Continent's pent-up jealousies, with which the United States had no concern. The *Lusitania* went down on May 7, 1915, with loss of 1,198 men, women, and children, including 128 Americans. Three days later he stood before a crowd of several thousand newly naturalized citizens in Philadelphia and said that "there is such a thing as a man being too proud to fight." On February 26, 1916, he announced that America "ought to keep out of this war." The only reason for entering would be "this single thing upon which her character and history are founded, her sense of humanity and justice." When this would stand revealed he did not say, and described how valor withheld itself "from all small implications and entanglements and waits for the great opportunity, when the sword will flash as if it carried the light of heaven upon its blade." Shortly afterward he told the League to Enforce Peace that the World War was far away and "With its causes and objects we are not concerned." In a note of December 1916 offering mediation between Allies and Central Powers, he infuriated the British government by saying that the objects of both sides were "virtually the same." As late as January 4, 1917, he confided to his close friend and adviser Colonel Edward M. House: "There will be no war. This country does not intend to become involved in this war."[18]

In the winter of 1916–17, just before the Russian Revolution of March 1917 that deposed the Tsar, and of course before American entrance, history may have reached a point where, if it were possible to play out events again, matters might have gone differently. A few years after the war Lord Grey confided to House that he had come to believe that the world would have been better off if the powers had made peace. Germany, he said, would probably have overthrown the Kaiser and become a democracy, and would have remained strong enough to maintain it. The Germans would have seen their military plans fail, and the lesson would have been enough, without the terrible destruction wrought in the war's final two years.[19]

At that moment the German government thought it could win,

and on the last day of January 1917 played what it believed its winning card. Its ambassador in Washington, Count Johann von Bernstorff, advised the American government that the next day Germany would commence unrestricted submarine warfare against ships entering and departing the British Isles.

The German government was not really acting against the United States but had determined to end the war's stalemate by starving the people of Britain, by cutting off Argentine and Australian food-stuffs. It was impossible not to extend the prohibition to American shipping, else the United States would provision the British. The German government anticipated American belligerency but expected no dire result. The U.S. Army was an insignificant force, smaller than the army of Portugal. If the Americans raised an army they could not train it and transport it to Europe in less than eighteen months. "And they won't come, either, because our submarines will sink them," the Minister of Marine, Admiral Eduard von Capelle, informed a committee of the Reichstag. Addition of the U.S. Navy to Allied naval forces would not change anything; the Allies already possessed a preponderance of naval force. America's military significance, Capelle said, would be "zero, zero, zero." In five months from February 1917 submarines around the British Isles would sink 600,000 tons of Allied and neutral shipping each month and win the war.

The German note of January 31 turned out to be the worst card the government in Berlin could have played. It changed the President's public position. He had thought out his course in detail in 1915 during a controversy over torpedoing of the British ship *Arabic,* when the Germans similarly had sought to wage unrestricted submarine warfare—sinking ships on sight, without provision for safety of passengers and crew. At that time he was courting the widow of a Washington jeweler, Mrs. Edith Bolling Galt, after his wife, Ellen Axson, died the month war began. Every day he wrote long handwritten letters to Edith. Sometimes he sent important government documents, and wrote about them as well as affairs of the heart. Mrs. Galt seems to have questioned him about German policy, and in reply he accused her of Bryanism, accommodation to the ideas of his recently departed Secretary of State, William Jennings Bryan, who had resigned rather than send a second and severe note to Germany after sinking of the *Lusitania.* "But you came near being corrupted there, young lady, by *Bryanism!*" he wrote. "It was your friend W.J.B. who took the ground that we must let Americans understand that they took passage on British ships, or any other ships owned by belligerents, at their own risk and peril. Beware of heresies! . . . we must base our claims of right on the undoubted practice of nations—for which Germany is showing such crass and brutal contempt. The road is hard to travel, but it lies plain before us."[20] By early March 1917 the President was hinting at what would happen. "We are provincials no longer," he remarked in his second inaugural. "The tragical events of the thirty months of vital turmoil through which we have just passed have made us citizens of the world. There can be no turning back. Our own fortunes as a nation are involved, whether we would have it so or not."

Had Machiavelli rather than a higher morality inspired President Wilson in April 1917, he would not have asked Congress for war. Sinkings were mounting and the Allies approached the brink of disaster, with no recourse other than to ask Germany for terms. But Wilson was in temperament an activist, "never satisfied with mere speculation or willing to apply slow-working remedies, but driven as if by demons . . . to achieve immediate and ideal solutions."[21] If the American people were bewildered, he knew their desire to stand up to Germany. It was Woodrow Wilson who carried that feeling to its logical conclusion.

CHAPTER 2

War

WHEN the United States entered World War I, the Allies stood in dire peril of failure—of losing the war. Fighting on the Western Front had stalemated. The Battle of Verdun had turned into a pounding battle of attrition in which the French Army lost hundreds of thousands of men, far more than it could afford, with German losses bearable only because Germany's population was half again that of France. The battle had commenced early in 1916 when the Imperial German Army captured two forts in front of the city, and ended months later with French recapture of the forts— by that time useless mounds of rubble with thousands of attackers and defenders entombed inside. Meanwhile the British Army had won 125 square miles of watery, useless ground along the Somme in fighting that took all summer.

The sheer weariness of both the British and French armies could be observed everywhere in the west as the new year, 1917, opened. The war promised to go on forever. Of what avail its inhuman losses? Allied and German troops that had begun fighting in August 1914 were mostly dead or else invalided home, replaced by conscript levies that reached into nearly every family in all three nations. Whatever the patriotism still evident on home fronts, where people said they were proud to have contributed their "boys" to the fray, life in the trenches was unbelievably squalid, what with rain, mud, rats, incessant roar of artillery, bad food, few decent places to sleep, accumulating human filth. Germany lay under a tight governmental control that reached out from Berlin, and perhaps it was German discipline at home as well as on the fronts that avoided open criticism of what was taking place. In France and England, societies less disciplined, morale was obviously slipping.

Verdun and the Somme bore messages of stalemate. The German Army was proving invincible. It fought on internal lines, easily shuttling from Russian front to Western Front. It was well, even brilliantly, led—as compared with the British and French, whose generals seemed able only to strut and pose, incapable of planning anything other than frontal attacks on impregnable positions or stupid battles of attrition. Early in 1917 the just-announced German submarine offensive promised to shut off Britain's food supply. In March a revolution in Petrograd displaced the Tsar and proclaimed a republic, a point much remarked by observers in Britain and the United States, but a sign of weakness rather than strength, evidence that government in Russia was insecure, that disorder might lead to chaos, forcing withdrawal of the Russian armed forces from the war —a prospect that became more evident as the year advanced, and turned into reality in November. The Bolshevik Revolution would enable Germany to concentrate its troops on the Western Front.

When the United States entered the war in April, the question became just what the U.S. Army could contribute to this rapidly deteriorating scene. It was not much of a question, for the U.S. Army was not much of a force. A minuscule organization with an aging officer corps and no experience in modern war, it was so weak that the European belligerents did not consider it a military force —among armies of the world it ranked seventeenth.[1] On April 1, it was able to muster 5,791 officers and 121,797 enlisted men. And from this group the War Department could have organized a mobile force, capable of fighting overseas, of only 24,000 and could have provided only enough ammunition for a day and a half. Rolls of the National Guard listed an additional 181,620 officers and men, of whom 80,446 had been called to federal service.

The Army in April 1917 was a home for old soldiers, a quiet, sleepy place where they killed time until they began drawing their pensions. Most officers above the rank of captain had entered the service before the Spanish-American War. Until just before the World War the Army was dominated by Civil War veterans, the last of whom, Colonel John Clem, the famed drummer boy of Shiloh, retired in August 1915. The officers of 1917 had grown up with old soldiers. Brigadier General Michael J. Lenihan saw U.S. Grant at West Point, and Sheridan and Sherman.[2] His experience was typical; Major General Charles D. Rhodes, while at the Academy, "presented arms" to the impressive funeral cortege of Grant, passed in cadet-review before the dashing Sheridan, received his diploma from the hands of a smiling Sherman. The Civil War was everywhere in the Army, and Rhodes looked forward to a humdrum life at a frontier post "where gray-haired captains were wont to gather daily about the post-trader's stove and chew plug-cut tobacco as they recited tales of their Civil War experiences."[3] Officers remembered soldiers older than the veterans of 1861–65; Peyton March recalled one of his early commanders, Colonel Horatio G. Gates, who had seen service in the Mexican War. Promotions were excruciatingly slow. Hunter Liggett remained a lieutenant for eighteen years. In October 1915, George C. Marshall was almost thirty-five years old. He had been in the Army since 1901, was a first lieutenant, and considered getting out.

Prior to April 1917, President Wilson seemingly took little interest in the Army, and he certainly was unwilling to change it. His first Secretary of War, Lindley M. Garrison of New Jersey, resigned early in 1916 because he could not get the President to effect any improvement. In place of the National Guard, Garrison proposed an auxiliary force that he called the Continental Army; but the Guard was a highly political organization, and Wilson deserted him on the issue and made peace with its many congressional supporters. Garrison's predecessor, Henry L. Stimson, years later after World War II described the President's behavior as a plain surrender.[4]

What could one expect from this unprepossessing organization? The Germans made up their minds that the Americans could do nothing to affect the course of the war.

What then happened, mobilization of a huge army of enormous fighting power, its transport to France in the nick of time to give a great victory to the Allies, is in retrospect simply amazing, one of the wonders of the present century, a development no seer could have foretold. It is not too much to say that creation of a great American fighting army, the American Expeditionary Forces, was the most decisive act by any nation in the war, the single act that determined the defeat of Imperial Germany in November 1918. If the Wilson administration had done nothing else in 1917–18 other than create the AEF, its reputation in history would have been assured. Had the Germans understood what sort of demonic force they were loosing in the United States, they never would have thrown down the challenge over submarine warfare; they would have made peace with Britain and France as quickly as possible, on the best terms they could get. Something protean, inexplicable in origin, moved the Americans. The reaction to the German challenge in April 1917 seems to have been instinctive—they would meet force with force. They did not know how they would equip the troops, how they would get them to Europe. They did not calculate, nor could they, how this army raised over the winter of 1917–18 would be ready to cross the Atlantic just when the Germans threatened to break through to victory on the Western Front in the fourth year of war. When the Soviet government made peace with Germany in the winter of 1917–18, surrendering what had been a second front, and Berlin moved troops from east to west and obtained a preponderance against the Allies, the German commander, General Erich Ludendorff, employed his new divisions in a series of blows that caved in the defensive line of the British Fifth Army and gave every evidence of a breakthrough. At that moment the Americans appeared.

When the United States went to war, the Wilson administration decided on a draft rather than volunteers, and here was the first move by which the war turned in favor of the Allies.[5] The British government had relied on volunteers until 1916, when it became evident that men who volunteered were often employed in jobs essential to the war and that the only fair way to raise a mass army was a draft. Before entrance into war, the administration moved slowly toward a draft; when someone proposed universal military service President Wilson countered with a proposal for universal voluntary service. Imminence of war brought a change of mind; on February 4, 1917, the President told Secretary of War Newton D. Baker he wanted a draft. He said nothing in public until after the war message and congressional resolution, but Judge Advocate General Enoch H. Crowder moved ahead with plans and Captain Hugh S. Johnson arranged for the Government Printing Office to produce necessary forms.

When the administration went to Congress for legislation, trouble arose, for key Democratic members in the House—speaker, floor leader, chairman of the Military Affairs Committee—refused support: Speaker Clark said he always had classed together the conscript and the convict! To introduce a bill it was necessary to turn to a Republican congressman, Julius Kahn of California. In the Upper House, a Democratic senator, James A. Reed of Missouri, predicted that blood would run in the streets if the government attempted to enforce a draft, just as in the Civil War. Senator Henry Cabot Lodge and other friends of ex-President Theodore Roosevelt took two weeks to amend the bill. They were stalling for time to authorize volunteer divisions of troops above and below draft age. Roosevelt, who had raised a volunteer regiment in the Spanish-American War, wanted to raise a division of volunteers now, even though Secretary Baker warned him a volunteer division would draw officers from units that needed them and create an elitism contrary to the basic idea of a democratic draft. After bitter debate both houses approved the Draft Bill by large majorities and the President signed it May 18.

The War Department organized the draft with care. Upon advice of Captain Johnson, who deserved much credit for the result, Crowder administered the draft from local polling places, which seemed less military than post offices, which the Army had used for recruiting. During World War II the Army again employed the polling place arrangement, and it lasted until the end of the draft in 1973. The Crowder-Johnson system went into effect June 5, 1917; between 7:00 a.m. and 7:00 p.m., 10 million young men, ages twenty-one to thirty inclusive, appeared at 4,000 polling places and registered before 12,000 registration board members aided by 125,000 registrars and assistants.

A series of lotteries followed, the first of which the War Department held on July 20, 1917. The method was fair and simple, and as with most games of chance fascinated the public. Each registrant had received a number, and numbers ran as high as 10,500, the total of men registered in the largest polling place. War Department officers placed each number in a small capsule and dropped it into a large glass bowl, and Secretary Baker, blindfolded, on July 20 pulled out the first one, number 258. For the next sixteen hours and forty-six minutes various officials received the honor of extracting fateful capsules, and drawing continued for all 10,500 numbers. After the Army took its first levy, it came back for more, a second drawing commenced, and another. In the drawing ceremonies the Army did its best to invoke patriotism. During the third lottery in September 1918, President Wilson extracted a capsule, wearing a blindfold made out of a strip of cloth from a chair used at the signing of the Declaration of Independence.

Eventually 23,908,576 men registered (not counting 325,445 in the territories), 44 percent of the male population. American manpower equaled that of Britain and France combined, and half as much again. Records showed 6,373,414 men available for service, of whom the Army accepted 2,702,687. Counting enlistments, a total of 4,271,150 men served in the Army in World War I: top strength, however, was 3.7 million. A total of 520,022 served in the Navy, including the Marine Corps. By the end of World War I, 4.8 million Americans had served in the military, 5 percent of the population, compared with 10 percent in the Civil War. World War I's smaller levy reflected the need for manpower in industry. Because of the draft's age restrictions and because of exemptions, few shortages arose of men essential to the civilian war effort.

Evasion ran to 11 percent—337,649—no figure to celebrate. Attorney General Thomas W. Gregory conducted dragnet raids to enforce the Selective Service Act, notably in New York City and vicinity. He used military personnel and members of a volunteer patriotic group, the American Protective League, to bring in "slackers," and the resultant outcry by newspapers such as the New York *World* and *The New York Times* gravely embarrassed the Wilson administration. Gregory wrote the President on September 9, 1918, that he took full responsibility and that it was impossible to round up draft dodgers individually.[6]

Authorities by mid-1919 had caught and dealt with half the evaders. For the others the government invoked a public punishment by listing names in newspapers. The champion draft evader proved a wealthy young man named Grover Cleveland Bergdoll, heir to a Philadelphia brewery fortune, who initially asked for exemption because he owned a farm.[7]

While the Army in midsummer 1917 enrolled its first levy it prepared to train them in camps known as cantonments, and by the end of the year it had housed, fed, and trained 1.8 million soldiers, equivalent to the population of Philadelphia. The War Department designated sixteen cantonments in northern states for the "National Army," its euphemism for units of drafted men. Another sixteen, mostly camps with tents, erected in the South for one-fourth the cost of wooden barracks, were for draft-swollen units of the National Guard. Each National Army cantonment quartered 40,000 men and cost $8 million. The basic military unit within a cantonment, a regiment of infantry, comprised 3,500 men and required twenty-two barracks. These frame structures accommodated 150 men. Each cantonment contained headquarters, quartermaster depot, kitchens, laundry, recreation facilities, post exchange (retail store), and base hospital of 1,000 beds. This meant 1,200 buildings per cantonment. In addition troops needed 5,000–11,000 acres for a rifle range and 2,000 acres for a drill ground. Constructing wooden cantonments was a gigantic undertaking. Across the United States twelve trains a day, each fifty cars long, brought in materials, and 50,000 carpenters and 150,000 other workmen labored incessantly, laying down enough roofing to cover Manhattan, Atlantic City, and a square mile more. Total Army construction costs to the time of the Armistice reached $800 million, and continuously occupied 200,000 civilian workers, or more than the combined strength of Union and Confederate armies at the Battle of Gettysburg.[8]

Camps sprang to life under the tread of their new residents, who learned the mysteries of the Army, a way of life known to be a bit peculiar (the Army said there was a right way and a wrong way and the Army way). The Army prized order ("what looks right is right"). Routines frequently made no sense, but draftees, full of patriotism, determined to endure the mysteries.

The Army cared for men in many ways. It provided clothing, board and room, the latter a cot in a barracks or tent. Pay was $25 a month, with $8 more for foreign service. Every enlisted man, as the Army insisted upon calling draftees, had to allot half his pay if he had a wife or child, and the government contributed an equal amount, with additional allowance for each child. An optional arrangement provided inexpensive life insurance, a novelty for soldiers in an era long before anyone heard of a G.I. Bill of Rights. Secretary of the Treasury William G. McAdoo presided over these first government insurance policies by which a soldier obtained coverage at $8 a year per $1,000 for as high as $10,000. He had tried to persuade private companies to carry the policies but their officials gazed at him gloomily, believing them risky; when he went ahead with government policies and every soldier did not die, insurance officials thought he was trying to take their business. In the end the four million government policies made life insurance popular and many years later almost every American bought a policy, whether he needed it or not, perhaps an acceptable arrangement for the companies.[9]

The Army and Navy both administered intelligence tests. The

draft provided a wonderful opportunity for academic psychologists to deal with a cross-section of the populace instead of their usual strange subjects, college students. Many years later tests had become so universal that no American could cross the street without taking one. Intelligence tests had had little respectability until 1916, when Lewis M. Terman of Stanford University revised a test drawn up by the Frenchman Alfred Binet. Terman made the letters IQ a part of the American language. Robert M. Yerkes of Harvard put together the Army tests, and he and assistants defined intelligence in college-oriented ways. The alpha test was for middle-class men of education:

The Overland car is made in	Buffalo	Detroit	Flint	Toledo.
Mauve is the name of a	drink	color	fabric	food.
Scrooge appears in	Vanity Fair	Romola	A Christmas Carol	Henry IV.

The beta test for dummies presumed the same background and asked soldiers to notice if the horn was missing from a phonograph or a net absent from a tennis court. Many beta examinees had never taken a written test. The psychologists declared a third of all World War I soldiers illiterate. Half the whites and 90 percent of blacks they announced as morons below the mental age of thirteen. Alvin C. York, the Tennessee sharpshooter who killed seventeen Germans with seventeen shots, captured 132 prisoners and thirty-five machine guns, and received the Congressional Medal of Honor, probably could not have passed the beta test.[10]

The Army's tests tended especially to discriminate against blacks. Initially a problem appeared in the beta test where median scores of whites and blacks were so similar that they indicated no significant racial differences in intelligence. The Army produced a revised beta that downgraded blacks. Then, in August 1918, draftees at Camp Lee took the tests, and companies of black Northerners scored considerably better than companies of southern white mountaineers. The resultant explanation was that the presence of masses of blacks in the South had lowered the intelligence of local whites! Carl C. Brigham of Princeton University explained the higher scores of northern blacks by a higher proportion of racial mixing, and that the more intelligent blacks had left the South.[11]

The tests received a mixed reaction among Army officers in World War I; many believed they allowed college graduates to avoid military service by pretending feeblemindedness. In January 1919 the Army abandoned its testing program.[12]

The War and Navy departments took measures, with mixed results, to ensure the moral well-being of their charges. They appointed chaplains, who ranked as officers. Concern arose over Christian Scientists, fear that they would counsel men against accepting medical care; Secretary of the Navy Josephus Daniels enrolled the first Scientist after church officials pledged cooperation. The War Department sought to make liquor unobtainable near Army camps, with considerable success, for the nation's prohibitionists seized upon the wartime shortage of grain to close saloons everywhere, and the public generally considered drinking and especially public drunkenness to be unpatriotic. Prostitutes congregated near cantonments or Navy bases and that problem too had its solution by prohibition.

The mayor of New Orleans outraged Secretary Daniels by refusing to close his city's "restricted district," known as Storyville, twenty-eight city blocks inhabited by 750 working girls (according to the mayor) and uncounted jazz musicians who played from 7:00 p.m. until dawn. In September 1917, Daniels declared war on Storyville, forcing the mayor to close it. Girls and musicians removed to St. Louis, Kansas City, and Chicago, and people credited Daniels with the spread of jazz, if nothing else, throughout the country. Perhaps the elimination of drink and prostitution spelled the need for physical exercise, and the Yale athlete, clock manufacturer, and picker of all-American football teams, Walter Camp, agreed to go to Washington and direct calisthenics for soldiers in the cantonments.[13]

Servicemen took their new military experiences in stride, although sometimes with a form of complaint known as griping. One aspect of Army life not alleviated by griping proved to be the Army's caste system, a hierarchy of privileges contrary to the democratic tradition. It was an arrangement that in theory freed officers' time for important problems of tactics and strategy without heed to petty details of existence. The Army also believed the caste system inculcated automatic obedience, so that men ordered into battle would not hesitate. For old Army officers the system was the foundation of their careers. They could not understand why draftees suddenly stooped to tie shoelaces to avoid saluting a colonel. Major General Leonard Wood saw nothing wrong with saluting and described it as a patriotic gesture: "You salute the lieutenant, the captain, the major, the colonel. They all salute me. I salute the Secretary of War. The Secretary salutes the President. The President salutes the flag. So, in saluting your officers, you are just indirectly saluting the flag."[14] To the horror of the Army's Chief of Staff, General Peyton C. March, someone spoke to President Wilson about saluting, obviously unimpressed by the logic behind the happy scene described above, and the President gingerly inquired if the War Department might abolish the salute. It did not, and March wrote testily in his memoirs that the salute was no different from what Wilson had experienced at Princeton when as president of the university he saw students recognize him by lifting their caps. Moreover, he remarked, warming to the subject, abolition of the salute was "the first thing adopted by the Bolshevik soldiers, after the Russian debacle of 1917, and was followed immediately by the complete disintegration of the Russian Army."[15]

Frederick P. Keppel, who became Third Assistant Secretary of War in April 1918 in charge of the life of the soldier in all its nonmilitary aspects (according to Secretary Baker), looked into the caste system after the war, and pronounced it "the main root" of soldiers' dissatisfaction. In an eloquent analysis he related how the Army had drawn both officers and men from a common economic and social reservoir, that never before was an army recruited with such a high average of education and social experience, or with officers superior to their men by so small a margin; yet differences between officers and men "in point of the privileges and social position conferred upon the former" had stretched to ridiculous proportions, with officers allowed and encouraged to claim and even monopolize advantages "in ways that have shown a total lack of the spirit of fair play." Soldiers of the draft army, he concluded, were "too wide awake, too critical by habit, and too well educated to concede special privileges that have no military significance or value to officers who are the mental and moral inferiors of half of their subordinates."[16]

Draftees griped about R.H.I.P. (rank has its privileges) and whenever possible struck back at tormentors. In AEF amateur vaudeville a question went: "What is your idea of a glorious sight?" The answer was "A shipload of second lieutenants sinking in mid-ocean."[17]

Such were the citizen soldiers and their cantonments, the arrangements made by the Army throughout the United States after the country went to war. In enlarging the Army to a size that would enable it to take part in the fighting in Europe, equally remarkable changes occurred in the War Department in Washington, in the monstrous mountain of masonry next to the White House—the old State, War and Navy Building put up in the era of President Grant, with its forest of chimneys, expanses of mansard roof, serried windows, antique pilasters, and, inside, the endless flights of stairs and high-ceilinged corridors and swinging doors; the building now houses the Executive Office of the President. In April 1917 the problems of the Army's high command in organizing the War Department for war were many and serious, and in subsequent months their solution or failure changed the lives—in some cases ended the lives—of young men in the camps.

The Cabinet officer who headed the War Department, charged with responsibility for bringing the Army into the twentieth century, was Newton Baker, an intelligent, hardworking official who took Garrison's place in March 1916. President Wilson had met Baker years before, during the early nineties, when the then Princeton professor had journeyed down to Baltimore to teach at Johns Hopkins and took meals at the same boardinghouse. Young Baker had gone to Cleveland, where he became a protégé of the reform mayor Tom Johnson, and succeeded Johnson as mayor. He served two terms (1911–15), fought for the three-cent streetcar fare and three-cent ice cream cone, sponsored public dance halls where for three cents boys and girls could enjoy a wholesome evening, and supported the municipal symphony orchestra with $10,000 out of the city budget, a much remarked piece of profligacy. He had supported Wilson in the 1912 convention and his former professor had offered him the office of Secretary of the Interior, but Baker had preferred to stay in Cleveland.

Baker was slightly over five feet in height, and sat at his War Department desk with one leg curled up under him on the cushion of his chair. Visitors noticed that on the desk invariably was a fresh pansy. The Secretary of War incessantly smoked a pipe. Secretary of the Treasury McAdoo remarked how boyish he looked posing beside tall, bulky generals, and the same was true of political figures of the time. The chairman of the War Industries Board, Bernard M. Baruch, towered over Baker, and because Baruch often was critical of the Secretary, he once burst out that "If I was a big fellow like

Baruch, they'd say I was a better Secretary of War."[18]

It is an interesting question whether Baker, with all his attractiveness, was a great Secretary of War. His administration of the department had much to commend. In dealing with people he displayed none of the coldness of his friend the President; he was warm and attentive, and visitors liked him. He expressed himself in clear, straightforward ways, spoke 225 words a minute (more than most stenographers could keep up with), and made excellent public addresses. Some of these qualities he had acquired in academic studies and some when mayor of Cleveland. But he drew one procedure from his Cleveland experience that did not assist him in the War Department and was remarkably like the modus operandi of President Wilson—as mayor he believed he held "a pastoral sort of office" in which "perhaps the most significant aspect was . . . the preaching function." It was his purpose to state ideals and persuade citizens to act.[19]

Baker's failure as Secretary of War was that, apart from presiding over the draft and arranging for men to enter cantonments, he allowed two not merely precious but almost decisive years to go by —March 1916 to March 1918—before he took measures to clean up his department, and moved only after criticism became so vocal and widespread that it threatened to drive him from office. He could not bring himself to change the Army's antiquated organization in Washington, the administrative arrangement known as the bureau system.

Secretary of War John C. Calhoun in 1817 had organized the bureaus in the War Department, and if at the outset, after the War of 1812, they had displayed some modest advantages, they had long since outlived their usefulness. Throughout the nineteenth century the Army's leading officer bore the title of Commanding General, and usually was in residence at Washington, where he presided over a group of bureaus—ordnance, signal corps, engineers, quartermaster, medical. A "chief" presided over each bureau. As years passed, the chiefs took on more independence until the War Department became like the Near East after Alexander the Great. Everything turned into confusion during the Spanish-American War, when the Army's supply system faltered—the Army backed up railroad cars outside Tampa, issued winter uniforms to troops for fighting in Cuba, and (the following delinquency was not as bad as it sounded) furnished the men with canned meat that troops described as embalmed beef. After hostilities President McKinley eased his Secretary of War, Russell A. Alger of Michigan, a goateed fuddy-duddy, out of the War Department and brought in the New York lawyer Elihu Root, who instituted reform. Because the efficient Germans had organized a General Staff, Root decided to have one, and in 1903, to accompaniment of much publicity, he established a staff of thirty or forty officers under a Chief of Staff who replaced the Commanding General. His successor in the department, William H. Taft, bounced responsibility back to the bureaus. Taft's successor, Stimson, took it away again and gave it to a strong Chief of Staff, General Wood, who served also under Garrison. By this time the bureau chiefs had learned to duck every time a reformer took aim. They popped up when no one was looking, and during the Preparedness agitation of 1916 arranged a piece of legislation, the National Defense Act, that prohibited the General Staff from engaging in administrative duties and brought them back into control. Baker meanwhile had succeeded Garrison and apparently did not understand what was going on.[20]

After mobilization of the citizen army in the summer of 1917 the bureau chiefs enlarged their satrapies, each in his own way, a procedure guaranteed to create chaos. General Wood, admittedly no disinterested observer of the Wilsonian War Department, remarked in his diary for May 21, 1917, that when the department touched anything it touched it with the dead, cold hand of inefficiency.[21] Colonel Robert L. Bullard passed through Washington early in June en route to Europe, and the War Department appalled this spirited officer who in the war's climactic point in 1918 would command the Second Army in France: "Of my stay in Washington the great impression left is that *if we really have a great war, our War Department will quickly break down.*"[22] By July the bureaus were hard at work competing with each other for scarce supplies in the open market. The Army's adjutant general filled the basement of the State, War and Navy Building with 12,000 typewriters. "There is going to be the greatest competition for typewriters around here," he explained to Baker, "and I have them all."

Without leadership the War Department bumped its way from one crisis to another toward disaster, with the bureau system out in front, doing its best.[23] But its procedures took time and Baker hustled the operation by allowing the Army's seniority system to foist upon him two ill-suited Chiefs of Staff, the incumbent in April

1917, Major General Hugh L. Scott, and Scott's successor, Major General Tasker H. Bliss. Both were able men but individuals of the nineteenth century; Scott was one of the last Indian fighters, and Bliss too had learned from the Indians. Scott belonged with the cavalry in the West. One day in October 1917, when the general should have had a few things on his mind, he spent his time talking to Indians; a subordinate peeked in his door at the department to see him alone with two Indians who stood in full tribal regalia in front of his desk, general and Indians talking sign language; the Indians had come from Arizona to tell their old friend they had heard he was going across the wide waters to kill his enemies, and they and their people wanted to go with him.[24] After retirement from the office of Chief of Staff, Scott in 1918 could not even command a training camp at Fort Dix and, with Baker's approval, had to be relieved. The general's papers, now in the Library of Congress, display his inadequacy—handwritten memos, large black-ink scrawling on tiny sheets of stationery. Scott was a colonel when Wilson became President, and the first military move the new Chief Executive made was to promote him to brigadier general. He had had a brother who was a professor at Princeton and had stood up for Wilson during the academic troubles there.[25]

Scott's successor, Bliss, possessed a disciplined mind, spoke French and Spanish, and studied the classics, which he read in their Latin and Greek originals. Had he not attended West Point he might have become a professor of languages at a small eastern college. Bliss impressed Bullard as a man who knew and cared little for soldiers and soldiering. In prewar years Bullard once spent a month under his command in camp, and in that time saw him with troops only during a practice march and maneuver of a week or so. He next saw him in combined maneuvers of the National Guard and Regular Army in Connecticut in 1912, an operation known as "controlled maneuvers," by which the Army guided and controlled each activity. Bliss arranged for everything to come off as planned, "although to accomplish this it was necessary to give far-fetched and improbable decisions and orders that strained the imagination to the limit and made troops and commanders dummies." On one occasion Bliss said to Bullard, who was acting as umpire: "Let the brigade halt here, upon this rut of the wagon wheel, not upon that other." The distance between two wagon wheels was three and a half feet.[26]

Something should have been done with these two Chiefs of Staff, but Baker was not the man to do it. President Wilson in 1917 sent Scott on a mission to Russia, and during Scott's absence Bliss became Acting Chief of Staff. Scott returned and served for a while and stepped down to the training command and Bliss took his place. Bliss went to Paris as American military representative on the Supreme War Council, and a little-known officer who regarded himself as unfit for the assignment, Major General John Biddle, became acting chief. Bliss returned in December 1917, relieved Biddle, and retired in January 1918. Biddle came back as acting chief.

Baker might have allowed this revolving-door situation to continue had not Republicans and Democrats in House and Senate, and millions of irate fellow citizens, nearly driven him from office because of the crisis in management of the war that arose in the winter of 1917–18. With the nation months into war, the war economy was not working; production was rising very slowly. There was no directing hand, the War Industries Board was a cipher, and the War Department hobbled along, with bureau chiefs attempting to secure ever more scarce supplies. Secretary Baker sent out each chief with a hunting license.

In this great winter crisis it was at first necessary to do something about war production, and President Wilson belatedly named Baruch as head of the War Industries Board. Baker then seized the opportunity to attend to the War Department, bringing back from France a superb officer, Major General Peyton C. March, as Chief of Staff.

Peyton March proved one of those extraordinary leaders who in crises in the history of the Republic have come out of obscurity. America has a way of producing such individuals and the U.S. Army has contributed more than its share. The Civil War raised up Grant and Sherman and Sheridan, and eighty years later came Marshall, Dwight D. Eisenhower, Omar N. Bradley, George Patton, Lawton Collins. When crisis arose they were ready, having sensed that sometime the nation might use them. A tall man with prominent nose, face set off by a short white beard, March had been in charge of General John J. Pershing's artillery, an assignment he enjoyed, pushing troops to the limit, turning everything toward efficiency. Word came to return to the United States and he sailed back with intense reluctance—perhaps the first requisite for anyone who becomes an administrator. His initial day in Washington he talked out his responsibilities with Biddle, who, he discovered, went home at five each afternoon. That night he strode back into the War Department, where he encountered a stygian darkness in the office of the Secretary of War, corridors resounding only to the echo of his own heavy boots. In the corridor outside the adjutant general's office rose a mountain of unopened mail sacks. No officer worked in the building save Major W. K. Wilson, sitting quietly at his desk in the code room. March flew into a rage, and next night hundreds of people scurried up and down halls, in and out of offices. Swinging doors flapped, typewriters clattered, big brass spittoons thudded and thumped. Years later, writing his memoirs, March described the scene triumphantly, so many lights gleaming from War Department offices that the building looked like a Christmas tree.[27]

This resolute Chief of Staff took the commonsensical procedures needed to bring order to any bureaucracy. He worked incessantly to straighten out lines of authority. Especially, he appointed the best men he could find, without regard to rank, seniority, age, anything but competence. He raised up Captain (by that time Lieutenant Colonel) Hugh Johnson to brigadier general. From France he brought back Colonel Robert E. Wood, who before 1917 had left the Regular Army to become an executive in Chicago. He made Wood brigadier general in charge of the quartermaster department. Such splendid appointments were accompanied by others; many of Wood's assistants were experienced civilians: "In food I had some of the packers from . . . Chicago, in clothing I got Louis Kirstein who was then the head of Filene's and who is one of the major men in retailing; and in the heavier materials and transportation I got men from General Motors and the big companies. So I got a group, a corps, of civilians who all knew their job."[28]

Ever increasing responsibility came to the desk of March's old West Point teacher, builder of the Panama Canal, George Washington Goethals, who had retired as a major general in 1916. Baker had brought Goethals out of retirement to associate the general's reputation with the War Department, take advantage of his well-known Republican connections, and in part use his genuine ability, but March gave him real work to do. Goethals possessed a mind like that of March, and as soon as the Overman Act in May 1918 conferred authority on President Wilson to override previous legislation and reorganize any government department at will, Goethals consolidated the War Department's supply operations into a single purchase, storage, and traffic division. As his assistant, Goethals brought in the former president of Montgomery Ward, Robert J. Thorne. With Wood in the quartermaster's office, Goethals recreated the organization with which he had built the Panama Canal, for Wood had worked for him there.[29] By the end of the war Goethals was destroying the bureau system as fast as he could. "I am making progress slowly with the organization," he wrote his son on November 3, 1918. ". . . We took over the Engineers on the 1st and are to take over Signal Corps on the 5th, Medical Corps on the 15th & Ordnance on the 31st. If the war ends I hope that the reorganized Army will include one Supply Corps, divided into supplies and finance."[30]

All the while General March rid the War Department of incompetents, such as Brigadier General Palmer Pierce. March told Goethals that Pierce would have to go and delegated Goethals to break the news that his new place was the War Industries Board. Goethals stayed awake at night painting a picture of gold, tinsel, and lace for Pierce's duties at the W.I.B. and was just starting to describe it to Pierce when March strode in. "Pierce," he announced, "I have cut your head off and ordered you out of the War Department." With such a framing the picture fell to pieces.[31] Pierce fled to the W.I.B., but the hand of March reached out, uprooted him, and sent him to France. According to Goethals, who was in on this exercise too, "Pierce was let down with a dull sickening thud, and though he has been saying all along how eager he was for service in France, he had tears in his voice, March said, when the news was broken to him, and this not too diplomatically. He sailed Tuesday, much to his surprise."[32] March tried less successfully to ship out General Crowder, an awkward subordinate, and proposed Crowder as part of a military mission to Switzerland. The judge advocate general and provost marshal general (Crowder had buttoned himself into both jobs) argued rather reasonably that his presence in Washington was more important than it would be in Switzerland, asked to take his case to Baker, and managed to stay on.

March's commanding presence penetrated every office of the department and out into the field. He shortened the West Point course to a year. He created an air service, tank corps, and chemical warfare service. He eliminated distinctions between Regular Army, National Guard, and National Army (the draftees). "Everywhere his quick, incisive decisions eliminated overlapping functions and intramural bickering while centralizing authority."[33] Typical was his reform of military intelligence, which in April 1917 consisted of two officers and two clerks; March worked it over into a large, modern operation of 282 officers, 29 noncommissioned officers, and 948 civilian employees. Not content with cleaning up affairs at home, he looked to the better functioning of Pershing's command. The AEF had cannibalized divisions in the United States for replacements, and March ordered special replacement camps for infantry, artillery, and engineers, so divisions could go to France intact. He sought to send Goethals to straighten out Pershing's supply problem, which was every bit as serious as that at home. Leonard Wood had returned from a tour of France with harsh words about Pershing's supply, and according to Goethals the report made "the desire to get my clutches on that work greater than ever."[34] Pershing flared at this proposed invasion of his authority and appointed a close friend, Major General James G. Harbord, who did the job. But it was March who forced the reformation.

The new Chief of Staff's achievement at the War Department in the last months of war, until the Armistice in November 1918, was to deliver the department from its past. In later years people forgot about Peyton March; in the twenties he sailed for Europe, where he stayed for several years, and returned home to publish a forthright (as one would have expected) book about his service in the war that lacked literary skill and made him seem petty. He lived on obscurely in Washington during and after World War II, a gaunt, white-haired figure striding into or out of the Army and Navy Club. When at last he died during the third year of the presidency of a man who had been a lieutenant colonel when he had worn the four silver stars of a full general, no one memorialized him, recalled what he had done in a war long past, the Army's machinelike efficiency during the final months of 1918, organizing, training, shipping huge fighting divisions overseas. In the eight months and one week he served as wartime Chief of Staff, over 135,000 more men (1,788,488) took ship for France than were in the entire Army in April 1918 (1,652,725).[35]

CHAPTER 3

Getting "Over There"

A NEWSPAPER editor from Raleigh, North Carolina, an adherent of the William Jennings Bryan side of the Democratic party, presided over the Navy Department in 1917–18—Josephus Daniels, a plump man with roundish face, of medium height, possessed of keen intelligence like his opposite in the War Department. Unlike Newton Baker, he was no man to push around. His immediate predecessors in the Navy Department had not made much of a mark on the office of Secretary. Appointed for good political reasons, they had known little about the Navy and its ways. They were not in office long enough to understand what was going on; only one of them, at the turn of the century, served a full four-year term, two were in office less than a year, one served three months. That was the way Navy officers liked it. Attempting to decide which of the Secretaries he admired most, Rear Admiral Bradley A. Fiske said he preferred the three-month man.

Daniels turned out to be a Navy supporter and developed a love for it that in the hierarchy of his affections came just after the Methodist Church and the Democratic party. But to Admiral Fiske's consternation, Daniels remained in office throughout the Wilson administration, eight long years. And he refused to let the Navy alone. He urged the admirals to throw away their cocked hats (they agreed, and after he left they got them out again), to get rid of words like port and starboard and use left and right (the admirals said he would have Navy navigators saying gee and haw), to install laundries

31

on new battleships, and as in Philadelphia, where there was not enough money to build two Marine barracks, to permit officers and men to live under the same roof. He established compulsory off-duty schools taught by officers for illiterate or poorly educated seamen, opened Annapolis to seamen, invited officers and men to the same social functions. He abolished the wine mess, the right of officers aboard ship to take wine with their meals; he considered it undemocratic because ordinary seamen received no wine. Daniels was an ardent teetotaler, which may have had something to do with his attitude toward officers' drinking wine on government property.

Daniels was full of reforming ideas, and favored women's rights at a time when American men were prejudiced. In 1917 he irre-pressibly decided that since no law said a Navy yeoman or Marine had to be a man he would invite women. Into the Navy he welcomed 11,000 yeomen (F) and 269 Marines (F), known as yeomanettes and marinettes. Perhaps to cheer up everyone after admitting women, he brought out of retirement the bandmaster of the Spanish-Ameri-can War, John Philip Sousa, whose quickstep tunes soon had every-one marching together.

Daniels's assistant was a rising Democratic politico, a tall young man named Franklin D. Roosevelt, who had entered the Navy De-partment because he liked ships and the sea and perhaps because in the nineties another Roosevelt had been Assistant Secretary of the Navy. The Hyde Park Roosevelt did not impress Theodore Roosevelt's friend Senator Lodge, who found him "a well-meaning, nice young fellow, but light." Elihu Root warned Daniels that F.D.R. might cause trouble, that whenever a Roosevelt rode, he wished to ride in front. Franklin confided to Eleanor that he could run the department better than his chief and informed a friend that the Secretary's Consulting Board, the group of scientists brought in to help the Navy, did not amount to much—"Most of these worthies are like Henry Ford, who until he saw a chance for publicity free of charge, thought a submarine was something to eat." Roosevelt's henchman Louis Henry Howe, in government employ, spread criti-cisms of Daniels's ineptitudes, rusticities, and Billy Sundayisms (Daniels and the revivalist were close friends). The Secretary knew his assistant was undercutting him, such as saying to Senator James W. Wadsworth that he was "disgusted beyond words" and was "simply holding on to save what he could from the wreck," but Daniels kept his irritation to himself, for he liked his young assistant and thought him a good fellow. In September 1918, Roosevelt conceived the idea of establishing himself in Europe as civilian coordinator of the Anglo-American naval effort. Daniels let the notion fall of its own weight.[1]

Despite the Secretary's effort to bring democracy to the Navy, and his assistant's belief that anything Daniels could do he could do better, neither of the civil heads of the Navy managed to change the Navy's strategic ideas until after war broke out in April 1917, and posed the urgent task of naval preparation—far more urgent than democratization, or substituting one personality for another in the Secretary's office. Over the years the Navy had concentrated on improving the battleship fleet and neglected the possibility of submarine warfare. Admittedly, by April 1917 it had had little time to change strategic ideas. Inventors had talked of submarines for decades, and tried human-propelled torpedoes during the Civil War, with fatal results to the humans, but oceangoing submarines had appeared only two years before the World War when in February 1912 the Navy commissioned the world's first practical diesel submarine, commanded by Lieutenant Chester W. Nimitz.[2] The admirals paid little attention to young Nimitz's ship (describing it as a boat); they went back to sleep and dreamed of hurling shells into the air off Santiago. Until 1917, when he died, Admiral of the Navy George Dewey presided over the General Board, listened to discussions of fleet action, and did nothing to prepare for German submarines; he and the board championed the battleship even after Jutland ended fleet action between the British and German navies in 1916. When the United States entered the war the Navy's plan called for fleet action in the Caribbean.

The U.S. Navy's fascination with fleet action stemmed from ignorance, a direct result of the studiously neutral behavior of the Wilson administration. The President was so careful to keep the country neutral that he regularly had denied Navy Department requests to send observers to England or the Continent to study the naval war at first hand. Already the admirals in Washington had gained a very poor impression of the ability of Britain and France to stand up to the Central Powers on the Western Front—the war there had seemed a succession of disasters. Similarly, the admirals could not understand why the British did not contain the enemy's submarines by blocking up their European bases, sinking blockships to prevent egress or else mining the immediate approaches to harbors. Both the Navy's high command and the President had the idea that submarines were akin to hornets. If one found the nest, wiping them out became simple. Neither understood how the Germans had made their bases impregnable by siting the approaches with heavy guns and filling the mouths with minefields. If a few Allied minelaying submarines got close, German trawlers simply swept up the mines.

With almost complete lack of understanding, U.S. admirals became so critical of the British (there was considerable anti-British sentiment in the Navy Department anyway) that the consensus was that the Allies might well be defeated, in which case the task of the U.S. Navy would be to prevent an attack by the German Navy along the Atlantic coast. An estimate of the Navy Department dated March 13, 1917, stressed defensive measures in American waters. The immediate threat would be German submarines operating against American merchant ships and the Atlantic Fleet. The Navy proposed to arm merchantmen, construct 110-foot patrol craft, and use nonrigid airships (blimps) to patrol from bases along the Atlantic littoral. The ultimate threat would come when the German High Seas Fleet crossed the Atlantic to take on the U.S. Navy after defeating the British.[3]

Once the U.S. Navy discovered that the real threat was German submarines operating in British waters at short range from Continental bases, this strategy had to be turned around 180 degrees. The Navy was forced to send as many of its destroyers as it could to European waters to assist in the fight against submarines.

Thus the Navy had to give up, at least momentarily, the doctrines of Captain Alfred T. Mahan. In the nineties and after the turn of the century the ideas of Mahan had dominated American naval thinking —carefully wrought theories that emphasized control of the sea and promised it to any large battle force willing to fight hard and well. Mahan had attracted attention in countries seeking to expand their navies—the U.S., Germany, Japan. Officers of the U.S. Navy had taken Mahan to heart, and to abandon him was most unattractive. Antisubmarine actions in British waters hardly constituted a strategy. Tactics necessarily were those of the British Navy's antisubmarine forces. It was even possible to contend that in 1917–18 the U.S. Navy had neither strategy nor tactics, and tagged along.

By World War II standards German submarine tactics in World War I were primitive, and perhaps this Indian ambush aspect had persuaded the battleship admirals that submarines were passing fads of a small group of wayward naval architects.[4] Having resort to lookouts only when searching for victims, the U-boats (*Unterseebooten*) enjoyed the advantage of a thin silhouette. Moreover, the U-boat lookout could see the masts of a steamer as far as fifteen miles whereas the steamer's lookout could discern the sub only at four. The Allies camouflaged their ships by painting weird triangles and lines over the hulls, lending a circus aspect to every harbor. Camouflage was supposed to fool the submarine by lessening visibility and blurring the edge of the target; yet it did not keep the prey from the hunter. The sub's best tactic was to line up a steamer's masts and submerge to periscope depth and lie in its course. When the steamer closed the range it was necessary for the sub to move back as far as 500 yards to the side at right angles, to fire torpedo tubes at its bow and stern. Torpedoes did not run straight, and the submarine could not stand farther away. When the steamer sailed without escort, the sub very likely would come to the surface and fire its deck gun in preference to expensive torpedoes.

Employing U-boats in this elementary way, the Germans came close to victory in World War I. Allied losses were horrendous, and for 1914–18 amounted to a row of 5,700 sunken ships. Lost ships ranked in size from the great *Britannic* and *Lusitania* to the smallest fishing smack.[5] Early in 1917 the German government resumed unrestricted submarine warfare and raced to accomplish the dismal purpose of starving the British. Tonnage sunk reached frightening proportions: 540,000 in February, 600,000 in March, 900,000 in April. Admiral Henning von Holtzendorff, chief of the German Naval Staff, estimated that Britain possessed 11 million tons, including neutral vessels, and if Germany sank 600,000 tons per month for five months and frightened into port 1.2 million of the 3 million available tons of neutral shipping, the British would lose two-fifths of their ships, an expenditure "final and irreplaceable."[6] When Foreign Secretary Arthur Balfour visited America in April 1917 and the London government cabled him news of the latest merchant ship losses, he said that submarines were "constantly on my mind. I could think of nothing but the number of ships which they were sinking. At that time it certainly looked as though we were going to lose the war."[7] Sinkings became so frequent that one large steamer in four departing the British Isles failed to return. Figures moved up and down, 600,000 tons in May, 700,000 in June, 550,000 in July,

500,000 in August, 350,000 in September, but as late as the summer of 1918 losses were high. In 1914 the Germans sank 310,000 tons of shipping; 1915, 1,301,000; 1916, 2,322,000; 1917, 6,270,000; 1918, 2,659,000. U-boats lost 5,000 men in destroying 5,000 ships. The total tonnage destroyed by submarines was ten times as great as that by mines, twenty times that of surface raiders. Planes, which looked to the future, sank 8,000 tons.[8]

The Germans might have done much better in the war if they had built more submarines. Fortunately for the Allies the German naval high command suffered the same illusions as did admirals of the U.S. Navy. The diesel-powered submarine was too new for admirals to understand; the Germans continued to think of surface fleet action, and even during the war poured enormous funds into battleships. The number of German submarines in commission in 1917–18, when for the first time the Germans had almost enough to inflict a deathblow on the Allies, did not change much. On January 1, 1917, they had 133, a year later 144. A third of this fleet lay on station, a third coming and going, and a third stayed in port under repair or provisioning. The Germans did not abandon the idea of a great surface fleet action until October 1918, when Admiral Reinhard Scheer obtained the cooperation of General Ludendorff for a submarine program, 376 more boats by late 1919. It was too late; Scheer described the program as "a twelfth-hour attempt to save everything."[9] Late in October the naval high command tried to take out the remaining surface ships for a *Goetterdaemmerung*, but this suicide mission came to nothing when crews refused to get up steam.

In the first weeks of 1917 the Wilson administration at long last began to address the sort of problems the Navy might encounter if the country entered the war. Initial deliberations were not promising. President Wilson sensed that battleships no longer ensured the nation's security and yet his understanding of submarines left something to be desired. He told Daniels it would be a good idea to have three motorboats on each Navy ship, and in smooth seas the ship could lower the boats to hunt submarines. When he had visited England before the war, he explained, he had seen annual festivals in rural areas where a shepherd stood in a circle of sheep and by calls and whistles herded three sheep into a pen. It was not difficult to manage two, the President said, but very difficult with three. The

Germans would expect a boat on each side of a ship but the third boat would confuse them.[10]

In the first days of March 1917 the President ordered guns and gun crews on liners and merchantmen, with questionable results. Rear Admiral William S. Sims, who in 1917–18 commanded American naval forces in Europe, later testified that arming merchant ships made them subject to torpedo attack, and that guns were futile against the small silhouette of a surfaced sub. In any event the Navy in early 1917 had no ammunition.[11]

The convoy proved the solution to German submarines, and its belated introduction by the Allies is too well-known a story to require retelling. Objections to convoying were not as senseless as they later appeared: convoys reduced speed of ships to the slowest, multiple arrivals in port jammed facilities, merchantmen might not be able to sail in close formation, and not nearly enough small craft were available for escort through the danger zone. By delaying ships, convoys reduced carrying capacity of Allied shipping by from 20 to 40 percent. But sinkings were becoming too numerous, and the British Navy was ready to try convoys when Prime Minister David Lloyd George pushed the issue early in 1917 in a visit to the Admiralty. President Wilson, despite his droll fondness for motorboats, easily saw the advantage of convoys. Sims, by then in London, reinforced the point. Success of a short-legged convoy between Gibraltar and England encouraged extension of such a system.

The U.S. Navy organized slow and medium-speed transatlantic convoys. Fast ships sailed by themselves, for submarines were extremely slow underwater. Every sixteen days a convoy left New York for the English west coast, and every eight days from Hampton Roads. As a convoy left the assembling port it picked up a cruiser or old battleship for protection against surface raiders, and ships spread out over as much as ten square miles, jogging along at eight knots—nine miles an hour—in columns of four ("Indian file"), 500 or 1,000 yards from ship to ship, groups abreast and a half mile apart. Twenty-four vessels, six groups, took a width of three miles and depth of one. Most valuable vessels or cargoes sailed in the center; least precious got the "coffin corners" at the rear. At the outset of the voyage to Europe a convoy was without danger—until summer 1918, when long-range submarines crossed the Atlantic and not merely attacked coastal traffic but raised the possibility of threatening embarking convoys. During the first part of the voyage captains obtained experience in columns with groups abreast, and practiced zigzagging, moving erratically to right and left so a sub could not line up masts. "Steering zigzag courses in formation under these conditions with the great unwieldy vessels one thousand yards apart," wrote Captain William D. Leahy, "left very few dull moments for the skipper. Our rudder jammed twice, once when the ship was rolling 25 degrees in a seaway." At night a ship in Leahy's convoy passed his own, the former German liner *Princess Matoika*, thirty yards astern.[12]

Once a convoy entered the war zone 300–400 miles off the British Isles or the Continent, fast destroyers with depth charges patrolled the crucial sides.[13] The shallow draft of the destroyers, nine or ten feet, protected them from torpedoes, which had to run fifteen feet underwater; closer to the surface, the force of the waves would deflect their path and they would not make a straight course. A destroyer could travel four to five times as fast as a submerged submarine, thirty to forty miles an hour versus seven or eight. If it spotted a torpedo wake it got up speed in unbelievably short time and raced to the far end of the wake, where the sub had fired, and began cutting a circle, right or left, dropping depth charges every ten or fifteen seconds in a circle wide enough to include the submarine, provided it had gone in that direction. If two destroyers were available—and this was frequently the case—one took off to the right, one to the left. Soon a plunging sea of geysers covered the area where the sub had fired, and charges blew sky-high. Submariners took comfort in the fact that a destroyer could not destroy one of their boats unless a depth charge exploded within fifty to a hundred feet of the hull. Because the sub might be anywhere from just under the surface to 200 feet down, misses could be vertical as well as lateral. But a depth charge was a fearful explosion, even if not a hit, for a single blown charge made a roar like a battleship's fourteen-inch battery fired at once. One can imagine taking the concussion of ten or twenty depth charges in succession—submariners were in shellshock for days, unable to think or work their cramped boat. The submarine's greatest enemy was the destroyer, inspiring Rear Admiral Caspar F. Goodrich to borrow words from Eliphaz the Temanite: "A dreadful sound is in his ears; in prosperity the destroyer shall come upon him."

Without American destroyers, transatlantic convoys would have been impossible. Although the British Navy possessed more than 400, the Grand Fleet required 100 in the Orkneys, and the Admiralty gave next preference to hospital ships, the Channel, and the Mediterranean, in that order. The U.S. Navy made the crucial difference, without which the Allies would have lost the war in 1917–18 for lack of American troops and supplies. Lord Robert Cecil cabled Balfour in Washington in April 1917 that the British government needed destroyers desperately. "Will you impress with great force upon U.S. authorities very urgent need for more destroyers being sent to assist us." Two dozen destroyers, he said, would help a great deal, "but we want as many as we can get. The matter does not brook of a moment's delay."[14] The first American contingent, a flotilla of six, steamed into Queenstown, Ireland, on May 4. On the day appointed for their arrival, word got around among local inhabitants, and people lined the shore, gazing out to sea. Slowly, almost imperceptibly, a tiny speck appeared on the horizon, then five more, and the specks enlarged into outlines of ships. On they came, six sleek destroyers, smoke pouring, spray flying, guns at ready. A contemporary painting, much admired during the war, showed the ships coming in. Underneath, the legend read: "Return of the *Mayflower*." By June 1 the U.S. Navy had twenty-four destroyers at Queenstown under command of the local British admiral. By the end of the war seventy-nine were in European waters.

The Navy did extremely well in arranging the transportation of troops to France. At the beginning of the war it possessed almost no transports, and its achievement was as noteworthy as was provision of destroyers for convoying. In April 1917, Vice Admiral Albert Gleaves commanded one unseaworthy transport plus the U.S.S. *Henderson*, not yet in commission. Federal authorities confiscated nearly 700,000 tons of German ships, in American ports since 1914, including sixteen passenger ships, one the largest ship afloat, the *Vaterland*, renamed *Leviathan* by President Wilson. German sailors made every effort to disable ships; on February 1, 1917, they received orders, and in the next two days broke crucial machinery. The Americans ingeniously reproduced broken parts, and cleaned up ships from stem to stern—the Germans had left them filthy. Half a million soldiers sailed to war on ships that had belonged to the enemy. The government seized neutral liners in American ports. Eventually Gleaves disposed of forty-two transports. All told, 2,080,000 troops arrived in France before the Armistice—952,581 in American ships, the remainder mostly in British. As Daniels proudly noted in his memoirs, the Navy escorted 82.75 percent of transports, the British Navy 14.125 percent, the French 3.125.[15]

Troops found the voyage thoroughly disagreeable. Commanders packed men into holds where they slept in awkward hammocks, breathing foul air. Frederick A. Pottle of Lovell, Maine, shipped aboard a miserable Italian vessel, the *Caserta,* and remembered how tiers of rough wooden bunks filled the middle of the ship, a dungeon with no portholes, light only from an open hatch in the deck far above; looking up, one had the impression of being in a well. In the tiers against the sides it was pitch-dark at all times, with none too much light anywhere. "Below decks it was stuffy and intolerably cramped, and when everyone was on deck it was equally cramped there." Ernest H. Ferrell of Custar, Ohio, sailed on the White Star Line's *Olympic,* sister ship to the *Titanic,* assigned to a cavernous lower deck where the smell of grease was sickening; he paid ten dollars to an enterprising member of the ship's crew, whom he presumed to be the captain, who sold canvas bunks in four-man staterooms. Food was especially bad aboard British ships. Joseph D. Lawrence of McBee, South Carolina, went over on the Cunard liner *Orduna* and remembered how from morning to night the food lines wound along deck corridors and up stairs to other decks. The food the men waited for was almost inedible. Toward the end of the war the British became extremely sensitive to complaints and gave American troops more than twice the rations provided to their own and sought American assistance in preparing and dispensing food.[16]

For officers the crossing was more pleasant, and it was possible to observe the larger scene, which was exciting. Enjoying top-deck accommodation with fellow officers aboard the White Star's *Baltic,* Colonel Horace Hobbs beheld nine big ships sailing through a calm, smooth sea, not even a breeze, skidding along silently at night in absolute darkness save for a masked stem light discernible only from the ship following directly behind. Hobbs counted troopships, cargo ships, and a great vessel transporting 5,000 Chinese laborers, all escorted by a British cruiser until early one morning seven destroyers pranced into view through fog and rain, a thrilling sight, long, lean, low in the water.[17]

With pride Gleaves wrote after the war that he had lost not a single soldier on the eastward transatlantic run. This was true, although other commanders lost ships and men—the *Tuscania, Moldavia,* and animal transport *Ticonderoga;* 13 deaths on the first, 56 on the second, 215 on the third. Gleaves lost four troop transports on the return voyage, which he did not escort heavily. The reason for light losses on transatlantic troop transports was that German submarine commanders concentrated on convoys of supply ships rather than transports. Two broad lanes for transatlantic convoys reached to Europe, with troopships taking a lane different from ships carrying supplies. Troops usually went direct to France, supplies to England. Each lane was 200 miles wide and difficult for submarines to cover. Supply-ship convoys were far more frequent (100 supply ships to every troopship), slower, less protected. The Germans also believed that American troops, trained by officers with no experience on the Western Front, would not affect the fighting.

The Germans erred in keeping submarines away from troopships, a huge human target. The Navy packed troops like sardines, especially after it discovered that men could sleep in twelve-hour shifts ("turn-in-and-turn-out"). It converted its nine best transports to shifts. Beginning in July 1918, 10,000 troops left the United States each day. Any sinking could produce inexpressible horror, and might have raised questions among bereaved relatives—parents, wives, children—about continued participation in the war. The transport carrying Private Darrel Scott of Fulton County, Ohio, took a torpedo at 6:00 p.m., in pitch-darkness, seas running mountain high. Scott was in the first lifeboat put down, with sixty men, and it tipped over. A good swimmer, he kept his head up for an hour and a half until another lifeboat came along, but was nearly frozen and barely got aboard. The next nine hours he spent in desperate cold, chilled to the bone, clothes frozen. Waves and wind then drove the boat on an island: "It was solid rock where we struck and our boat was dashed to pieces in just one second."[18] Valford S. Clark of Toledo was aboard the *Tuscania* and had come from supper and was standing on the lower deck singing and laughing with friends. He turned to two of the boys and said, "Let's all get off this deck before we get hit with something," and had hardly gotten the words out of his mouth when there was a loud boom and everyone cried, "There she is!" The ship shook from stem to stern and all lights went out. Soldiers rushed for the main stairs and upper deck, saying to each other, "Take your time, men." In line they got into the lifeboats. Clark's boat stayed afloat, but he saw boats upset and men go down, destroyers striking boats and killing passengers, red rockets in air, men crying for help, now and then the submarine coming to the surface. At long last English patrol boats came out and rescued survivors.[19]

Years afterward Captain William V. Pratt, the wartime Assistant Chief of Naval Operations, contemplated what could have happened—what pressure on the Navy Department, the Wilson administration—if the Germans had torpedoed the Leviathan, which carried 14,000 men: the icy, stormy Atlantic, lifeboats smashed, thousands of soldiers swimming, thousands more trapped aboard the plunging liner.[20]

Another possibility worried the Navy, that the Germans might send battle cruisers into the troop convoy lane. Sometimes three huge convoys were at sea loaded with troops, not to mention fast ships like the Leviathan, Northern Pacific, and Great Northern that sailed alone. A single convoy carried 48,000 men. The Germans were aware of these arrangements and could have raced battle cruisers into the Atlantic and sunk transports like cornered rats. Enemy cruisers might have fled to Spanish ports. A division of the latest American battleships, oil burners, steamed to Ireland, and another took station at Halifax. The Navy asked for a loan of British battle cruisers, which the British refused. The Japanese fleet would not leave the Pacific to help the Americans, or for that matter the British. The Navy then formed a plan and issued instructions whereby a code word, flashed into the Atlantic, would cause every convoy under U.S. supervision to break and scatter, later to rendezvous south of the Azores and Madeira. In October 1918 a British delegation led by the First Lord of the Admiralty, Sir Eric Geddes, came to Washington and agreed to lend battle cruisers. As it turned out, by this time morale in the German surface fleet was poor, and the Germans never did attempt a battle cruiser raid.[21]

The Germans failed to send long-range submarines to American coastal waters until the summer of 1918, and even then made only a few U-cruiser visits. Using torpedoes, guns, bombs, and mines, these submarines sank several dozen ships, mostly of small tonnage —the total was 167,000. But a mine sank the heavy cruiser San Diego, and another nearly sank the battleship Minnesota.[22] Mine-laying raised the specter of having to protect American coastal waters, a task that would have required hundreds of vessels. And it opened other unattractive possibilities, reflected in a proposal by the British government in August 1918 to shift slower troop transports from American coastal ports to the St. Lawrence, to Montreal and Quebec, forming convoys at Halifax.[23]

If the Germans could have used long-range submarines all along the transatlantic passage, they might have caused grave difficulties. Destroyers were operating only in the danger zones a few hundred miles off England and France: how protect convoys all the way across the Atlantic? The U.S. Navy was hard-pressed to escort convoys during the last leg of the crossing; it could not take convoys all the way without drawing its own and British destroyers from other tasks. In the absence of destroyers in the narrow waters—the Channel and the Mediterranean—German submarines might have wreaked havoc there. Dozens of long-range submarines spread across the Atlantic also would have forced zigzagging all the way, slowing convoys. And it would have created a morale problem among convoy captains and crews, fearful of attacks far out at sea. Men could survive in open boats within 200 miles of the U.S. and Canadian coast but in mid-ocean their plight would be hopeless.[24]

By the autumn of 1917 it was becoming clear that the German submarine menace in the Atlantic was under control, and despite later losses of merchant ships and transports the danger of the first months of 1917 had disappeared. Such was not the case in the Mediterranean, where until the end of the war the Allies suffered heavy losses, mostly from German submarines based in Austrian ports, partly from Austria's own submarines. Here the trouble lay in lack of cooperation among the Allies. The British and Americans both sought to interest the French and Italians in the antisubmarine tactics that worked so well in the Atlantic, but French and Italian naval officers and government leaders refused to risk ships and men, preferring to let the submarines do their will, knowing also that many of the losses were British ships. It was a thoroughly unsatisfactory situation. For a while the United States tried to organize the Mediterranean, and with British concurrence proposed an Allied "admiralissimo," but the plan came to naught.[25]

U.S. naval operations in 1917–18 included laying a mine barrage from the Orkneys to Norwegian territorial waters to prevent submarines based in North German ports from exiting into the Atlantic through the North Sea. The idea of using mines against submarines was as new as underwater vessels. At the outset of the war, mines used by all the powers proved highly unreliable. Nearly two-thirds of British mines in 1914–16 turned out to be defective. But then they improved dramatically and the Royal Navy constructed fields in the Dover strait and initially closed it in April 1918; the navy also tried to block Zeebrugge and Ostend, the ports of Bruges, by laying down mines and blockships and blowing canal locks. Penning submarines in the North Sea at first appeared too grandiose a project, too American. The sheer number of mines required seemed astronomical; mines had to be close together, and because the open sea was deep they had to be in layers to prevent submarines from diving under them. The Americans in 1917 nonetheless examined the possibility, and an electrical engineer from Salem, Massachusetts, Ralph C. Browne, working with Commander Simon P. Fullinwider, produced a mine with horizontal horns and two vertical seventy-foot copper antennae, a huge improvement over British contact mines. Subcontracting to the automobile industry, the Navy Department mass-produced the Browne-Fullinwider mine and proposed a series of fields 240 miles across the North Sea, the distance between New York and Washington. The British made a show of support. Laying the northern barrage, as the U.S. Navy called it, began June 8, 1918, and the Navy designed it as a deterrent rather than barrier. By autumn 1918, notwithstanding "teething troubles" of the Mark VI mine—premature explosions—the U.S. and British navies had laid a series of extended barrages, 70,263 mines, of which the British laid 13,652. The Norwegian government on October 7 closed its territorial waters, effectively shutting off the Atlantic. The barrage might have proved its worth in 1919 if the war had continued. During its short operational life its mines sank two German submarines, possibly three more.[26]

All the while, and in addition to the U.S. Navy's construction of a North Sea barrage, convoying, and transporting troops and supplies, it was necessary to restrict neutral commerce to prevent supplies reaching the Central Powers via neutrals. Regulating neutral commerce was, of course, an embarrassing task. The United States had been the advocate of neutral commerce since 1776, and fought the British over neutral rights in 1812–14. During the Civil War, when the South claimed neutral rights, the U.S. Navy blockaded southern ports and acted like the British Navy. Technically it was not a blockade because the Lincoln administration had not formally recognized the Confederate government. On land federal forces treated captured Confederates according to the laws of war. In 1914–17 the Wilson administration refused to surrender an iota of neutral rights, and sought to enlarge them by demanding that warring nations respect the right of Americans to travel aboard belligerent ships.

The United States in 1917–18 continued to act in accord with neutral rights, even though a major belligerent, and years later when a historian made an examination of American wartime behavior toward the neutrals he found not a single violation.[27] Part of the reason was that beginning in 1917 the number of neutrals dramatically declined; eight Latin American nations declared war on Germany, and five more severed relations. With remaining neutrals, Latin American and other, no serious problems arose. The initial federal agency dealing with export control, the Exports Administrative Board, in October 1917 became the War Trade Board, and under its able head, Vance C. McCormick, issued licenses to cover all American and neutral exports and imports. It gave or withheld supplies in American ports—oil, coal, and ships' stores. Known as bunker control, this tactic had three objectives. The first was to prevent aid from reaching the enemy, directly or indirectly, and to this end no ship could sail or carry cargo without board consent; no one could buy or sell a ship accepting supplies without consent; such a ship could send no questionable wireless communication; the board could dismiss master, officers, and crew; the ship could not carry cargo to blacklisted firms; no enemy subject could take passage without authorization; no ship could acquire surplus supplies without authorization; no sailing vessels could take ships' stores into the danger zone, where a submarine might obtain them, nor could an unarmed and unconvoyed steamer take deck cargo useful to raiders; if one ship of a shipping line misbehaved, the board blacklisted all. The second purpose of bunker control, perhaps most important, was conservation of tonnage. Refusal of stores to sailing ships desiring to enter the war zone forced such vessels into the coastal trade, which needed them, and a similar tactic for coastal steamers drove them into transoceanic routes; vessels had to load to capacity; the board discouraged unnecessarily long hauls, such as voyages to South Africa; no ship could lay up, except for repairs; the board often mandated return voyages, and cargoes, a tactic especially useful with neutral ships. The third purpose of control was to secure essential commodities, by requiring a vessel to bring them back; this rule produced a corollary, that the shipper must keep freight rates within reason, effective with Spanish steamers and ships engaged in the coffee trade with Brazil.

Blacklisting had infuriated the Wilson administration when the British government used a blacklist against American firms in 1914–17. But blacklisting was an undeniable exercise of domestic jurisdiction. After the United States entered the war it published its own blacklist, and Ambassador Sir Cecil Spring Rice in Washington found the occasion amusing: "The blacklist is now published and is far more extensive than our own. *The New York Times* which raged over ours publishes the American list almost without comment."[28]

The North Sea mine barrage hardly accorded with freedom of the seas, and here a technicality saved the American position. The United States in 1914–17 had not protested British and German mine laying, merely entering a reservation of rights. Presumably those rights continued even as the U.S. Navy violated them.

After the war Admiral Sims raised a heated public argument over the Navy's general conduct of the war at sea, charging the Navy Department with gross incompetence. Sims was a tall, handsome officer, with a white Vandyke, who for years had fought against desk officers, even though in twenty-five years of duty he was afloat only nine. After the Battle of Santiago in 1898 he had studied the aim of naval gunners that Sunday morning in July when the Spanish came out and three American ships put 5,752 shells in the air. Strikes for various guns ranged from 1.1 percent to 3.1. Only two twelve- or thirteen-inch shells struck home.[29] He made a report to the Navy Department that someone pigeonholed, whereupon cockroaches ate part of it. Insubordinately he wrote President Theodore Roosevelt, who appointed him an aide and forced the Navy to mend its ways. Ever afterward Sims looked for monkey business in the department and in 1917–18 was sure he had found it. During the war his London headquarters staff increased to 200 officers and 1,000 men, directing twenty-three stations along the Irish, English, French, and Italian coasts; 75,000 officers and men; 368 ships, including the division of 5 oil-burning battleships in Ireland in case German battle cruisers put to sea, another division of coal-burning battleships (oil was in short supply) that reinforced the Grand Fleet in the event of another Jutland (also allowing the British to lay up 5 deteriorating predreadnought battleships of the *King Edward* class), 79 destroyers, 128 submarine chasers, and 85 auxiliary vessels. Unhappy with this experience, he accused Secretary Daniels and the Chief of Naval Operations, Admiral William S. Benson, of sheer inability.

When Sims raised his sixteen-inch guns against Daniels and Benson he fired off in every direction. Daniels's democratic measures in the department bothered him, and he fired away at them and ignored the Secretary's judgment and organizational skill and honesty, and his ability to make the Navy's case on Capitol Hill.[30] He criticized Benson and Daniels for holding destroyers to protect the battleship fleet at Hampton Roads, forgetting that it was impossible to take every destroyer away from the battleships—what if German battle cruisers, accompanied by destroyers and submarines, had gotten into the western Atlantic?[31] The Navy's weakness in destroyers did go on too long; even as German submarine successes were piling up, the Naval Act of 1916 was authorizing another great battleship building program—$315 million for ten battleships, six battle cruisers, and support vessels. After entrance into war the department was slow to scrap the Act of 1916, revising its priorities only on July 20, 1917. Thereafter it did its best, opting for $25 million worth of wooden submarine chasers, buying yachts of all classes and descriptions—in the market for anything that would float. It contracted for $250 million worth of destroyers, and by the war's end new four-stackers were coming down the ways, 44 completed during the war, 223 after.

Hearings by the Senate Committee on Naval Affairs ended in May 1920 and findings appeared a year later, a majority report by three Republicans agreeing with Sims, a minority report by two Democrats disagreeing. The Harding administration could have seized on the majority report and blamed Daniels, Roosevelt, and every other Democrat in sight. It wisely chose to take no action.[32]

CHAPTER 4

The AEF

T HE American Expeditionary Forces, as the Army in Europe was
known, were stamped with the personality of their commander,
General Pershing, a tough, unrelenting officer. Without him it
hardly seems possible that the 2,080,000 American soldiers in
France could have been turned into a great fighting army. Critics
remarked how Pershing gave the impression he was alone in France,
reminiscent of Finley Peter Dunne's description of Lieutenant Colonel Theodore Roosevelt in Cuba. There was point to the criticism,
for in World War I the organization of the AEF could not possibly
have been the work of one man. Many years later another general,
Douglas MacArthur, judged Pershing as neither a strategist nor
tactician and added that he was not as smart as Chief of Staff Peyton
March.[1] The appraisal was correct, albeit coming from a man who
believed himself to possess the qualities he denied Pershing. But if
the AEF's commander in chief had many assistants and was not the
complete general, the enormous achievement was accomplished
under his leadership, built out of nothing in a year and a half, based
on what MacArthur admitted was Pershing's "strength and firmness
of character." For that accomplishment Pershing has stood high in
the annals of modern warfare.

The tall officer with the trim mustache and sharp eyes was born
in Missouri in 1860 into a family originally named Pfoersching.
Young Pershing graduated from West Point in 1886, thirtieth in a
class of seventy-seven, about the same rank as Ulysses S. Grant. He

took all military class honors, each year gaining the highest rank possible for a man of his seniority: first corporal, first sergeant, first captain. He relished the first captaincy. "No military rank that has ever come to me gave me quite the satisfaction that I felt that day," he said, and during the World War he told another first captain, MacArthur, that "We old first captains, Douglas, must never flinch."[2] His career moved slowly at the outset, and in the early nineties he commanded cadets at the state college in Lincoln, Nebraska, where he met such local people as Willa Cather and Charles G. Dawes, future Vice President of the United States in 1925–29. Pershing and Dawes ate at Don Cameron's fifteen-cent lunch counter, where they often joined another young man, the rising politico W. J. Bryan. Pershing in his mid-thirties and still a lieutenant once asked Dawes if he should leave the Army and become a lawyer. "I'd stick with the Army for a while," said Dawes.

Pershing went to Cuba and fought at Santiago, and afterward sailed to the Far East to help put down the Filipino rebellion, where tough officers seemed the only alternative to a United States withdrawal from the islands. Although only a captain, he proved so effective in the Philippines that word got back to Washington, where President Theodore Roosevelt told anyone who would listen that Pershing and Leonard Wood were the two best men in the Army and, "by George," he intended to use their abilities. In 1906, when Pershing was forty-six years old, Roosevelt jumped him over 862 senior officers from captain to brigadier general. A year earlier Pershing had married the daughter of Senator Francis E. Warren of Wyoming, chairman of the Military Affairs Committee, and the marriage did not hurt his career. After commanding 11,000 troops in the Villa Expedition of 1916, he became the natural choice, among a small group of major generals of the Regular Army, for command of the AEF.

His appointment in 1917 was early evidence of the administration's policy of "no politics" in naming officers. It was a good policy, considering the nature of war in Europe. Walter Millis has written that in the Spanish-American War officers moved up and down lines, hats on the tips of their swords, shouting, "Follow me, boys!" They did this kind of thing and charged up a hill toward certain death and survived. In the World War a gallant officer charged up a hill toward certain death and met it. The administration decided to appoint field grade officers from the Regular Army; captaincies

and lieutenancies went to men out of the Plattsburg training camp
or its equivalents in civil life, or the Army chose enlisted men to take
three months of special training and thereby become "ninety-day
wonders," second lieutenants. Pershing was not without political
opinions, and was no supporter of President Wilson, especially after
the *Lusitania* went down. "What do you suppose a weak, chicken-
hearted, white-livered lot as we have in Washington are going to
do?" he growled to his wife. A few days later Wilson said there was
such a thing as a man being too proud to fight and Pershing's
disposition verged on apoplexy: "Isn't that the damnedest rot you
ever heard a sane person get off?"[3] Whatever he thought in those
timid days, he kept his mouth shut and made himself available for
preferment in 1917.

Having set a rule in favor of professionalism, the administration
considered requests from former President Roosevelt and General
Wood, both of whom wished to command troops in France. The
Roosevelt case came up first, Wood's case a year later, and in the
first Wilson and in the second Pershing belatedly decided against
both Rough Riders (Wood and Roosevelt had been colonel and
lieutenant colonel respectively of the famous Spanish-American
War regiment). The President and Pershing handled the cases awkwardly and neither spoke frankly; both lacked the courage to look
the ex-President and ex–Chief of Staff in the eye and say what they
thought. In Roosevelt's case his appointment as a major general
would have undermined the professionalism the Army so badly
needed to establish, and the President should have said so. Instead
he showed rigid unwillingness to grant anything to a man who had
opposed him politically.[4] Most of Wood's detractors resided in the
Army, where he had rubbed them the wrong way. He once had been
an Army surgeon who had not attended West Point and career
officers did not like his background, though the difference was to his
advantage, for he received his degrees from Harvard. When he was
Chief of Staff he fought the bureau system to what he presumed
was its death, and bureaucrats spread calumnies about him. They
claimed him physically unfit and liked to remark how he walked with
a limp, even though that problem had a simple explanation—after
the war with Spain he inadvertently had struck his head on the sharp
point of a hanging lamp, an injury that gave rise to a brain tumor
that caused the limp. Although Army doctors in 1918 declared him
fit, critics continued to capitalize on his infirmity and circulated a

story about epileptic seizures. As if military enemies were not enough, Wood created political enemies as well. He seemed to delight in talking about the President—in a small group that included men he did not know, he referred to the President as a rabbit. An excellent Chief of Staff, he had grown disgruntled with the Democratic Wilson administration and openly criticized it. When Pershing dealt with him in February 1918, turning down his request for command in France by describing him as a political general, there was truth to the remark. Wood went to the President, who listened courteously and did nothing, and the general afterward told the President's secretary, Joseph P. Tumulty, that "I know who is responsible for this. It is that man Pershing." True enough, but if Pershing had not done the job, Baker and Wilson would have.[5]

The Wood case called attention to one of Pershing's traits that reduced his effectiveness as a commander: his desire to dominate. If Wood was the political general Pershing claimed him to be, he was also a former Chief of Staff, a large personality with a civilian and military following, and hence an awkward subordinate. Pershing did not want people in his command who might treat him as their equal; the AEF had one full general, and he was it. To admirers, mainly men younger than himself, Pershing displayed heroic proportions; with peers he was uncomfortable. "Always the ambition, the air of moral superiority, the coldbloodedness, the feeling that he would expend men like cartridges, the knowledge that he demanded an uncomfortable degree of personal loyalty and that he considered his own judgment nearly infallible," Allan R. Millett has said of him.[6] Pershing did not want Wood in France because he would have had trouble dominating him. The AEF's commander watched his prerogatives. He exercised command of field troops far beyond the time he should have. Able subordinates like Hunter Liggett and Bullard, who commanded respectively the First and Second armies and were the only men in World War I to receive the rank of lieutenant general, obtained their commands late in the war, on October 16 and November 1. He tried to reach back to Washington and dominate there too. March was junior to Pershing, and before returning to Washington had been in his command, and Pershing never forgot it. He liked to believe that he, Pershing, was senior general in the Army and that the Chief of Staff was a subordinate, operating a supply bureau for the AEF. As he wrote in his memoirs, "It remained, then, for the War Department simply and without cavil to support our efforts to the fullest extent."[7] Through most of 1918 he carried on a frosty cable correspondence with March, trying to push him around. Pershing's feud went to great lengths, including his choice of the Sam Browne belt with a strap over the right shoulder that looked smart, helped with avoirdupois, and distinguished officers of the AEF from supply officers at home. Sir Samuel Browne had fabricated his invention when he was in India during the seventies, and the expedition to Afghanistan used it in 1879; British officers wore it during the World War, and Hitler and Mussolini later wore it. March pronounced it a waste of scarce leather and instructed his military police to strip it from all of Pershing's officers landing in the United States.[8]

If Pershing could occupy himself with such trivial problems— Baker once described him as "the only combination of telescope and microscope I know"—he spent much time on serious issues. One of the ways he stamped the Army in France as his creation was by establishing the size of overseas divisions. Appointed AEF commander in May 1917, he and a small staff decided in favor of basic units of unprecedented size, 27,000 men and 1,000 officers, which with support troops brought the divisional slice to 40,000 men, twice or three times a European division in 1917–18. He opted for the "square division" of four infantry regiments. As organized by Pershing's staff, each American division was larger than the entire Regular Army twenty-five years before. They did not set divisional size with public relations in mind—so that when European and American newspapermen described battles by divisions and tended not to mention that an American division equaled a European corps, American divisions would look good in newspaper accounts. They took the decision because the large division allowed ample replacements during battle, and because of scarcity of field grade officers.

Having agreed to large divisions, Pershing asked for many of them, and made changes in his requirements that baffled officers in Washington, whose task it was, he said, to equip and send the men he asked for. After he and his staff went over on the *Baltic*, late in May 1917, 11,000 men of the First Division followed, but strength in France did not rise rapidly for months, partly because troops were not available, partly because of scarcity of shipping. At the end of September 1917, AEF strength stood at 61,531. After the Italian defeat at Caporetto and the beginning of the Bolshevik Revolution, an Allied conference at Rapallo in November 1917 set a figure of thirty American divisions for 1918. During the great German offensive in March–May, the British government suddenly found shipping, and when it offered to bring over as many Americans as could be crammed aboard, Pershing upped his requirements to sixty-six divisions, a suspect figure as it seemed to double his first goal and was close to being two-thirds of an attractive round number, a hundred. Then he went for the round number. The Allied commander in France, General Ferdinand Foch, suggested it late in June when the German Army's strength had mesmerized the Allies. Pershing seized on the suggestion and passed it to Washington with his fervent recommendation. In his memoirs he slyly admitted it was a tactic, that he hoped for more troops and asked for far more than he would get. It indeed was a great many; calculating 40,000 men for each division, including support troops, 100 divisions meant 4 million men, with extra replacements 5 million, an army one-fourth larger than the British and French armies combined. Alone, it was enough to defeat the Germans. Horrified, the War Department compromised at eighty divisions; President Wilson agreed to that plan on July 26, 1918. Pershing dreamed of more, and when Baker visited the front in September he found the staff planning ninety-six divisions, not far from the round figure. March sharply cabled that the official program was eighty. Pershing cabled back that although the eighty-division program might be "convenient" to the War Department, it was inadequate for Europe, and the AEF should plan its own goals.

By the time of the Armistice the AEF had grown to forty-two divisions, which proved enough. The United States had more troops in France than did Britain; another three months and there would have been more American than French soldiers under arms in their own country. Beginning in the late spring of 1918, troops streamed in by the hundreds of thousands: in May, 245,945; June, 278,664; July, 306,350; August, 285,974; September, 257,457. The Germans had fairly accurate figures for strength up to March 1918 but not thereafter, and both high command and common soldiers were astonished when it turned out that 10,000 men a day were coming in. Most of those troops headed straight for the front. One day a German prisoner at Le Havre beheld a vast throng coming off ships and turned to an American soldier to ask how many men he was looking at right then. The answer was 40,000 or 50,000. *"Mein*

Gott in Himmel!" was the response, and tears came to the German's eyes.[9]

First sight of French shores was likely to be something men in the AEF never forgot. Private Philip C. Jessup beheld a dim outline on the horizon, then a lighthouse, then gradually "the land in all its glory. Every imaginable shade of green was spread out down to the bare cliffs, and here and there a brilliant patch of orange gorse or brown and yellow mustard. The houses were beautiful—all stone and plaster with tile, stone, or slate roofs." Fishing vessels crowded the harbor mouth with "fantastically rigged sails of red, yellow, brown, black, or white."[10]

Once ashore and passing along rail lines in little cars marked HOMMES 40, CHEVAUX 8, men retained their initial impression, according to Corporal William L. Langer. Apart from the cramped, altogether uncushioned inconvenience of the "40 & 8" cars, the trip was delightful, Langer remembered. France seemed a veritable garden land, "soft hills, the clear-cut fields of waving wheat or the trim vegetable patches, the groups of red-tiled stone houses, the canals and the white roads, both lined with fabulous lines of splendid trees, all these are memories ineradicably impressed on our minds."[11] Frederick Pottle remembered buttresses of the cathedral of Le Mans in the distance as his train lay in the squalor of the yards, the broad Loire at Tours shimmering in sunset, "the placid pastoral beauty of France, apparently untouched by war, unrolling itself so sweetly before us, as though we were mere tourists!"[12]

Then arrival and assignment to "billets," as the French put it, and the impressions wore off. Pershing took over a château as befitted his status, near the old French garrison town of Chaumont, 135 miles southeast of Paris. Headquarters officers and troops established themselves in the local cantonment vacated by French troops, a somber square of barracks with a parade ground. As divisions came into ports and up rail lines in horse cars they poured into towns and villages where officers took rooms in small, cramped houses of local people and men bedded down in barns and outbuildings. A division stretched through several villages and farm areas. Local people long had lived amidst soldiers and managed to get along with the new guests and sold vegetables, chickens, eggs, and wine. Troops made friends with the natives and adjusted their expectations to the straitened nature of their circumstances.

The commanding general of the AEF watched each division pass

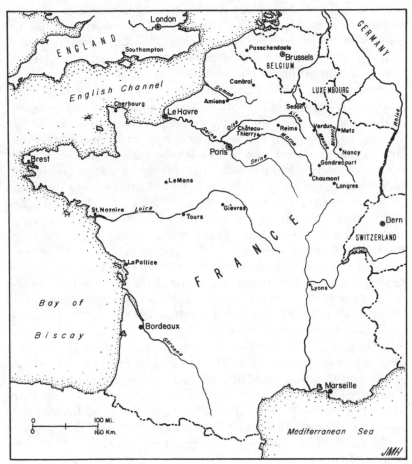

"Over There," 1917–18

under his command, and troops saw his big staff car traveling forty
or fifty miles an hour down country roads with chickens flying and
livestock scattering as he headed for inspections or meetings. He
came to France a major general and Congress in October 1917
awarded him four stars, first American commander to hold such
rank since Grant, Sherman, and Sheridan. Rank made his situation
easier with British and French opposites. His task remained—obtaining a fighting force, training enough troops so that when Americans went into action they would acquit themselves well.

The c. in c. took time getting his army into action, for he sensed
how low the prestige of the United States would fall if troops failed
on the battlefield. He maintained that to put one division in line he
needed four: a division in line, he said, required a backup division
for rotating; moreover, casualties might be high, so he needed two
more. Considering his divisions' size, this meant eight to twelve by
European standards. In any event buildup was slow, four divisions
by December 1917. After a contingent of the First Division had gone
over in June 1917, the rest of its troops followed, along with men
of the Second Division, which contained a brigade of Marines, the
Twenty-sixth Division from New England, which was the first National Guard division to cross the Atlantic, and the Forty-second or
Rainbow Division of National Guard units from many states.[13] Units
of the First Division moved into a quiet sector of the front near
Nancy on October 21, 1917, and two days later, at 6:05 a.m., fired
first shots. In early November the Germans raided the division's
trenches and killed three soldiers. About the same time American
medical and engineer detachments were caught in a German coun-
terattack at Cambrai. In March 1918, Pershing assigned two divisions to the French for combat; the result, incidentally, was another
trench raid on the Twenty-sixth at Seicheprey, with 634 casualties,
including 80 men killed and 130 prisoners.

The AEF's commanding general spent months training his divisions. Field grade officers went to a general staff college at Langres.
Company grade officers attended schools for weapons and tactics—
artillery, small arms, gas. The result should have helped the AEF;
General Bullard took command of the First Division in December
1917 and remarked later how schools replaced what the Army had
known as drill, for "little of our previous training, except discipline,
fitted the special conditions that were before us."[14] Still, one wonders about all the schooling, whether the AEF's commander was too

academic. Secretary Baker came over on an inspection trip in February 1918, when General March was about to take over the War Department, and was unsure of the schooling but hesitated, typically, to interfere with Pershing's plans. It turned out that a lot of training was not absolutely necessary; during the Battle of St. Mihiel the Forty-second Division threw in 9,000 replacements from America and they did well, and Brigadier General MacArthur found one soldier of conspicuous merit with less than two months' training in the United States.

Behind Pershing's concern that his men make a showing lay another reason for his eagerness to send them to school: training for open rather than trench warfare, which was contrary to prevailing military doctrine in Europe. The French and British armies had accustomed themselves to trenches, a complex way of fighting as practiced on the Western Front, for it involved construction and maintenance of several trench lines, and men had to know when to raise heads, fire, patrol. Pershing and his generals admitted trench warfare required training, but fundamentally detested trenches. The problem in Europe, they maintained, the reason for stalemate on the Western Front, was this strategy. The French rushed instructors to the United States, and tried also to teach the AEF. Premier Georges Clemenceau told Colonel House that if the Americans did not permit the French to teach them, the Germans would.[15] But Pershing's friend Harbord wrote in his diary January 28, 1918, how the French "mother us in the matter of training. Our 1st Division suffered from this for months, absorbing nothing but defensive warfare from them, whereas only offensive warfare ever wins a war."[16] British instructors acted more circumspectly, for Ambassador Spring Rice in Washington advised Balfour that on all matters, diplomatic and military, Americans were touchy and "It cannot be too often insisted that to be useful we must be inconspicuous." The British newspaper magnate Lord Northcliffe prescribed flattery and self-abnegation.[17] But British instructors proved no more successful than the French, for Americans refused to learn defensive doctrine.

Stressing offense, Pershing announced a tactical principle, marksmanship by individual soldiers. A marksman had courage to get out of a trench. The AEF was not well prepared for gas war. It possessed almost no understanding of tanks, and had few. Its commanders had worked with artillery in the Old Army and quickly learned to use French 75s. If Pershing recognized that machine guns often proved decisive, he believed his troops could rush them with acceptable loss of life. But he placed his trust in individual marksmanship. As Harbord described the commander in chief's premier tactical principle, "When even one soldier climbed out and moved to the front, the adventure for him became open warfare, a war of movement, and the essentials of minor tactics were then in play."[18] In 1917 both the British and French armies on the Western Front each used less than a billion and a half rounds of rifle ammunition. For 1918, Pershing put in for 6 billion.

AEF commanders may have misjudged the importance of rifles and open warfare, and yet one cannot be sure. Years later when Pershing published his memoirs he made his point again and took a swipe at his supply general, March, for ignoring it: " . . . training methods at home had not improved, as preparation for trench warfare still predominated. All this was discouraging . . . , disastrous to morale, threw upon the AEF an extra burden of training, and resulted in our having a number of divisions only partially trained when the time came to use them."[19] For this and other judgments March hastily composed a book to show how foolish Pershing was, and Baker privately entered the argument by writing March, "Am I not right in feeling that his insistence on our training troops for open warfare finally proved useless? Did his army ever really get the Germans into open warfare? My recollection is that the Germans retreated from trench to trench . . ." Remembering Pershing's requests for cavalry late in the war, Baker added that "great sweeping cavalry movements" never took place.[20] He was right in venturing that the Germans retired from trench to trench. But at the end of fighting, the Americans were getting out into open country. And another aspect of fighting justified the rifle. Harbord liked to speak of the need for élan, willingness to take chances when logic advised a trench. Because of élan French and British troops took appalling losses in the war's first year. They had turned very cautious by 1917 when the Americans came into the war. Americans entered the line in 1918 trained in Pershing's ideas, really the spirit of 1914–15. Their élan surprised German commanders, and when added to the immense numbers of American troops may well have persuaded the Germans to give up.

Provisioning the AEF proved almost as difficult as organizing and getting it in place. The first two generals in charge of the Services of Supply failed with the job. The third, a good staff officer, Major

General Francis J. Kernan, laid out things well but tied himself to headquarters at Tours. The fourth, Harbord, put his headquarters aboard a train likely to turn up anywhere to survey a local operation and replace an inept commander. By the end of the war Harbord's 670,000 men, a third of Pershing's entire force, were unloading ships much more promptly and getting material to the front.

At the very outset American officers discovered total confusion in the ports, and Goethals's later assistant, Robert Wood, who had gone over with the Rainbow Division, received the task of straightening things out. Turn-around was terrible—ships at St. Nazaire took forty days before starting to unload, at a time when a ship was worth its weight in gold. When Pershing asked Wood to correct the situation, he said he could do it in thirty days but needed two pieces of information: first, a list of ships en route and their dates of arrival two days before same; and second, the general nature of the cargo. He went over to London where Sims gave him a naval officer with a code, and he received the two pieces of information. Thereafter it became only a matter of distribution. Before Wood took over, all convoys had gone into St. Nazaire. Wood opened Bordeaux and Brest and later La Pallice, Le Havre, and Marseilles. "In thirty days I had it all straightened out, just by distributing the load." If a ship carried locomotives, he sent it to a port with big cranes. "They all thought I was really very good, but any man who'd had experience in commercial shipping could have done that. When I had the ports of Panama and Colón they would wire me from San Francisco stating just what kind of ship would arrive and what it had on it, and then I was all ready for it."[21]

Even after distribution of ships, French ports proved grossly inadequate for rapidly increasing demands by the AEF, and American engineers changed them beyond recognition, enlarging them, modernizing them. Quays of the old ports were not long enough. Most cranes were antiques. At St. Nazaire railroad tracks along the cement piers moved freight without crossovers or practical turntables. Workers pushed little cars around, or a single animal hauled them. Tiny turntables stood in pairs, and with a car on one the French turned it by hand at right angles, pushed it across a short track to the parallel track, and again turned it; if they wanted it on the same track they pushed the turntable 180 degrees.[22] At Bordeaux not more than two ships of any size could unload in a week. To handle the enormous traffic of an overseas army, engineers virtually rebuilt Le Havre, Cherbourg, Brest, St. Nazaire, Bordeaux, and other ports. By early 1918, Bordeaux boasted docks a mile long and electric cranes; soon fourteen ships unloaded simultaneously, speed determined only by available stevedores.

Likewise the same problems existed with rail lines out of ports. Initial supply of the AEF over French lines proved chaotic. Communication by telegraph or telephone was primitive. Once out of port areas, French railroads did not keep track of rolling stock and strewed cars all over France. Each *chef de gare* was monarch of all he surveyed and could stop any train and take off a car. Trains to Gondrecourt, where Americans dropped troops and materiel, came in with cars missing and the only recourse was to send men back to check each station. Once they found cars they might not get them back. Colonel Johnson Hagood in November 1917 watched fifty carloads of flour stand at Bourmont for a month, and finally gave the flour to the French.[23] The solution was to bring in American railroadmen, including the vice president of the Pennsylvania Railroad, William W. Atterbury, who became a brigadier general. Americans revamped hundreds of miles of track from ports to front, and strengthened it to take their own big locomotives and cars.

By the spring of 1918 supply in Europe was turning around, well before Harbord's appointment. Notable was the huge supply plant at Gièvres, which Hagood, by then a brigadier general, looked over and found arranged in a diamond, six miles from end to end, with engineer, medical, quartermaster, ordnance, and gas depots—256 storehouses, 4.5 million square feet of covered storage, 225 miles of track.[24]

Beginning in May 1918 a new problem beset AEF supply officers. Tonnage of supplies from the United States dwindled alarmingly as increasing numbers of troops arrived. It began to appear as if reorganized port facilities and rail lines might have little to receive and transport other than men. Arrival of supplies dropped from forty-nine pounds per man in April to twenty-two in September, a fall so abrupt that Secretary Daniels, then in Europe, told three congressmen just after the Armistice that Pershing had to favor a cease-fire because his supply system was about to break down.

Throughout the war Pershing's friend from Nebraska days, Dawes, helped keep supplies coming up to the front. Having been appointed general purchasing agent in August 1917, Dawes had discovered ships arriving in France half empty because of inadequate control at docks in the United States, and authorities at home infuriated him by considering an increase in cargoes to Latin America. He could do little about these delinquencies other than complain, but undertook to brighten the corner where he was. He started with the presumption he could do what he wanted, and discovered many AEF necessities available in Europe. He found that in 1914, when the Germans occupied Belgium, the Belgian Army had evacuated 800 locomotives, which thereafter stood unused on rail lines in northern France. General Atterbury disliked these little engines and angrily told the Belgians they were gold bricks and gave them back, but Dawes got them back again, calculating that the negotiation saved 100,000 tons of shipping.[25] He turned up huge amounts of material in most unlikely places. He found more machine tools than the Army could use. He saw a requisition for 400,-000 railroad ties, with 2.4 million needed in all, and dazed Army engineers by getting an offer of 145,000 in Portugal, 50,000 in Spain, even some in France, "just as a starter."[26] He found 10-million ship tons (forty cubic feet equals a ship ton of supplies) in Europe, as compared to 7.6 million received from the United States.

The Services of Supply also supervised medical arrangements of the AEF, which proved adequate in the autumn of 1918 when tens of thousands of wounded men, many in serious condition, came back from the front. By the end of the war, AEF hospitals contained 283,553 beds. Of 200,000 officers of the AEF, 16,000 were doctors.

At the beginning the medical bureau in Washington was in poor shape, despite its able head, Major General William Gorgas, the conqueror of yellow fever in Cuba and Panama. The famous surgeon of Boston Dr. Harvey Cushing had served as a volunteer with the British Army, and went down to the capital to sort out equipment; he was flabbergasted to find shortages of instruments of all sorts, no new ones immediately available because instrument makers had taken on war work. Standard medical chests dated from the Civil War or Spanish-American War. Laid over supplies in one box, someone told Cushing, was a newspaper announcing Cervera's fleet off New England.[27]

Gorgas worked hard to change things. He realized he could not depend on the Army's small group of doctors, almost all without experience beyond elementary problems of peacetime Army medicine. He commissioned such outstanding civilian doctors as Cushing, George W. Crile of Cleveland, and Charles and William Mayo of Rochester, Minnesota. The AEF eventually received the best medicine the country could provide. Crile became Pershing's medical troubleshooter. Not merely a superb surgeon but a superb organizer, he brought order to front-line medicine, "observing, recommending, picking up a group where there seems to be an unnecessarily high mortality rate, changing this or that method of handling, until they get better results."[28] He investigated the time a wounded man could go without attention before being endangered by tetanus, and saved soldiers from amputations. AEF surgeons amputated only 700 hands or feet, 600 arms, 1,700 legs; there was not a single basket case. Crile arranged for the Red Cross to publish a journal for AEF doctors, *War Medicine*, distributed free, and wrote unsigned editorials.

In 1917–18 deaths from battlefield causes proved far fewer than in past wars. So were deaths from disease; in the Mexican War in the medical dark ages, disease killed more than one-tenth of the Army in a single year; in the Civil War, it was sixty-five men per thousand; in World War I, fifteen. Little evidence appeared of incompetent treatment. Crile wrote in his diary that he "saw over 20,000 bed hospitals yesterday; much good surgery, some bad; some needless amputations."[29] Hugh Young of Johns Hopkins, the genitourinary specialist who was a colonel on Pershing's staff, discovered his brother-in-law dead of pneumonia because of incompetent treatment by a Regular Army doctor.[30]

Venereal disease, dread malady of armies of the past, worried Pershing almost as much as battlefield casualties and, knowing he could not prevent the one but could do something about the other, he took stringent measures. No ideologue in this regard, during the Villa Expedition he had set up a *maison tolérée* in Mexico, but feared the worst from the AEF, far from home for an indefinite period. During passage on the *Baltic*, Hugh Young showed him horrible pictures of results of sexual promiscuity, and Young's lectures may have been inspirational. Another persuasion was the experience of the British and French, who had gotten nowhere with v.d.; the disease reportedly afflicted one-fourth of the men of a British division. If Americans had done nothing, they might have filled twenty base hospitals, 20,000 beds. Each French prostitute infected dozens of men.[31] Premier Clemenceau offered to solve the problem by official houses of prostitution. That was no solution—Pershing gave Clemenceau's letter to the War Department's special assistant for troop morale, Raymond Fosdick, who showed it to Baker, who read it twice and said, "For God's sake, Raymond, don't show this to the president or he'll stop the war."[32] Young cleaned up ports under AEF control and Pershing moved relentlessly against offenders of Young's rules; on top of papers awaiting him each morning lay the venereal report of all units. Years after the war an AEF general related a story of battalion commanders who in reply to Pershing's question during an inspection said there was only one case of such disease in their command. The c. in c. curtly said, "One too many."[33] By draconian measures Young reduced the AEF rate to less than that of Americans at home.

In addition to medical attention the AEF enjoyed ministrations of service organizations—Y.M.C.A., Red Cross, Salvation Army. The "Y" became a subject of wrath in the Army on which it was difficult to be neutral. The usual comment about "that damned Y" was that its secretaries were clergymen or draft dodgers who took it easy fraternizing with officers while men suffered. Clergymen held too many prayer meetings, the men said, and refused to let soldiers play cards in Y huts; meanwhile the draft dodgers flourished.[34] When General March was in command at Valdahon he inspected the Y and saw husky young men who could have been soldiers. When he discovered that their venereal disease rate was higher than that of any unit under his command, his disposition, never placid, turned choleric, and he sent a bristling report to Pershing. Officials of the Y rushed down from Paris and begged him to withdraw his indictment, but he declined, telling them that not merely did he think the military should take over all service organizations but that women should do their work. Irving Berlin's *Yip Yip Yaphank* offered a tune, "I Can Always Find a Little Sunshine in the Y.M.C.A.," but doughboys added a verse to "Mademoiselle from Armentières":

> The Y.M.C.A. went over the top,
> They thought they heard a nickel drop.

Tales of the Y multiplied—overcharging, demands for cash before tired soldiers received cigarettes, Yanks who bought boxes of Y chocolate to find in the bottom a card from a mother to her son in France. Nor did the Red Cross fare much better; Colonel Carter Harrison IV, former mayor of Chicago, wrote his wife about "an awfully cheap bunch, nice enough fellows for the most part, but of the calibre I would have made bureau heads of in the City Hall."[35]

Most men in the AEF preferred husband-and-wife teams of the Salvation Army that confined activities to sewing buttons and serving pies, doughnuts, pancakes, and coffee. For the rest of his life Captain Farley Granger, Sr., sent the Salvation Army five dollars each year. Elmer Sherwood of Bloomfield, Indiana, wrote that Salvation Army workers had wings sprouting that would carry them to heaven after the war. "Officers take their places in the line which forms before the S.A. canteen just the same as privates. A major took his place in the line behind me this morning and having no mess kit, took his flapjack in his hat."[36]

Other volunteer groups offered services. An association known as the Purple Cross urged Harbord to appoint an embalming officer to each division staff. Nothing came of the proposal. The War Department asked Pershing's opinion, which was negative, because of lack of shipping for coffins, and without coffins the professionals of the Purple Cross would have wasted their skills.

CHAPTER 5

Victory

AT last in the spring of 1918 preparation came to an end and fighting commenced, at a time of deadly peril for the Allies. More than anything else, the event that gave advantage to the Germans was the collapse of the Russian front, which offered an opportunity to transfer half a million German troops, perhaps even a million, to the Western Front. The republican government in Petrograd had tried to keep troops in the field; after an offensive against the Austrians in the summer the effort proved too much, and by November, when the Bolsheviks took over, war weariness was so omnipresent that the Soviet government had little choice save to make peace. The Bolsheviks did not want to continue the war and probably would have made peace even if the military situation had been favorable. Conviction and exigency reinforced each other and the Treaty of Brest-Litovsk, signed in March 1918, marked Russia's defeat and withdrawal.

Three other developments in 1917 helped gain the Germans the advantage. In March 1917 a new French commander, General Henri Nivelle, had opened an offensive that collapsed so rapidly that nothing could hide the defeat. Losses were not extraordinarily high by the front's standards of ferocity; perhaps 15,000 men died and 70,000 were wounded. But something snapped within French morale, and troops in many divisions mutinied. Draconian measures, including executions, quelled the outbreak, but for the rest of the year the French Army's élan was severely diminished.

Alarmed, the British commander in France, Sir Douglas Haig, organized a series of offensives in Flanders to take pressure off his French ally. Haig pushed his troops, but the terrain along northern France and into Belgium was marshy, impossible for construction of trenches more than two or three feet deep, requiring troops to pile sandbags in front. Moreover, he threw troops against impregnable defenses; the Germans had been on their lines so long they had fortified them admirably. Artillery fire from both sides destroyed drainage and turned no-man's-land into a swamp of brown mud and water. The battle became known for the ridge of Passchendaele, a dread name thereafter in British military annals. Years later, when Winston Churchill in his memoirs criticized Haig for stupidity, the field marshal wrote the *Times* that he had had to attack, that the mere suggestion of a pause had brought Nivelle's successor, General Henri Pétain, to beg for another effort without delay, not to leave the Germans alone a week on account of the "awful state" of French troops. Whatever this postwar argument and the wartime conversations of Pétain with Haig, one point was absolutely clear by the end of 1917. The British had advanced four miles on a narrow front, attaining weaker positions than they left, inflicting 270,710 casualties and suffering 448,614, including 150,000 men killed. At the end of 1917 the British Army was as tired as the French.

By that time the Italian Army had collapsed at Caporetto. The Italians in October 1917 lost 275,000 prisoners, 2,500 guns, and tremendous quantities of equipment; the Germans and Austrians drove forward seventy miles. The Italian Army reconstituted the front on the Piave River, and held only after the Allies rushed in reinforcements—two army corps, one British and one French. To some observers it seemed that if the Germans had forced Italy out of the war the result would not have been tragic, for the Italian Army had not been much help. Still, Italian territory adjoined southern France, and if Italy left the war the French would have to put strong forces on the frontier. Because of pressure on the Western Front no forces other than the two corps were available. Throughout the war the Allies worried about a second German front in the west, a front in the south after collapse of Italy or, perhaps, a violation of Switzerland, as had happened with Belgium.

Meanwhile after analyzing infantry tactics from the fighting fronts the Germans had gone over to what sometimes have been known erroneously as Hutier tactics, so-called for General Oskar von Hu-

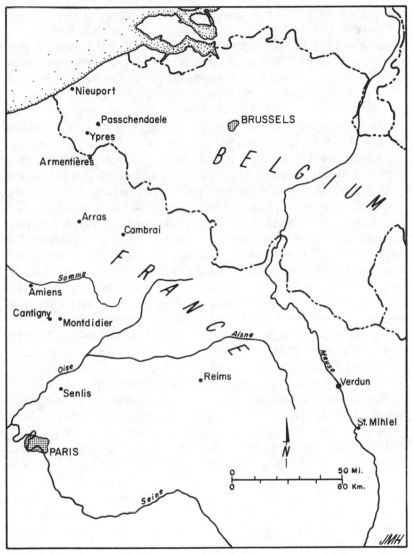

The Western Front

tier, victor of an attack against Riga in 1917. Authorship of the new tactics lay more properly with men and officers throughout the German Army. After the battles of the Somme and Verdun in 1916, it became clear that the Central Powers needed offensive tactics of a different sort, and the result was collection of data from many commanders and staff officers, including small-unit leaders in the trenches. After analysis the data first appeared in a series of manuals in the winter of 1916–17. Constantly modified, the basic technique now became infiltration. To gain territory, surprise was essential; without it, local commanders delayed attack. First came a sudden, massive barrage of gas and high-explosive shells aimed at enemy artillery, not their field fortifications. Then storm battalions—hand-picked and specially trained units of men in each attacking division —moved forward, shielded by an artillery technique that produced a rolling curtain of shells, fired at a predetermined rate, immediately ahead of the troops. Equipped with special light-artillery batteries and mortars, these storm troops ignored the enemy's strong points and units at the flanks, leaving them for the second wave, and boldly infiltrated small groups until they reached the enemy's artillery. Expanded to include masses of tanks and planes, these procedures became standard infantry tactics during World War II and later conflicts. The German high command refined the new tactics in a manual, *The Attack in Position Warfare*, which appeared on January 1, 1918. Loosed upon Allied armies in France in the spring of 1918, they proved fearfully effective. When an Allied commander accustomed to setpiece tactics of trench warfare tried to make a short and orderly withdrawal, more often than not it turned into a rout.[1]

The Germans launched their first blow against the British Fifth Army on March 21, 1918, and before its commander, Sir Hubert Gough, sensed what was happening, they infiltrated his force of 200,000 men, rolled its rear lines against the front in melees of disaster, took 80,000 prisoners, and penetrated twenty-four miles to the outskirts of Amiens. The Germans began to bombard Paris with long-range guns, dropping shells indiscriminately every few minutes, massive explosions that blew up buildings, often killing dozens of people. The British called in French troops, threw in all reserves, and after agonizing delays managed to hold a very weak line against the attackers.

Next, the German high command—in the main, General Ludendorff, although technically he was subordinate to Field Marshal Paul von Hindenburg—hurled dozens of divisions against the French, in a second battering offensive that began on April 9. After an excruciating delay the exhausted French barely held.

Then came a crushing blow beginning May 27. It was in this awful moment of devastating breakthrough, when the road to Paris lay wide open, that the French called in the Americans.

In the spring, summer, and autumn of 1918 the U.S. Army at last rolled into action. When the Germans opened their first offensive against the British, Pershing offered all his troops to the Allies. Anglo-French forces managed to plug the gap in the line. On May 28 the First Division sent a reinforced regiment into Cantigny, a crossroads close to Montdidier on the northwestern bulge of a salient between Arras and Rheims, and General Bullard's troops took the village, which lay on a plateau from which the Germans had ranged artillery. At the same time came the Germans' Chemin des Dames offensive, bringing much larger counteraction by the U.S. Army. By late summer hundreds of thousands of young men from the New World were battling to redress the balance of the Old.

American participation in the Chemin des Dames hardly compared with what came later at the Aisne-Marne and especially St. Mihiel and the Meuse-Argonne, but it marked an initial test of Pershing's rifle tactics. The testing tended to focus on the U.S. Marines at Belleau Wood; through an oversight, the AEF censor in Paris permitted identification of troops in that area as Marines, because they represented a different service. Army leaders long afterward remembered the glorification, the failure of newspapers at home to take account of the Second Division's other brigade, of Army troops, which also distinguished itself. Many years later in World War II, General MacArthur refused unit citations to Marines on Bataan because, he said, the Corps had received more than enough attention.

The offensive of the German Army along the Chemin des Dames on May 27 shoved back the French front from Rheims in the east to Soissons and beyond in the west, and seemed destined for huge success. A French general had held the Rheims-Soissons portion of the front with ten weak divisions, four of them British. Instead of deploying behind several lines of trenches with a lightly held area at the front to receive any artillery barrage, he placed most of his men at the front. Pétain had advised a careful distribution, but failed to check on his subordinate. When the Germans came over with

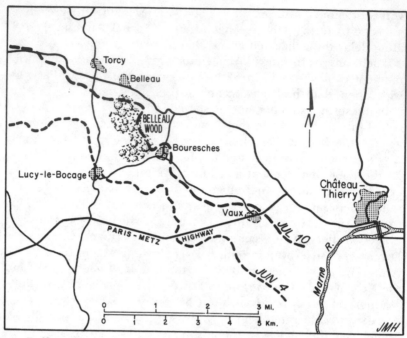

Belleau Wood, Vaus, and Château-Thierry, May–July 1918

325,000 men in twenty-five divisions, the attack succeeded beyond all expectation, ten miles in a day, troops moving forward without resistance. Nothing like it had been seen on the Western Front since 1914. In Allied lines, troops gained the sinking feeling that this time the Germans would break through. Pershing's representative at French GHQ, Major Paul H. Clark, spoke with General de Barescut of the Operations Bureau, who described the battle as the greatest, most important, of the war. The deep penetration, a V-shaped salient, required huge numbers of troops to stop. The Allied generalissimo, Foch, who had received his appointment after the Fifth Army's debacle, considered shortening his lines, pulling British troops to the north back to the Somme, or abandoning the eastern part of the front from Rheims to Switzerland. The British probably would have resisted withdrawal, and the more expedient alternative was to abandon Rheims-Switzerland. The Operations Bureau anticipated the worst. When Clark asked three officers what would happen if Paris fell, all doubted the war could go on.[2] At Chaumont,

Pershing issued secret orders anticipating evacuation. Trucks stood outside the American embassy in Paris. Hundreds of thousands fled the capital. As in 1914, the French government prepared to evacuate. A secret meeting of the Chamber of Deputies considered an armistice. Nor was France's ally, Britain, more confident; the War Cabinet discussed abandonment of the Channel ports and withdrawal from France.

Chaos prevailed in front areas as German troops swept through Château-Thierry to the Marne and entered such localities as the square-mile area known as Belleau Wood. Then something electrifying happened, for suddenly the roads between Provins and the front toward Meaux and Coulommiers filled with endless streams of Americans, an "inexhaustible flood of gleaming youth in its first maturity of health and vigour." It was the huge American Second Division, really a corps, mile after mile of singing Americans, trucks hurling dust high in the air, bumper to bumper, on they came. Ensuing months offered similar scenes but none would match this. Harbord, then brigadier general in command of the Marine brigade, never forgot it and the very thought brought tears to his eyes.

For the French, Churchill wrote in *The World Crisis*, the effect was prodigious. They felt they were present at "the magical operation of the transfusion of blood," reanimating the mangled body of a France bled white by four years of innumerable wounds. The Americans were "half trained, half organised, with only their courage, their numbers and their magnificent youth behind their weapons," and were to buy their experience at a bitter price, but this they were quite ready to do.[3]

When the Americans arrived at Belleau Wood near the Paris-Metz highway on June 4, 1918, they found no line, only thin groups of retreating Frenchmen. The division commander flung a brigade forward on either side of the road, stretching it as far as he could, Marines to the northwest, Army to the southeast. They were five miles west of Château-Thierry. No one knew what to expect save that Germans were coming on fast. By the time the Marines spread out, the Germans were moving into Belleau Wood, almost on top of the Americans.

What happened thereafter was a somber baptism in fire, and many of the men who sang as they rolled along were soon dead or badly wounded. In long rows they walked through tall, green wheat toward machine guns, without artillery or tanks. A preliminary shelling, a barrage of gas, a few tanks in front, maybe one tank, could have knocked out the German guns. It was sheer heroism. The correspondent Floyd Gibbons took a bullet in the eye, but before he fell sent a dispatch about Sergeant Dan Daly, already a two-time winner of the Congressional Medal of Honor, who shouted at a platoon, "Come on, you sons of bitches, do you want to live forever?"[4] In Belleau Wood the Germans linked machine guns with supporting fields of fire—the place was a huge machine-gun nest. Marines took those guns by frontal assault. A single company advanced twenty yards into sixteen heavy and thirty-five light machine guns. Each enemy gun presented a different set of problems. A little group of men might lie in the wheat under the muzzle of a German gun that clipped stalks around their ears and riddled combat packs, fired high by "a matter of inches and the mercy of God." Under such circumstances life ceased to be desirable and the only desirable thing was to kill the gunner. Before one gun a corporal named Geer said, "By God, let's get him!" One man seized the spitting muzzle and upended it on the gunner, losing a hand, and bayonets flashed in, and a rifle butt rose and fell.[5] It was desperate, desperate fighting, a "bloody tangle of brush and rocks made horrible by the stench of rotting bodies, the unceasing crash of great shells, the vicious whine and snap of machine gun bullets." The enemy was fiendishly crafty, trees and rocks alive with snipers, grenades suspended against low-hanging branches, everywhere small ground mines.[6] The Marines took Belleau Wood, but it was an appalling victory. Out of 8,000 men, 5,183 men were killed or wounded.

Other commanders at the time, and later, questioned why the Marines had to go in at once, why they could not have waited for artillery. The front, critics said, was stabilizing. Major General Joseph T. Dickman of the U.S. Third Division, one of Pershing's best officers, wrote in his memoirs that it was magnificent fighting but not modern war, a glorious but unnecessary sacrifice.[7] General Matthew B. Ridgway in 1956 described Belleau Wood as "one of many prize examples of men's lives being thrown away against objectives which were not worth the cost . . . a monument, for all time, to the inflexibility of military thinking in that period."[8] The Marines in June 1918 saw things differently, for like the French government in Paris they did not believe the front was stabilizing. They also saw Belleau Wood as a test of American arms. So did an opposing German commander. In an order to his troops he beheld "not a question of the possession or nonpossession of this or that village or woods, insignificant in itself" but "a question whether the . . . claim that the American Army is equal to or even the superior of the German Army is to be made good."[9]

Army troops during the Chemin des Dames took 3,200 casualties and were as good as the Marines, and at one point considerably better; the Second Division's Army brigade on July 1 fought brilliantly at the little town of Vaux between Belleau Wood and Château-Thierry, making a mechanically perfect assault that was the result of planning so notably absent in tactics of the Marines. Vaux was a town built of stone, whose every house could be turned into a fort. Briefed by picture postcards, aerial photos, and the memory of the town stonemason, who built up a model of every street and alleyway, the Army moved with care. Commanders allotted a group of men to each house. The artillery preparation opened at 6:00 a.m., July 1, fired for twelve hours, and abruptly shortened to a creeping barrage in front of the infantry, who moved in just behind. When they reached the edge of town, the barrage lifted to the other side to deflect German reinforcements. Men rushed forward to assigned houses and caught defenders in the cellars—where they had gone to take cover from the shelling, after which they thought they had time to get up and lock in the machine guns. The Army took Vaux in twenty minutes, with forty-six men killed.

After the Chemin des Dames the AEF followed with elimination of the Aisne-Marne salient, elimination of the St. Mihiel salient, and the grimmest engagement of all, the great Battle of the Meuse-Argonne. Each battle represented increasing involvement although not always increasing difficulty of execution. The Aisne-Marne proved more difficult than St. Mihiel, where German troops were pulling out when Americans entered the salient; St. Mihiel became known as the operation where the Americans relieved the Germans. But there could be no doubt of the scale of the Meuse-Argonne, and for years afterward the very mention of that hyphenated word conjured forbidding terrain tenaciously defended, troops fighting from line to line, commanders relieved one after the other, dreadful casualties.

The Aisne-Marne offensive almost failed to open because three days earlier, on the morning of July 15, the Germans had begun an offensive from this salient created during the Chemin des Dames battle, pouring out of its east side where the Marne entered and crossed. Again the French had packed troops into forward positions. This time, however, the German Army came up against a regiment of Americans under an aging colonel named Ulysses Grant McAlexander. The colonel had seemed an unlikely commander. For years he had drilled cadets at small colleges in Iowa and Oregon. He actually had lost command of another regiment because of refusal to accept advice from senior officers. He received reinstatement with the 38th Infantry Regiment, and thus found himself and his big unit, 4,000 men, in a highly exposed, and crucial position just before the Second Battle of the Marne. Sensing the danger, he had disposed his troops to take advantage of every piece of terrain, and when the Germans began coming over he coolly stopped them. The regiment stood like veterans from 3:00 a.m., July 15, until noon on July 16, bearing the full brunt of attack, only retiring after being outflanked on both sides. The delighted Pershing, not given to praise, spoke of the regiment's "brilliant conduct" and promoted McAlexander to brigadier general.

Meanwhile French General Charles Mangin ranged troops on the Soissons side of the salient for the attack scheduled July 18. Undeterred by German action, he had the prescience to see that if his divisions could attack toward Soissons they could push in the side of the Aisne-Marne salient and cut the main German supply road and railroad to its tip, and turn the Second Battle of the Marne into victory.

Until the last minute it was uncertain whether American troops that constituted the bulk of the Allied attacking force would get into line in time to catch the barrage scheduled to open at 4:30 a.m., July 18, and seven hours before the attack Harbord's Second Division— he now was major general in command—was still trying to come up, with no one in line except artillerymen. Weather was terrible, raining hard, the road almost impassable, everywhere "trucks, artillery, infantry columns, cavalry, wagons, caissons, mud, MUD, utter confusion."[10] The forest was Plutonian in darkness and, when forced off the road, the men walked among the trees, each with a hand on the shoulder of the man in front. At 3:00 a.m. the Fifth Marines and Ninth Infantry were coming through the forest; at 4:00 a.m. it was almost certain they would make it, and men began to run and moved in behind the rolling barrage just as it opened.

The first day saw large American gains, but on the second defenders stiffened. Machine guns rattled, with a crackling din of rifles and

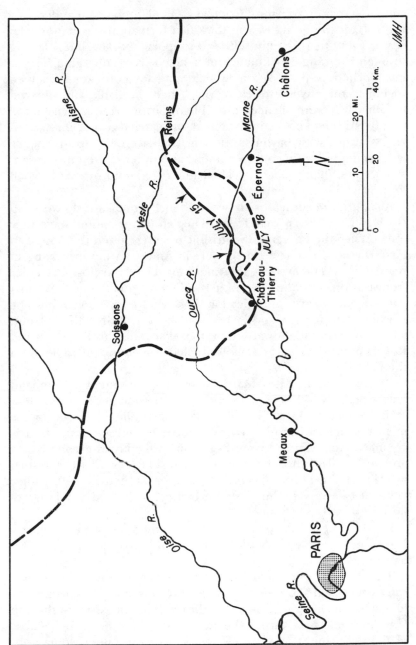

Soissons, July 1918

coughing roar of grenades. Company and platoon commanders lost control, for the going was so thick that formation was impossible. It was every man for himself, "an irregular, broken line, clawing through the tangles, climbing over fallen trees, plunging heavily into Boche rifle-pits." A Maxim held until someone got a few men together and crawled to left or right, gained a flank, and silenced it. Guns also were silenced after blind, furious rushes that "left a trail of writhing khaki figures, but always carried two or three frenzied Marines with bayonets into the emplacement; from whence would come shooting and screaming and other clotted unpleasant sounds, and then silence."[11] The battle raged until August 2, when French troops took Soissons.

Again the question arose of whether such frontal attacks were too costly, for Americans went forward in platoon formation, wave after wave. When the Fifteenth (Scottish) Division relieved the American First Division, it saw dead soldiers in American uniform lying in regular lines. The French said Americans stayed too close. A soldier from Boston, Horatio Rogers, passed by on July 29 and saw men still lying there, groups of dead in short windrows, mowed down by machine guns in the woods. Almost all lay face down, rifles in front, killed while running toward the woods. Packs had broken open and Rogers noticed letters and photographs from home spilled out onto the field.[12]

Reduction of the Aisne-Marne salient marked a notable command failure of the New England Twenty-sixth Division under Major General Clarence R. Edwards, a Regular Army officer beloved by his men, who lost track of an entire brigade for three days. Edwards commanded a National Guard division weak in field grade officers and ran his division without the taut control necessary to keep such a sizable force going. General Liggett excoriated him, Brigadier General Charles H. Cole, and several colonels, and Pershing relieved Edwards in October.

But the Americans won at the Aisne-Marne, whatever the failures. It was their first major battle, and everything considered, the AEF had managed well.

The Aisne-Marne offensive was more decisive than the Americans, concerned about performance of troops in a pitched and prolonged battle, imagined, and after the war it became evident that the U.S. Army may have turned the tide in mid-July, even though defeat of the German Army on the Western Front required four more months. In his memoirs Ludendorff described August 8 as his black day, the point when Germany lost the war, when reinvigorated British troops in a massive offensive broke his line with tanks; like Cambrai in 1917, they drove for miles into back areas and, unlike Cambrai, held them. But the German Army and civil government had hoped for great results from the Second Battle of the Marne. Chancellor Georg von Hertling anticipated "grave events" in Paris at the end of July. Instead the Germans came up against soldiers like U. G. McAlexander, and when 75,000 Americans and thousands of French and French Moroccans jumped off against the side of the salient, Hertling realized Germany had lost the war.[13]

After the Aisne-Marne, the U.S. Army undertook a large operation entirely on its own, pinching out the St. Mihiel salient, a sixteen-mile wedge in French lines to the right of Verdun between Fresnes and a point east of the Moselle that had stood four years. St. Mihiel was the first large American operation and involved the First Army, under Pershing's direct command. The Allied generalissimo, Foch, hesitated about authorizing St. Mihiel, but Pershing insisted and the battle opened September 12. German divisions in the salient had alerted higher headquarters of the imminence of the attack, but headquarters proved unsympathetic, with the result that the Germans started withdrawal of heavy artillery two hours prior to the American bombardment, and American guns caught columns on the road, causing great confusion. Incensed over the dilemma in which the higher command had left them, front-line troops put up a halfhearted defense. Everything was virtually over in a day and a half, by September 14, although the Americans did not reach the top of the salient until two days later. The First Army took 16,000 prisoners and 443 guns, a respectable showing.[14]

Like the Aisne-Marne, St. Mihiel contained its disappointments, but no battlefield is a tidy place and mistakes are unavoidable. Premier Clemenceau in 1917–18 frequently journeyed to the front, as it was close to Paris and he liked to see what was going on. At the height of St. Mihiel he happened into Thiaucourt, where a monumental traffic jam of trucks, guns, and troops caught and held his car for hours. Years later he remembered the logistical incompetence of the Americans. General Liggett admitted that his troops had gotten into trouble, which, he said, was not as bad as Clemenceau had made out. Following the war Pershing and Dickman asserted that a directive from Foch had prevented capture of Metz,

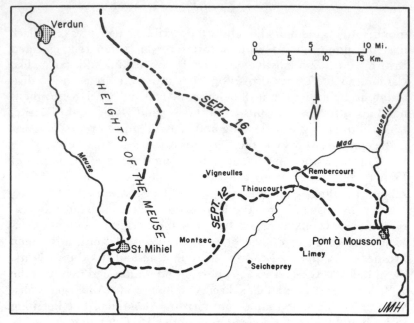

St. Mihiel, September 1918

fifteen miles to the north of the St. Mihiel salient. Liggett maintained that such an advance would have been possible only if the U.S. Army had been a well-oiled, coordinated machine, which in early September 1918 it was not.[15] Apart from St. Mihiel's logistical problems, the reason Foch refused to allow capture of Metz was that the American high command had only twelve days after the fighting before the Meuse-Argonne offensive.

Planned by the generalissimo as the American contribution to a huge British-French-American attack that would roll up the front from its top at Nieuport down through Ypres-Arras-Rheims-Verdun to the Swiss border, the Meuse-Argonne was a gamble. The AEF had to shift 300,000 men from the right of Verdun—St. Mihiel flanked Verdun—to sixty miles on the left toward Rheims where they joined fresh divisions for the attack. The shift involved a tremendous movement of men and equipment; it required night marches to escape detection; Foch may have wondered if the Americans could handle it, having heard from Clemenceau about Thiaucourt. Moreover, the proposed American sector, twenty-four miles from the Meuse River on the right across to the Argonne Forest on

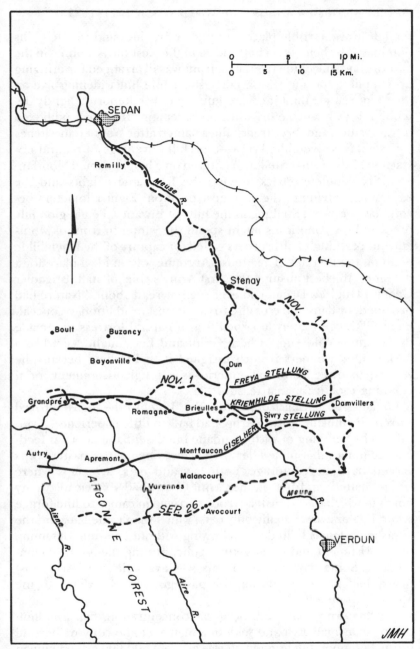

Meuse-Argonne, September–November 1918

the left, was a terrible place—a tangle of ravines and wooded hills dominated by heights on both sides, in the west the Argonne, in the east the far bank of the river. The front was ill arranged for bringing up supplies, starting with a fairly short line but widening like an inverted triangle until it covered ninety miles. Reported lightly defended, it was capable of swift reinforcement. Its wired, pillboxed front position and three trench lines named after Wagnerian witches —Giselher, Kriemhilde, Freya—took full advantage of natural obstacles. The Giselher Stellung centered on a height named Montfaucon. Six kilometers back loomed the Romagne heights and the Kriemhilde Stellung, the strongest position. Eight kilometers beyond lay the Freya Stellung in the hills of Buzancy. Pétain gloomily predicted the Americans might spend the winter in front of Montfaucon. Pershing's battle orders called for capture of the Kriemhilde Stellung the first day. The Meuse-Argonne was an ideal place for a defender, the best position the First Army's chief of staff, Brigadier General Hugh A. Drum, had ever seen or read about: "Nature had provided for flank and crossfire to the utmost in addition to concealment."[16] Liggett later described it as a natural fortress that made the Virginia Wilderness where Grant and Lee fought seem like a park.[17] One wonders if Foch assigned it to Pershing because he wanted to give the proud Americans a tough assignment, or if Pershing took it for that reason.

Logistics of getting troops from St. Mihiel to the Meuse proved extremely difficult, for the Army had had so little experience. Typical was its handling of such mundane but essential matters as feeding the horses that pulled heavy vehicles. The quartermaster corps should have stored forage, both hay and oats, at camps where troops halted, and horses then could have had sixteen to twenty hours in which to eat. Instead troops arrived in camps to find forage several miles away, usually only oats, which then came late, and the famished animals bolted it, swallowing without chewing, obtaining no nourishment and often getting colic, putting them out of commission. Some days not even oats was available. The Army lost nearly half its horses during the passage from St. Mihiel to the Meuse-Argonne.[18]

Yet the Army managed the great concentration, half a million troops in a small area and seldom a man seen, no convoys beyond normal number, but at night all was active, "500,000 armed human beings accompanied by acres of guns—paraphernalia covering the earth—a blanket of destruction ten miles deep, thirty miles long, gliding by inches, skulking by inches—hundreds of thousands of my fellow beings are dragging and tugging this vast carpet of destruction toward the enemy; thrusting its sharp and explosive edge into the enemy."[19]

The battle opened on September 26, and continued until the Armistice. In a day and a half the Americans captured Montfaucon and the Giselher Stellung. Then enemy reinforcements streamed in and fighting turned fierce. Americans took the Argonne Forest by October 10, but the fight was hard; the enemy brought in forty-three divisions, with estimated strength of 470,000, and suffered 100,000 casualties. The American First Army, with 135,000 French troops under its command, reached a strength of 1,031,000. Casualties totaled 122,063, including 26,277 American dead, almost a full division. Americans took 26,000 prisoners and 874 guns.

The Meuse-Argonne proved a long agony, for week after week men fought through mud and rain, death everywhere, coming at any time in indescribable form. Bishop Charles H. Brent wrote how the prospect of glorious death pro patria loomed far more glorious at a distance than near at hand.[20] A half century and more later the traveler in that awful country still can see what happened—everywhere the cemeteries, small German plots along the road with several hundred close graves marked by stone walls, somber iron gates, black-lettered wooden crosses, many bearing the word "Unbekannt"; the American cemetery at Romagne with nearly 16,000 graves arranged in eight squares set off by paths along the grass, long rows of marble crosses and occasional stars of David, marching curiously toward the onlooker, markers bearing names so familiarly American they could have been friends or acquaintances of yesterday. The Meuse-Argonne recalls the past; the traveler gazes at grain fields, the wooded hills, and knows there are untold stores of metal and bones underneath. Hawks perch on telephone wires and look inquiringly as if they too know the history of the place.

In the Meuse-Argonne, Americans went to their deaths without ceremony, farewells as far from chivalric romances as they could be. Charles B. Merritt wrote his mother that if she ever received his letter she could know he was dead; he could see smoke from dozens of bursting shells, unmarked graves in almost every fence corner along the roads for miles, and such might be his fate. He was killed on September 30.[21] Lieutenant Elden S. Betts wrote his family October 4 that in case "I get mine tomorrow" he was writing a few lines to say good-bye and God bless them all, they had been the best of families and whatever he had won or was he owed to them. He told them not to grieve, as he was sure they would meet "on the shining sands on the other side." He hoped they would be proud of him. "Now goodbye, and thank you Pop, Edie and Margie, and love to all the family as well."[22] Elden Betts was killed five days later in an attack on Hill 240.

The battle seemed never-ending. Weather was cold, rain continuous, men without shelter. Roads were few and artillery churned them and rain made them so slippery that big guns and other heavy equipment slid off. The traffic jam became a mark of the American Army, and at one point vehicles of the First Corps jammed up for six miles, tailgate to tailgate. Liggett, who had replaced Pershing as commander of the First Army in mid-October, estimated 100,000 stragglers; for two weeks in October operations virtually ceased while he tightened control. Some men were lost, others lost themselves. George B. Duncan took over the Eighty-second Division and found that on October 21 he had 3,208 riflemen out of a full rifle strength of 12,250.[23] On October 29, after stringent measures, he had 3,540. Divisions wore out after a few days, and Pershing took them out of the line and threw in new ones. He relieved three divisional commanders and Major General George Cameron, who commanded a corps. Bullard, whose corps was next to Cameron's, pleaded for his neighbor to close up the flank, not easy as Cameron's Seventy-ninth Division was in front of Montfaucon. Cameron did not move fast enough for Bullard or Pershing.[24] Commanders who did not drive their men went to the classification depot at Blois.

Pershing shoved commanders who shoved men, for any failure might bring taunts from Haig and Foch and Pétain, who almost openly speculated what the Americans could have done with better leadership. How much better, they thought, to have brigaded Americans with British or French divisions. Haig never liked Americans, Pershing less than most, and believed that the Meuse-Argonne justified his opinion. With his typical economy of words, which may have been a cover for vacuity, he suggested during an Anglo-French meeting at Senlis that the American Army was "incompletely organized" and would be of little use until the spring of 1919. Pershing heard of the criticism and Sir Douglas felt obliged to write an apology, denying he had implied that the Americans were failing in the Meuse-Argonne.

During the battle Pershing displayed a hard, tough exterior and readily defended his troops, but was none too sure the AEF would make it. At one point, when riding in his staff car, he broke down, buried his face in his hands, uttered his dead wife's name (she had died in the Presidio fire in San Francisco in 1915), and murmured, "Frankie . . . Frankie . . . my God, sometimes I don't know how I can go on."

At last success crowned the battle. Just before the Armistice the Americans reached their assigned ninety-mile line at the top of the inverted triangle. AEF artillery blasted the four-track railroad near Sedan that supplied German troops all the way up to the Channel.

Near the end of fighting, November 6–7, the First Division made a rampaging effort to seize Sedan, the worst tactical "atrocity," Liggett said, that came to his attention during the war; the division lunged across the sector of the Forty-second Division in an attempt to reach Sedan ahead of every other American outfit and especially of the French, who were planning a sedate, ceremonial entry into the city lost to Germany in 1870. In the comingling, First Division troops of Brigadier General Frank Parker took the Rainbow Division's Brigadier General MacArthur prisoner—MacArthur looked like a spy because he wore a rakish outfit including a regulation cap without stiffening. The First Division was part of the Fifth Corps under Major General Charles P. Summerall, a Pershing favorite, and one can guess that the c. in c. told Summerall to get Sedan any way he could. After the mixup he and the neighboring corps commander, Dickman, sorted out the troops. Dickman wanted a court-martial for Parker and Summerall. Pershing seemed a bit upset.[25] The task of taking Sedan was given to the French.

On November 1, 1918, the AEF commander formed the Second Army under Bullard and became an army group commander. He had forty-two divisions in France, twenty-six in the line.

Then, suddenly, the war was over.

CHAPTER 6

Money and Food

A T the beginning of the war it was impossible to know how much it might cost. Few economists guessed anywhere near what the actual expenditure came to. When E.R.A. Seligman of Columbia University estimated $10 billion the first year, his colleagues greeted him with incredulity. The entire cost of the United States government from 1789 to April 6, 1917, had been $24 billion, and the federal budget for the preceding three fiscal years, July 1913 through June 1916, averaged $737 million in receipts and $718 million in disbursements. Yet it was necessary to go ahead with raising money, and Treasury officials decided to avoid estimates and concentrate on procedure. They proposed to raise most of the war's cost through bonds rather than taxes—two-thirds bonds, one-third taxes. The decision was correct, even though a large inflation occurred. Raising everything through taxes would have been extremely difficult. Prior to 1913 and the first assessment of income taxes, most federal government income had derived from the tariff. The war interfered with foreign trade and hence tariff revenues, and only the new income tax enabled the Treasury in 1914–17 to meet regular federal obligations out of taxation. To have paid all the cost of participation in the war out of tax revenues would have required a steep rise in the income tax, and many other new taxes. In the spring of 1917, pushing new taxes through Congress was very unattractive. The government also feared the effect of taxes upon businessmen, whom it could not safely discourage; as matters turned out, the wartime excess profits tax aroused great complaint. When in the last months of the war the demands of war financing reached their height, the administration might have ameliorated inflation by imposing heavier taxes, departing from the formula of two-thirds bonds, one-third taxes, going to one-to-one. Not enough time remained to draw up a new tax program and get it through Congress.

And so the Wilson administration set the lines of war finance in ways that compel admiration. In retrospect matters might have gone differently, with better results. Practically there was not much choice.

Secretary of the Treasury William G. McAdoo presided over war finances, and it was well that a person of his talents was in charge. He possessed the necessary imagination and drive. Tall, wiry, with a sharp nose, he had married President Wilson's daughter Eleanor in 1914, inspiring his enemies to attribute his successes in government to what they regarded as a tactical move. But this appraisal was unfair; McAdoo had made a name for himself and received the Treasury well before he made his dynastic marriage. A high-level promoter in New York City, he had succeeded with the Hudson Tubes at a time when many engineers and even more businessmen believed it impossible to tunnel under the Hudson and lay railroad tracks in a subterranean hole. He went on to success in the stock market. Almost anything he touched he made work. He was competent and knew it, and did not hesitate to let the President know, pointing out what Wilson well knew, that in Europe the finance ministers were principal advisers of government.

McAdoo was ambitious, perhaps too much so, and eventually he lost out in striving for the single prize he wanted most out of life. He yearned for Wilson's job, suitably, upon the President's retirement. During the war he kept his political prospects in mind, and gained a reputation for being willing to speak on all occasions and even (to use Mr. Dooley's remark) no occasion. The journalist Mark Sullivan, who did not like him or his fighting speeches, once wrote that someone should tell the Secretary of the Treasury the old story that ended with the saying, "All we want out of you is silence, and damned little of that."[1] Wilson came to distrust him, and did not lift a hand to help him obtain the Democratic nomination in 1920. In 1924, McAdoo deadlocked the convention against Al Smith, a deadlock that led to nomination of the ineffectual John W. Davis on the hundred and third ballot.[2]

As Secretary of the Treasury in 1917–18, McAdoo managed to stay closely to the plan of two-to-one—taxes during the fiscal years 1918 and 1919 brought in $8.8 billion, a little more than a third of total expenditure.[3] The remaining two-thirds—$15.5 billion—he raised by bond drives, four of them happily named Liberty Loans, the fifth conducted after the war by his successor, Carter Glass, and even more happily known as a Victory Loan. Indeed the five loans from May 1917 to May 1919 raised $21.4 billion, and the Treasury used the excess for loans to the Allies. McAdoo sought to spread ownership of bonds, to soak up buying power and give Americans the feeling that they had a stake in the war. In his typically fighting idiom he thought a financial front comparable to a military front. It was on May 14, 1917, that he announced the first Liberty Loan, $2 billion, with interest rate at 3½ percent, bonds to run thirty years but redeemable after fifteen, exempt from taxes except estate and inheritance, and convertible by purchasers to any bonds of a subsequent issue that might bear a higher rate; books closed with 4 million subscriptions and the Treasury had met its goal. The second loan, launched October 1, $3 billion, carried a 4 percent rate, without the tax-free features of the initial loan; lists closed October 27, with 9 million subscriptions, totaling $6 billion. The third loan, in the spring of 1918, $3 billion, with interest a bit higher, 4½ percent, but without the conversion privilege of the first two issues, closed May 4 with 18 million subscriptions, $4.1 billion. The fourth loan opened September 28, 1918, $6 billion at 4¼ percent; it produced 23 million subscriptions, $6.9 billion. Sixty thousand women sold $1 billion in bonds for the second loan; for the fourth, between 700,000 and 800,000 women obtained $2 billion. The Victory Loan offered April 21, 1919, $4.5 billion, also was oversubscribed.

At the same time as these campaigns, the Treasury enrolled the children of America. Children saved pennies and nickels to buy twenty-five-cent "thrift stamps" that they could accumulate into interest-bearing savings certificates, and by the end of the war the sale of these stamps totaled $834 million. Adults told children to save the stamps. Perhaps it was the lullaby that did the trick:

> Hush little thrift stamp,
> Don't you cry;
> You'll be a war bond
> By and by.

Loan campaigns hurt savings banks, whose depositors drew out funds, and to keep banks going the government created the War Finance Corporation, with capital of $500 million. Its operating procedures stipulated by Congress, the W.F.C. charged going rates for its loans, according to areas around the country, from 5 to 8 percent. It undertook to protect the market for Liberty Loans by buying and selling bonds, and at the end of the war had purchased $378 million worth of bonds and sold $272 million, at a profit of over $2 million.

Altogether McAdoo's campaigns constituted a tremendous accomplishment of salesmanship and public participation. They employed newfound techniques of what people afterward described as Madison Avenue public relations—slogans; appearance of vaudeville and motion picture stars such as Douglas Fairbanks, Mary Pickford, and Al Jolson; hanging out flags and banners and huge thermometers with the mercury of contributions rising—all the pressure and push of American salesmanship in later times.

Total direct cost of the war to the United States was $35.5 billion —$24.3 billion in the nation's own expenditure, and the remainder, $11.2 billion, in wartime and immediate postwar loans to other nations, mostly the Allies. Total cost of the American war effort hence reached the same cost as the first hundred years of the federal government. It amounted to $2 million an hour during the war. The fiscal years 1918, 1919, and 1920, from July 1917 through June 1920, each cost eighteen times as much as a prewar year.

Compared to other belligerents in World War I, expenditure of the United States was modest. Total for all belligerents, in 1913 dollars, was $82 billion, and of that cost Americans accounted for from $24 billion to $35 billion (if one counted debts owed the Treasury by foreign nations). Cost per capita in the United States was one-third the cost in Britain and far less than in France, Germany, and other countries. War expenditure of the United States equaled 8.7 percent of estimated national wealth, compared with France at 19 percent, Germany at 32, Great Britain at 35.

In surveying World War I's cost, most Americans understood the reason for the Wilson administration's basic expenditure, $24.3 billion, and appreciated the fact that it was a good deal less than that of European countries, but in the twenties and thirties criticism arose over the $11.2 billion in foreign loans. In World War I the Treasury considered them assets, which led to trouble when debtors first insisted upon renegotiating the interest rates and then, with the exception of Finland, defaulted during the Great Depression. But there was much to say for the loans. Throughout 1917 and until the late summer of 1918 the Allies had engaged in almost all of the fighting, and the least the Americans could have done was to give financial support. The loans also were not total losses if only because the Allies used them to buy war supplies in the United States and profits went into American pockets. Moreover, the Wilson administration was conscious that indebtedness brings responsibility, for in July 1917 the President wrote Colonel House that "England and France have not the same views with regard to peace that we have by any means. When the war is over, we can force them to our way of thinking, because by that time they will among other things be financially in our hands." Although that hope did not come to much, things might have worked that way. A special point of later criticism was that it was silly to ask for repayment, because the debtors could not pay, and hence it would have been better to make the loans into gifts, hoping that generosity would bring thankfulness. As for the latter contention, matters usually do not work that way, in either personal or international affairs. As to the former, the Wilson administration could not have given the money away. International finance at that time did not conduct itself that way. In any event, American taxpayers would not have allowed such an arrangement when they were lending money to their own government.

In regard to the loans it is also necessary to point out circumstances of the Morgan overdraft, an indebtedness by the British government to J. P. Morgan and Company that reached the proportions of a crisis shortly after the United States entered the war.[4] In the mid-thirties a Senate committee headed by Gerald P. Nye of North Dakota investigated the pre-1917 munitions trade and raised a possibility that the Wilson administration went to war because American bankers needed to protect their Allied loans.

Before April 1917 the British certainly had strained their credit in America. Morgan had been handling the sale of British and French bonds and in January had informed the two governments that not merely had the bond market dried up but that it was not possible to float a large unsecured loan as the firm had hoped, and it could meet Anglo-French needs only by short-term loans against collateral. On April 3, the day after the President's war message, one of the leading members of the British government, Bonar Law, told the Imperial War Cabinet that entrance of the United States gave hope that Britain would not have to go off the gold standard. When Congress passed the Loan Act on April 24, the first loan went to the British the next day, $200 million. At that moment Britain was purchasing in the United States at a rate of $75 million a week and the British Treasury possessed less than $1 billion in gold, together with $219 million in American securities. In anticipation of more assistance, the British went ahead with purchases, shipping $125 million in gold in June and selling $10 million in securities. American banks withdrew over $100 million from their sterling balances, apparently to buy bonds in the first Liberty Loan. The dollar securities of the British government, beyond those pledged against loans, sank to $166 million, and it was impossible to get them quickly. London had $45 million in gold in Canada and $650 million in gold elsewhere. At that point the gold in possession of the United States Treasury totaled $3 billion.[5]

By late June the British had run up an overdraft with Morgan of $400 million, and Morgan presented it to the Treasury. McAdoo was out of the city on the bond drive, and his assistant, Oscar T. Crosby, refused it and suspended all loans to Britain. Balfour cabled House on June 28: "we seem on the edge of a financial disaster which would be worse than a defeat in the field. . . . You know I am not an alarmist: but this is really serious."[6] Lord Northcliffe, then in New York City, cabled London, "If loan stops, war stops."[7]

The suddenness of the crisis alarmed House, who in irritation wrote in his diary that he had told officials in London and Paris to let the American government know before they were in extremities. "They did not do this, but bluffed it out almost to the end. It is nothing short of criminal, and I cannot understand the statesmanship that inspired such a course."[8]

Because of the Morgan overdraft, the Wilson administration found itself in an extremely awkward position, having to bail out J. P. Morgan, else the war might stop. Less than a quarter century earlier, after the Panic of 1893, another Democratic administration had gone to Morgan to guarantee gold holdings of the Treasury, and it was said at the time, although there was no truth in the story, that Morgan had made a great deal of money by taking government bonds at a remarkable discount in exchange for gold. The crisis of the nineties infuriated the nation's farmers, together with millions of other debtors who believed in the greed of Wall Street and the special greed of J. P. Morgan. The gold crisis of that time cost President Grover Cleveland control of the Democratic party and gave William Jennings Bryan the presidential nomination.[9] In the new crisis the Morgan overdraft required great care; Wilson supporters in Congress were up for reelection in 1918. As it happened, a young British subject resident in New York, a secret service operative, consulted the anglophile governor of the New York Federal Reserve Bank, Benjamin Strong, who offered to help McAdoo out of the difficulty. Over the following months in 1917-18, the Treasury quietly paid Morgan piecemeal for the overdraft.

Records of the State Department used for the Nye hearings of the thirties revealed that Ambassador Walter Hines Page in London was deeply concerned about Britain's solvency. In a cable of March 5, 1917, to the State Department, Page had said that the Allied financial situation was so desperate that termination of all purchases in the United States was imminent, that this would cause a panic in the United States, that the crisis was "too great and urgent for any private agency to meet," and only funds from the Treasury could save the situation. According to international law, Page said, a neutral government could not make a direct grant of credit to a belligerent, and hence "perhaps our going to war is the only way in which our present preeminent trade position can be maintained and a panic averted."[10]

But the Nye hearings were unable to show that the Wilson administration had given any attention to the warning of its London ambassador. Wilson had appointed Page in 1913 for reasons not altogether clear, perhaps simply because he liked him and both were Southerners. Page had gone to England and fallen under the influence of the government to which Wilson had accredited him. He thereby lost all influence at the White House, inclining the President to believe almost the opposite of anything Page recommended. No evidence ever has appeared that Wilson saw the British financial situation as serious prior to its undoubted crisis in midsummer of 1917. Hearings of the thirties drew the attention of the well-known historian Charles A. Beard, who popularized them in articles and in a thin volume entitled *The Devil Theory of War*, essentially an argument that the America of his own time should not go to war again. The belief that the Wilson administration went to war in 1917 to save American bankers fit the ideas of a generation convinced that bankers would do anything for money.

Americans helped win the war by lending to their government, which used the money both at home and abroad. In addition the government promised to send grain, meat, and other products of American farms to the people of France, Italy, and Great Britain. Food supplies in those countries had been contracting since early in the war. In 1914, Turkish control of the Dardanelles and German control of the Baltic had cut off exports to Western Europe from Russia. Between August 1916 and January 1917 the Central Powers had seized almost all of Rumania, another source of grain. Surpluses from India, Australia, and the Argentine had become increasingly difficult to obtain because of scarcity of shipping. India was quite far—and roughly speaking, 15,000 ship tons from Australia and 10,000 tons from Argentina delivered the same amounts because of the difference in length of the voyages. So did 5,000 tons from North America. The problem was serious well before German announcement of unrestricted submarine warfare early in 1917. Subsequent sinkings brought a food crisis. French stores dwindled alarmingly, Italian cities survived by running stocks down to a day or two prior to arrival of grain ships, and Britain's very survival depended on American food.

President Wilson made the best possible choice for food administrator when he sent for Herbert Hoover, who came home from Europe, where he had been in charge of Belgian relief. Under the Food Control or Lever Act of August 10, 1917, Hoover received power to buy and sell food, offer guarantees to farmers, prevent hoarding and speculation, fix trade margins, suspend exchange trading, and organize the food industry to eliminate waste. With his customary intensity, his feeling that whatever he undertook was critical to the fate of the nation and the world, he threw himself into the task, sweeping aside formalities, jettisoning procedures, moving to control food under the slogan of "Food Will Win the War—Don't Waste It."

The government's food administrator decided at the very beginning upon a voluntary effort. He accumulated a small volunteer staff, and at first needed only a few rooms in the New Willard Hotel; eventually his Washington group numbered 1,900. But everywhere —in Washington and in states, counties, municipalities (outside Washington the staff numbered 9,000)—were volunteers; only clerks and office helpers received pay. Commercial interests of the country, he said, could provide the only people who knew anything about food, and he intended to enlist them and not create a group of unimaginative paid bureaucrats. He hated bureaucracies—he was a mining engineer, turned government expert. He said he had seen too many problems in Europe arising from rationing and heavy-handed bureaucratic solutions, and that there must be "no professors on the job." As he afterward commented on another of his operations, "We had the usual plague of theorists, who wanted to make charts with squares and circles showing the relation of each job to the other, along with descriptions of particular functions and authorities. Nothing could raise my temperature faster than charts for an emergency organization which shifted daily."[11]

For the United States to send grain abroad in enormous quantities required, first of all, conservancy. A man who "knew how to get things done," Hoover began to tell his countrymen how to save food. He estimated that from the American harvest year ending July 1918, the Allies needed 1.85 million tons of animal products including fats, 8.8 million tons of cereals, 1.5 million tons of sugar. He thereupon preached a gospel of the clean dinner plate. Soon his picture was in newspapers, magazines, and pamphlets. Shortly after the war Charles Seymour of Yale published a popular history of the Wilson era and wrote how Hoover became a benevolent bogey for the nation, with broad forehead, round face, compelling eyes.[12] To Hooverize the plate became a national habit: "Eat plenty, wisely and without waste." He called on patriots to observe meatless and wheatless days. Fathers and mothers denied children a spoonful of sugar on their cereal "because Mr. Hoover would not like it." His ukases reminded critics of Russia under the tsars; he invaded details of existence as if they were his own. In January 1918 he established the "fifty-fifty rule," whereby licensed retailers had to require every purchaser of wheat flour to buy an equal amount of corn, oats, rice, barley, or other cereal. He announced on February 11, 1918, that Americans should kill no hens until May 1. Then he said they should eat no meat of any sort. On March 29 he suspended the meatless order for thirty days and on May 26 relented to propose a limit of two pounds per person per week, still a punishment for people of his time, the meat-and-potatoes era. Toward the end of the war he dealt with cheating in public places and gave out twelve rules for restaurant eating, including no bread until after the first course, one kind of meat, a half ounce of butter per person, no sugar bowl (sugar only in small cubes, two half lumps per meal, one pound for forty-five meals). These injunctions led the old humor magazine *Life* to remark that adults had to watch children: "Do not permit your child to take a bite or two from an apple and throw the rest away; nowadays even children must be taught to be patriotic to the core."

The Food Administration sent slogans and page brighteners to farm journals:

Food is sacred. To waste it is sinful.

The Wheat Sector was taken by the Soldiers of the Commissary in the Spring Drive.

Don't let your horse be more patriotic than you are—eat a dish of oatmeal!

Wheatless days in America make sleepless nights in Germany.

If U fast U beat U boats. If U feast U boats beat U.

Let wheatless and meatless be kickless and whineless, lest all days to come be soul-less and spineless.

Serve beans by all means.

Herbert Hoover—the Autocrat of the Breakfast Table.

Everywhere—public buildings, railroad stations, libraries, highways—signs spread the message. Outdoor signs, painted and electric, urged conservancy. Posters spoke dramatically of saving food; Howard Chandler Christy produced a popular poster, "In Her Wheatless Kitchen." Railway coaches displayed 50,000 posters, express wagons 100,000; 50,000 streetcars used thirteen different cards and changed them every month. The American Chicle Company printed food slogans on gum wrappers. The Lydia E. Pinkham Medicine Company ran conservation ads; whiskey from scarce grain, of course, gave vigor to its female remedy. The nation's movie industry produced shorts for theaters, one of which, a cartoon entitled *He Had to Be Told*, displayed a smug young gentleman sitting at a table taking one lump of sugar after another and dropping them into his coffee, saying all the while, "I would like to join the Army, or Navy, or Marines, or do something to help win the war." Finally Uncle Sam came out of the sugar bowl and answered, "Why don't you help save sugar?" Slides urged the patriotism of food: "There are four great problems: FOOD—men—money—ships. If we fail in one we shall have lost the war. *But* we shall win with your help."

Food Administration experts estimated that a third of Americans consumed more than they needed, largely because of inefficient buying and cooking and failure to use substitutes for breadstuffs, meats, fats, and sugar. It was essential to teach elemental nutrition to American women, through whose hands passed almost all the country's food. An official of the Food Administration saw no "royal road" to "put over" food propaganda, but noted that in Germany, "the most masculine country in the world," instructions read: "Work with women. Never forget them for an instant. Put all your efforts on the women and use women all you can." The Food Administration inaugurated a pledge campaign to attract American women. Twenty million Americans, mostly housewives, signed the pledge: "I am glad to join you in the service of food conservation for our nation, and I hereby accept membership in the United States Food Administration, pledging myself to carry out the directions and advice of the Food Administrator in the conduct of my household, in so far as my circumstances admit." Signers received buttons to wear, stickers for windows. Their names appeared in newspapers.[13]

Occupants of the White House—the President and Mrs. Wilson, the President's daughter Margaret, and his cousin Helen Bones—cooperated with the Food Administration. Mrs. Wilson signed a pledge card, and placed a Food Administration sticker in the window of the Executive Mansion. She planted (here was another aspect of the conservancy program) a "war garden" of easy-to-grow vegetables. In a gesture that caught national attention, the President arranged for a flock of Shropshire Downs sheep to graze on the grounds behind the mansion, first time such a thing had happened since the early nineteenth century, a bucolic era when no one thought it strange to see sheep on the grounds. The Red Cross received ninety-eight pounds of wool from the sheep and distributed it among forty-eight states, Puerto Rico, Hawaii, and the Philippines, where officials auctioned it for $100,000. All the while the women of the Wilson household knitted, and in the evenings the President held the yarn while the women rolled it into balls.[14]

Conservancy meant saving fruit and vegetables through canning or dehydrating. Bryan went out on the lecture circuit and, despite his own well-fed appearance, advised farmers to "Plant what you can and can all you can." Mrs. Robert Lansing, wife of his successor as Secretary of State, gave a luncheon consisting entirely of dried foods, and it was reported that everything served from soup to dessert was "most delicious and delicate."[15]

Children appear to have admired the so-called war bread that used whole grains or substituted corn for wheat. As in the thrift stamp program, perhaps the rhymes attracted them:

> Little Jack Horner
> Sat in a corner
> Eating bread at a terrible rate;
> As he passed up for more
> He said, "Mother, this war
> Bread's the best bread that I ever ate."

And again:

> Little Boy Blue, come blow your horn!
> The cook's using wheat where she ought to use corn.
> And terrible famine our country will sweep,
> If the cooks and the housewives remain fast asleep.
> Go wake them. Go wake them. It's now up to you.
> Be a loyal American, Little Boy Blue.

State and local officials sometimes virtually compelled people to do what Hoover asked, and one of the Food Administrator's assistants, Ray Lyman Wilbur, later president of Stanford University, became uncertain of tactics in such states as Indiana, although he admitted that Indiana possessed the best food conservation program. People in Indiana believed in whatever Washington decreed, whether meatless or wheatless. They inquired into the loyalty of uncooperative citizens such as bakers or hotelkeepers. Where letters failed, Indiana patriots invited delinquents to talk matters over with the county or federal district attorney. During interviews the attorney made a statement, followed by a question: "The Government has a definite program for war purposes on the food question. Are you for it, or against it?"[16]

To achieve the other part of its purpose, to increase production, the Food Administration asked farmers to increase their acreage of food crops. In 1917 the shortage of wheat in the United States was alarming, because of low yields and European purchasing in the Chicago grain market. Average prewar production totaled 690 million bushels, with export of 105 to all countries (54.6 to France, Italy, and Britain). In 1916 the American wheat crop was 637 and in 1917 the same. Considering the rise in America's population from prewar, to 103 million on January 1, 1918, even without exports the 1917 crop would not have allowed prewar per capita consumption. Because of three years of war, the Allies in 1917 were producing only about half their prewar wheat crop and needed 600 million bushels. Early in the spring of 1917 each of the Allied governments as well as the neutral countries entered the May futures market on the Chicago Board of Trade and raised the spot price of wheat from an average of $1.80 per bushel in December 1916 to $2.40 in April. Speculators came into the market, and on May 11, No. 2 Red Winter sold in Chicago for $3.45 in a wild scramble of "shorts" to cover their sales. Next day the Board suspended trading. A total of 620 million bushels of the 1916 crop already had gone to market, nearly all the crop. Food Administration officials saw a possibility that the price of wheat would skyrocket, benefiting only speculators. In just a few months the latter had taken $200 million in profits.

The wheat shortage required several measures, but mainly, of course, increased production. Conservancy helped. So did curbing of speculation; after an agonizing delay, during which much wheat moved to market, Congress ended speculation with the Food Control Act, under which Hoover organized a Grain Corporation that bought up all wheat. As mentioned, total production in 1917 was only 637 million bushels. The Food Control Act guaranteed a minimum price high enough to stimulate production. Even with drafting of hundreds of thousands of farmers, and the winter of 1917–18, the coldest in fifty years, and a withering drought in the summer of 1918, production rose to 921 million bushels. In 1917 exports to Britain, France, and Italy were 187.4 million bushels, and Canada exported 49 million more, for a total of 236.4 million. In 1918 figures were 170.2 million bushels and 66.9 million, totaling 237.1 million. In 1917, adding 41.6 million bushels from India, 55.2 million from Australia, and 32.5 million from Argentina, exports reached 365.7 million, and in 1918, 316.2 million (15.8 million from India, 12.4 million from Australia, 50.9 million from Argentina). Control of the world's premier foodstuff barely fed the Allies, but it worked. The effort had been "no child's play," an economist for the Grain Corporation concluded. A few false steps might have brought far-reaching consequences, even "the loss of the Allied cause itself and the consequent changing of the future history of the world."[17]

In such ways the Wilson administration conducted its two large campaigns for money and food, and with high success in both. The reason undoubtedly lay in the President's choice of two excellent administrators. Interestingly they were quite alike, in that both were intense, talented, high-strung. Both also were amateurs—McAdoo a promoter rather than financier, Hoover an engineer rather than agricultural expert. Both achieved their successes largely through enlisting volunteers. They also used the new science of public relations, helping fasten it upon subsequent generations of Americans whom the war accustomed to drives, slogans, and other persuasive methods. And the two wartime programs were to have other long-range results. The bond sales of McAdoo accustomed Americans to purchasing paper instruments of value. In 1917 one adult American in seven owned stocks, but McAdoo changed that, and laid the foundation for the Big Bull Market of the twenties. Hoover's food conservancy program forced housewives to think of food substitutes such as fruits and vegetables, to learn of canning and dehydrating, and from such experience came interest in calories and vitamins, proteins and carbohydrates, permanent change in the nation's food habits. The other part of the Hoover food program, increased production, depressed farm values through the twenties and perhaps inspired the overproduction that has afflicted American agriculture ever since.

CHAPTER 7

Ships and Arms

W HEN Lord Northcliffe visited America in the summer of 1917
he beheld war production rising like a skyscraper. Watching
the building of a skyscraper, he afterward wrote, the uninformed
observer feels that the thing will never begin. "For some time there
is a blasting of rock, crowds of men appear with strange machines,
nothing much seems to happen." Then gradually a great steel skeleton arises, and the passerby finds to his astonishment that although
lower stories are in skeleton form, exterior walls of the seventeenth
or thirtieth story are finished. Another delay, and lo! the skyscraper
is done, and housing its ten or fifteen thousand busy workers.[1]

Here was a pleasant simile, and yet war production did not arise
like Northcliffe's skyscraper. Throughout 1917 it suffered from lack
of a plan. No one could decide what the program should be. Clearly
the nation needed ships—the merchant marine was inadequate for
a great transatlantic war. Likewise arms for the new Army. But
without a plan no one knew how much raw material—steel, copper,
tin, rubber—to reserve from stocks or current and forthcoming
production. Officials of the Wilson administration did not offer
suggestions and took refuge in routine. Volunteer skyscraper builders flocked to Washington and moved from office to office inquiring
how they might serve the government without compensation as
"W.O.C. men," perhaps receiving a dollar a year. Lines of private
cars waited on sidings in Union Station. The Metropolitan Club,
according to one observer, looked like a second edition of Wall

Street.[2] Volunteer builders usually managed to obtain positions and soon were attempting to rouse the government, seeking out officials whom they considered men of decision, sometimes building support for ideas through newspapers or journals of opinion. The task eventually frustrated; almost none had worked in government, many never in large enterprises. In the spring of 1918, administration officials at last began to sense the urgency of industrial mobilization, the need for closest cooperation between government and business, the complexity of a gigantic task. By this time it was too late to build a skyscraper, for the war ended in November.

The administration made a mighty effort to obtain ships, and if the war had lasted into 1919 or 1920 the shipping program might have produced a mighty result. Instead it had almost no effect upon the war, except to consume great quantities of scarce supplies and labor. The United States Shipping Board, organized in January 1917 under the Shipping Act of September 1916, possessed general authority over procurement. In April 1917 the shipbuilding industry was in a decrepit state caused by decades of neglect, and it found itself with much to do. In 1810, American tonnage registered for foreign trade had stood at 981,000. In 1861 it was 2.5 million. Confederate raiders drove it down to 1.5 million. By 1914 it had dropped to 1 million.[3] But in the single month of April 1917 German submarines sank close to 1 million tons of Allied ships. The Shipping Board therefore announced a vast program of new yards, with expenditure of $750 million. In April 1917 the entire United States contained 37 yards with 142 ways for steel vessels and 24 yards with 73 ways for wooden vessels. These yards employed 45,000 workers. In subsequent months the board spent $270 million and built 341 yards with a total of 1,284 ways, more than double the ways in the rest of the world. By the end of the war American yards employed 380,000 workers.

Trouble plagued government shipbuilding because of clashes over programs and personalities. A businessman, William G. Denman, at first headed the Shipping Board, and General Goethals headed the board's operating subsidiary, the Emergency Fleet Corporation. Denman and Goethals embroiled themselves in a virtually public argument over their respective authorities. Goethals had insisted on a separate operating corporation so as to avoid what he described as the excellent hot air artists on the Shipping Board.[4] Denman maneuvered against the general, becoming certain he had "the old son-of-a-bitch sewed up."[5] Goethals resigned in July 1917 and the President accepted his resignation and that of Denman, and replaced the latter with Edward N. Hurley, a businessman. In April 1918 direction of the Fleet Corporation passed to the steelmaker Charles M. Schwab.

Under Schwab, an erstwhile lieutenant of Andrew Carnegie, who had founded Bethlehem Steel, the shipping program picked up. If the war had lasted into 1919 it would have been a triumph, for the Fleet Corporation planned on a grand scale. At Hog Island in the Delaware River near Philadelphia, the greatest of all the yards went up in the midst of a swamp beginning in the autumn of 1917, costing $65 million and employing 34,000 men, 846 acres with 250 buildings, eighty miles of railroad track, and fifty ways on which fifty ships were under construction while twenty-eight more were fitted out at the piers. Hog Island was larger than the seven largest shipyards in England. At the height of its operation, the editor Hamilton Holt wrote a graphic description.[6] In the summer of 1917 he had seen a flat stretch of land circling back from a mile and a half of waterfront, nothing but "a dismal, soggy, salt swamp inhabited only by muskrats and mosquitoes." When he saw the shipyard it was "a beehive of industry," indeed "one of the great manufacturing cities of the world." Giant cranes unloaded huge pieces of steel and logs from freight cars. "Donkey engines were puffing. Sirens were blowing. Those titanic human woodpeckers, the compressed air riveters, were splitting the ears with their welding." A half-dozen scows dredged the river, pile drivers descended with "giant whacks" upon logs at the water's edge, men walked along with mud-encrusted shoes, begrimed faces, laughing and shouting, singing and swearing.

At Hog Island a man applied for work and then went to school to learn all about a cross-section of the middle of one of the ships he was going to work on. Men in school continually erected and took down the cross-section. When a man proved himself he graduated from school to a ship.[7]

One gang laid the keel, another worked on the ribs, another did bulkheads, another decks. Gangs worked on five ways, laying the keel on way No. 1, moving to way No. 2, whereupon a second gang came on way No. 1 to raise the ribs. As soon as they finished, the first gang had completed the keel on way No. 2, and rib erectors moved on to way No. 2 and the keel layers to way No. 3. By the time the keel was laid on way No. 5 the ship on way No. 1 had been launched, and the gang of keel layers moved back. The rotation instilled a spirit of competition.

Hog Island held contracts for 200 ships, of two types, 4,600-ton cargo ships and 5,000-ton combined cargo-carriers and troop transports. Cargo ships had a speed of eleven to twelve knots and transports fifteen to sixteen. All were oil burners of latest design and used practically no wood, even down to metal furniture.

Each way had eight cranes, four on each side, so that at least two could reach any part of the ship, eliminating delay from breakage of a crane.

Each ship contained 250,000 parts. Engineers drew and designed parts and sent patterns all over the country to factories. Parts arrived at Hog Island by railroad and passed into the distributing yard with its 250,000 piles.

Engineers calculated that each ship needed more than half a million rivets, of which 200,000 were for bulkheads. They arranged for platforms beside ships where men erected bulkheads, which cranes hoisted into the ships, allowing more men to work on each ship.

The plan was to launch a ship in eighty-seven days, and take thirty to thirty-five more to finish the interior, such as installation of engines. When all ways were working, the yard could launch a ship every other day.

To push the ship program Schwab moved the Fleet Corporation's headquarters out of Washington to Philadelphia, nearer Hog Island, and with characteristic energy ventured forth in his private railway car to visit and exhort workers at yards all over the country. Known as a company man and a rich man, he spoke to crowds of workers, saying nothing memorable but doing it in a memorable way, awarding service badges to men who gave four months in the yards and bars for additional service ("With these service badges you can walk through the crowds, meet the boys of the Navy and the Army, and hold your heads high"). Every month a "competitive department" under Rear Admiral Frank F. Fletcher evaluated each yard's performance and presented a red flag to the best yard, white flag to the second best, blue flag to the third, and medals of gold, silver, and bronze to outstanding men in each winning plant. With his own money Schwab established a $10,000 bonus to men in the plant producing the most tonnage above the scheduled program and persuaded several yard owners to match his award, among them the youthful W. Averell Harriman, chairman of the Merchant Shipbuilding Corporation.[8]

By the midsummer of 1918 ship production was rising rapidly and on a single day, July 4, 1918, the yards launched ninety-five ships with tonnage of nearly 300,000.

Few of those ships helped win the war. Hog Island did not launch its first ship, the *Quistconck* (Indian for Hog Island), until August 5, 1918, nor deliver it until December 3. Many ships used during the war were confiscated from belligerents—notably Germany—when America entered the war, or obtained from neutrals who had laid up ships in American ports. Twelve ships came from the Great Lakes, bisected so as to go through the Welland Canal and put back together for ocean service. In August 1917 the Fleet Corporation commandeered 431 steel ships then under construction. It contracted for 1,741 additional steel ships, 1,017 wooden, 50 composite, and 43 concrete ships. Wooden ships were not easily usable for ocean traffic but could carry coastal trade, such as the New England coal trade and the West Indian trade, and make steel ships available for transatlantic runs. Composite ships combined steel frames and wooden plates. Yards delivered 664,000 tons of all sorts in 1917 and 1.3 million in 1918, a miserable performance considering that German submarines were sinking hundreds of thousands of tons each month. By the Armistice the Fleet Corporation had finished only 107 steel, 67 wooden, and 4 composite vessels. It canceled contracts for 941. Much construction mindlessly continued and the last emergency ships went down the ways in February 1921.[9] The government sold the ships to private owners and almost all became financial losses. Most of the wooden and composite ships never went to sea; the Fleet Corporation in 1922 auctioned for $750,000 218 wooden ships and 9 composites that originally cost $300 million, and a salvage company removed usable machinery and burned the hulls to the waterline.[10]

As for arms for the U.S. Army, the problem proved roughly the same as for shipping—lack of planning before entrance into the war, and then inability to translate programs in time for use on the Western Front.

Before April 1917, political leaders and military officers had contemplated industrial mobilization, but it had seemed too theoretical to take seriously. The Spanish-American War did not last long enough. In 1914–17 the European nations went to war with no more thought than the United States in 1898, and it became necessary to take many measures to mobilize economies. The Wilson administration gave them almost no attention. The Preparedness movement beginning in 1915 was mostly preparedness for the presidential election the next year. In Washington the Navy Department brought together a Consulting Board of scientists including Thomas A. Edison. Howard E. Coffin, vice president of the Hudson Motor Car Company, became a member of the Edison board and arranged for a public relations man, Grosvenor B. Clarkson, to distribute inventory forms to discover the country's industrial resources. Owners of 30,000 plants returned the forms. Many did not. In August 1916, Congress created a Council of National Defense, a Cabinet committee, with an Advisory Commission of prominent citizens working without pay: Coffin; Bernard Baruch; president of the Drexel Institute of Philadelphia, Hollis Godfrey; president of the Baltimore and Ohio Railroad, Daniel Willard; president of Sears, Roebuck, Julius Rosenwald; president of the American Federation of Labor, Samuel Gompers; secretary-general of the American College of Surgeons, Dr. Franklin H. Martin. The commission met in December 1916 and appointed as its director a statistician of the American Telephone and Telegraph Company, Walter S. Gifford.

After the declaration of war, the theoretical began to become real, and yet not for a while—throughout the spring and summer of 1917 the nature of the country's part in World War I remained unclear and seemed to be mostly a continuation of assistance to the Allies in the form of money and food and for the rest of it help in the realm of morale, the New World coming to the aid of the Old. Not until the autumn, when the Italian front collapsed and the Bolshevik revolution gave evidence that the Russians would leave the war and that the Germans would have an enormous advantage on the Western Front in the spring of 1918, did the Allies and Americans come to an understanding that a massive American army would have to go to France.

Meanwhile industrial mobilization had not gotten very far. After April 6, each member of the C.N.D.'s Advisory Commission had formed a committee to supervise a part of industrial mobilization. Soon there were 150 committees. A British observer wrote of the commission's parent group, the Council of National Defense, that "a more amorphous body was certainly never established to assist a government."[11] The C.N.D. also created a General Munitions Board under the president of the Warner and Swasey Company of Cleveland, Frank A. Scott, and it became the War Industries Board, headed in succession by Scott, the railroad executive Robert S. Lovett, and Daniel Willard. In the War Department, Secretary Baker let the bureau chiefs run loose, and they ordered everything in sight, without any idea of how large the AEF would be, how complicated the procedures of production were, or how much shipping would be available to take materiel to France.[12] Even as the War Department expanded, the new officers in the bureaus, whether from the Regular Army or brought in from civil life, tended to take on the colorations of the bureaus—the idea was to get everything for one's own bureau. The only coordination between the bureaus came when they faced the would-be civilian managers in the C.N.D. and W.I.B. On such occasions War Department representatives turned into a solid phalanx of obstructionism, demanding a cooperation from the civilians that was nothing less than subservience. The War Department told the civilians what it wanted, and assumed those requirements were not subject to question, for military professionals had established them.

The inability of the administration and the Army to organize production became apparent in the winter of 1917–18 with a railroad tie-up of massive proportions. Once the War Department and to a lesser extent the Navy and the Shipping Board obtained scarce supplies, they requisitioned railroad cars. The railroad supervisory organ, the Railroads' War Board, on July 20, 1917, by Bulletin 22, provided tags for expediting this freight, and its agents tagged everything and sent it to the east coast, causing colossal tie-ups, cars backed up to Buffalo and Pittsburgh. The War Department requisitioned warehouse space on docks and even ships. Nothing seemingly could resolve the mess. The Railroads' War Board depended on voluntary measures; each railroad refused to permit its own engines to operate on another railroad's tracks, and hoarded cars. In November roads undertook "revolutionary measures" to move engines and cars. President Wilson seized the roads effective January 1, 1918.[13]

All the while coal production went down, supplies 6 million tons short each month. The President had fixed bituminous coal prices at $2 a ton when $3 probably was necessary to operate marginal mines; the Food Administration had set minimum prices to increase production, but the Fuel Administration had set maximum prices. Mid-December 1917 brought the coldest winter in fifty years: −20° in Boston, −16° in Albany. On January 5, 1918, winds of fifty-five miles an hour brought the first of two massive storms to the Midwest; a fifteen-inch snowfall blocked railroad terminals. A second blizzard came six days afterward. The head of the Fuel Administration, President Harry A. Garfield of Williams College, son of the martyred President, ordered a five-day embargo on use of coal in almost all factories east of the Mississippi, beginning January 18, after which nonessential industry was to go on a five-day week, shutting for nine "heatless Mondays" from January 28 until March 25. At first he gave no explanation and belatedly announced that the embargo was to break the coal shortage at eastern ports that had immobilized scores of ships. Garfield quickly lost any popularity he had ever obtained, and was known nationally as "the professor." He had had no understanding of the coal industry. The President had chosen him as fuel administrator because he knew him at Princeton, where he had hired him as a faculty member before Garfield went to Williams. In lost wages and production the coal embargo's estimated cost was $4.3 billion; a coal journal calculated that it saved 3.4 million tons but measured against losses the cost per ton was $1,256.94.[14]

With little coal, a harsh winter, and the railroad tie-up, popular attention turned to Washington. At first the problem seemed to be Secretary of War Baker, whom Colonel House schemed to get out of the way, appointed as private secretary to the President. In his place House had in mind a "forceful fellow" like McAdoo or Hoover.[15] Men of every shade of political opinion, the colonel wrote privately, condemned the war organization. He arranged for Baker to come to New York and spend a day drawing up a plan. Senator George E. Chamberlain of Oregon, Democratic chairman of the Military Affairs Committee, scheduled hearings, and witnesses paraded before the senators, each describing another part of what seemed an unending tapestry of incompetence.[16] Chamberlain asked for a new Cabinet department, a Department of Munitions, perhaps headed by a Republican. Then he realized that Democratic Cabinet appointees would surround such an official, and so another Chamberlain bill proposed a War Cabinet of "three distinguished citizens of demonstrated ability" with almost unlimited jurisdiction, superseding Baker's War Department.

Behind the effort to "get" Baker lay intense feeling about the

President himself. Wilson, even the friendly House believed, had allowed industrial mobilization to slip from his hands. "It is one of the things I have feared the President would sometime do. He seems to have done it. I have never heard such a storm of protest."[17] Senator Henry Cabot Lodge of Massachusetts hardly admired Wilson, and tended to express himself privately with hyperbole, but his commentary at this time to his British friend, the former ambassador in Washington, Lord Bryce, reflected widespread opinion. "The fact is," Lodge wrote, "that the President has no administrative capacity. He lives in the sunshine. He wants nobody to tell him the truth apparently and he has a perfect genius for selecting little men for important places."[18] Baker handed in his resignation, and the President refused it. House wrote that the Secretary "seems to be getting deeper into the mire, and the President cannot see it. Baker's mind is so sympathetic with that of the President's that the President does not realize that he is no more of an administrator than he is himself."[19]

It was at this point that Wilson turned to Baruch, the forty-seven-year-old New York financier ("Hebrew Wall Street speculator," opined House), $50,000 contributor to the Democratic party in 1916, a handsome man, prematurely white hair parted down the middle, round face, twinkling eyes.[20] In the letter of appointment the President denominated him "the general eye of all supply departments in the field of industry."

In the short time that remained before the war came to its end—Wilson appointed Baruch on March 4, 1918—the new W.I.B. administrator followed the same voluntary procedures of McAdoo and Hoover, seeking to obtain cooperation and good will. [21] Actually, of course, he had no time to assemble a large bureaucracy with which to compel industrialists to do their part. His staff numbered 750 and included the president of the American Vanadium Company, J. Leonard Replogle; vice president of International Harvester, Alexander Legge; vice president of John Deere and Company, George N. Peek; and Wall Street investment banker Clarence Dillon. The W.I.B. organized the nation into twenty-one production zones, assigning businessmen to resource advisory committees. By the end of the war manufacturing centers were sending lobbyists to Washington to keep in touch. It was efficient use of local talent. An unanticipated result of such decentralization was that businessmen obtained intimate views of the government's problems.

The W.I.B. managed some achievements that at the time and later were much celebrated, and doubtless helped the war effort. A key word in its judgments was "essentiality"—whether a product had immediate war use. Its conservation division set specifications for products that might waste commodities, standardizing baby carriages and coffins, reducing bicycle designs (saving 2,000 tons of steel), taking stays out of corsets (allegedly obtaining enough metal for two warships). It induced tailors to reduce the size of sample wool swatches, saving 450,000 yards; forced substitution of paper wrappers for 141.8 million pasteboard cartons and 500,000 wooden packing cases of hosiery and underwear, freeing 17,321 freight cars; asked thread manufacturers to put 200 yards on each wooden spool (they had reduced yardage to 150 to hold the price during inflation) and saved 600 freight cars.[22]

Baruch technically did not have control of prices, which belonged to a Price Fixing Committee headed by Robert S. Brookings, but he assumed that power to allocate priorities included prices. Whether because of his work or that of Brookings, the commodity price index during the war's last three months did not change. The metals group index, to which Baruch gave special attention, fell from 330 (July 1913 through June 1914 equaled 100) in July 1917 to an average of 211 for 1918. In March 1918 the index for all commodities was 188, at the Armistice, 201.[23]

The W.I.B. acted as purchasing agent for the Allies, and in London created "joint executives" for such items as nitrates, tin, wool, leather, platinum. The executives served as exclusive buyers, and then allocated these commodities.

But behind the facade of achievement, creation of organization, lay the basic unwillingness of the Army to give up procurement. Whatever went on at higher levels in the W.I.B., its major activity ground away on the level of the so-called commodity sections, committees that passed on priorities and production quotas for such basic items as wool, rubber, steel, hardware. In the commodity sections sat representatives of both the W.I.B. and the Army. Here the Army conducted a sort of guerrilla war with the civilians. In the spring of 1918 when the sections were not working well at all, General March relieved their principal military coordinator, General Pierce, and gave coordination to Hugh Johnson.[24] March was contemptuous of the W.I.B. and expected little from his new coordinator, who himself went over to the W.I.B. with an intense suspicion of civilians. But unlike March, Johnson's suspicion was not based so much on the supposed superiority of Army professionals as upon, as he later admitted, sheer ignorance. He quickly saw the problem, and also found himself drawn to Baruch and the latter's assistant, Peek, both of whom he came to admire because of their intellectual agility and decisiveness. He created parallel commodity committees within the War Department. And he did his best to bring Army representatives in the W.I.B. commodity sections into cooperation with civilian opposites. For a while he thought things were working, and then discovered they were not, partly because Army representatives had other duties in the War Department, also because in an apparently sensible effort to assert the primacy of civilians in industrial mobilization Baruch had given paramount authority to the chairmen of the commodity sections, all of whom were civilians. Army representatives had done what came naturally, which was to cease almost all efforts to cooperate, on the theory that the civilian heads were paying no attention to Army needs anyway. It probably was true that the heads were acting arbitrarily. Johnson arranged for decisions to be put back into the sections as a whole, taking them away from the chairmen. Johnson's task again became one of working out cooperation, which he was beginning to accomplish late in the summer of 1918 when he asked for and obtained a brigade command.

In the short time that Baruch had to make changes in industrial mobilization he could not manage enough to dominate the Army. Control worked the other way—the Army controlled the W.I.B. Under claim of military necessity the Army simply told the W.I.B. what to order. It is illuminating to read how on May 13, 1918, the chairman of the W.I.B. wrote sharply to Edward R. Stettinius, then the War Department's "surveyor general" of purchases. Baruch admonished Stettinius that he had heard the department had placed orders far in excess of reasonable requirements. Five days later, a long time considering that the letter had passed only from one Washington office to another, Stettinius responded that he did not know any specific cases of overproduction in excess of requirements laid down by the General Staff and General Pershing. The response, of course, was no response at all.[25]

In procurement of rifles and machine guns the Army and W.I.B. —or perhaps it was mostly the Army—did not do badly. Problems had appeared with production at the beginning of the war, when the inventory of rifles showed 200,000 Krag-Joergensens, good only for training, and 600,000 Model 1903 Springfields. The Springfield was the most accurate rifle in the world, but artisans manufactured it and their work was impossible to imitate on an assembly line. In April 1917 several plants in the United States were producing Enfields for the British Army, and ordnance officers decided to adopt the Enfield but modify its bore to use Springfield cartridges. By August the modified Enfield, known as the Lee-Enfield, was in production; by the end of December factories turned out 5,000 a day. All together American manufacturers produced 2.5 million rifles—313,000 Springfields, the rest Lee-Enfields. The latter proved slightly inferior to the Springfields.

Machine guns were at first much tighter, 1,500 guns of four types on hand in April 1917. The Army needed them badly, for experience on the Western Front had demonstrated their value: in 1912, Congress had sanctioned four machine guns per regiment; in 1919 new Army plans would provide 336 machine guns per regiment, an increase of eighty-four times. Fortunately machine gun requirements were met. For most of the fighting in France the Americans used British Lewis guns or the French Chauchat, known as the Sho-Sho, the Sure Shot, or, when it jammed as it regularly did, the Sure something else. By February 1918 the United States began to produce the best gun anywhere, the Browning. Brownings were standard equipment in World War II and Korea. General Pershing received 29,000 automatic rifles and 27,000 heavies and was so proud of them he did not allow these guns on the Western Front until a few weeks before the Armistice, for fear the Germans would capture and copy them.

Artillery constituted one of the embarrassments in arms production, not merely because of a total production failure but for a reason discovered only in March 1918. Ordnance officers had hoped to produce a gun designed in 1916 and known to its critics as the Crime of 1916. After long confusion they gave up and decided on the gun known as the French 75. Problems arose in getting blueprints, for the French were secretive, and one exasperated officer vowed they would rather lose the war than reveal the secret of the *soixante-quinze*. The French also relied on artisans, and the Americans had to put rigid tolerances into drawings for assembly lines. The war ended before delivery of a single 75. The irony of the long effort to produce an artillery piece was that the American

Model 1902 three-inch gun turned out to be a far better piece than ordnance officers thought, and would have served the purpose in France. Officers of the School of Fire at Fort Sill discovered that the 1902 gun was as accurate as the 75, sturdier, and simpler to put in position. Meanwhile the French provided 1,828 75's for the AEF.[26]

Another failure was in tanks. The enthusiasm for tanks displayed by the British Minister of Munitions, Churchill, did not touch American officers, and more than anything it was their failure to understand tanks that accounted for the lack of them. The War Department received no clear appreciation from Pershing and did not push the tank program until it was too late. The AEF's commander showed a peculiar indifference to tanks as late as August 1918, when he cabled the War Department for eight mounted cavalry regiments. Only in the summer of 1918 did the Ford Motor Company begin to build six-ton vehicles, and none got to France. The AEF's chief of staff, tank corps, "due to fear that he would never get into the fight if he waited for tanks," went on duty with the engineers. Pershing's troops received 227 light tanks from the French and 64 heavies from the British. At St. Mihiel the tank corps entered battle with 174 and came out with 131. About eighty were ready for the Meuse-Argonne, and by October 11 were down to forty-eight. The First Army began its final offensive in early November with sixteen light tanks, one per 40,000 troops. In a lecture after the war Pershing's chief of tanks, Brigadier General S. D. Rockenbach, said he had "miserably few available." American divisions relied on frontal assaults by infantry. Lawrence Stallings wrote after Belleau Wood that a single British Mark IV tank would have unlocked the gates to that enclosure in fifteen minutes. In 1935, Colonel George Marshall wrote Harbord that in the Meuse-Argonne in early November, the AEF could have captured 100,000 prisoners if it had possessed tanks.[27]

It was in planes and powder, however, rather than artillery and tanks, that industrial mobilization displayed essentially wrongheaded approaches by the Army and the Wilson administration. In the matter of planes both the Army and the administration guessed wrongly over requirements and procedures. In powder, once the crisis became apparent, the Army displayed more prescience about a program and procedures than did the administration, but the latter then entangled itself in a populist contention as to whether new plants would be built by the government or private industry and precious months passed before a decision. With such confusions the wonder was that the entire war industrial mobilization did not go into a tailspin. By the time of the Armistice it was close to that, albeit for several other reasons (shortage of shipping, failure of the War Department bureaus to gather reliable statistics and control their orders, Pershing's incessant changing of his requirements).

Production of planes began with high hopes. At the outset the U.S. Army possessed hardly any planes. Pershing had used training ships during the Mexican Expedition, although not well, for their engines could not perform efficiently over mountainous terrain. Wooden propellers cracked in the dry heat of the Southwest. Soon all eight planes were out of commission. In April 1917 the signal corps had fifty-five serviceable planes, fifty-one of them obsolete, the others obsolescent. Secretary Baker, mesmerized by planes, announced he would ask Congress for $600 million for "the greatest air fleet ever devised" and told the President he was "thoroughly fascinated by the possibilities of the thing" and that it would be "perhaps America's most speedy and effective contribution to the Allied cause from a military point of view." Colonel House similarly advised Wilson: "If you will give the word, and will stand for an appropriation of one billion dollars, the thing is done." Wilson gave the word and Congress voted the money.[28]

It was necessary to start from scratch and all sorts of production problems appeared. For an airframe the Army needed as much as 5,000 feet of lumber to get 500 feet with no cross or spiral grain. Flax for airplane linen—planes in those days were mere wooden frames, over which builders stretched cloth—proved impossible from Ireland in quantities of 250 to 500 yards. Although cotton was a feasible substitute, the dope used on linen would not work as well on cotton, and forced invention of nitrate and acetate dopes.[29] Engines seemed no problem, for in a few days of concentrated effort in a suite in the New Willard Hotel in Washington two engineers designed the excellent Liberty engine. Pershing could not decide what sort of plane he wanted and kept cabling advice and each modification took the Liberty engine back to the drawing boards. In the spring of 1918, John D. Ryan was put in charge of aircraft production and told manufacturers to make no more changes, resulting in production of 13,547 twelve-cylinder Liberty engines, of which 4,435 went overseas. Few planes went over. Baker had promised 20,000. The figure went down to 17,000, 15,000, 2,000, finally 37. The War Department announced on February 21, 1918, that "the first American-built battle planes are today en route to the front in France." Actually a lone plane had gone from the factory to an aviation field (in America) for a radiator test. Of the 6,364 planes used by the Army in France, evenly divided between service and training types, most were foreign-built: 4,874 French, 258 British, 19 Italian. Pershing received 1,213 American-made De Havilland-4's, an English model powered by the Liberty engine, a good all-round plane with poor visibility. The De Havilland's fuel tank tended to explode in a crash, and the plane was known as a flying coffin.

Stories kept appearing of malfeasance among manufacturers or devious dealings between Army procurement officers and manufacturers, and President Wilson incautiously allowed an amateur in plane production, the sculptor Gutzon Borglum, to investigate the aircraft industry. Borglum was a man of large ideas, and later carved Mount Rushmore to prove it, but his bizarre inquiries about aircraft threw everything into turmoil. The President called on his opponent in the election of 1916, Hughes, and released the latter's report on October 31, 1918, showing confusion, lack of central responsibility, incompetence, minor violation of law, but no thievery.[30]

In looking back at the failure of the plane program it is an interesting fact that even if the Americans had produced armadas of planes, these new instruments of warfare might not have been used effectively. Throughout World War I the nations of Europe failed to understand the plane's importance. The attacking Germans in 1914 desperately needed to know where their troops were. Advancing too fast to set up field telephones, with wireless not yet working over long distances by land, they could have used planes, but instead lost the First Battle of the Marne and perhaps the war when a general staff officer at a crucial moment advised an unnecessary withdrawal. As the plane developed mechanically the Allies and their opponents employed it for observation, spotting for artillery, or reconnaissance of terrain and troop movements. After the Dutch builder Anthony Fokker in 1916 installed machine guns by synchronizing their fire with revolutions of the propellers, planes became instruments of harassment, able to appear suddenly and to machine-gun troops in open fields or to keep them down in the trenches. Planes made themselves attractive for another reason; by engaging in spectacular duels and dogfights, and attacking well-defended observation balloons, pilots in planes equipped with machine guns introduced an attractive sort of individual valor into warfare on the Western Front. Massive use of planes for bombing of civilians or their houses or industry was never an American objective in World War I. Secretary Baker was against "promiscuous bombing upon industry, commerce or population."[31] Use of planes for bombing just behind the lines or along the trench lines might have raised havoc with troops and even turned the war of position into a war of movement long before the last weeks of the war when troops did get out of trenches. Far more imaginative use of planes at sea might have made a difference—when the fleets of Britain and Germany drifted into battle in 1916 it was without knowing each other's position, nor for that matter where their own units were. Admiral Sir John Jellicoe heard the firing upon Sir David Beatty's battle cruisers and said plaintively to his staff: "I wish someone would tell me who is firing and what they're firing at." His retreat a little later because of a possible submarine attack on his battleship line that never came broke off a battle that he might have won. Nor did the Allies ever try to counter the submarine threat by hunting subs with planes, which could have seen silhouettes far sooner than lookouts from masts.

Failure of the American plane program, like the ship program, became a tragedy because of its immense consumption of materials and labor. One has, however, the haunting feeling that even if the planes had become available the U.S. Army and the Allies might not have used them to much avail.

Procurement of powder for the Army marked another example of how industrial mobilization did not go smoothly in 1917–18, although the reasons for trouble were somewhat different than in the case of the plane program.[32] At the beginning of American participation in the war the Army placed no extra orders on the American powder industry, for it did not anticipate sending a large body of troops to Europe. The principal powder maker in the United States, E. I. du Pont de Nemours and Company, was busy anyway with Allied war orders, which had booked Du Pont's entire production until September 15, 1917. Not until October did the Army realize its possible powder needs. Nor did Du Pont itself sense them, for the same reason as the Army.

When in October it became apparent that new plants would be required, the Army's representatives quickly came to an agreement with Du Pont, for relations in the past had been excellent and the mutual trust that had developed made everything easy. Du Pont executives knew exactly how to construct a plant, having already increased their production of the three principal military explosives —smokeless powder, TNT, and picric acid—from almost nothing (and in the case of picric acid, nothing) in 1914 to large levels because of Allied war orders. They had exact ideas of costs, and the negotiating Army officers agreed with them, and it was an easy arrangement: $90 million for new plant, $155 million in initial orders, combined total of $250 million.

But six days after the Army signed with Du Pont, a telegram arrived in Wilmington from Secretary Baker, calling everything off until further notice. Baker had taken alarm at the contract, the largest government contract in American history. It called for complete government subsidies for the proposed new plant—the government was to pay for everything including a 15 percent commission, $13.5 million on the projected plant cost of $90 million. In addition Du Pont would obtain a profit of perhaps ten cents per pound on production of 1 million pounds of powder a day, approximately $30 million a year (and with the plant commission, a total profit of $43.5 million) as calculated by a hostile government investigator, Robert Brookings. In 1914–17 the Du Pont Company had made enormous profits on Allied business, as Du Pont was an extremely efficient company and the Allies desperately needed the powder. The president of the company, Pierre S. du Pont, a very able manager, had constantly kept in mind the probability that ammunition plants would be useless after the war, for their conversion to peacetime use seemed unlikely, and so he had entirely amortized the plants—Du Pont would not be caught with them after the war. But Baker and his chief, President Wilson, had become suspicious of the Du Pont Company, believing it to be nothing less than what in the thirties was known as a "merchant of death." The prospect of Du Pont's making millions out of U.S. Government orders was too much for the Secretary of War and the President.

In discussions between Pierre du Pont and Baker, the Secretary's point of view became altogether clear, much to the disgust of the patriotic munitions maker. In one of the first interviews the Secretary said frankly that "I have just come from the White House. I may tell you that we have made up our minds that we are going to win this war without Du Pont." Baker had in mind not merely government ownership of new powder plants, but their construction by a company or companies other than Du Pont, and their subsequent running as government plants, not Du Pont plants.

What Baker and Wilson did not understand was that no company in the United States, other than Du Pont, knew how to put up an efficient powder plant. It was a case, really, of losing the war without Du Pont. In December, Baker went to an able Western mining executive, Daniel C. Jackling, and put him in charge of the government's powder program. Jackling immediately went to see Pierre du Pont in Wilmington to ask cooperation of the Du Pont Company, which the company's president promised even for a non-Du Pont program. Jackling gave a contract to the Thompson-Starrett Company, a huge construction firm. The company admitted it needed Du Pont assistance, and refused to accept more than half of the powder-factory construction program, taking only a contract for construction of a plant called Nitro at Charleston, West Virginia. Meanwhile Pierre du Pont began to have second thoughts about his proposed contract with the Army, now rejected; he knew that his proposed net profit was quite reasonable, considering the risk that somewhere along the line some government official might object to an item or items in the plant cost and then everything would be thrown into the courts where Du Pont might easily lose, but he began to see that if Du Pont stayed out of the government's powder program because of a contention over profits it would look very bad for the company, especially if the war was lost. Baker began to see that his own position, which was that of Wilson, had been doctrinaire in the extreme. He and the Du Pont Company hence came to a compromise that Du Pont would construct a plant at Nashville, Tennessee, accepting the other half of the powder program and 400,000 pounds a day more (making a total capacity of 900,000 pounds), for a total cost to the government that was reasonable enough—one dollar. But the argument over free enterprise versus government enterprise, however interesting as a piece of political philosophy and perhaps political science, had taken four months, October 1917 until January of the following year.

In the event everything worked out all right, and the Du Pont plant at Old Hickory was in production by the end of the war, though not up to capacity. The rival Thompson-Starrett plant at

Nitro, symbol of government enterprise, was just getting in production on the day the war ended. In addition to being speedier, Du Pont had built its plant for less money if one calculated unit cost. Had the war lasted into 1919 or 1920 these two huge plants would have ensured a supply of ammunition for the AEF, even if Pershing had increased the size of his forces, as indeed he hoped to do, to 100 divisions.

The development of the powder program, different in detail from the airplane program, was nonetheless similar in its general proportions, a story of delay and confusion, of erroneous positions taken sometimes by the Army, sometimes the administration, sometimes both.

Failures with ships and arms, one may conclude, occurred principally because World War I was for the United States the first modern war, requiring mobilization of industry, not merely conversion of plants (as in the Civil War) but construction of new plants. Baruch and his W.I.B. associates, such as Peek and Johnson, had a considerable vision of what industrial mobilization really was about. If the war had lasted into 1919 or 1920, American industry would have turned out astonishing quantities of ships, artillery, tanks, planes, and ammunition, enough to have satisfied whatever requirements Pershing and his supply service, the War Department, might have dreamed up. Even for 1917–18, in rifles and machine guns, the Army did well and deserved credit.

And yet to come to a conclusion that constitutes a sort of absolution to everyone involved, by remarking that they were taking part in such an immense novelty that, after all, one could not expect them to triumph on every hand, is hardly sufficient. It is not enough to say that World War I came too soon to permit the close understanding between men of politics and economics, between government and industry, that usually—the point can be argued—marked national achievement in later years of the present century.

The essential, foundational fact to which the War Department bureau generals and the highest civil officials of the United States Government needed to address their attention, when they contemplated industrial mobilization, was that in 1917–18 there was only one sector, one place, in the United States where the necessary expertise lay, and that was private industry. Only here was it possible to find experience—organizers and operators of the world's greatest industrial machine, who had taken the new and often complicated processes of manufacture and arranged for construction of plants, employment of work forces. They had brought together the means of transportation, raw materials to the plants, finished products to consumers whether in the United States or abroad. They were accustomed to holding the strings of complexity, to arranging and if necessary rearranging according to what balance sheets proved or forewarned.

Neither the bureau generals nor Baker and Wilson understood the nature of business experience, how special it was. Goethals did —the Panama Canal was one of the great engineering feats of all time. So did his young assistant Robert Wood. Otherwise the War Department's generals (and Pershing in France, who also had his supply problems) were, and one uses the word with hesitation, ignoramuses. So were Baker and Wilson, for the former had been mayor of a Midwestern city, the latter president of a small college and governor of a tiny state. They thought that because they could write requisitions or make speeches, were clever at posing in uniform or presenting themselves before Congress, they could manage industrial mobilization by, so to speak, the seats of their pants, putting a little more energy, a few more requisitions, more speeches, into the task and by some sort of legerdemain, which they did not bother to investigate, the necessary ships and military hardware would come out of the large end of American industry's cornucopia. In understanding of industrial mobilization the War Department's bureau generals and the government's Secretary of War and President were children, compared to industrialists such as Pierre du Pont. The president of the Du Pont Company was no politician, and when in the midst of his contention with the Wilson administration he leaked his troubles to the Chamberlain committee he proved that fact. But this was a small delinquency compared to the dilettantism of the nation's military and political leaders.

CHAPTER 8

The Allies

WHEN Napoleon once was asked against whom he would prefer to wage war, he replied, "Allies." World War I proved no exception to his rule, for both sides fought in alliance and often found their allies' company unbearable. The Germans had trouble with the Austrians, and only the combined force of their irritabilities held them together. The common language in the courts of Berlin and Vienna drove them apart—insults required no translation. Emperor Charles succeeded Francis Joseph in 1916 and surreptitiously sought a separate peace, and the Germans thereafter watched the Austrians closely. The British and French disliked each other out of enmities that reached back to Louis XIV—the Anglo-French entente antedated the war by only ten years, and its negotiation proved so delicate that the negotiators kept its details from both national parliaments. Italy entered on the side of the Allies in 1915 not because of admiration for Britain and France but out of desire for the territory of its weak neighbor Austria-Hungary: the Central Powers had nothing to give the Italians, the Allies did.

Relations between the United States and the Allies were often difficult. In the year before the United States entered the war, the British government had tightened its rules in regard to blockade and expanded the blacklist, and President Wilson in exasperation declared the blacklist the last straw; Admiral Benson told Sims the country would as soon fight the British as the Germans, and the President felt the same way. When in April 1917 the nation entered on the side of the Allies, it was with no thought of a formal alliance such as the Treaty of London of 1914 between Britain and France, and in his speeches and diplomatic exchanges Wilson soon was saying that the United States was an "associated power." In July 1917 he told the British secret service operative William Wiseman that the United States was now ready to take its place as a world power, but that his countrymen desired a "lone hand" and no alliance.[1] London and Washington soon were arguing over how much to charge for transporting American troops to Europe in British ships; the British asked for $150 a person (not including food, the President said).[2] The two governments settled for $81.75, a figure based on the actual war risk loss of ships rather than assumption of an arbitrary rate of 5 percent on their total valuation. All the while soldiers in France were conducting arguments. Relations frequently were awkward, and the line between witticism and insult was thin. After American troops arrived in Europe a British soldier might ask if AEF stood for After Everything's Finished, and the American might reply, no, it stood for After England Failed.

Between French and American troops the language barrier prevented remarks, but as members of the AEF walked or rode along they sang dozens of unprintable verses about "Mademoiselle from Armentières" that ended with "Hinky Dinky Parlez-Vous." They described Frenchmen as "frogs" because Frenchmen ate frogs' legs. They noticed manure piles outside country and village houses, substitution of perfume for bathing, lack of indoor plumbing. They believed that people who sold vegetables, chickens, eggs, and wine at high prices were citizens of a government that took advantage in larger ways such as charging rent for the trenches. And not merely the soldiers believed that canard; President Wilson said privately that the French wanted to charge rent for the trenches. By the end of the war relations between the troops had improved and November 11, 1918, brought a burst of enthusiasm, but delay in bringing home the AEF, many men not getting back until the summer of 1919, revived wartime irritabilities.[3]

In the first months of war not much happened in formal diplomatic relations with the Allies other than ceremonial visits to Washington by missions, as they were called, and opening of the Treasury to loans. The first of the visitors, Foreign Secretary Arthur Balfour, made a large impression. He seemed to like everything he saw. He carefully praised President Wilson; after a visit to the White House he said, "I cannot see how he is inferior to Lincoln."[4] It was the Foreign Secretary's second visit to America, after forty years, and perhaps the country's growth since the seventies, its size and strength, overwhelmed him. Everywhere he expressed faith in America, not least in a much noticed address to the Senate.

The French mission proved far less effective, if only because of its head, René Viviani. The morning after arrival he flew into a rage because a manicurist whom he had engaged was not on hand at 6:00. When he promised a speech to the Senate he refused to appear unless President Wilson was present, and then gave the speech entirely in French. After he concluded, Marshal Joseph Joffre stepped forward with a beaming smile and said, "I cannot speak English—*Vive l'Amérique!*" and the whole chamber shouted with enthusiasm.[5] But then Viviani and party traveled across the country, and Viviani kissed the mayor of Kansas City.

The Japanese government sent Viscount Kikujiro Ishii, who sought recognition of his country's sphere of influence in East Asia; he told Secretary of State Lansing that Germany three times had sought to persuade Japan to forsake the Allied cause. The result was the ambiguous Lansing-Ishii agreement, which the Japanese promptly translated unambiguously into Chinese; the phrase "special interests" became "paramount interests," and the Japanese refused to consider them limited to economic concerns. Later Ishii wrote in his *Diplomatic Commentaries* that he and Lansing were only "performing the role of photographers, as it were, of a condition," Japan's paramount situation in the Far East. "Even though Americans may destroy the print because it is not to their liking," he explained, "the negative will remain. And even if the negative also be destroyed, does not the substance of the picture remain?"

With the defeat of the Italian Army at Caporetto late in October and the Bolshevik Revolution in Petrograd in early November, President Wilson decided to send an American mission to Europe, led by Colonel House. The colonel went to "iron things out," as House was wont to describe his diplomatic endeavors; he sought to create "liaison," a word that entered American speech during the winter of 1917–18. He already had made trips in the guise of a private person bearing letters from the President, letters that had opened the doors of Europe. He was susceptible to flattery, like most men, and did not know the affairs of Europe as well as he knew American domestic politics. The Europeans may have smiled when he came to ask their points of view and describe those of Washington. But he was a shrewd man, a good listener and observer, and if his auditors smiled they did so inwardly, else House would have reported the merriment.

House arrived in London on November 7, two days after the Petrograd Revolution, and remained until November 21, when he went to Paris to attend a conference of eighteen nations, a group with membership ranging from Belgium to Siam. There he found chaos, and not merely because of the many delegations; the Allies had called the meeting without preparation—no program or purpose, only a hope that something would happen. At Paris, as at London, there was no agreement, or even effort to agree, on war aims. David Lloyd George had come over to make a speech, after which he intended to go home. Having divined the Prime Minister's purpose, House moved to thwart it: "We arranged it so he could not speak, therefore he went home . . . " Clemenceau, who had just become premier of France, had no program. The Italians, like the Americans, had expected proposals. This gave House his chance to seize control: "As for ourselves, being newcomers and never having sat in before at such a conference, it would have been indelicate to have taken control of it more than we did. As a matter of fact, we did control it, and made possible whatever good results may be accomplished."[6] The colonel organized interallied committees on war purchases and finance, maritime transport, navies, food, petroleum, and munitions. The Allies believed such organization unnecessary, and André Tardieu wrote later that "when Americans fall in love with an idea, even if their enthusiasm does not last, it is always intense."[7] At the time the Allies could say nothing, for the United States Treasury was extending loans. For the resultant reformation of procedure the Allies eventually were grateful. The machinery of economic cooperation created at Paris ensured a far more effective supply than had shopping lists and filling of individual orders. The Allied economic committees functioned under a Supreme War Council created by the British, French, and Italian governments at a preceding conference at Rapallo.

In one respect the Americans disappointed the Allies at the Paris conference, and this was House's refusal to establish political liaison. Having represented the United States in economic matters, he departed, installing the counselor of the Paris embassy, Arthur Frazier, as a "listener." Frazier fulfilled that limited role until October 1918, when the question of a German armistice arose.

The issue of military liaison became unavoidable during the spring of 1918. At this time of high peril to the Allies it seemed necessary to amalgamate the AEF with the troops of Britain and France.[8] The issue first appeared in December 1917, when after the Bolshevik Revolution it became evident that the Germans might be able to move divisions from east to west and overwhelm the Allies. At that time the situation was unclear; the German threat was just appearing. Perhaps for that reason the War Department in faraway Washington sent Pershing an ambiguous cable on December 18 and told him to cooperate, and then allowed the American commander to interpret the cable to mean he could continue to create an American army under his personal command. He cabled back that the position of the United States at the eventual peace conference would be incomparably better with an American army in the field, noted national habits and the ancient antagonism between the Americans and British, the language barrier with the French, the perverse dedication of the Allies to trench warfare, how tired they were and how their defeatism would affect American troops. He was not above referring to British and French commanders who had become inured to sacrifices on the Western Front and might send foreigners to their deaths. Indeed, throughout the war, he made this point. In the early summer of 1918 he noticed carefully how the French, whose front adjoined that of the AEF, and who were in combined operations with the Americans, cared little for American lives, failed to bring up artillery with high-explosive or gas shells to support the Marines at Belleau Wood, and in the Second Battle of the Marne deserted four green companies of the Twenty-eighth Division and let the remnants fight their way back to American lines.

When the Germans opened their great spring offensive in March 1918, broke through the lines of the British Fifth Army, and threatened to end the war, the issue of amalgamation suddenly became the all-consuming problem of relations with the Allies. Lloyd George was desperate for American troops, and showered cables upon the new British ambassador in Washington, Lord Reading, who had replaced Spring Rice. He managed to find shipping to assist the U.S. Navy in bringing them over. He then wanted the Americans without equipment, as many infantrymen and machine-gun units as could cram aboard. Day after day, week after week during the month of April, the British with great difficulty closed up their line with the adjoining French.

At the outset Pershing had offered his divisions, but as soon as the gap began to close he took the offer back. He did not seem to care that the German Army under the capable Ludendorff might soon strike some other place, probably against the weak French. The AEF commander managed to obtain support not merely from Secretary Baker but from President Wilson, who took the position that he was the man on the spot and they should not tell him what to do. At one point Lord Reading in Washington thought he had gotten a contrary commitment out of the President, but soon learned how securely Pershing controlled the situation—or, perhaps one might say, how all American high officials believed in creating an AEF and not permitting the Allies to amalgamate it. Reading seems to have cabled what he interpreted as Wilson's agreement at a time when Baker was in Europe. The President learned that Allied statesmen were quoting him wrongly and on his portable typewriter with the wide spacing and telltale blue ribbon typed a note to Assistant Secretary of War Benedict Crowell: "Please cable to the Secretary of War that I agreed upon no details whatever with Lord Reading. I told him that I had agreed to the proposition of the Supreme War Council *in the formula proposed to me by the Secretary of War by cable* and that I could assure him that we would send troops over as fast as we could make them ready and find transportation for them. That was all. The details are left to be worked out and we shall wish the advice of the Secretary of War as the result of his consultations on the other side."[9] At that moment, to be sure, Baker was consulting with Pershing, and the President knew what advice the general was giving Baker.

By this time, the beginning of May 1918, Pershing was in fighting form—that is, was arguing with Allied statesmen and generals as if they had no right to tell him what to do. Years later in his memoirs he recounted what he said, and the details are perhaps correct, as memoir accounts on the British and French side are equally pungent. The American general related that he was not about to make the U.S. Army a recruiting agency for the Anglo-French. He would not allow them to turn his army into cannon fodder. At one point Foch had said, "You are willing to risk our being driven back to the Loire?" The answer was immediate: "Yes, I am willing to take the risk. Moreover, the time may come when the American Army will have to stand the brunt of this war, and it is not wise to fritter away our resources in this manner. The morale of the British, French and Italian armies is low, while, as you know, that of the American Army is very high. It would be a grave mistake to give up the idea of building an American Army in all its details as rapidly as possible." Right after that Pershing had sat down with Lloyd George, Clemenceau, and Italian Prime Minister Vittorio Orlando. Lloyd George said, "Can't you see that the war will be lost unless we get this support?" The other two prime ministers echoed the question. Pershing responded, with the greatest emphasis, "Gentlemen, I have thought this program over very deliberately and will not be coerced."[10] This may have been the meeting at which the prime ministers told Pershing that the President of the United States was back of them in this matter. Pershing said he did not give a damn who was back of them.[11]

On May 4, Lloyd George cabled Reading in complete frustration. Pershing, he said, was an obstinate man. Foch had tried to talk to him and was "intensely depressed and disgusted." The prospect was bleak to the point of despair. "It is maddening to think that though men are there issue may be endangered because of short-sightedness of one General and failure of his Government to order him to carry out their undertakings." The French reported that American troops fought bravely but officers were untrained and staff officers lost their heads. It was a terrible prospect, Lloyd George cabled Reading, "if a large amateur U.S. army is built up without men and regimental officers being first put through the furnace under guidance of more experienced general officers."[12]

The Allies' demand for American troops abated, until the new crisis arose at the end of May. By that time Pershing was ready to commit his divisions.

Meanwhile, on January 8, 1918, President Wilson in Washington had announced the Fourteen Points for European and world peace. The collapse of the Russian government into communism and the Soviet regime's release of the texts of Allied secret treaties to a reporter for the Manchester *Guardian* raised the need of a statement of Allied ideals.[13] The American President was the logical man to announce those ideals, for two reasons. For one, an American was necessary for the task. The European Allies were tired, they could not grasp large issues; the war had locked them in mortal combat with the Central Powers, from which they could hardly raise their eyes to larger prospects. For another, no European leader could speak with the authority of Wilson. Prime Minister Lloyd George had made a speech about war aims on January 5, but he did not hold a commanding position in Allied counsels and was far more of a politician than statesman and could not have managed the task. Nor could Clemenceau, who had just become France's premier.

It was possible to contend that Wilson nominated himself for the role of peacemaker. The President admittedly desired an international role. Many years later a friendly biographer suggested this desire in a subtitle: *Woodrow Wilson: World Prophet.* And yet someone had to accomplish the task.

It is true that he did not consult the Allies. But they had shown no desire to consult with him. And they might have comforted themselves, had they known that he did not consult with his own advisers in any systematic way. He held a ten- or fifteen-minute conversation with House on December 18, 1917, after the colonel returned from the interallied conference, and the colonel was nonplussed—"I never knew a man who did things so casually." Wilson wrote his message on the basis of a memorandum of December 22 given him by a group of college professors and other experts in history and geography and economics known as the Inquiry, a group House had brought together. He sought advice from the Serbian minister in Washington, Milenko R. Vesnić, which he rejected. He went over a mass of memoranda supplied by American representatives in Europe that House brought to Washington. He did not consult the State Department, and read the text to Lansing the day before he spoke to Congress. Lansing accepted it with a few suggestions as to words, which Wilson adopted. The President's private secretary, Tumulty, knew nothing of the speech until two hours before its delivery. Three Cabinet members learned of it several hours afterward.[14]

The Fourteen Points are among the best known of all Wilson's utterances and need no explanation in detail. Apart from points (1), open covenants of peace openly arrived at, (2) freedom of the seas, (3) removal, "so far as possible," of trade barriers, (4) reduction of armaments "to the lowest point consistent with domestic safety," (5) equitable adjustment of colonial claims, and (14) a league of nations, the points dealt with territory: (6) evacuation of Russia, (7) evacuation and restoration of Belgium, (8) return of Alsace-Lorraine to France, (9) readjustment of Italian frontiers "along clearly recognizable lines of nationality," (10) "autonomous development" for the peoples of Austria-Hungary, (11) evacuation of Rumania, Serbia, and Montenegro, with access to the sea for Serbia, (12) reduction of Turkey to territory containing only peoples of Turkish descent, (13) independence of Poland, with access to the sea. These points the President later supplemented with the Four Principles of February 1918, in which he announced that the balance of power was forever discredited; the Four Ends of July 4, which foreshadowed a League of Nations to establish "the reign of law, based upon the consent of the governed and sustained by the organized opinion of mankind"; and the Five Particulars of September 27, which announced egalitarianism among states.

The most important of the territorial points, (10) autonomous development for the peoples of Austria-Hungary, came apart in subsequent months. Americans had felt little hostility for the decrepit imperial government in Vienna and declared war only in December 1917, when creation of the Supreme War Council raised the possibility of taking part in decisions involving the Italian front. At that time President Wilson thought the Habsburg monarchy would survive the war in attenuated form, the empire's Czechs perhaps receiving an autonomous regime centered in Prague that was akin to the "dual monarchy" created for the Hungarians in the mid-nineteenth century. But the Czechs opted for their own dual state, themselves and their fellow Slavs, the Slovaks. A revolt of Czech prisoners in Russia beginning in April 1918 led to an anabasis of 50,000–75,000 Czechs who took over the Trans-Siberian Railroad and made their way to Vladivostok, where they asked transportation to the Western Front to fight on the side of the Allies. Their movement across Siberia inspired widespread newspaper accounts and a campaign by Americans of Czechoslovak descent, eventually successful, to ensure independence of a new state in Eastern Europe.

People later said, without exaggeration, that Czechoslovakia was "made in America." The nation's future president, Thomas G. Masaryk, repaired to the United States via Siberia, and received a great welcome among the 100,000 Czech-Americans in Chicago. He raised $1 million to finance the cause, most of it in Chicago. Masaryk used this modest sum to advantage; he recalled that he inverted the Czech proverb, "Little money, little music." Although fewer Slovaks than Czechs had emigrated to the United States, he was himself a

Slovak and arranged an agreement in Pittsburgh on June 30, 1918, that promised Slovaks in a future Czechoslovakia their own administrative system, legislature, and courts, with Slovak as an official language. A former professor, he interviewed Wilson at the White House, and remarked afterward, "We understood each other fairly well—after all, we had both been professors." On September 3, 1918, the United States recognized the Czecho-Slovak National Council in Paris as a de facto belligerent government. Masaryk thanked Wilson in a letter, remarking that after arrival in the United States he had visited Gettysburg and read the address about government of, by, and for the people; he said he was happy Wilson "shaped these principles for the foreign policies of this great Republic as well as those of the other nations." The President replied that the letter gave him a great deal of gratification. His work in America not quite complete, Masaryk prepared a Czechoslovak Declaration of Independence and gave a copy to Professor Herbert A. Miller, who cut it into a hundred pieces and reassembled it in a style "to give a vigor of statement that would appeal to Americans." On October 26, 1918, Masaryk read a Declaration of Common Aims from the courtyard behind Independence Hall in Philadelphia. That same day a cable from Europe announced his election as president of the provisional state.[15]

Not everything was arranged with democratic tidiness during creation of Czechoslovakia, and millions of people found themselves under alien rule. Aboard ship en route to the Peace Conference, Wilson learned of a mass of Germans in northern Bohemia. "Why," he said, "Masaryk never told me that."[16]

By the early autumn of 1918, with Austria-Hungary falling apart and Germany suffering attacks on the Western Front, everything was going well. The President allowed the nationalities of Austria-Hungary to do what they pleased, content to make peace with whatever regimes appeared. He seems not to have cared about long-term results, whether Central Europe needed economic unity. Destruction of Austria-Hungary in World War I led to international disaster in the thirties. But probably no one, not even the American President, could have put the Habsburg monarchy back together.

As for the plight of Germany, Wilson similarly but more wisely let it take care of itself, and did not care if the military collapsed or the civilians lost their nerve, so long as someone in authority asked for peace.

Quite contrary to what Hitler said in the thirties, Germany's request for an armistice in 1918 came not because of a "stab in the back" of the German Army by a panicky civil government in Berlin, but because of the dire threat of military collapse. As early as the Soissons counteroffensive in July, Chancellor von Hertling knew the war was lost; and on August 8, when the British Army opened its attack, Ludendorff knew. When the U.S. Army began the Battle of the Meuse-Argonne on September 26 there was sheer emergency; Ludendorff said two days afterward he was unable to furnish a guarantee against a collapse in the west. He sent Major Hilmar von dem Bussche-Haddenhausen to Berlin to meet with political leaders on the morning of October 2, and the message of the high command's emissary was shocking, for among other things the major said Germany had no more reserves. By virtue of American help, he explained, the Allies were in a position to replace their losses. American soldiers were of no particular value—despite large numbers, the German Army turned them back whenever they made gains by mass attacks—but it was of critical importance that this sluggish soldiery was able to take over and hold long stretches of the front, enabling more experienced British and French divisions to go on the offensive and feel certain that in case of difficulty they had almost inexhaustible reserves.[17]

For Germany early in October 1918, militarily everything was far from lost, if the high command had been willing to abandon huge stocks of arms and munitions in France and Belgium, accumulated over four years of warfare, and retreat behind the German border. Foch at the end of August reportedly said, pointing to a map, that the Germans could still escape if they did not mind leaving their luggage. The high command had the means for such a withdrawal, time fuses for exploding mines or shells that could retard explosions not merely for days or weeks but months and would have sealed roads and railways in front of their line and held up any advance—the Allies would have had to construct new roads and rail lines. Having pulled back, Germany would have given up all French territory, the single cause that kept France in the war, likewise Belgian territory, the avowed reason Britain was fighting. The Allies would have risked 2 million more casualties by taking the war into Germany, and probably would have made peace.[18]

The high command refused to give up the arms, munitions, and territory. Ludendorff could think of nothing other than confessing his loss of confidence. The result was a dissolution of civilian morale that brought the end of the war.

A peculiar domestic political situation had existed in Germany throughout the war. The Chancellor in April 1917, Bethmann Hollweg, an honorable man, had lost out that summer in a contest with the nation's military leaders, Hindenburg and Ludendorff, who then installed as Chancellor an almost unknown Prussian bureaucrat, George Michaelis. After some months Michaelis gave way to the Bavarian premier (Bavaria was a kingdom within the German Empire), Hertling. It is quite possible to contend that during the last two years of war Germany was a military dictatorship, under Hindenburg and Ludendorff. And yet this perhaps was not the case, for to the German people the two military men were heroes. They gladly accepted them as interpreters of what the military situation required, which the generals said was support from the politicians. And behind that situation lay another, namely, that Germany's position in the war and its future as a great power would not have been much different whatever the leadership, military or civil. The principal problem of the German Empire in 1914–18 was that German military power was too weak—despite its great strength—to overwhelm Germany's enemies. The dream was of world power, not simply European, and the means to the dream was conquest or at the least dominance of enemies such as France and Britain and, beginning in 1917, the United States. Personalities, military or civil, had little to do with the dream, for almost all Germans shared it. And because the German Army was such a magnificent fighting machine, standing off the combined forces of the Allies, with a slight assistance from Austria-Hungary and Turkey, the hollowness of the world-power dream did not become apparent. Few Germans, civil or military, could see through it. Hope of victory led the weary German troops, their leaders, and the German people.[19] Then, with finality, everything fell to pieces: the high command confessed to failure. American divisions were coming across, huge divisions, hundreds of thousands of men arriving in France each month, 40,000 ashore at Brest in a single day, a reality that Major von dem Bussche revealed. It was impossible to fight this kind of force.

It is interesting to contemplate how German strength, through belief in victory, turned into weakness, once victory became impossible. The war had required mobilization of the masses, and the problem was to win mass support without granting influence over policy. Leaders of all the great powers managed to stay in power by promising victory. The human costs of war continued to rise, as well as the physical costs, and it was necessary to promise ever more rewards. As promises increased, the power of government to fulfill them decreased, and the prospect of domestic revolution grew.[20] There were plenty of problems within Germany in the summer and autumn of 1918. The German people were suffering, bread had become short, the possibility arose of meatless weeks. Shortage of cloth was appalling; in early July the government confiscated table linen from hotels and restaurants, and authorized communities to force surrender of unused clothing and to take anything decorative from houses, such as curtains. Shoes were difficult to obtain. Soap was scarce; miners could not wash, nor housewives keep clothes clean.[21] The moment was bearable, more sacrifice was possible, but after four years the high command said victory was impossible; the word spread through Berlin and the country, and the result was devastating, for the German nation no longer possessed the inner strength to carry on.

Berlin officials took the measures necessary to surrender, and negotiated with President Wilson, not the Allies. Hertling gave way to Prince Max of Baden, cousin to the Emperor, who on October 5 made an eloquent address to the Reichstag proposing immediate armistice, with the Fourteen Points as a basis. Next day he sent a note to Wilson, prepared by his predecessor and the high command. The saying in Berlin was that "Max equals Pax." Wilson's response of October 8, sent through the Swiss government, produced an acceptance on October 12. The President had asked if Max was "speaking merely for the constituted authorities of the empire who have so far conducted the war," and the Emperor on October 15 issued a decree that the military were now subordinate to civilians, that as Emperor he gave orders only after consulting the Chancellor. Eleven days later William II dismissed Ludendorff, curtly informing him that his resignation would be acceptable. The same day the Reichstag completed a revision of the imperial constitution, making Germany a democratic monarchy like England, and the new clauses came into force October 28. On October 30, Admiral Scheer ordered the High Seas Fleet to sea without approval of Emperor or Chancellor; 100,000 sailors at Kiel and Wilhelmshaven rose in revolt. Max resigned and the leader of the Socialist party, Friedrich Ebert, became Chancellor. Negotiation meanwhile had reached its climax. After Count Max's original note, the President received and answered six messages before he transmitted to the Allies the German armistice request that promised to evacuate occupied territory, avoid destruction as troops retired, and said the Berlin government spoke for the German people. On Wilson's side the correspondence had hinted at the need for the Emperor's abdication, and William fled to Holland on November 9.

After the President transmitted his correspondence, all that was necessary was for the British and French to agree to the Fourteen Points, but at the outset this was not so easy. Months earlier, relations between Wilson and the Allies had begun to deteriorate, turning down if only because the President had announced Allied war aims without the slightest consultation. European statesmen did not know Wilson, indeed had never met him—although contact might have done harm, for he was fundamentally out of sympathy with their national purposes and also was an awkward negotiator whose self-righteousness would have ruffled them.[22] During the months after the Fourteen Points address Allied leaders spoke disparagingly, and word got back. By August, Colonel House was writing in his diary that Lloyd George and Clemenceau disliked the President "and the President dislikes them, and all of them are partly justified in their feeling."[23] In October Wilson again antagonized the Allies by negotiating privately, even if their antagonism was not because of lack of information; the cable exchange passed through Switzerland, and French intelligence decoded it. But upon transmittal of the correspondence the irritation came out. Clemenceau said he had just read the Fourteen Points. Active in politics for half a century, he disliked instruction from a man who until 1911 had been a college professor. Lloyd George offered a few similar remarks; months earlier he had made his own statement of peace terms, and hardly desired to negotiate on the basis of Wilson's. In late October the First Lord of the Admiralty, Sir Eric Geddes, just returned from the United States, filled the Prime Minister's ears with what he wanted to hear, about how silly the President was, getting flattery from people around him, even Britishers such as Reading, whom Geddes described as glib-tongued, and the "sycophant" Wiseman.[24] In America, Geddes had given every evidence of admiring the President and had dealt pleasantly with Reading and Wiseman.

Shortly afterward Colonel House arrived in Paris to displace Frazier at the Supreme War Council and iron things out. He had to use a hot iron indeed. In a meeting on October 29 he said that if the Allies persisted in their arguments over the Fourteen Points, upon which Germany had based a request for an armistice, Wilson would have to tell the enemy they would not accept his conditions. The question would arise as to whether America would discuss issues of peace directly with Germany and Austria-Hungary.

"That would amount," said Clemenceau, "to a separate peace between the United States and the Central Powers."

"It might," House replied.

"My statement," the colonel cabled the President, "had a very exciting effect on those present."[25]

Next day, the British and French with exception of reparations and freedom of the seas accepted the Fourteen Points, and House framed the acceptance in a memorandum of November 4 and cabled it to Wilson, who forwarded it to the Germans, informing them they could receive terms from Marshal Foch.

Negotiation of an armistice was not without a remarkable intervention by Pershing in the Supreme War Council, in favor of continuing the war. During a meeting of Allied commanders at Senlis on October 25, the American commander in chief had supported a proposal of a fairly harsh armistice, but then appears to have become concerned that President Wilson might be too lenient. Privately to his friends Lloyd C. Griscom and Charles G. Dawes, then in a letter to the Supreme War Council on October 30, he came out in favor of unconditional surrender, and told Griscom and Dawes and the Council that the military situation made it possible—apparently he had in mind the imminent formation of the Second Army under Bullard and what his divisions might accomplish if they broke into open country, which they did during the first week of November. He also had in mind a cable from Wilson apprising him that if he had any disagreement with an armistice he should discuss it with House or otherwise bring it to the President's attention, and thus not very subtly was trying to undercut his own commander in chief.[26]

Many factors ensured the failure of Pershing's proposal. Allied military strength was not as remarkable as he believed. British and French troops, like American, had been defeating the Germans, but had no stomach for continuing the war; they had been fighting more than four years. The Americans, so Haig, Pétain, and Foch thought, were not yet a first-rate force. The British and French governments also knew that the longer the war, the larger the military and political role of the Americans. Foch chose not to back Pershing, staying aloof from a conflict that could produce quarrels and perhaps challenge his authority, which was none too certain. Lloyd George and Clemenceau disliked Haig and Foch and were glad to take decisions permanently out of their hands. Colonel House was unwilling to back him, perhaps because he feared to remove Wilson's Fourteen Points from negotiation after the Anglo-French and Germans had agreed to them. President Wilson of course favored a reasonable armistice. Lastly, Pershing soon realized that Foch's terms, which were harsh, would prevent the Germans from renewing the war. Foch demanded evacuation of all occupied territory, the left bank of the Rhine, bridgeheads at Mainz, Cologne, and Coblenz, reservation to the Allies and the United States of right to claim damages, surrender of submarines and internment of the German fleet, abrogation of the treaties of Bucharest (which forced Rumania out of the war) and Brest-Litovsk, destruction of German planes, tanks, and heavy artillery, maintenance of the blockade until conclusion of peace, return of prisoners and deported civilians, and 150,000 railway cars, 5,000 locomotives, and 5,000 trucks.

American soldiers in France were happy to see the war end, and would not have favored Pershing's proposal had they known of it. Many years later an AEF doughboy remembered how one day in 1918 a plane came along over his unit and dropped copies of the Army newspaper, Stars and Stripes, containing a statement by former President Taft sternly warning against any compromise and advising that Americans must fight on to Berlin. "I still remember the rage I felt," he wrote. "I fear my rage was totally illogically associated with Taft's corpulence. 'Yes, you fat old so and so,' I thought, 'I wish you were here for the march on Berlin.' "[27]

Pershing's idea of continuing the war disappeared, left for eventual discussion by historians who tended to characterize it, as did Lloyd George and Clemenceau, as political and theatrical. At 11:00 a.m. on the eleventh day of the eleventh month of 1918, the American air ace with twenty-five confirmed kills, Captain Edward V. Rickenbacker, flew his Spad over the American lines to see what was happening and a half century later recalled the sudden silence. On one side he saw little khaki-clad figures emerging from holes and trenches and moving cautiously toward a line of gray-clad figures from the other side, and the lines came together.[28]

In the United States truck drivers cut ignitions and turned on the "juice" to make engines backfire. And everywhere the hand-lettered signs, as in Chicago where a little girl wrote them down:

To hell with the Kaiser.

The Kaiser has "Flu."

The Kaiser is in Dutch.

Deutschland ueber Alles/Alles is ueber mit Deutschland.

Closed—Gone to Kaiser Bill's funeral.

Closed for the day, You know the reason why.

For sale, the German Empire, Apply to Gen. Foch.

Long Live Peace.[29]

President Wilson announced the Armistice with the eloquence of which he was a master, and his message moved the American people: "The armistice was signed this morning. Everything for which America has fought has been accomplished. It will now be our fortunate duty to assist by example, by sober, friendly counsel, and by material aid in the establishment of just democracy throughout the world." In the exhilaration of Armistice Day, President and Mrs. Wilson drove to the Italian Embassy that evening, where a ball celebrated the birthday of the King of Italy, and Wilson toasted the health of the King. The presidential couple stayed an hour. Upon return to the White House they found the emotion of the day had excited them too much to sleep, and they kindled a fire and sat on a large couch and talked until early hours of the morning. The President then read a chapter in the Bible and went to bed.[30]

1. President Woodrow Wilson reading his war message to Congress, April 2, 1917.

2. Wilson and his Cabinet, 1917. Front row, l. to r.: Secretary of Commerce William C. Redfield, Secretary of State Robert Lansing, Secretary of Agriculture David F. Houston, the President, Secretary of the Treasury William G. McAdoo, Postmaster General Albert S. Burleson. Back row, l. to r.: Secretary of the Navy Josephus Daniels, Secretary of Labor William B. Wilson, Secretary of War Newton D. Baker, Attorney General Thomas W. Gregory, Secretary of the Interior Franklin K. Lane.

3. The President and Mrs. Wilson leaving D.A.R. Hall in
Washington, July 20, 1917.

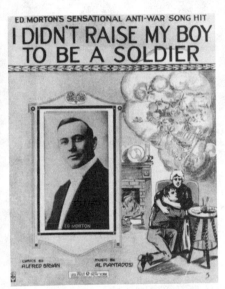

4, 5. A popular song and its sequel.

6. The poster to shame all able-bodied males.

The better the Soldier
The better the Salute

7. Military discipline.

8. "We have an oil stove and the cussed thing smokes like Vesuvius. It smells like a refinery and tastes like quinine in here now. I guess if we get good and smoked and eat about a peck of sand every day, we'll be hard-boiled and bomb-proof when we get to Berlin. The wind isn't blowing today and we are all very happy." (Lieutenant Truman to Bess Wallace, Camp Doniphan, Oklahoma, October 21, 1917.)

9. First Lieutenant Harry S. Truman, Missouri National Guard, 1917.

10.   Assistant Secretary of the Navy Franklin D. Roosevelt and friends doing calisthenics, Washington, August 1917.

11. Major Generals Tasker H. Bliss and Hugh L. Scott, Assistant Chief of Staff and Chief of Staff, U.S. Army, Washington, May 2, 1917.

12. General Peyton C. March, Chief of Staff, 1918–21.

13.   Transports in convoy to France, October 1918.

14.   General John J. Pershing, commander in chief, AEF, Chaumont,
October 19, 1918.

15. Troops moving toward Montsec, St. Mihiel, September 1918.

16. Black infantrymen advancing along screened road, Meuse-Argonne.

17. Men of 18th Infantry, First Division, under shellfire, Exermont, Meuse-Argonne, October 7, 1918.

18. 64th Infantry Brigade, Thirty-second Division, near Romagne, Meuse-Argonne, October 18, 1918.

19. Sergeant Alvin C. York arriving back in United States, May 22, 1919. Winner of the Congressional Medal of Honor, the most decorated soldier in the AEF, York had killed seventeen Germans with seventeen shots, and captured 132 prisoners and thirty-five machine guns. He had joined the Army with reluctance, because of his religious convictions. While in training he was amazed by the poor marksmanship of his urban comrades in the Eighty-second Division ("they missed everything but the sky"). A Tennessee mountaineer, he had learned to shoot by hunting wild turkeys. "Of course, it weren't no trouble nohow for me to hit them big army targets. They were so much bigger than turkeys' heads." In the Meuse-Argonne he and his squad came under fire from a German machine gun, and he worked his way around to a good position and waited for each member of the gun crew to raise his head—whereupon he "jes' teched him off." When a German lieutenant and seven men rose out of cover and charged with fixed bayonets, they made the mistake of attacking in column, and York dealt with them as if they were turkeys, shooting the last one first, so that those ahead would not take alarm and scatter.

CHAPTER 9

Peace

DURING heady days of war the President of the United States dreamed of the Peace Conference when he, leader of the American people, would make straight the way. His country's war aims differed from those of the Allies, and he avoided arguments over them, for once war was over he hoped to hold the Allies economically and militarily in his hand. Then he could assert America's purposes, those of the world rather than Europe, of peoples rather than governments and statesmen. Especially must there be none of the sordid grabbing for money and territory that had disgraced peace settlements in the past. In the spring of 1918 the President spoke to a group of foreign correspondents off the record and described his course. According to one of his auditors who made a summary from memory and sent it to Balfour, the talk ended as follows: "As to the Peace Conference which must come some day, the position of the United States may be summed up as this: 'Gentlemen of the Conference we come here asking *nothing for ourselves* and we are here to see *you get nothing.'* "[1]

Wilson indeed had his vision, his dream, of how much he could accomplish at the Peace Conference. He would not have been human, had he failed to be exhilarated by the possibility of reorganizing Europe and the world. But it is necessary to say that during the war months he also thought carefully about the difficulties of the forthcoming meeting. He knew it would not be easy and might contain many disappointments. In the event he found it in some ways markedly unsatisfactory. He did obtain the League of Nations and generally decent territorial and other settlements. Perhaps his major problem with it was not so much what it did but what people thought it did—his contemporaries exaggerated the supposed surrenders and compromises, and some exaggerations were so far-fetched as to be ridiculous (Lord Bryce said it was "the most hideous diplomatic failure of which history holds record").[2]

The American leader made a series of tactical errors just before and at the beginning of the Peace Conference, and they had something to do with the result. The first error was the decision to go to Paris as head of the American delegation. It was an unprecedented action. President McKinley had wanted to tour Europe after the Spanish-American War, but did not feel legally able to go out of the country for an extended period. Roosevelt visited the Panama Canal Zone in 1906, but that was virtually American property, not foreign soil. Taft gave up annual summer vacations at Murray Bay in Canada; he did cross the Mexican border once to visit with the president of Mexico, Porfirio Díaz. And there was a special advantage if Wilson had stayed at home. During the war he had contemplated remaining in Washington during the Peace Conference, as a god on Olympus ("veiled in all the remoteness of the Grand Lama from which elevation he could have dictated his own terms").[3] He told Stockton Axson he would not go to Europe: "House will be there and with his powers of observation and his ability to give clear, cool reports, I shall be able to keep well informed of the daily proceedings." It was not customary, he said, for the titular head of state to negotiate. Axson also sensed that he knew himself well enough to realize that he had unusual talents for declining to compromise an issue.[4] Then he changed his mind. Secretary Lansing was against attendance, and so were Tumulty and the President's physician, Rear Admiral Cary T. Grayson. But Wilson no longer hesitated. He wrote Senator Key Pittman of Nevada, whom he had asked, together with Senator Peter Gerry of Rhode Island, to sound opinion on whether he should go, that he really did not think personal prestige was worth anything if one could not expose it to the experience of the workaday world. "If it is so sensitive a plant that it cannot be exhibited in public," he said, "it will wither anyhow, and the sooner the better."[5] In less than a month he was on his way.

In retrospect the point stands out: it would have been far better had he remained at home, from where he could have taken credit for accomplishments of his representatives, or disavowed inconvenient agreements. If for some reason he was bound to go to Europe, he should have made a ceremonial appearance and retired back to the United States.

He compounded this error with a second: the choice of Paris as the seat of the conference, to please the French who had suffered most in the war. Paris was ill chosen, dedicated by generations of patriots to France's military and imperial past, everywhere monuments to battles won, territory conquered. Baron Georges Haussmann had razed medieval buildings in favor of great avenues, and the greatest, the Champs Elysées, led to the Arc de Triomphe, the world's largest arch for inscribing glories of the past. How much better to have met in a small Swiss city with modest hotels and restaurants and a nearby lake and mountains to remind delegates of the peaceful world of nature. The original idea was to have the Peace Conference in a neutral state and Switzerland seemed available. At the last minute Wilson and Lansing threw over the plan apparently because of rumor of Bolshevist propaganda in Switzerland. House was in Paris representing the President and, after meeting with Clemenceau, agreed on the French capital.[6]

A third error was the choice of the peace commissioners, a weak group: House, Lansing, Bliss, and a lone Republican, the retired diplomat Henry White. House's appointment was a blunder, as the colonel came to see, for it made him prominent; he needed to work behind the scenes. Lansing was a weak man whom Wilson had placed in the State Department because he desired a figurehead; the President had talked with House for months about how stupid Lansing was and of the need to replace him.[7] The choice of Bliss made no sense other than the general's attendance at the Supreme War Council.[8] Appointment of White was absurd; he had spent years outside of the United States, possessed no importance in the Republican party, and was old and tired. Ray Stannard Baker, ardent supporter of the President, admitted that White had "grown sweet and mellow, full of human kindliness, with an immense acquaintance among men who no longer count, a wide familiarity with methods and forms which no longer govern the world."[9] The President might have appointed such eminent Republicans as Taft, Root, Hughes, Lodge, or Senator Philander C. Knox, a former Secretary of State. Bryan asked to be a peace commissioner and Wilson should have chosen him. None of these figures in American politics would have subordinated himself to the President's will.

Wilson ignored the tactical errors—the decision to go himself, choice of Paris, weak commissioners—for after the Armistice he stood at the height of his powers. The British economist John Maynard Keynes wrote that "never had a philosopher held such weapons wherewith to bind the princes of this world."[10] The U.S. Army was at its peak in numbers, discipline, and equipment. Europe depended on American food and financially, as Wilson expected, lay at his mercy.

The President accepted the moment for what it was. When the former German liner *George Washington* backed out of its berth at Hoboken, a warship fired a salute and opened up with its big siren, and as the ship stood down the river the ferryboats and tugs tied whistle ropes down in such a blare it was impossible to talk. In every window of buildings along Manhattan handkerchiefs waved and fluttering paper filled the air. When the ship passed down the lower bay a big naval dirigible swung out and sailed directly overhead. Upon reaching open water the liner took on its escort—the battleship *Pennsylvania* steamed out in front, smoothing a path through the winter seas, and ten destroyers spread out to right and left.[11] The great ship reached Brest on December 13; the President slowed it to arrive that day, for thirteen was his lucky number—his name had thirteen letters. The day was a Friday.[12] During the last night at sea nine American battleships and twenty destroyers and an equal number of French ships joined the liner, and when dawn broke that glorious morning the ocean was a living mass as far as the eye could see.[13] A galaxy of admirals and generals, foreign and domestic, took part in welcoming ceremonies at Brest. Next day came reception in Paris, the greatest the capital had ever held. Houses, trees, roofs were black with people, all along the Champs Elysées. At 10:00 a.m. a big gun boomed and the avenue under the Arc turned black as the advance guard of cavalry appeared. After it came the President of the United States and the President of France, Raymond Poincaré, bowing and smiling. Wilson did not bow his thanks in a formal way but smiled happily and waved his hat in all directions enthusiastically with great sweeps of the arm, as if he would embrace all Paris, Europe, the world.[14] Two million throats roared "Voodrow Veelson!" and "Veelson *le Juste!*"

A fourth problem emerged in making peace. During preceding weeks Wilson had believed that arrangements for the approaching conference would take care of themselves. Choice of a staff had fallen to Lansing, who should have inquired as to the President's pleasure but instead appointed men who proved unacceptable. The staff's secretary, Joseph C. Grew, was an able choice, but neither strong-willed nor, because he was a career diplomat, capable of resigning. His assistants, Leland Harrison and Philip Patchin, had the same weakness. Wilson told House to start all over and build an organization, and House pleaded that Grew, though unsuited for the secretary's post, was a gentleman, while Grew pleaded for Harrison and Patchin, and all three stayed; the President remained hostile to his staff and was inclined to ignore it. In Paris a great infusion of unemployed military officers then swelled the staff to 1,300. "The fact is that you can't move about this hotel now without stubbing your toe on an army officer," Lansing wrote Undersecretary of State Frank Polk. "They are as thick as flies about a jam pot, although we have got rid of quite a number."[15] Waiting to go home, the officers might as well have worked at something. But their presence produced efforts by two brigadier generals, the chief of the Paris military district and the chief of military intelligence, to bring military staff under their personal control, and the President watched with an annoyance that verged on contempt; he relied on House to gather a dozen officials and twice as many stenographers, relegating remaining members of the staff, military and civil, to busy work. "I have such a large force and there are so many meetings held in my rooms," House wrote, "that it has been necessary to add to them from time to time. I now have the entire tier on the third floor front and one tier back. I have twice as many rooms as all the other Commissioners put together."[16]

Another difficulty developed (although it was hardly the President's fault), the loss of nearly a month after Wilson arrived, from December 13 until January 18, when the conference opened. He needed to get on with peacemaking, but the Allied leaders were not ready, and the President therefore made two state visits. In England he found a government and people moderately interested in his presence, typified by the grumpiness of King George V because the visit broke up a holiday the monarch had planned at Sandringham. In Italy, Wilson held no conversations of importance. Little occurred except adulation. *"Evviva il President! Evviva Veelson!"* At a railroad station en route to Rome the mayor, giving a speech, compared Wilson's visit to the second coming of Christ. In Milan the President read banners announcing himself as Savior of Humanity, God of Peace, Cavalier of Humanity, and the Moses from across the Atlantic. He autographed menu cards after a dinner, and Grayson noticed many people kissing the signature and pressing it to their hearts.[17]

At last the conference began, and organized itself reasonably well. It wisely held only six plenary sessions, for to bring together seventy-two delegates accomplished nothing. A much more manageable group, the Council of Ten, consisted of Wilson, Clemenceau, Lloyd George, Orlando, and the foreign ministers, together with two Japanese representatives; including secretaries and interpreters, the group comprised thirty people. For a little over a month it met every weekday, save one, until February 14, when Wilson left Paris to return briefly to the United States and sign legislation produced by the closing session of Congress.

The Council of Ten decided what subjects the Peace Conference as a whole would consider, a worthy task, and gave "auditions" to representatives of smaller nations, which may have been necessary but was time-consuming for the President and premiers. Although it had asked delegates of smaller states to put territorial and other claims in writing, for reasons involving personal prestige this did not suffice, and it allowed delegates to make points orally; fourteen such auditions took place in February. At one a Syrian named Chekri Ghanem read through his horn-rim glasses a long account and plea of pathetic eloquence that took two hours and a half to deliver and translate. Wilson got up and wandered over to the other side of the room and stared out the window, hands in coattails. An assistant had slipped him a note that Ghanem had not visited Syria for the last thirty-five years, having lived in France.[18]

As the Peace Conference ran its course, a smaller group, the Council of Four, decided high policy. It first met after Wilson returned from the United States, late in March. When Orlando was absent for several weeks, it became the Council of Three. Initial meetings took place without any secretary, only a translator, Paul J. Mantoux, to assist Orlando. Lloyd George on April 19 brought in the secretary of the British Cabinet, Sir Maurice Hankey, to take notes, not knowing that Mantoux was also taking notes.[19] Altogether it held 149 sessions.

Major figures, whether ten, four, or three, could not easily resolve technical questions, and the result was the creation of sixty commissions of experts. On January 29, after a wearing session of the Ten, the President suggested that two American experts confer with British counterparts and submit joint reports; other council members approved and gave their experts the task of coordination, and the American experts thus became negotiators. Considerable power passed to the Inquiry, the group that had met since September 1917, sponsored by House under the direction of his brother-in-law Sidney E. Mezes, president of the City College of New York. Mezes's duties eventually fell to the geographer and later president of Johns Hopkins University, Isaiah Bowman. Before its members went to Paris as technical advisers, the group had maintained a small headquarters at the American Geographical Society in New York, with divisions—Eastern Europe, Austria, Turkish Empire—at Harvard, Yale, and Princeton, and economic research in Washington. Inquiry members exerted a considerable influence at Paris, although perhaps not as much as they thought. At one point the professors asked Colonel House to tell the President that he, Wilson, had a chance to inflict a blow on the "old diplomacy" of Europe, and Wilson tartly told House to tell the inquirers that what he wanted was information, not decisions, that as the boys at Princeton used to say about their cigarettes, "I roll my own."[20]

Officially the Paris Peace Conference was known as the Preliminary Peace Conference, and a German delegation did not appear until May 7, when the formal Peace Conference, or Congress, came briefly into being. In January some of the Allied delegations had talked of a preliminary treaty settling military and economic issues, after which the conference might turn to the League of Nations, frontiers, and reparations. Wilson insisted that it deal immediately with the League. Chaired by the President, the League Commission finished the Covenant in mid-February. Wilson went back to the United States, and when he returned March 13 refused to consider a preliminary treaty that did not include the League of Nations. This may have led to trouble, for the commissions of experts drew up the conference's more harsh arrangements, notably reparations, as maximum demands, assuming a long negotiation with German delegates. Instead the conference in early May presented a virtually complete treaty to the Germans, with only slight possibility for change, giving the former enemy an opportunity to accuse the Allies of a *Diktat,* a dictated peace.

After signature of the Treaty of Versailles, Allied representatives signed treaties with representatives of the other Central Powers on the grounds of Versailles or in the environs of Paris: the Treaty of St. Germain with Austria (September 10, 1919), Neuilly with Bulgaria (November 27), Trianon with Hungary (June 4, 1920), Sèvres with Turkey (August 20, 1920). To negotiate these treaties, three American peace commissioners, White, Bliss, and House, together with a small staff, remained in Paris after conclusion of the German treaty. Undersecretary of State Frank Polk went over to head this remaining group.

The first major issue before the Peace Conference was the project for a League of Nations, a complicated negotiation that deserves analysis in detail.[21]

Next came penalties against the Central Powers, mainly Germany. The French took back Alsace and Lorraine, and received the coal fields of the Saar Valley for fifteen years. They asked for a buffer state in the Rhineland, like the Saar an area indubitably German, and here Clemenceau came under intense pressure from Foch and Poincaré, who generally favored harsh treatment of Germany. At one point during a plenary session and while Foch was speaking, Clemenceau came over to Wilson and said, "You must save me from these two fools."[22] In the end they decided on an Allied occupation of the Rhineland for fifteen years, rather than a buffer state. From Wilson and Lloyd George, Clemenceau also obtained bilateral treaties of guarantee of France's border, an inexplicable arrangement other than its being a necessity of French domestic politics; one suspects that when Clemenceau signed the guarantee treaties he knew they would come to nothing in the American Senate, the British treaty depending on ratification of the American.[23]

President Wilson had much to do with the reparations bill against Germany, claims that plagued international relations throughout the twenties. Late in March 1919, British, French, and American experts submitted figures respectively of $55 billion, $31 billion to $47 billion, and $25 billion to $35 billion.[24] General Jan C. Smuts of South Africa, with whom Wilson was friendly, "very much impressed" the President by suggesting inclusion of the cost of Allied military pensions and separation allowances, even though American experts unanimously advised against it as contrary to the Fourteen Points. They said logic also was against it. "Logic! Logic! I don't give a damn for logic," Wilson replied. "I am going to include pensions!" The conference passed the total reparations bill to a commission that in 1921 asked Germany for $33 billion, a high figure in view of Germany's financial situation. More than half the figure was pensions. The American financial expert Thomas W. Lamont believed the Allies might have gotten $12 to $15 billion in reparations; in the event they obtained $9 billion over fourteen years, 1918–32, not even the interest on their total reparations bill of $33 billion.[25] The United States submitted a small claim for reparations to pay for the minuscule American army of occupation that remained in Germany until 1923. Meanwhile, to reinforce the request for huge reparations, the conferees had written into the Versailles Treaty an assertion of German war guilt that stirred European politics for a generation, "the war imposed upon them by the aggression of Germany and her allies."

The Allies established two other penalties for the defeated enemy: disarmament, and distribution of Germany's (and Turkey's) colonies in the form of mandates. They announced disarmament as a principle and singled out Germany to disarm first, presumption being that the victors would follow. The Treaty of Versailles permitted an army of only 100,000, with enlistments of twelve years to avoid any buildup of reserves; forbade tanks, planes, or poison gas; limited the German Navy to ships of 10,000 tons displacement and prohibited submarines. The Germans, however, had already disarmed their navy. Secretary Daniels visited Scapa Flow early in June and Vice Admiral Sir Roger Keyes showed him the interned High Seas Fleet, a magnificent sight—eleven battleships, five battle cruisers, eight light cruisers, fifty destroyers. Keyes pointed out disdainfully how three trawlers guarded them. Not long afterward, on June 21, at 1:00 p.m., officers of Vice Admiral Ludwig von Reuter scuttled the fleet.[26]

In a secret treaty of 1917 the British and Japanese had awarded themselves Germany's Pacific colonies by a line drawn along the equator, Japan to receive the Marshalls, Carolines, and Marianas, island groups that proved difficult for American Marines to capture during World War II. South-West Africa, close to the Union of South Africa, passed under mandate to the Union. According to the

Sykes-Picot Agreement of 1916, the British and French divided the Middle East provinces of the Turkish Empire—Syria, Lebanon, Palestine, Iraq—with the British taking a lion's share. The Italians received part of Turkey in accord with the secret agreement of St. Jean de Maurienne in 1917. The Peace Conference offered the United States a mandate of Armenia, carved out of Turkish Anatolia, and President Wilson accepted it subject to Senate approval. The President did not even submit the agreement to the Senate.[27]

Punishment of Germany, through taking the Saar coal fields, reparations, unilateral disarmament, and disposition of the colonies as mandates, became a much remarked point, and critics said the statesmen at Paris displayed poor judgment, that they should have made a far more generous peace. The critics, one must say, did not understand how the people at home hampered each of the Big Four. Statesmen were hardly free agents, and there was something ironic over the fact that a people's peace, anticipated by Wilson, turned out to be rather vindictive. Popular opinion forced Clemenceau to include the war guilt clause and prevented a reasonable sum of reparations. He resisted Foch and Poincaré on dismemberment of Germany, and the resistance cost him the presidency of France, for which he ran unsuccessfully shortly after the Peace Conference. Whenever Lloyd George suggested more moderate treatment of Germany, the Northcliffe press asked for his head. Orlando was willing to compromise over the Adriatic, and lost office in June 1919. American voters repudiated Wilson in 1920 largely because he had seemed willing to surrender America's national interest to foreigners. Aboard the *George Washington* he had told a group of advisers that the men with whom he was about to deal did not represent their peoples, but in fact the punishment of Germany in the Versailles Treaty was at the time a popular measure.[28]

Another task of the Peace Conference was to apply the principle of national self-determination. The phrase became one of the most enduring ideas of the conference because it expressed hope for democratic governments, for which the war had made the world safe. Colonel House characterized it as "the gladdest and yet, in some ways, the maddest" principle in history. People overlooked everything else, he wrote, in the effort to be free—for nations so affected "sufferings and hardships of the war seemed to fall from them in this hour of joy."[29] Lansing afterward described self-determination, more dourly, as "the dream of an idealist who failed to realize the danger until too late . . . What a calamity that the phrase was ever uttered! What misery it will cause!"[30]

Finland and the Baltic states of Latvia, Lithuania, and Estonia had established independence before the conference, because of the presence of German troops. Finland actually invited the Germans. During subsequent years the four million Finns were among the happiest people of Europe. The Baltic states managed a precarious independence until incorporated into the Soviet Union during World War II.

The independence of Poland was not a contentious issue at the Peace Conference, as both the Allies and Central Powers had favored a Polish state. Each side hoped for a friendly Poland, and two sets of Polish leaders arose, Roman Dmowski and the world-famous pianist Ignaz Paderewski, who looked to the Allies, and Jozef Pilsudski, who supported Germany and Austria-Hungary. During a trip to the United States, Dmowski had organized Americans of Polish extraction, and Paderewski flattered Colonel House, whom he said God had sent to deliver Poland, to whom he spoke as honestly as to his God, whose hand was everywhere helping Poland, who had converted Britain to the Polish cause, who was the only man since Napoleon who understood the importance of Poland to the peace of Europe. Paderewski played Chopin at the White House for the President and Mrs. Wilson, and noticed that the President in numbering the Fourteen Points awarded Poland his favorite number, thirteen.[31] The President was well disposed; en route to the Peace Conference he had remarked that the Poles could have "any government they damned pleased."[32] At first everything worked out well; Pilsudski, who had more support within Poland, went over to the Allies, and brought Dmowski and Paderewski into his government; but then they remained only long enough to receive an American relief delegation headed by Herbert Hoover, after which Pilsudski expelled them. Poland's eastern frontier with Russia later became a matter of dispute, resulting in a Polish-Russian War; the Treaty of Riga in 1921 established the boundary far to the east of the so-called Curzon Line, a roughly ethnographic line proposed by the postwar British foreign secretary, Lord Curzon. The Russians did not forget the unfavorable arrangement of Riga, and after World War II pushed the Polish boundary back to the Curzon Line. At the Peace Conference of 1919 the Poles asked a boundary with Germany that included the rich industrial area around Breslau, known as Upper Silesia. The conference eventually arranged a plebiscite, bound to favor Germany, for during preceding decades the Germans had colonized it heavily. The Poles in 1919 considered a plebiscite in Upper Silesia as legalizing an injustice, and the Germans considered it an insult. President Wilson hoped that the League of Nations would solve the issue in the years ahead. "At least, House," he said, "we are saving the Covenant, and that instrument will work wonders, bring the blessing of peace, and then when the war psychosis has abated, it will not be difficult to settle all the disputes that baffle us now."[33]

The conference became executor of the Habsburg estate, for the empire died just before the conference. Here perhaps was the reason for remarks by Lansing to Undersecretary Polk halfway through the conference on March 14. The "game of grab goes merrily on," he complained, and every European nation, old and newborn, was trying to get every foot of territory and every economic advantage. "It really disgusts one to see what is being attempted."[34] Perhaps it was the Habsburg estate that also led to an exchange between Clemenceau and Wilson. The Premier told the President he had a heart of steel, to which Wilson punned, "I have not the heart to steal."[35] Austria, once the empire's center, stood by itself, shorn of imperial possessions. The Peace Conference forbade any linking of Austria with Germany, unless with permission of the League Council. The principal succession state, Czechoslovakia, did well with its inheritance.[36] Two small neighboring nations, members of the Allied coalition, also took what they wanted—Rumania gained Transylvania from Hungary, and Serbia transformed itself into Yugoslavia, acquiring Croatia, Slovenia, and Montenegro. Many countries were disappointed—such as Italy. Foreign Minister Sidney Sonnino desired the Dalmatian littoral. The British and French felt that after Caporetto the Italians deserved nothing. But by the end of the war Italy basked in the glow of the Battle of Vittorio Veneto, begun on the anniversary of Caporetto, October 24, 1918, in which the Italians won against the Austrians because the subject nationalities refused to fight. Sonnino thereupon sank his teeth into Dalmatia—an important point of behavior, as Clemenceau once wrote, because Sonnino never let go of anything, once he got his teeth into it. Shortly after the Armistice, Prime Minister Orlando sent 12,000 troops into the Yugoslav city of Fiume—which was not included in the Treaty of London—where a core of 20,000 Italians lived (Orlando said 30,000). Italy already held Trieste, and Fiume remained the only other large port on the eastern side of the Adriatic, which was why Orlando wanted it. Sonnino cared nothing for Fiume, neither did Orlando for Dalmatia, but at Paris the two Italian statesmen compromised with each other and asked for both. They stood impervious to logic. President Wilson told Sonnino that New York City had a larger Italian population than any city in Italy, but he would not cede New York to Italy; the Italian did not even smile. Sonnino and Orlando failed to get either Dalmatia or Fiume, went back to Rome and sulked, and returned for the conference's final weeks.[37]

The conference reached no agreement about Russia and in effect avoided the issue. The "Russian problem" continued wearily on into the twenties and thirties and forties, down to the present time —and would engage countless commentators. Historians looked back to the Paris Peace Conference's inability to resolve the problem and said that there, in a single failure, lay the fundamental reason the conference failed. The Bolsheviks acted as spoilers of peace during the twenties, flirted with the League of Nations in the thirties by joining it, and sided with Hitler in 1939 and permitted the Nazi attack on Poland and the opening of World War II.

In retrospect the American wartime and immediate postwar behavior toward the new Soviet regime was difficult to understand. For years scholars argued over why the Wilson administration joined the Allied military intervention in Russia in the summer of 1918. The British and French clearly had their own understanding of the Russian problem—anticapitalist propaganda, refusal of the new government to recognize tsarist debts, most of all the collapse of the front in the east and all it meant for the Western Front during the spring and early summer of 1918. American intervention, however, seemed to have had several possible purposes—to prevent occupation of large parts of Siberia by the Japanese, to rescue the Czech Legion that was fighting its way across Siberia to Vladivostok, to combat bolshevism, to combat Germany's effort to suborn Russia through German agents.[38]

An especially interesting interpretation was that Wilson may have been considering the possibility of a new liberal order in the world, the need for an intellectual halfway station—which he would create in the League Covenant—between militaristic German imperialism and a radical Bolshevik revolutionary world. The threat of revolution certainly concerned the principal negotiators at the Paris Peace Conference. Wilson's thoughts must have been filled with fear of a Bolshevist world unfriendly to American purposes and the need to bring the forces of order, which in the past had been largely reactionary, into cooperation with the forces of movement, which were heading toward revolution. The President was aware of his supporters in all the countries of Europe—former enemy and neutral as well as Allied countries. He always had beheld the Covenant of the League, and for that matter the entire Paris settlement, as not for any group or people, not expressive of any Allied point of view, but for all of Europe, indeed the world, a vision of the future not the past, of revulsion against the prewar international anarchy. And while he was not a student of international economics, he knew that politics reflected many other matters, notably economics. He saw himself as a champion of the best of the past, perhaps of liberalism in the nineteenth-century English sense, assuredly not the extremes of militarism or bolshevism. Seen in this light many of Wilson's beliefs and actions about bolshevism made much sense, his desire to oppose it with a view of his own.[39]

And yet was not the President's purpose in sending troops to Russia much more simple, namely, because the Allies asked him to do it? Wilson had refused a half-dozen requests to join in a military intervention. At last, in July 1918, pressure became unbearable. Years later Newton Baker recalled that he had convinced Wilson intervention was unwise, "but he told me that he felt obliged to do it anyhow because the British and French were pressing it on his attention so hard and he had refused so many of their requests that they were beginning to feel that he was not a good associate, much less a good ally."[40]

In retrospect the above reason for intervention seemed unbelievably simple. So did the President's apparent view of the Russian problem as a whole. In October 1918, three months after intervention began, he told Wiseman that Russia was an impossible place like Mexico, and the only decent policy was to let the dust settle. "I believe in letting them work out their own salvation," he said, "even though they wallow in anarchy for a while."[41] How could he have looked at this major problem of Europe and the world, of wartime and Peace Conference diplomacy, and resolved it with so flip an explanation? Should he not have been moving heaven and earth to find some arrangement by which the United States, not to mention the Allies, could enter into decent relations with the Russian people and their government?

But what else could he reasonably have done during and after the war? Having made one bad decision because of Allied insistence, he was not about to make another. At the Peace Conference he expected the Anglo-French to request more intervention, and knew that American public opinion and congressional sentiment adamantly opposed such a course. It would be equally impossible to recognize a regime that had made peace with the Germans to the immense peril of the Allies, pronounced a curse on capitalism everywhere, and murdered tens of thousands of dissidents among its citizens.

At the Peace Conference the Big Three conferred about the Russian problem but by and large did nothing. Attempts to communicate with Russia's new leaders came to naught. Meanwhile the Wilson administration withdrew its 14,000 troops from North Russia and Siberia—a minuscule intervention force, considering that it had intervened in France with 2 million.

As matters turned out at Paris, resolving the Japanese problem was almost as difficult as dealing with that of Russia. Here the initial awkwardness was disposition of German political and economic rights on China's Shantung Peninsula. Japan's representatives at Paris insisted on obtaining those rights, for several good reasons, so the Japanese said. The forces of Japan had taken Shantung in 1914, and the Chinese under duress confirmed the transfer the next year. The Chinese in September 1918 secretly gave Japan two more railway concessions. Meanwhile, in 1917, Japan and Britain signed a secret treaty confirming the passage of Germany's rights in China to Japan. France and Italy also signed the treaty. At the Peace Conference the young Chinese nationalist Wellington Koo sought to get the concessions back. He contended that China's entrance into war in 1917 had invigorated its rights to Shantung, "the Holy Land of the Chinese, the Home of Confucius." But Japan was strong, China weak, and according to a Chinese proverb Koo's request amounted to negotiating with a tiger for its skin. The Japanese refused to give Shantung back to the Chinese. What was President Wilson to do? The two Japanese delegates taking part in the Council of Ten threatened to leave the Peace Conference if they did not obtain confirmation of their country's new position in China.

The Japanese in effect proposed a trade-off for Shantung—if they remained in Paris, Japan would duly become a member of the League of Nations. If only further to make their point, but also to advance an idea that was itself worthy of statement in the proposed new world constitution, Baron Nobuaki Makino asked the League of Nations Commission at its last session in mid-February to endorse a declaration favoring rights of all nonwhite nations, "just treatment in every respect, making no distinction, either in law or in fact, on account of their race or nationality." Some weeks later he sat quietly while the Australian representative on the commission fought a watered-down version of this declaration, "the principle of equality of nations and just treatment of their nationals," and said little when Wilson and the British representative, Lord Robert Cecil, abstained in the vote, resulting in the proposal's failure because of need for unanimity.[42]

Wilson easily got the point about the League. When the Italian delegation to the Peace Conference later walked out over Dalmatia and Fiume, the President found himself in an impossible position, for "if the Italians remain away and the Japanese go home, what becomes of the League of Nations?" The Japanese were not bluffers, he said, "and they will go home unless we give them what they should not have."[43] This Far Eastern issue perplexed him, he told Ray Baker, and he could not sometimes see where his own principles applied; with a smile he said he had been reading over the Fourteen Points to refresh his memory. Every few days, he told Grayson, a new secret treaty seemed to turn up. In a meeting of the Ten he gave Shantung to the Japanese, and informed the American delegation afterward. It had been a tiring business, he explained to Grayson, who had proposed an automobile ride. "I am sure to fall asleep as soon as I get into the motor, for last night I could not sleep —my mind was so full of the Japanese-Chinese controversy. But it is settled this morning, and while it is not to be a satisfactory settlement, I suppose it could be called an 'even break.' It is the best that could be accomplished out of a 'dirty past.' "[44]

As for the Japanese point about racial equality—again, what was the President to do? He had tried very hard to get an antidiscrimination article in the League Covenant. The Japanese delegates at Paris were under intense pressure to obtain a statement about racial rights, both from their government in Tokyo and from Japanese public opinion as expressed vociferously in newspaper editorials. The failure of this proposal was not lost upon the leaders of Japan.

They later grouped it with refusal of the American Congress in the mid-twenties to grant Japan an immigration quota. When added to other concerns, such as support by the United States for the Chinese Nationalist government during the thirties, the result was war in 1941.

Leading delegates at the Paris Peace Conference of 1919 could not, unfortunately, look far beyond their own time, and took the moment for what it was—the opportunity to end World War I. In the presence of hundreds of top-hatted diplomats and bemedaled soldiers, they signed the German treaty in the Hall of Mirrors at Versailles on June 28, 1919. The day was overcast, but before President Wilson reached the palace grounds the sun broke through the clouds. Guns boomed, airplanes dipped, and for the first time since the war, the fountains outside the palace played; water rose high in the air and splashed into surrounding pools. After the ceremonies the Big Three strolled outside, and crowds burst through the cordon of troops and bore in on them, shouting "*Vive* Clemenceau!", "*Vive* Lloyd George!", "*Vive* Veelson!" For a moment they swept the leaders along the terrace, top hats bobbing uncertainly, until a platoon of the Garde Republicaine came up and rescued them, preserving decorum during this final moment at Versailles.

Looking back on the Peace Conference in long retrospect, one wonders what went wrong at Paris, what kept the Treaty of Versailles from being a longer-lasting document and thereby preventing World War II. Could it have been flaws in the principal negotiators of the German treaty, the Big Three? The Italian prime minister, Orlando, did not count in the equation, for he was an inconsequential statesman. His concerns were territorial, his emotions tearful. While in attendance he stood apart from much discussion because he did not understand English. Clemenceau, admittedly an important negotiator, appeared as too much the protector of his country. An old man, he had been a reporter during the last days of the American Civil War, and married an American girl, Mary Plummer, from whom he long since had separated. He lived in the past, and no event had touched him more than France's surrender to the Germans in the war of 1870–71. He had been in Paris during the Commune and never forgot the spectacle of Frenchmen fighting each other in the presence of Germans. The 1914–18 war had redeemed France, but he distrusted his countrymen, feared the future, determined to do what he could to keep Germany down. The flight of the Emperor and announcement of the Weimar Republic did not impress him; the Germans would try again.

Lloyd George also had a point of view based on history, but it was a much shorter history. He had become prime minister late in 1916 after his predecessor, Asquith, proved incapable of leading Britain to victory. He took over when his country approached defeat, and with energy and administrative force pulled it back, with help from the Americans. Unsure of what the United States wanted from the peace, willing to appease anyone—Frenchmen, Americans, even Germans—to prevent another war, he trusted to his ability to talk adversaries around. He was aware of his hold on the British electorate, demonstrated in the so-called khaki election of December 1918, held while many Britons still were in uniform. He trusted to that hold, together with Welsh nimbleness. "He is slippery as an eel," Wilson told Grayson, "and I never know when to count on him." And again: "He is the most unsteady individual you can imagine. . . . He is unstable. He is constantly turning somersaults. He is an impossible, incalculable person to do business with."[45]

As for Wilson, observers of the Peace Conference long remembered how Clemenceau's sarcasm had produced several versions of perhaps an original remark that focused on the negotiating inability of the President. "God gave us the Ten Commandments, and we broke them. Wilson gave us the Fourteen Points. We shall see." Or, "How can I talk to a fellow who thinks himself the first man for two thousand years who has known anything about peace on earth?" Or, "Wilson talked like Jesus Christ but acted like Lloyd George." A few years after the Peace Conference, Charles Seymour was talking about peacemaking with Colonel House, who emphasized that Wilson was up against the two most skillful negotiators he, House, had ever seen. No one in the United States compared with them. Unlike Wilson, they understood personal appeal in conducting relations. Wilson always felt that if he had logic on his side, that sufficed. But to be right, House insisted, was only a small part of politics. Wilson had hypnotized himself by the beauty of his words and the effectiveness of his presentation, but this did not affect Clemenceau and Lloyd George, who probably did not even listen.[46]

Within a few months of the treaty's signature, Keynes brought out *The Economic Consequences of the Peace,* the book about the Peace Conference that dealt principally with finance, with which he was familiar, but it was his portraits of the Big Three statesmen in the book's opening pages that caught the attention of readers. Clemenceau, he said, was an intense, clearheaded old man whose first and last thought was the safety of France, whose understanding of foibles and poses was so large that in an instant he saw through deception and superficial concern, concentrating on his purpose. Lloyd George he drew as a Welsh witch, a sorcerer, whose long blade flashed and skewered, a man with a sixth sense of what people had in mind, possessed of powers no human imagined. Wilson was an old Presbyterian "bamboozled" (the American word intrigued him) by flattery who needed to be debamboozled. The latter effort he said was impossible.

The personal appraisals were interesting, almost believable, even to individuals who ought to have known better, and Smuts in 1948 told Keynes's biographer Roy Harrod that "the portrait of Wilson was absolutely truthful, but Keynes should not have written it; after all Wilson was our friend."[47]

Perhaps the conference failed not because of personalities but because of atmosphere. Here again Keynes described the scene, as in a nightmare; everyone, he said, was morbid, catastrophe overhanging frivolity, "the futility and smallness of man before the great events confronting him; the mingled significance and unreality of the decisions; levity, blindness, insolence, confused cries from without,—all the elements of ancient tragedy." Seated amid the theatrical trappings of French salons, he wondered if the visages of Wilson and Clemenceau, with their fixed hue, were "really faces at all and not the tragic-comic masks of some strange drama or puppet-show."[48]

Years later Keynes's countryman Harold Nicolson published an account of the conference that, if not so tragic, was equally critical. Nicolson beheld confusion as the problem—lack of organization, of procedure.[49] However gifted the participants, they could not bring their purposes into focus because staff work was poor.

Literary descriptions of ineptitude, morbidity, and confusion have the advantage of single issues, and in the hand of a skillful writer each becomes convincing. Yet all have the fault of simplicity. Failure at Paris occurred because of world forces too large for simple literary analysis. One of these forces was economic.[50] Long before 1919 the spread of the Industrial Revolution out of England, where it first appeared, into Germany and the United States, and the beginning of industrialization in other countries, skewed the power balance of nations. Hence some of the miscalculation that brought World War I. The cause of World War II was similar miscalculation, refusal to anticipate the Great Depression of the thirties. Forces that brought the depression were so novel—economic changes that reached back into the nineteenth century, disarray caused by World War I, financial excesses of the twenties—that the men at Paris perhaps could not have anticipated them. In any event the Peace Conference dealt largely with territorial and military matters and barely touched economic. The reparations clause made no real economic sense, and the tangle of debts and reparations did not help. In this respect Keynes was right. But he himself did not understand what was to come and after the American stock market crash in 1929 at first described it as a minor readjustment of the marketplace. The crash tipped over the economies of Europe and brought Hitler to power and so palsied the wills of Western democracies that the Third Reich passed from triumph to triumph and nothing stopped it short of World War II.

The second force that the Peace Conference failed to deal with was what Wilson, employing a then new psychological term, described as the "war psychosis." The President liked to talk about it, and believed it a major problem in world affairs. He never had admired military solutions; although he disliked Germany and favored the Allies, he looked with horror on the coming of war. He feared the sights of war; when he went to the Peace Conference he believed that this "war psychosis" might overwhelm him if he toured the battlefields, as Allied leaders, his advisers, and Pershing urged him. Eventually he went for a day or two.

The President was correct in sensing the war psychosis, but as an American he could never fully appreciate it. The war had gone on too long—battle losses had mounted, and hatreds with them, until clear thinking about peace had become almost impossible. Wilson could only sense what the war had done to Europe, a war in which Germany suffered thirty-six times as many deaths in battle (1.8 million) as did the United States (50,300), Russia thirty-four times (1.7 million), France twenty-eight times (1.4 million), Britain nineteen times (950,000). The American population was 35 million larger than Germany's, twice that of Britain, more than twice that of France. Not a town or village or rural area in Western Europe but young men failed to return. After the war great battlefields like Verdun became cemeteries; at Verdun the French government constructed an ossuary for 100,000 men. Churches placed long lists of names on plaques; towns put up monuments. The village of Kreuth near the Tegernsee in Bavaria erected a monument that displayed village losses in wars beginning in the early eighteenth century, and listed as many men dead in 1914–18 as in two centuries of preceding wars; World War I names on Kreuth's monument showed several groups of brothers. For Europeans the war of 1914–18 was impossible to forget; bitterness made peace unlikely.

CHAPTER 10

The Senate and the Treaty

O NE comes, at last, to the central question about Woodrow Wilson and World War I: why the President of the United States almost perversely insisted upon losing the fight, to use his word, for the League of Nations and thereby became the Great Architect of World War II? By sheer stubbornness, or so it has seemed, Wilson reestablished the international anarchy of prewar years. He championed a Covenant that was anathema to his domestic political opponents; he insisted upon a nontraditional League that would have enforced peace rather than slowly increased the rule of law. And this when the design of the League really did not matter. American support for a League would have to evolve, whatever the design. What the country needed was a turning of attention to Europe's political problems—where the danger of future war lay. A League with or without reservations might have done just that, which was all that mattered.[1]

This President who possessed one of the keenest intellects ever to ponder affairs of state could behold neither the country's best course nor his own. The treaty's failure brought his great political career to a pitiful end. After the Western tour in 1919 in support of the Covenant he suffered a stroke that turned him into a shell of a man, incompetent to occupy the office of President. He should have resigned immediately in favor of Vice President Thomas R. Marshall. Instead he clung to the presidency for nearly a year and a half, October 2, 1919, to March 4, 1921.

In retrospect it is clear that the United States should have joined the League in whatever form was possible. The Covenant as Wilson drew it was a far stronger instrument than the later U.N. Charter, for it provided effective sanctions. It would have been more effective than the U.N. even if the Senate had removed the document's sanctions, for the international climate in 1919 was far better than in 1945; the initial months after the Armistice marked a sort of suspended moment when all the major powers favored peace, unlike the period after World War II when two superpowers vied for supremacy. Moreover, Americans for at least a considerable time after the Armistice desired to take part in world affairs; by common agreement of observers the League Covenant would have passed the Senate in the summer of 1919 if it had come to a vote. For years thereafter the American people yearned to reorganize Europe and the world, a yearning symbolized by establishment of private peace organizations and societies, a peace movement. Unfortunately this peace movement had no direction, because the country remained outside of the League. It pursued a series of hopeless projects for preserving peace. During the twenties it focused on the World Court, the Kellogg-Briand Pact, and disarmament conferences, in the thirties on reciprocal trade treaties and neutrality acts.[2]

If the United States had joined a "toothless" League, and if for some unlikely reason some sort of sanctions had proved necessary, the Americans themselves could have done the job. In 1919 the United States was strong enough to have made the world safe for democracy. It possessed one of the richest portions of the globe, the world's largest economy, had created the largest army, and was building the largest navy.

In one respect League membership might have encouraged the coming of World War II. During the twenties the dominant members of the League, Britain and France, disagreed over treatment of Germany, the British believing in conciliation of the many "good Germans," the French relying on force. At the end of the twenties the French tired of trying to convince the British. If Americans had joined the League, they might have taken the British side and produced a resurgent Germany under Hitler a few years earlier.

But then one must not underestimate the possibilities of reformation and redemption, national as well as personal. Good treatment for the Weimar Republic might well have ensured its survival beyond the dismal year 1933 and preserved the world from Hitler. In the years after World War I there was enormous need in Europe for perspective, for disinterested analysis and advice. Also, to be sure, a helping hand. Americans in the twenties and thirties were a thoughtful as well as energetic people, geography had insulated them from Europe's petty arguments, especially from the war psychosis, and if the idea advanced by Wilson, that Americans understood all peoples because they comprised all peoples, possessed any merit, it might have made a crucial difference.

The question arises as to why Wilson refused to compromise with the Senate—why did he stick, as indeed he did, for every jot and tittle of his view of the proper form of the Covenant, and thereby ensure its failure? The President, of course, was a very ill man after the stroke, which might explain his rigidity when the treaty came before the Senate. But it was more than that. Months earlier, in drawing up the Covenant in Paris, he had shown an extraordinary stubbornness. Friends warned him that such a Covenant would get into trouble in the Senate, but he did not think so, and believed he could face it down. He looked forward to a fight with the Senate. In a brief conversation with Colonel House as he left Paris for the final time, a conversation repeated by writers ever since House published it, the colonel pleaded that Western civilization was built on compromise. Wilson opined that he had found he never could obtain anything worthwhile without fighting for it.

Why the saddening, maddening misjudgment? Perhaps something in Wilson's Presbyterian soul, or his Princeton experience, or the times in which he lived, made compromise difficult if not impossible. His life from its beginning in the manse at Staunton to his academic duties at Princeton had taught him to stand for what he believed, and in deciding what to believe he did not always choose well. He was warmly enthusiastic, even hotheaded. When he took up an idea, he said, he caught fire like a field of grain. Some of this behavior could have come out of Calvinism, some out of Princeton, where small issues loomed. Princeton may have dominated—twenty years on that campus. He once said in another much quoted phrase that all the politics he ever knew, he learned on the Princeton campus. The times, too, the high Victorian Age in which he came to manhood, may have reinforced his impulse to take a stand. It was an age of principle, whatever the practice, indeed so much reliance on the spoken and written word that believers were in danger of succumbing to their own eloquence. Words perhaps lay at the core of Wilson's behavior. He excelled on the platform, "a spellbinder during a time when the American people admired oratory above all other political skills."[3] The resonant voice, meticulous pronunciation, seemed the soul of logic. He attracted students and voters with what appeared coldly logical or hotly convincing words when, in fact, he could be voicing a position not altogether thought out. He wrote in an involuted style that appeared gracious and hence believable, and when he warmed to a subject took readers to the mountaintops of emotion whence they beheld the small, simple world below.

Other explanations for Wilsonian stubbornness are possible. In April 1917, the President became a war leader, and the experience may not have assisted relations with Congress, which sadly deteriorated. He addressed Congress after little or no consultation, failing to talk with Democrats and Republicans alike.

He may not have sensed the imminence of disaster with the Senate because of luck in getting out of failures with the War Department and the war economy—General March took over the War Department, and the Allies furnished ships, artillery, planes, and ammunition.

Everything considered—the manse, academe, the Age of Principle and Words in which he lived, his war leadership, his escape from blame for the War Department and the war economy—it is clear that Wilson's complacency made him unaware of the potential of losing the League fight. But it is possible that another factor entered: increasing physical and mental debility. Long before he reached the White House, Wilson may have suffered at least two strokes. In 1896 he suddenly lost control of his right hand. The hand recovered, though there was recurrence in later years. Then in 1906 he awoke one morning blind in his left eye. He never regained much more than peripheral vision. That year the distinguished Philadelphia ophthalmologist Dr. George F. de Schweinitz diagnosed arteriosclerosis, progressive mental deterioration, "premature old age," the malady that killed his father. The prognosis horrified Wilson's family. The patient carried on his duties at Princeton and to everyone's surprise nothing more happened, although Wilson's health was fragile until 1910.

The stroke theory of Wilson's behavior over many years, at Princeton as well as during the League fight, has much to recommend it. Arthur S. Link and his scholarly fellow editors of *The Papers of Woodrow Wilson* have found it by far the most convincing explanation for the egregious errors during the last part of Wilson's presidency of Princeton, between the years 1906 and 1910— behavior that defied common sense, differed markedly from the way in which Wilson acted before, and almost inspired a search to discover physical reasons for it. The White House years, too, displayed a similar divergence—generally excellent judgment and masterful handling of Congress during the first term, 1913–17, and then a gradual failure to deal with Congress during the second term that with the end of the war and the making of peace turned into debacle.

Certain it is that Wilson husbanded his strength in the White House, as if he almost feared another collapse. His White House physician, Grayson, watched him incessantly, as if the President's strength might not be up to the demands of his office. At the outset Grayson placed him on a strict regimen. Wilson had long suffered from an uncomfortable combination of nervousness and indigestion, known in those days as dyspepsia, and Grayson took away his stomach pump and put him on a bland diet. But the doctor also saw to it that in every possible way he conserved his strength. He spent only three or four hours a day in the office, and relaxed in afternoons, taking frequent automobile rides that lasted several hours, or playing golf. Saturday nights he went to the theater, often Keith's on G Street between Fourteenth and Fifteenth near the Treasury. Sundays he attended church and rested.

During the presidency Wilson's summers passed without much attention to public business. Indeed during one summer, that of 1915, the President occupied his time by falling in love. In August of the previous year his first wife, Ellen, had died. He had pined away because of remorse and melancholy. Then he discovered Mrs. Galt. He courted the widow assiduously, so much so that the White House usher, Irwin H. (Ike) Hoover, believed the President did nothing that summer but write longhand letters to the woman he loved; one missive ran to forty pages. The letters were deeply, effusively Victorian, almost offensive to a present-day reader—"my dream come true," "a flood of tender happiness," "my heart's desire filled to the utmost," "heart full to overflowing," "exquisite charm and loveliness," "soft caresses," "unspeakable tenderness." All with underlinings, exclamation marks, and in the midst of pressing public business. He admitted to Edith that, what with the European war, the ship of state had sailed into dangerous waters, and said he felt like a pilot who had to hold his attention, indeed rivet it, else the ship would strike a reef; for that reason, he said, he needed Edith in the pilot house. Marriage in December 1915 eased this problem.

Illness marked the summer of 1916, and Wilson spent the autumn at an estate, Shadow Lawn, on the Jersey Shore—albeit campaigning much of the time, making speeches at Shadow Lawn and going out on tours.

In 1917–18 the half-day regimen did not change, though the President in 1918 often spoke of fatigue. His wife taught him solitaire, with which he spent an hour before lunch each day. Golf and motoring continued, and few appointments on Cabinet days, Tuesdays and Fridays, with correspondence in the evenings but also theater.

Then came the Peace Conference and too much work, and in April 1919 a collapse from what Grayson diagnosed as influenza and likely was. After recovery he spent the remaining weeks in Paris in harried meetings, and upon the conference's end sailed for home next day. And in two months he started on a month-long speaking tour in support of the League, the tour with which he thought he could turn the American people against errant senators refusing to accept the Covenant in the form he deemed right and proper.

But if the reason Wilson refused to compromise with the Senate was increasing physical and mental debility over a long period of time it is, alas, impossible to establish. His medical records disappeared years ago. The records of de Schweinitz were burned in the fifties. The internist Alfred Stengel, whom he also visited in 1906, passed his records to his son, who burned them. Wilson appears to have consulted the neurologist Francis X. Dercum, whose records were destroyed under the terms of Dercum's will. Grayson kept a diary; it covers only the months from December 1918 to September 1919 and contains nothing about earlier strokes nor of de Schweinitz's diagnosis of arteriosclerosis. The patient's letters to relatives and friends, and other letters, testify uncertainly about health, apart from nervousness, indigestion, and Grayson's prescription of leisure.[4]

All one is left with is the stubbornness. It would be fascinating to know what caused it. Historians love to get to the roots of problems, and it is exasperating to confront a major personality out of the present and previous century and have to admit that analysis leads to nothing provable. We do not know what caused it. Perhaps it was an innate quality. All one can say is that it certainly was there. Friends and foes testified to it. The President's brother-in-law, Stockton Axson, was thoroughly cognizant of it. Senator Lodge may have counted on it to prevent acceptance of reservations to the Covenant, which meant failure of the treaty.[5]

Until the last year of the war the President dealt very carefully with the increasingly popular movement to establish a League of Nations after the war. He took a public position that was entirely in agreement with the ideas of his countrymen. For many years they had groped for a way, a path they liked to call it, by which or through which they might participate in world affairs. In the Hague Conferences of 1899 and 1907 they had codified international law and considered arbitration of international disputes. They had supported Pan-American Conferences and bilateral treaties of arbitration and conciliation. They beheld international relations primarily as unorganized, and hoped that the example of a great democracy in the New World would bring rationality and order. The American way of ensuring international order was gradual, conservative, one step at a time, and did not contemplate a new constitution for world peace.[6] In a burst of enthusiasm former Secretary of State Bryan suggested a postwar organization in which any signatory that went to war before submitting its problem to a special conciliation council, if nonjusticiable, or an international court, would find itself at war against this proposed League. He backed away from his own notion because it involved force. The plan nonetheless circulated in the United States among members of the League to Enforce Peace, an organization of college presidents and professors and international lawyers and public-spirited citizens that formed in 1915, and Lord Bryce championed the idea in England.[7] In May 1916, Wilson addressed a Washington meeting of the League to Enforce Peace, with Senator Lodge on the platform, and favored a world organization for part of such a process—to make certain of delay before a member nation went to war. Lodge seemed in agreement. In January 1918, in the last of the Fourteen Points, the President proposed "a general association of nations," whatever that meant. On March 28, 1918, he saw the two leaders of the L.E.P., President A. Lawrence Lowell of Harvard and former President Taft, and opposed a forceful league. He said that nations might guarantee each other's integrity and territory and if violations occurred or threatened it might be necessary to call a conference. This would be slow business. But it had built the common law. A small seed would grow, law must precede the policeman. He did not think the Senate would enter an agreement by which a majority of nations could tell the United States to go to war.

It is true that on two occasions before 1918 the President had mentioned to his brother-in-law his interest in an association wherein all nations should guarantee the territorial integrity of each. In early August 1914, after return to Washington from the funeral of his first wife, Ellen, or perhaps it was in February 1915, he told Axson that something might happen on the seas that would make it impossible to restrain the American people, and he had been thinking a good deal about Napoleon's remark that "nothing was ever finally settled by force," and had decided that four things were necessary for ordering the world. One was that never again should nations acquire a foot of ground by conquest. Another was equality of nations, large and small. Third was that governments, not individuals, should manufacture munitions. Fourth and last was the association of nations, with a mutual guarantee. In 1916, Axson reminded him of the conversation and asked if he still saw the world that way. "You bet I do," was the response.[8] Here was the embryo of the Covenant of the League. If Wilson later had to drop the idea of munitions manufacture by governments, so as to protect small nations, he wrote the rest of these principles into the Covenant. But nothing concrete came out of this interesting and private drawing of the League of Nations.

Then, in the summer of 1918, he began to edge toward a novel program of peace. At first he spoke only to House, who had said that the President had to do something about a League, that he should put his ideas together. After the Fourteen Points address, the British government had organized a committee under the international lawyer Sir Walter Phillimore, to draw up a constitution for a League. The President in July told House the Phillimore Committee's ideas lacked virility and that the colonel should draft a constitution. House drew a loose document, an organization to codify international law and to discuss problems. Wilson worked it over and struck out the proposed international court, wrote in economic sanctions and military force, and kept House's proposal of a qualified mutual guarantee of political independence and territorial integrity. In mid-August he conferred with House at the latter's summer place in Magnolia, Massachusetts, and told Wiseman, who was present, that he did not like Phillimore's draft because it had no teeth, but asked that the British government not publish the Phillimore constitution because he did not want to focus public attention until after the war. Wiseman inquired what his own ideas were and he said he had two principles, that there must be a League of Nations, and it must be virile, not a paper League. Wiseman cabled London that despite his own affectionate admiration for the President, Wilson was a most difficult person as head of government, his attitude lately had tended to become more arbitrary and aloof, and at times he seemed to treat foreign governments hardly seriously.[9]

All the while Wilson was taking almost no precautions with his Republican opponents, and in the 1918 congressional elections openly challenged the G.O.P., asking for a Democratic Congress. He said a Republican majority would "certainly be interpreted on the other side of the water as a repudiation of my leadership." He thereby insulted the patriotism of Republicans throughout the country, who had supported the war as much as had Democrats. The result was return of a Republican majority. The reason for the Republican triumph was complex, in no sense simply a rejection of the President's appeal. The Democratic National Committee had urged an appeal. Elections generally were over local issues, but a few larger problems worked against the Democrats. Midwestern wheat farmers had resented a price ceiling while southern cotton was uncontrolled. A Congress dominated by southern Democrats dissatisfied the North. The administration's heatless, wheatless, meatless days had wearied the entire country. The Armistice came too late to help the Democrats on November 5. The "in" party almost always loses strength in congressional elections during years without presidential contests. Then in the Senate, where results were crucial, several Republicans won by close margins.[10]

The G.O.P. triumph had deplorable consequences. Republicans won the Senate by two seats, 49 to 47, enough to make Lodge chairman of the Foreign Relations Committee, which he filled with Wilson's enemies.[11] Even worse, leaders abroad, taking the President at his word, assumed that the American people had repudiated him.

Wilson stubbornly continued with his ideas of an international organization that broke with tradition. After the Armistice he should have sought to discover how much support his new ideas might have; he should have tried them out on the Cabinet, and asked leaders of opinion across the country. The British embassy cabled London that the President was doing nothing to focus opinion—that both parties resented that he had not consulted the Senate and had left the country in the dark.[12] He was as secretive as he had been about the war message of April 1917, which he composed himself, or the Fourteen Points speech, or negotiation with the German government. Aboard ship for the Peace Conference, Secretary of State Lansing learned that the President was basing the new international organization "on the principle of diplomatic adjustment rather than that of judicial settlement." The Secretary pointed out that a mutual territorial guarantee backed by economic and military sanctions (the proviso most debated in the United States; it became Article 10 of the Covenant) was dangerous if a simple majority of League members invoked it and unworkable if it required unanimity. "It is simply loaded with dynamite," he wrote privately, "and he must not go on with it." Lansing urged a self-denying or negative covenant, a promise of "hands-off" in case of an aggressor.[13] Wilson paid no attention to this suggestion.

During the month that the President was in Europe before the conference opened, his views took on a publicly rigid form. In England he told Asquith the old story of Lincoln's Cabinet where a chorus of "Noes" greeted an issue, after which the President said "Aye" and that "The ayes have it!" He said his wife considered him the most obstinate man in America and nothing could induce him to yield in regard to the League of Nations. In an address at the Sorbonne on December 21 he announced "a great wind of moral force moving through the world, and every man who opposes himself to that wind will go down in disgrace."

Throughout January and early February the President put his League ideas through several drafts. In the first week of January, having read proposals for a League by Smuts, he wrote what amounted to a third draft (House's July 1918 draft was first, Wilson's initial revision second). He circulated it to the American peace commissioners and the delegation's legal expert, Hunter Miller, and after proposals from European sources wrote a fourth draft that went to the printer on January 20. Lord Robert Cecil had drawn a draft close enough to Wilson's fourth that it now seemed worthwhile trying for an Anglo-American draft, and House, Miller, and the British legal expert Cecil Hurst tried what amounted to a fifth draft, but Wilson did not like it and instructed House and Miller to revise his own text with a few Anglo-American points, producing a sixth draft; Miller stayed up all night and arranged it. When the British protested, Wilson moved back to the Anglo-American fifth draft. Through all this drafting the President held firm to the principle of diplomatic adjustment rather than judicial settlement.

The Covenant passed in review before the committee set up by the Peace Conference on January 25, the League of Nations Commission, which met daily February 3–14; therein the Covenant took final shape. The committee made a few changes. The resultant twenty-six articles, models of brevity and expression, contrasted markedly with the 111 articles of the U.N. Charter drawn up a quarter century later. Important articles were 10, the territorial guarantee; 11, any threat to peace was a concern to all members; and 16, economic sanctions, which looked to military sanctions. The heart of the Covenant, as Wilson later described it, was Article 10: "The members of the League undertake to respect and preserve as against external aggression the territorial integrity and existing political independence of all Members of the League." The President in mid-February left Paris for home, and during the voyage carried a copy of the Covenant in the breast pocket of his greatcoat; once when he was climbing to the ship's bridge his coat blew open and Ray Baker saw the copy. At a dinner for congressional leaders in Washington on February 26, Wilson explained the Covenant. To the Democratic National Committee two days later he described those individuals who did not admire the Covenant as "blind and little provincial people," a characterization that quickly got back. The President's opponents among Senate Republicans found their suspicion confirmed that he was trying to make it difficult for them to reject the Covenant by writing it into the peace treaty, that he hoped to crush opposition under the weight of popular demand for peace. That indeed was his purpose. Senator Lodge just before midnight on March 3, 1919, the day before the session of Congress was to end, read to the Senate in a clever maneuver a round-robin statement signed by thirty-seven Republican senators and senators-elect (two other Republican senators added their names by telegraph the next day) that advised that "the constitution of the league of nations in the form now proposed . . . should not be accepted by the United States," and that the proposal for a League of Nations should be taken up for discussion at Paris only after the conference had negotiated peace terms with Germany. In a speech in New York the next day, March 4, Wilson refused. Back in Paris he proved willing to change the Covenant slightly, excluding any question affecting the Monroe Doctrine, making it possible for members to withdraw, exempting domestic matters from the purview of the League (he left determination of such matters to the League Council).

The final trip home proved uneventful and on July 8 the presidential party landed at Hoboken amidst another procession of dreadnoughts, airplanes, and dirigibles. The President crossed to New York on a cool, exhilarating, windy summer day, to decorated streets and cheering crowds, and entrained at Pennsylvania Station; he arrived in Washington late that evening to find 100,000 people gathered in and about Union Station to welcome him. From there he drove to the White House. It was a beautiful night, the city ablaze with lights, public buildings floodlit. The wife of Secretary Daniels expressed regret to the President that everything was illuminated but the Capitol. "It never is," was the response.[14]

On July 10, Wilson presented the Treaty of Versailles to the Senate, in a speech that he read; it lacked spontaneity, except for the peroration in which he told senators the light streamed ahead, the Covenant would lead the way. Just before the speech, with the treaty under his arm, he had started to march into the Senate Chamber, and Senator Lodge, who was walking by his side, inquired, "Mr. President, can I carry the treaty for you?" The President smiled and said, "Not on your life." Everyone laughed.[15]

During the next month and a half the President moved toward a fight between himself, leading the people, and the Senate, a trip out West to take the issue to the people, but remained in the city in hope that he could bring the Senate to his point of view. He talked with senators individually or in groups. He invited the Foreign Relations Committee to luncheon on August 19 and preceded the meal with three hours of questions and answers. The President's auditors felt ill at ease, as if in a kindergarten, and did not speak out, as they should have. Wilson chafed. Years earlier he had written his first wife, Ellen, before they were married, that he had a sense of power dealing with men collectively but did not always feel so in dealing with them singly, that he felt no sacrifice of pride in seeking to please a group. It was a glimpse of the future, part of the reasoning behind the President's decision to go to the country.[16]

The trip west to talk to the people was just too much. It would have taxed a well man. For Wilson it was impossible—twenty-two days beginning September 6, 8,000 miles, the jolting train, standing in swaying automobiles for a dozen parades, thirty-seven hour-long speeches, auditoriums packed, fetid air overwhelming on the high speakers' platforms. At the outset a stopover at Columbus, Ohio, was very unsatisfactory, for the President had a severe headache and Grayson considered him in "none too good a physical condition." At Indianapolis he found 16,000 to 20,000 people jamming the fairground auditorium, a place not intended for speechmaking, with just a platform in the center of the building, no sounding board, "and it was a physical impossibility for any one human voice to fill this space." Governor Goodrich introduced him and talked too long. When Wilson started, he could not be heard, and people moved toward the doors, which made matters worse; at that point a stentorian-voiced usher asked all who wanted to leave and who could not hear to pass out of the hall, and attendants closed the doors after two hundred people left, and Wilson resumed; at the beginning his voice was a trifle husky, but in five minutes he had the crowd under control. Acoustics in the St. Louis convention hall were splendid and the President did well. In the coliseum at St. Paul everything went off beautifully, especially when the mayor jumped up on the platform after the President's address and shouted, "All those in favor of the ratification of the Treaty without a single change will vote Aye!" A thundering volume of Ayes reverberated. A bare twenty-five voted No. When the President left the hall the crowd was on its feet cheering. As the trip progressed, the President's headaches seemed ever more troublesome. He could not sleep well because of asthmatic attacks, which he had suffered ever since the bout with influenza during the Peace Conference. Grayson noted increasing tiredness en route to Bismarck. Tumulty wanted Wilson to speak at every little stop and said he could stand the strain, but Grayson objected. In Seattle the President was not feeling well. Two days later, September 15, the strain showed, and it required all of the doctor's skill to keep him fit to meet his engagements. September 17 in San Francisco he had a splitting headache all morning and Grayson doubted he could make his address, but he carried it off, and felt much the better for it, as he was on the home stamping ground of Senator Hiram W. Johnson, one of the League's bitterest opponents.[17]

A very serious problem during the western trip was that in every place where Wilson spoke, save one, his voice received no amplification. He had to shout, gesticulate, virtually do handsprings to hold crowds. In San Diego on September 19 he spoke to 30,000 people using a "voice phone," the new loudspeakers—what Grayson described as "an electrical device designed to spread the human voice broadcast." He said it was the most difficult speech he ever delivered; he could not be free and natural, having to remain in one place so his voice carried into the "megaphones." But the audience heard every word, with the exception of those in one spot directly opposite him at the far end of the stadium.[18]

Unfortunately the ways of the future were not those of the moment. Within a year the President also could have resorted to the new medium of radio, which "came in" during 1920–21. A spellbinder in auditoriums, he might have been as effective on radio as his successor of the thirties, Franklin D. Roosevelt.

As the tour progressed, enthusiasm increased; signs appeared that the President was gaining rapport with his audiences. But people seemed unsure of the Covenant, and he could not easily inform them about that abstract document except to lead them with words. The latter were not very good. Wilson had prepared nothing before his train had departed Washington, and dictated as he went along. The words did not come, as in the Pueblo speech of September 25: "We have accepted the truth and we are going to be led by it, and it is going to lead us, and through us the world, out into pastures of quietness and peace such as the world never dreamed of before." These were tired words, not Wilsonian; they were patched-up street phrases.[19]

The President pushed himself beyond endurance. After the Pueblo speech and a sleepless night on the train he collapsed. He told Tumulty, who related his words to Grayson, that "I don't seem to realize it, but I seem to have gone to pieces. The Doctor is right. I am not in condition to go on. I have never been in a condition like this, and I just feel as if I am going to pieces." He choked, wept as he turned away to look out the window.[20] The train sped back to Washington, where in a few days he suffered the massive stroke from which he never recovered.

The stroke on the morning of October 2, 1919, made Wilson an invalid, unable to use the left side of his body and affecting vision and sensation on that side. "My God, the President is paralyzed!" cried Grayson upon emerging from the President's quarters.[21] For a while he hovered between life and death, his kidneys refusing to function. Recovering, he lay flat in bed for five or six weeks. By Christmas he could work or concentrate for five or ten minutes. For the rest of his days in the White House his routine was to remain in bed until ten o'clock, when a servant placed him in a chair and rolled him to the south grounds or in bad weather to the porch or some room; at noon he saw a movie in the East Room; and after lunch at one o'clock he went back to bed, where he remained until the next morning.[22]

It was during these sad months that Wilson isolated himself—or guardians of his sickbed, Grayson and Mrs. Wilson, isolated him—from outside influence, from anyone who might tire or disturb him by disagreement. Few people talked to him; his appointment list for this period is now in the Library of Congress and has almost no names. Cabinet members could not speak with him. Vice President Marshall never saw him until the inauguration of Harding in 1921. Mrs. Wilson doughtily refused access. "The welfare of the country depends upon our presenting this case to him in person," said one delegation's leader shortly after he became ill. Mrs. Wilson drew herself up to her full five feet nine inches and, according to Grayson, replied: "I am not thinking of the country now, I am thinking of my husband." When Wilson had improved enough she took matters to him, priding herself on her ability as a reporter—her mother had trained her to accuracy as a child by telling her to observe anything she saw or heard in the town of Wytheville, Virginia, and repeat it to one of her grandparents, an invalid.[23]

In 1919–21 many people said Mrs. Wilson was the first woman President of the United States. A White House correspondent, Charles T. Thompson, wrote of "the Mrs. Wilson regency," and Mrs. Wilson herself described it as "my stewardship." Feeble jokes circulated to the effect that she was the Presidentress and had changed her title from First Lady to Acting First Man. Between the stroke and the President's resumption of attendance at Cabinet meetings, 180 days elapsed. In the annals of presidential incapacity the case closest to Wilson's occurred many years later when President Dwight D. Eisenhower in 1955 suffered a heart attack that hospitalized him for 49 days. If one considered the illnesses of American Presidents that led to death, none lasted as long as Wilson's illness: William Henry Harrison was bedridden seven days, Zachary Taylor five, James A. Garfield eighty, McKinley eight, Harding four. Wilson in 1919 must have known he was a wreck of his former self, for he swore Grayson and his wife to secrecy, that they should tell no one of his condition.[24] The highest officials, including Marshall, knew nothing even about the nature of his illness (Grayson spoke of a nervous breakdown) until February 10, 1920, when the Baltimore *Sun* carried an interview with one of his attending physicians, Hugh Young of Johns Hopkins, who said the trouble was cerebral thrombosis. Cabinet members meanwhile saw he could not perform his constitutional duties. For five and a half months Lansing convened Cabinet meetings, twenty-one times. At the outset the Secretary of State asked Tumulty to certify to the President's incapacity, or have Grayson certify. Both refused. Marshall would not take over, the Cabinet did nothing, Congress refused to act because the Democrats did not want to expose a scandal, the Supreme Court seemed powerless. The heads of departments and Tumulty ran the government.

During the President's illness his judgment deteriorated sadly; he acted willfully on the slightest provocation. He refused to receive Sir Edward Grey, who despite increasing physical disability (he was losing his sight) came to Washington as ambassador. Grey hoped to assist passage of the treaty and spent four months in the capital. But when he refused to dismiss a young embassy assistant who, Mrs. Wilson believed, had made unseemly remarks about her at parties, the President refused to see him.[25] Wilson finally broke with House, for the colonel's prominence at the Peace Conference had ruffled him. House returned to New York in mid-November 1919 and sent word to the White House that he desired to call. "Don't let us discuss that any more," the President said to Axson. "He is out of my life. The door is closed."[26] The colonel sent letters that the President failed to acknowledge and may not have read or even known about—many years later, in 1952, scholars at the Library of Congress opened some of the letters. His advice no longer asked, House shuffled off into obscurity. After inquiring of friends and acquaintances he came to believe that the President had not tired of his advice but somehow he had irritated Mrs. Wilson.[27] The ill President early in 1920 savagely dismissed Lansing. To the Foreign

Relations Committee the Secretary had testified of dissatisfaction with the Shantung settlement, and a disgruntled member of the peace delegation told the committee of his private conversations about the League Covenant. There was also fear that he would stir up war with Mexico over the so-called Jenkins case, the imprisonment of Consul William O. Jenkins by the Mexicans. Perhaps Lansing's unforgivable error was the attempt to certify the President's incapacity. It may have been Lansing's independence in other ways.[28] To the first Cabinet position Wilson appointed a lawyer, Bainbridge Colby, who wrote well and could compose state papers, was doggedly loyal, and possessed no national or international distinction.

At this saddening moment in the history of the presidency the treaty came before the Senate for a vote.

Much has been written on the Senate and the League of Nations, and it is necessary to reduce the ideas and procedures of the Upper House on this subject in 1919-20 to essentials and not deal with personalities. It is customary to describe Wilson's senatorial opponents as bigots who could not see beyond party loyalty. "Bungalow minds" was a Wilson expression. Minds of senators who would not vote for the League in any form, the so-called irreconcilables, perhaps contained "varying amounts of traditionalism, ignorance, bigotry, fear of the untried, prejudice, personal pique, partisanship, political ambition, and a natural bent for destructiveness." Former President Taft beheld the vicious narrowness of Reed of Missouri, explosive ignorance of Miles Poindexter of Washington, ponderous Websterian language and lack of stamina of William E. Borah of Idaho, vanity of Lodge, selfishness, laziness and narrow, lawyerlike acuteness of Knox of Pennsylvania, emptiness and sly partisanship of Frederick Hale of Maine, utter nothingness of Albert B. Fall of New Mexico.[29] Wilson, in turn, had alienated Democratic as well as Republican senators by his own near total lack of tact. But there was much more to the League fight in the Senate than the personalities of individual senators: there was principle, the desire of more than a third of the senators to preserve the traditional foreign policy of the United States, to take the traditional way in America's international relations, which meant arbitration, conciliation, and conferences for codification of international law. Americans always had refused to enforce these processes. During and after World War I the limited use of force to accomplish arbitration advocated by the

League to Enforce Peace represented the extreme position of the minority of Americans who supported the use of force.

Since the Covenant did not reveal clearly how League members should deal with a transgressor and Wilson's rhetorical explanations did not help, it gradually became evident—and embarrassing evidence it was—that the President was willing to let the League use force. Article 10 did not employ the word "guarantee," only that League members undertook to "respect and preserve." The latter phrase perplexed such acute observers and skilled lawyers as Root and Taft. Both had been cautious about the L.E.P., Root unwilling to join, Taft unsure of enforcement of process, although he agreed that the notion contained "some snap."[30] Root was much less friendly to the Covenant than was Taft; he wanted to eliminate Article 10, whereas Taft was willing to go along. But both considered a territorial guarantee, however worded, a political rather than a legal act and therefore contrary to American tradition. The very thought of agreeing to force, a political act, was awkward constitutionally and probably impossible in advance of a specific situation when Congress and the President had to declare war. Wilson said that in each case of aggression Article 10 allowed Congress to retain its authority to decide whether to send troops, but also said many times that Article 10 was the heart of the Covenant, the kingpin of the whole structure. He only confused his opponents by claiming it was not a political or legal but a moral pledge. When Senator Harding asked about the difference, he said a moral pledge was more binding than mere legality. When he spoke of legal obligation he meant an individual bound to do a particular thing under certain sanctions. A moral obligation was of course superior, had greater binding force, carried the right to judgment "as to whether it is indeed incumbent upon one in those circumstances to do that thing." In every moral obligation was judgment, in a legal obligation no element of judgment.[31] Later, on the western tour, he gave the impression that Article 10 was a legal pledge.

To Republicans, presidential explanations of the League came close to dissembling. To be sure, Root and Taft cordially disliked Wilson. But they were also trying to do what was best for the country. Lodge, often drawn as the worst of the President's opponents, agreed with the senior statesmen. He detested the President for "his utter indifference to principle, his lack of generous emotion, his entire subjection to his own personal animosities and his deep-rooted timidity—to use no harsher word." As majority leader of the Senate he had to keep Republicans together. But surely on this issue of international organization he placed patriotism beyond politics. "It is the most momentous question ever presented to the country," he wrote a friend. To another he remarked, "We must hold the reservations for they alone make the treaty safe or reasonably safe for the United States." He meant it—that the League was a turning point into intervention in Europe and probably elsewhere, and could produce a far different international order from what he and his contemporaries had known.[32] Senator Borah of Idaho, one of the most resolute of the irreconcilables, disliked any proposal he did not originate or amend, and was one of the most mulish of men. Once President Calvin Coolidge allegedly gazed out a White House window and saw Borah riding by on horseback, and remarked that it was curious that both horse and rider were going in the same direction. But behind the ambition and contrariness was a desire, on the League issue, to continue America's traditional policy of abstention from international political commitments. This was the view of such irreconcilables as Senator Johnson.[33]

Wilson refused to understand the concern of his opponents. He seemed to want to have nothing to do with them, for fear that in some way they might corrupt his ideas. Seldom was there such a theorist, such unwillingness to deal with human beings—although years later Stockton Axson told Ray Baker that back in the eighties Wilson had written his first book, *Congressional Government,* a study of relations between Congress and the presidency, without ever visiting Congress. He wrote the book in Baltimore.[34] It is clear that if the President had tried, even a little, to understand his opponents, the Covenant would have passed the Senate.[35] When in February 1919 he returned from Paris for two weeks in Washington, he seized every private opportunity to make fun of the Senate. At Philadelphia he visited Jefferson Hospital to call on his daughter, Mrs. Francis B. Sayre, where he had a first view of his new grandson, Woodrow Wilson Sayre, born February 22. The baby, plump and well formed, lay with eyes tightly closed and mouth wide open, which amused the President. The nurse remarked: "I wish he would open his eyes so you could see how beautiful they are." The President replied: "With his mouth open and his eyes shut, I predict that he will make a Senator when he grows up."[36] Aboard ship back to the Peace Conference the President caught cold in an ill-ventilated room where he watched a movie, and after being examined by Grayson he ventured that the doctor had misdiagnosed his problem. "My trouble is this, and I have worked it out myself," he said. "I am suffering from a retention of gases generated by the Republican Senators—and that's enough to poison any man."[37] Back in Paris he took Lodge's round-robin suggestions with ill temper, and gave in to forms of words that did not really address the senators' major concern. In Paris he did not think of compromise but said to Ambassador John W. Davis, who had come over from London, that as soon as the Peace Conference ended he was going home to "lick those fellows in the Senate," after which he would have time to rest from the weariness that he admitted.[38]

The reservations the Republican senators wanted might not have made much difference in the Covenant, even if the President had accepted all of them—an act that would have astonished his opponents, and might have been a clever move. Wilson would have had to watch his own statements prior to accepting all the reservations, but if he had left open an avenue for retreat and then suddenly in the summer of 1919 accepted all the Republican reservations, it would have cut the ground from under his opponents.[39] Lord Grey eventually gave up the mission to Washington and went back to London ("There is no one with whom I can discuss anything effectively in Washington. My time spent here is useless . . ."),[40] and wrote a letter to the London *Times* that the Allies should give in to whatever reservations the Americans desired, that cooperation was more likely if the Americans entered "as a willing partner with limited obligations" rather than "a reluctant partner who felt that her hand had been forced." By this time the President was recovering from his stroke in a minor way, but if he had been in his right mind, or perhaps one should say a more sensible frame of mind, he could have allowed his Senate supporters to vote for all the reservations to the Covenant.[41]

Then, too, the President might have seized upon a remarkable suggestion that Lodge toyed with, namely, of two leagues, one in Europe, the other in the Western Hemisphere, with the United States in control of the latter. Such an arrangement would have catered to tradition and yet in the hands of a real leader might have moved the American people closer to an international viewpoint.[42]

Instead of arranging a reasonable compromise the President let everything slip into confusion—whether willfully or from ignorance, it is difficult to say. He may not have wished to make his position too clear. He certainly did not seem to know the difference between the several ways in which the Senate could express itself—an amendment, a reservation, or a resolution.[43] An amendment required renegotiation, and he refused any amendment (he believed, incidentally, that an amendment required a two-thirds vote in the Senate, when in fact it required a majority vote). A reservation did not change the text and other nations could accept it without formal acknowledgment. Between July when he presented the treaty and November when it first came to a vote, it became evident that the Senate would not pass the treaty without a reservation on the use of force. Wilson secretly gave four "interpretative reservations" to his leader in the upper house, Gilbert M. Hitchcock of Nebraska, to use at discretion and if necessary incorporate, he said, in a separate resolution. The latter part of the proposal, however, confused the difference between a reservation and a resolution. A reservation by definition had to be attached to the instrument of ratification to be legally binding; the Supreme Court in *Fourteen Diamond Rings*, one of the "insular cases" concerning the relation of the Philippines to the United States, had so ruled. A resolution would have been only an expression of opinion, without force, what Secretary of State Richard Olney in 1896 described as merely an "expression of opinion by the eminent gentlemen who vote for it." Lacking assurances of a reservation on the use of force, it was impossible to obtain support of mild Republican reservationists against the G.O.P.'s strong reservationists and irreconcilables. On November 19 the treaty came up for two votes, first with fourteen Lodge reservations, drawn mostly in the Foreign Relations Committee and refined by Lodge and confederates on the Senate floor, circumscribing Article 10 and other parts of the Covenant and treaty. It failed, thirty-nine senators in favor, fifty-five against. The second vote was without reservations, thirty-eight for, fifty-three against.

A group of senators led by a mild reservationist, Frank B. Kellogg of Minnesota, and a strong reservationist, Harry S. New of Indiana, sought to draw up reservations acceptable to two-thirds of the Senate, but late in February 1920 a senator asked the President if he would sign the treaty with reservations, and Wilson said he would pocket it if it contained the Lodge reservations. Lodge had been working with Kellogg and New, and the remark raised a question of how much they might accomplish. When the Democratic leader,

Hitchcock, visited the President and said the time perhaps had come to extend the olive branch, the sick man replied in deadly voice, "Let Lodge extend the olive branch." The treaty came up again on March 19, loaded with the fourteen Lodge reservations and a fifteenth expressing sympathy with Ireland's aspirations for independence. Twenty-one Democrats deserted the President and joined Republican mild reservationists and strong reservationists in favor, but it failed again, forty-nine for, thirty-five against, seven votes short. If it had passed, the President would have refused to ratify.[44]

News of the Senate's final action went to the ill man in the White House, and Grayson saw Wilson several times that night.[45] At about three in the morning the patient said, "Doctor, the devil is a busy man." Later he asked Grayson to read from 2 Cor. 4:8–9: "We are troubled on every side, yet not distressed; we are perplexed, but not in despair, persecuted, but not forsaken; cast down, but not destroyed . . ."

CHAPTER 11

Readjustment

ONCE the war was over, the first order of national business other than peacemaking was to get men out of the Army. The War Department proposed to retain soldiers who if discharged would have trouble finding civil pursuits. Keeping men in the Army in an orderly way, however, proved impossible, and General March opted for demobilization by units without regard to employment. The only procedures Army authorities followed thereafter were such small matters as discharging men from camps nearest their homes and making sure they were in decent physical condition and left camp with a railroad ticket and $60. Better than after any previous wars, the government in 1918–19 organized the task of fitting soldiers back into what the Army described as civilian life. The United States Employment Service placed representatives in every camp, set up bureaus in cities and towns, and worked with such local voluntary bodies as the Red Cross and Y.M.C.A. In ten months the service placed 474,085 men, out of 758,574 registrants. Still, organization was more apparent than real, for early in 1919 when the service faced an inundation of job-seeking veterans and asked Congress for a deficiency appropriation of $1.8 million, it received $272,000, and reduced branch offices from 750 to 56, little more than one per state. No one thought of a G.I. Bill of Rights in 1918–19, although Congress in 1924 passed the Adjusted Compensation Act to make up the difference between service pay and wages of war workers. It provided compensation on the basis of $1.25 a day for overseas service and $1 for service in the United States. It scheduled payments for 1944, but during the Great Depression advanced the date to 1936.

The easiest task was to release men from cantonments in the United States, where the Army discharged 600,000 at once. For the AEF it was first necessary to bring the men home. Withdrawal of Allied ships from American service after the Armistice, to serve national needs, threw the burden of homeward transit on the U.S. Navy, which converted all possible vessels into troopships—cargo transports, battleships, cruisers, ten enemy ships; it expanded the troop fleet to four times its size on Armistice Day, 174 vessels accommodating 419,000 passengers. But 2 million men needed to come home. Most of the doughboys had to wait until the spring and summer of 1919.

During the AEF's long wait discipline relaxed and threatened to collapse, for men were in an irritable mood, remembering the thought that inspired them in the autumn of 1918—Hell, Heaven, or Hoboken by Christmas. Pershing inveighed against "relaxation in discipline, in conduct, in appearance, in everything that marks a soldier," and tried to keep his divisions busy with calisthenics, drills, and all manner of schooling. The program produced far more harm than good; men refused to cooperate, obeying officers with faint enthusiasm and increasing contempt. Officers in Paris, concerned about morale, organized the American Legion, but that group veered off in other directions, toward antiradicalism and 100 percent Americanism at home. Morale in Europe continued to go down. The men changed Pershing's supposed remark (actually Captain C. E. Stanton made it) in Paris before Lafayette's tomb, "Lafayette, we are here," to "Lafayette, we are still here." They believed their government had forgotten them, or their presence assisted generals reluctant to go home and reduce themselves to peacetime ranks of colonel or major. No one knew how long they would stay:

> Rumors are flying about fast and furious,
> Some good, some bad and all of them curious;
> We're leaving next Christmas, or maybe this evening.
> Or any damn day of the time intervening.

Captain Harry S. Truman of Battery "D" of the 129th Field Artillery Regiment attached to the Thirty-fifth Division wrote his cousin

Ethel Noland that he was "very anxious that Woodie cease his gallivantin' around and send us home at once and quickly." Most of the AEF, he said, "don't give a whoop (to put it mildly) whether Russia has a Red Government or no Government and if the King of the Lollipops wants to slaughter his subjects or his Prime Minister it's all the same to us." He saw no point in keeping troops around to "browbeat a Peace Conference that'll skin us anyway." Peace soldiering, he wrote, was a disgusting operation run by West Pointers, Regular officers who wanted men to curry horses, feed chaff out of the hay, and if necessary salt it (though there was no salt), and soft-soap harness. All because some old general had gone horse crazy and sent out inspectors—staff colonels and majors who never got their feet off the desk during the war.[1]

Gradually the AEF went home, with initial shipment of 26,000 in November. Through winter and spring, across the cold, wind-swept north Atlantic, ships made their way. Captain Truman and his Kansas City battery went back on the former German steamer *Zeppelin,* a rough rider, everyone seasick, two weeks rolling and wallowing, men shooting craps and putting aside enough money to buy their captain a loving cup; on Easter Sunday morning, April 20, 1919, they sailed into New York harbor. Peak month for return was June, when 360,000 left the Old World. On a Sunday in June, Private Ernest Ferrell's ship moved up the river in Philadelphia, where he saw riverbanks filled with bathers who waved at the men who waved back. By the end of August only 40,000 logistical troops and the occupying force in the Rhineland remained.

Reunions were tearful and joyous, and frequently returning soldiers entered into a state of matrimony. Captain Truman, mustered out May 6, set the day of marriage to Bess Wallace of Independence, Missouri, for June 28, by chance the day for signing of the Treaty of Versailles. He married his Bess in Trinity Episcopal Church and after a wedding trip to Chicago, Detroit, and Port Huron, the couple returned to live with Bess's mother at 219 North Delaware Street, Independence.

As befitted the commander of the AEF, General Pershing waited for his own return until September, when his great army had disappeared. He came back on the *Leviathan,* and on the way learned that Congress had bestowed upon him the special rank of "General of the Armies" that carried a permanent four stars. After a tumultuous reception in New York City he journeyed down to Washington to review a reconstituted division—24,000 men equipped with field guns, limbers and caissons, ammunition trucks, rolling kitchens, ambulance trains. For the occasion the Army shipped in horses and mules from posts as far as Kansas and Texas. Men required four hours to pass in review, planes roaring overhead, an observation balloon swaying above the White House. Caterpillar treads of the tanks gashed asphalt streets as they wheeled past the reviewing stand. It was the same route taken by Civil War veterans in their Grand Review fifty-four years before. General March and other dignitaries watched from the stand. March looked on sourly, in anticipation of departure from his post as Chief of Staff and replacement by his rival Pershing. As in 1865, the commander in chief who had led the nation through war was not present, for Wilson was on the western tour in behalf of the Covenant, on the threshold of personal tragedy even grimmer than Lincoln's.[2]

As the great majority of men left the Army, an occupation force established itself in a sector of the Rhineland that included Trier and Coblenz. French, British, and Belgian troops occupied adjoining sectors. Only an eighth of the AEF, 240,000 men, originally took part in the occupation. Pershing gave his best troops the honor of marching into Germany. Among them was the Second Division, whose Marine brigade had stood at Belleau Wood and Soissons. Lieutenant John W. Thomason walked along sadly with his men, twelve hundred men marching, most of them new to the brigade, replacing men who had fallen in rows in the wheat fields. Ghosts walked silently with the new men, Thomason thought, as the mist rolled around the column.[3] Captain Frank Murphy, later mayor of Detroit and associate justice of the Supreme Court, similarly marched with his division into Germany, an arduous operation, hills of southern Germany "charming to look at but fiendish to climb" with heavy packs and walking in the rain. Murphy's right toe came through his shoe, men marched on stone roads in bare feet. He was the only captain in his battalion who walked all the way to Hoenningen northwest of Coblenz, 200 miles in fifteen marching days.[4]

Soldiers long remembered time spent along the Rhine at Coblenz, a small residential and government city, where they gazed across the river at the huge American flag flying from the local fort, Ehrenbreitstein. It was the largest flag the commander of occupying troops, General Dickman, could find in the entire AEF, and he flew it from the tallest staff of the fortress, 500 feet above the water.[5]

The Rhineland Occupation

Colonel T. Bentley Mott, a Regular, recalled how troops at Manila twenty years before had raised Old Glory over the capital of the Philippines, and Mott felt a lump in his throat as he looked up at the battlements—"suddenly all that this flag meant. . . . Pride, a thrill of patriotic awe, and then a sense of utter happiness—happiness in the power it told us of, the mighty protection it signified for everything we loved. In that one glance I could see, crowding behind this symbol in the German sky, millions of soldiers pouring into France . . ." Fading photographs of half a century and more show posed groups of soldiers along the Rhine, in front of paddlewheel boats with straight stacks, and behind and rising into the heights the masonry of Ehrenbreitstein and above the fortress the flag.

The other memory of the occupation was homesickness. It was possible to while away time purchasing souvenirs, including *"Gott mit uns"* belt buckles, German insignia, and more iron crosses than the Emperor possibly could have awarded. Doughboys were so souvenir happy they assaulted German policemen to obtain spiked helmets. But as in the case of troops in France after the Armistice, there was not much to do. It was said that men were in an "army of no occupation." The thrill of entering Germany wore off. Few members of the occupying force opted to remain in the Regular Army; all they wanted was to go home. By the autumn of 1919 the force was down to a division, by 1920 to 16,000, by end of 1922, 1,200, and this remnant went home in January the next year.[6]

Having demobilized wartime soldiers, and most of the half million wartime sailors, the Army and Navy's leadership, military and civil, cast around for a proper peacetime organization. Europe seemed secure, and because Japan had fought on the side of the Allies no danger appeared there. Vague dangers lurked, revival of German militarism, increase in Japan's power, but such fears were hardly the stuff from which to argue a large peacetime Army and Navy. Almost all the two services had to go on was hope that their wartime establishments had created a constituency from which to support more public outlays.

Increasing the peacetime Navy appeared easier than enlarging the Army, for the Navy had been popular since the eighties, and a tradition of strength at sea went back to the time of the Revolution and Captain John Paul Jones. The Navy, moreover, did not require large numbers of men; its principal expenditures went for ships and maintenance. The Naval Act of 1916 stood on the books and, even if most of the ships were still on the drawing boards, sentiment envisioned a Navy "second to none"—larger than Great Britain's. "Let's build a navy bigger than hers and do what we please," Wilson had said in 1916 when the British blacklisted American merchantmen. During and just after the war the Navy watched every opportunity to ensure its future strength, and everything seemed to be going well. Wartime differences with the British encouraged Navy leaders to think they could go ahead with the 1916 program. In September 1918 the Navy Department's General Board recommended an even larger program of capital ships, a total (including ships in the Act of 1916) of twelve new battleships and sixteen new battle cruisers.[7] At the Peace Conference the President spoke encouragingly of a naval race, in the event the British and French refused to support the League of Nations. When the treaty went to the Senate, naval circles at first thought all was lost, but then it failed and that appeared to mean an increase in the Navy—League supporters had argued that an increase would be necessary if the United States stayed out of the world government.

Contrary to the Navy's hopes, postwar opinion refused to support a building program. During the war the Navy had constructed destroyers and submarine chasers, and to go ahead with a program meant costly battleships. If comparison with the British Navy, forty-two first-line capital ships to sixteen for the United States, alarmed the admirals, it alarmed the American public when converted to dollars. The national debt had soared to $24 billion. Even *The New York Times*, usually big-Navy, saw no reason for a contest with Britain, and announced the Atlantic coast as secure as if Europe possessed no fleets, that it was grotesque to talk of British aggression.[8] Professional circles were blue with discouragement and pessimism well before Congress's fiscal 1921 appropriation of $432 million. The appropriation for 1922 passed with an amendment by Senator Borah calling for a naval disarmament conference, which met in November 1921 and fixed the Navy at its pre-1916 level.

Naval leaders continued to show only slight interest in submarines, preferring battleships. If the Navy had gone ahead with the Act of 1916, not to mention the plan of 1918, the resultant force might not have amounted to much in terms of future naval war. Nor did naval circles concern themselves over what the airplane might do to war at sea. In the latter case they had reason for indifference;

in early postwar years the plane had not developed mechanically to where it constituted a serious naval weapon. Three Navy seaplanes undertook to fly from Newfoundland to England in 1919, by way of the Azores and Lisbon, and Daniels proudly wrote in his report of the Navy's achievements that year that when an airship could fly from America to Europe in a few hours the ocean no longer afforded dependable protection. But the NC planes did not have easy passage, only NC-3 made it, and Benson told Assistant Secretary of War Crowell, "The Navy doesn't need airplanes."[9] It did not create a bureau of aeronautics until after Brigadier General William Mitchell's fliers in the summer of 1921 sank the German battle cruiser *Ostfriesland* off the Virginia Capes, and roused itself at that time perhaps to obtain funds for planes that otherwise would have gone to the Army. The Navy prided itself that when Mitchell's bombers came over, the ship was dead in the water; with a crew aboard, under way, antiaircraft guns firing, it might have stayed afloat. When the Washington Naval Disarmament Conference limited battleships, the Navy converted two battle cruiser hulls to aircraft carriers, the *Lexington* and *Saratoga*, but the admirals' hearts were not in the task.[10]

The postwar Navy took much more interest in dirigibles than in submarines or planes. German dirigibles had bombed London—awesome sights as their huge shapes floated over the city at night outlined by searchlights. Their hydrogen-filled containers had become easy targets for incendiary bullets, but the prospect of noninflammable helium made dirigibles appear feasible. "Lighter than air" ships could attack a faraway enemy, carrying twenty-five to thirty tons of bombs for 211 hours at forty-five miles per hour. Early in the war an American diplomat had envisioned New York City held for ransom of $1 billion by a German zeppelin.[11] The Germans actually built such a dirigible, the L-72, for use against the United States. The British R-34 made the transatlantic crossing in December 1918 while Wilson was en route to the Peace Conference, and crowded him off the front pages of American newspapers. The Navy tried hard to develop dirigibles, until a series of tragic disasters brought the experiment to a close.

The postwar Army became a public issue at the same time as debate arose over the Navy, and the result was similar—another defeat. The Army's need was obvious enough, a corps of trained men—the Regular Army—and a massive Reserve instructed by

Regulars, from which to create another citizen army if necessary. Therein lay its difficulty: it needed men, as compared to the Navy's need for ships and maintenance. Years earlier General Wood had seen that a mass Army was a matter of public relations, and if Wood had been Chief of Staff in 1919–21 he might have managed those relations, and at least would have tried.[12] The effort lay beyond March, who in his abrupt way settled on an impossible approach, a skeleton organization that in wartime would absorb citizen levies. For the skeleton he asked a half million men, four times as many as the pre-1917 Army.

The March plan never had a chance. This huge Regular force seemingly would allow the riffraff of American life to enroll in an organization that would pay them to do nothing, since peace ensured nothing to do. Everyone knew the veterans could return to the colors, springing to arms in the way William Jennings Bryan had predicted. Secretary Baker supported the plan. But because it was the plan of the Chief of Staff, General Pershing would not support it.

The result was the Palmer plan. In October 1919 one of March's subordinates, a former member of the AEF, Colonel John M. Palmer, appeared before the Senate Committee on Military Affairs, and, sensing that the March plan could not pass Congress, he decided, as he put it, to "kick over the traces." In an hour of testimony he tore the March plan apart, arguing that it not merely was too large but "not in harmony with the genius of American institutions." He spoke for a citizen Army rather than the professional skeleton. After his testimony he prepared for a transfer to Siberia, if American troops were still there, and knew March would gladly have buried him alive, but Senator Wadsworth asked him to advise the committee and the resultant bill became the National Defense Act of 1920. It created nine Corps Areas within the United States, in addition to the three territorial departments existing before the war—Panama Canal Zone, Hawaii, and the Philippines. Palmer arranged for the new Army to have three field armies. He hoped for universal military training, several months for all youths, which proved impossible, and redrafted his proposal to substitute voluntary for compulsory citizen training.

The postwar Army veered back toward the insignificant force it had been in April 1917. Palmer had thought a 300,000-man Regular Army would be enough, and Pershing agreed. The National De-

fense Act established a Regular Army of 297,500 officers and men.
In January 1921, however, Congress forbade the Secretary of War
to recruit more than 175,000. When Wilson vetoed the bill it passed
over his veto, 217 to 16 in the House, 67 to 1 in the Senate. By this
time relations between the Army and Congress had deteriorated
sadly. Senator Wadsworth wrote President-elect Harding that if the
House of Representatives had had the chance it would have torn the
Army to pieces. By mid-1923 the Army was down to 131,254 officers
and men, close to the 127,588 of April 1917.[13]

What Congress rearranged in size, General Pershing, who became Chief of Staff in 1921, rearranged in organization: he returned
it to what he had known before the war. Indeed he returned it to
1817, extending the bureau system to combat arms by creating
chiefs of infantry and cavalry.[14] He made one innovation, the Sam
Browne belt.

Along with demobilization, generally a happy if belated experience, and failures in postwar organization of the American military,
readjustment to peace included three developments that marked off
the immediate postwar years as unattractive to many Americans and
tended to sour feelings about victory in World War I. The Milwaukee Socialist Victor L. Berger said that all the United States got
out of the war was flu and Prohibition. He might have added economic troubles—internationally, failure to expand into markets that
businessmen beheld during the war, hitherto dominated by the
British and Germans; nationally, a horrendous price inflation.

The word "influenza" is Italian for "influence." To millions of
people not merely in the United States who fell ill from influenza
late in 1918, its mysterious comings and goings were as vaguely
ethereal and indefinite. Known as Spanish flu, from its alleged origin, it caused 20 million deaths, making it easily equal to the Black
Death of the Middle Ages and any other visitations from time im-
memorial. In the United States, 300,000 people died in eight weeks
beginning in mid-September 1918, among them 25,000 soldiers,
equal to half the American battlefield deaths of World War I. Early
in 1919 the epidemic vanished as mysteriously as it had come, but
left a train of Bright's disease, cardiac problems, and pulmonary
tuberculosis.

The epidemic of 1918 was horrible in its particulars: not a street
in cities and towns without hasty funerals; children and old people
left untouched, but the ablebodied between ages twenty and forty

slaughtered. In October 1918 troop convoys became floating hells as soldiers en route to France sickened and died. Charles Sawyer, Secretary of Commerce in the Truman administration, sat on the upper deck of a transport as it left New York in the late summer of 1918 talking with Branch Rickey, afterward a great man of baseball, then a major in the chemical corps. Sawyer and Rickey noticed three coffins on the foredeck and hoped they would have no use. After the ship put to sea, flu broke out, men died by the dozens, thirty or forty a day, burials every afternoon at three o'clock, bodies heaved overboard without coffins. Medical men ran out of iron weights to make corpses sink, and laid them out on the top deck. When the ship arrived at St. Nazaire after fourteen days it was difficult to pick one's way across.[15]

In his isolated cantonment at Camp Funston in Kansas, General Wood visited pneumonia wards in the base hospital, a sad sight, men dying everywhere, ninety deaths one day, death very prompt.[16] Physicians at Camp Sherman in Ohio recorded 25,000 cases of flu, 3,500 of pneumonia, 1,100 deaths in less than three weeks. At Sherman the ambulance drove up to the hospital barracks every hour bringing in four pneumonia cases, taking out four bodies. Medics filled the morgue, and then deposited bodies in warehouses.[17]

Just before the congressional election of 1918, Claude Bowers spoke in Angola, Indiana, a ghastly experience, for he looked out on an audience that wore masks because of the flu epidemic.[18]

In Washington it proved impossible to remove bodies fast enough from houses. One afternoon a young girl called up a district commissioner, Louis Brownlow, said she had three roommates, two bodies in her room, the third roommate dying, and would someone please come; she herself, she said, was the only one not stricken. Police arrived to find four dead girls.[19]

As flu brought tragedy to many Americans, so the second result of the war, Prohibition, brought fury. It was, of course, peculiarly objectionable to Berger's fellow citizens of Milwaukee. The Prohibition movement had been growing for years because of the disreputable nature of saloons and problems with public drunkenness. It was not difficult to show untoward results from drinking—John Wilkes Booth and Charles J. Guiteau both had been drinking just before they performed their violent acts; Leon Czolgosz was the son of a saloonkeeper and had been living in a saloon when he set out

to assassinate McKinley; John N. Schrank, who shot but failed to kill
Theodore Roosevelt in 1912, was a saloonkeeper and bartender.
Immigrants frequented saloons for friendship and cheer, and native-born Americans supported Prohibition for that reason. In a
country filled with the reforming zeal of the Progressive Era, liquor
attracted attention especially of women, who prefaced their fight for
the right to vote by the fight against alcohol.

The Anti-Saloon League, founded in 1897, proved the great engine of Prohibition. It sponsored state-wide laws, and between 1907
and 1917, twenty-seven states prohibited liquor. Where the League
could not make a state dry, it pushed local option. Active also in
Congress, it arranged the Webb-Kenyon Act in 1913, forbidding
shipment of liquor into dry states. Then, to seize the last stronghold
of liquor, the cities, the League sponsored a constitutional amendment.

Judging from the number of dry congressmen elected in 1916,
Prohibition could have come without war, but war, which took 4
million men out of circulation, centralized authority in Washington
and made easier what many people then and later believed an invasion of their rights. Most important, it brought into the movement
such non-prohibitionists as Theodore Roosevelt and Herbert
Hoover, who advocated Prohibition to save grain. Bryan argued that
7 billion pounds of foodstuff had gone into liquor in 1916, one-third
whiskey, most of the rest beer, a little wine, enough to feed 7.5
million men.[20]

During the war the handwriting was on the wall of every saloon
in the country. Use of edible grains for distilled drinks ended September 8, 1917. The Eighteenth Amendment mandating Prohibition went to the states for ratification in December. Beginning February 1918, maltsters ceased purchases of barley and other grains
for malting. All this moved Finley Peter Dunne's Mr. Hennessey to
gloomy reflection, conversing with his friend Mr. Dooley, whose
place of business was a saloon on Archey Road in Chicago: "King
Alcohol no longer rules th' sea or th' land. Th' ladies have got that
binivolent o' dishpot on his knees beggin' fr mercy . . . Take a
dhrink, me boy, whether ye need it or not. Take it now. It may be
y'er last." Senators had trouble getting drinks at essential times;
Brandegee of Connecticut told Alice Longworth that one afternoon
Senator Knox, former Secretary of State, came into Brandegee's
office announcing someone had stolen his stock of whiskey, and

took a stiff drink from Brandegee's supply.[21] Federal marshals secured great amounts of illegal alcohol and the question arose of what to do with the precious confiscation. In Cabinet the President told of whiskey put in a bucket at an Army canteen and given to a mule—the mule got its head in the bucket and drank and drank and became so drunk it kicked over everything, "but did not kick the bucket." In the ensuing discussion Postmaster General Albert S. Burleson, a citizen of Texas, declared it a sin to pour out good whiskey.

After the war there was no stopping the Eighteenth Amendment and its enforcement apparatus, the Volstead Act, which defined intoxicating liquor as any beverage containing more than half of 1 percent alcohol. As Senator Harding told a constituent, it was to be a long trail across the desert.[22] The Wilson administration did not favor Prohibition, the President preferring manufacture and sale of beer and light wines, which he believed would make easier enforcement of the amendment in its essential aspects. He vetoed the Volstead Act, which passed over his veto. The evening before Prohibition, January 15, 1920, saw everywhere obsequies for John Barleycorn. A New York restaurant arranged a dance at which each guest received a miniature casket as a souvenir. At Norfolk, Billy Sunday staged a ceremony beginning at the railroad station where the "corpse" of Barleycorn arrived in a coffin twenty feet long on "a special train from Milwaukee," and passed through the streets to Sunday's tabernacle, where the evangelist preached to 10,000 people. In Washington, Bishop James Cannon, Jr., of the Methodist Church South, Secretary Daniels, Senator Morris Sheppard, and Congressman Andrew J. Volstead held a watch-night service at the First Congregational Church to celebrate "the Passover from the old era to the new." Bryan began to speak at 11:20 and talked until midnight, when his auditors rose and ushered in dry America by singing the doxology.[23]

Prohibition proved a trying experience for many Americans, and influenza wreaked havoc, but the principal concern of the American people after World War I was the economy. At the outset there was much talk of getting rid of wartime regulation, and on the domestic side of the economy that was exactly what happened. The Wilsonian idea of war had been instant, immediate conversion of farms and factories, and the subsequent changeover was likewise. Those who wanted to continue some formal mechanisms of government control lost out. The War Industries Board ceased operations with the Armistice; Baruch felt it no longer had public support. "Let's turn industry absolutely free. Everything that made us possible is gone —the war spirit of cooperation and sacrifice—the vast purchasing power of the government—the scant legal authority we have had— and the support of public opinion."[24] As the W.I.B. closed down, so did the Food Administration, Fuel Administration, Railroad Administration, War Trade Board.

The government had been active considerably longer in foreign economic policy than in domestic matters.[25] Since the turn of the century the economy's growth had encouraged American businessmen to sell abroad, to "restock the empty shelves and to fill the empty larders of four continents and many archipelagos."[26] America's share of world trade in 1913 stood at 11 percent, compared with 13 percent for Germany, 15 percent for Britain. That year more finished manufactures went abroad than agricultural produce, and exporters began to clamor for government support and assistance. Wilson was sympathetic. He arranged the Underwood Tariff on the assumption that Americans would have to import if they were going to export. Together with Secretary of the Treasury McAdoo, he also spoke with characteristic energy of the need for a larger merchant marine. In 1916 he signed the Merchant Marine Act, creating the United States Shipping Board and providing it with funds for construction of a commercial fleet large enough to carry much of America's foreign trade. A year earlier Wilson had quadrupled the Department of Commerce's budget for the Bureau of Foreign and Domestic Commerce, allotting an unprecedented sum, $50,000, for study of trade with Latin America. Under aggressive leadership of Secretary William C. Redfield, the Commerce Department became a veritable engine for promotion of foreign trade. It organized business for cooperative development of overseas markets. It provided both exporters and investors with a variety of important services. It coordinated foreign trade policy with such private groups as the National Association of Manufacturers and the National Foreign Trade Council; together with these groups, it lobbied Congress for changes in maritime, banking, and antitrust laws. By the time the United States entered the war, something like a partnership had developed between government and private firms interested in foreign trade.

Yet in this area too, government support and intervention had proved at best a tenuous, awkward enterprise. The Shipping Board had not created its operating agency, the Emergency Fleet Corporation, until entrance into the war. Few ships came down the ways until after the Armistice, and those turned out proved too costly to operate or unsuitable for commercial purposes. During the war the Commerce Department had lost much of its jurisdiction in foreign trade to the War Trade Board, and Redfield's subsequent resignation and the preoccupation of policymakers with the peace and the battle for passage of the treaty through the Senate limited new efforts to coordinate and expand foreign trade. Credit facilities had long been inadequate, and government officials balked at schemes that would use public funds to underwrite postwar private trade. Nor were they ready to cancel war debts of the Allies and raise taxes to finance reconstruction of export markets in Europe. Making matters worse, exporters and bankers, small and large firms, often could not agree on the best way to encourage overseas trade and investment. The European conversion to peacetime production also lessened the demand for American goods. Tariffs shut American producers out of some markets, and a growing demand for retaliation and protection raised the possibility of another tariff hike in the United States.

In addition to practical difficulties in government assistance of foreign trade, there was the intellectual framework within which both government and private business leaders operated. They wanted the government to participate in rebuilding the international economy, but without sacrificing such traditional verities as political noninvolvement and private initiative. Their goal was a cooperative relationship between the public and private sectors that fell somewhat between the old laissez-faire and outright government domination. The former could not provide industrialists and bankers with the government help they needed. The latter ran the risk of bureaucratic inefficiency and dangerous foreign entanglements. The middle way they envisioned was symbolized by the Webb-Pomerene Act of 1918, under which the government suspended the antitrust laws for private interests who combined voluntarily in the export trade. The act permitted open associations of private exporters rather than the closed system of state-supported cartels so familiar in prewar Europe. The Edge Act of 1919 also fell within this framework. It provided for an unspecified number of private, federally chartered investment cooperatives on the assumption that such combinations could underwrite European recovery and American trade without recourse to government loans or controls.

A business-government partnership nonetheless developed during the Wilson administration that carried over into the Republican ascendancy of the twenties. During that decade the Anglo-American acrimony that typified the last years of Democratic rule gave way to an interesting pattern of economic collaboration between British and American bankers and businessmen. Supported informally by governments, the private arrangements worked out for developing oil resources, regulating radio and cable communications, controlling loans, and financing Europe's revival squared with the American idea of an international economic cooperation that stopped short of political entanglements and government domination. It was an intelligent effort, and while the pattern of cooperation began to break down even before the Great Depression of the thirties, American leaders would again try to carry it out after World War II— unilaterally through the Reciprocal Trade Agreements Act, multilaterally through such agencies as the General Agreement on Tariffs and Trade, the World Bank, and the International Monetary Fund.[27]

The principal economic concern after the Armistice until near the end of 1920 was not foreign trade or even freeing the domestic economy from government regulation—it was an aspect of the domestic economy known as HCL, high cost of living. HCL was constantly in the headlines. By 1919 the cost of living had risen 77 percent above 1914. In 1920 it went to 102 percent. Young Americans might sing catchy tunes about always chasing rainbows and forever blowing bubbles, but life was not that good. Wage earners in factories barely managed to stay up with inflation; in 1919 annual real earnings were 5 percent above 1914, and the figure rose to 6 percent in 1920, 8 percent in 1921. For farmers HCL was endurable because of high agricultural prices. For people living on dividends from common stocks, HCL was no problem. For anyone tied to the fixed income of bonds and for increasing numbers of Americans in white-collar jobs and tied to salaries, HCL was a nightmare.

HCL of course revealed an excess of demand over supply, too many dollars chasing too few goods. The question was what created the chase. Here there seem to have been several causes. One of them was the wartime and postwar demands of labor for increased wages—but the requirements of labor do not seem to have been a major factor in HCL. At the beginning of American participation in the war the wages of millions of nonunion laboring men and women were appallingly low. Many of them had long before learned to accept whatever wages they could get, partly because immigration had created a pool of cheap labor, partly because ever since the Civil War the South had suffered from disguised unemployment. When the government took over the railroads McAdoo found wages as low as ten cents an hour. Half the employees (the roads' payroll totaled 1.5 million) received no more than $75 a month. Ex-President Taft, co-chairman of the War Labor Board, created to reduce or eliminate employer-employee disputes dangerous to war industry, could not believe what he found: "Why, I had no idea! How can people live on such wages!" Taft and his co-chairman, Frank P. Walsh, ordered wages doubled and tripled.[28]

During the war union labor was modest in its demands. The A.F. of L.'s perennial president, Samuel Gompers, an intense patriot, took pride in the opportunity that had come to him in his adopted country (he had emigrated from England in 1863 at the age of thirteen). He sat on the Advisory Commission of the Council of National Defense. One of his A.F. of L. organizers, Hugh Frayne, headed the W.I.B.'s labor division. The board's seal combined eagle, stars, shield, ships, and soldiers, with two hands clasped in a handshake, sleeves showing one an employee, the other the employer, under a pennant fluttering from the beak of the eagle and bearing the inscription, "Together We Will Win." Significantly, labor's hand was on the right. The president of the A.F. of L. also remembered how union membership had languished for two decades prior to the war, how such organizations as the Knights of Labor grew rapidly and lost out through misjudgment. He was pleased by rapid wartime increase in union membership from 2.6 million in 1914 to 3 million in 1917 to 5 million by 1920, but expected a depression and believed that, quite apart from the requirements of patriotism, the A.F. of L. needed a good war record to prepare for retrenchment.[29]

Wartime businessmen were careful with unions, appreciating the restraint of union demands. Businessmen may have been careful for another reason, their own extraordinary profits, no time to push down workingmen. The United States Steel Corporation, capitalized in 1901 at $1.4 billion, enjoyed a net income of $224 million in 1917, not approached again for thirty-seven years. E. I. du Pont de Nemours and Company in 1916 earned in excess of $82 million, and paid out more than $62 million in dividends on common shares, a return of exactly 100 percent. During the four years preceding the World War the Bethlehem Shipbuilding Company earned an average profit of $6 million; during four years of war it averaged $49 million.[30]

After the Armistice union laborers tried, for the most part unsuccessfully, to better their position. Four million industrial workers, one out of every five, engaged in 2,600 strikes during 1919, an unprecedented number, never surpassed or approached in later years. A bituminous coal strike occurred in November-December 1919. A steel strike in September 1919, the biggest the country had known, lasted until January of the following year. The steel strike, which was for union recognition, began Monday, September 22, and in terms of men off the job proved a tremendous success, half the industry's work force, a quarter of a million. Many more went out, probably double the number that had joined during the organizing drive, for pressure to strike was from the men, tired of the industry's long hours—more than a third worked a seven-day week, twelve hours a day. But then the strike turned into a long and, for the men, disappointing duel. Ever since failure of the Homestead strike in 1892 no unions had organized the steel industry. The intransigent Judge Elbert H. Gary represented the owners as president of the Iron and Steel Institute. His credo was the Golden Rule in business (he sought to be "unselfish, reasonable, fair, sincere, and honest"). A veteran labor agitator, a white-haired old lady of eighty-nine, "Mother" Jones, urged the cause in the Pittsburgh area, and asked at Homestead whether the mill "belongs to Kaiser Gary or Uncle Sam." In December three nationally known Protestant clergymen representing the Interchurch World Movement waited upon Gary, who talked for two hours and prevented the group from bringing up their proposals for a settlement.[31] The strike failed for several reasons—a sympathy strike by Great Lakes seamen began after ore supplies from the Minnesota ranges had reached a pre-winter peak in anticipation of freezing of the lakes, the national coal strike began after steel companies had accumulated large coal stocks, and the independent-minded railroad brotherhoods refused to strike short switching lines such as the Union Railroad and the McKeesport and Monongahela Railroad connecting mills to main railroads. Companies opened mills with a few skilled workers and 30,000 strikebreakers.

The war and immediate postwar years were not a happy time for laborers, and the principal cause or causes of HCL clearly lay else-where.[32] One cause certainly was the fact that when war came to America the economy had achieved virtually full production, with no slack to take up either increasing consumer demand or increasing war production. In immediately preceding years the growth rate of the economy had been quite small. In the third quarter of 1918 production had risen only 17 percent above 1914. In the third quarter of 1919 it reached 19 percent, where it remained into 1920. The principal accomplishment of the W.I.B., apart from organizing industry out of the chaos that War Department, Shipping Board, and Allied purchasing had driven it into, was to divert one-fourth of the economy from consumer to war production; almost no increase came in national product itself.

Inability of the economy to expand, despite the torrent of war orders, may have been due in part to a well-intentioned move by the Wilson administration, the Revenue Act of October 1917, which imposed an excess profits tax on businesses. The act focused on profits that exceeded net earnings of 1911–13, and taxed them at from 20 to 60 percent, according to the rate of excess profit to invested capital. It penalized undistributed earnings. Corporate tax-payers received exemption equivalent to not less than 7 percent nor more than 9 percent of capital, so as to guarantee reasonable return. The tax was equitable, and brought in $2.2 billion in the fiscal year ending June 30, 1918, but raised the cost of investment and re-stricted production.

During the war the Treasury Department acted according to the arbitrary calculation that at first seemed sensible, two-thirds of the war's cost from bonds, one-third from taxes. Inflation soon proved the formula far too low on taxes, and the administration should have acted immediately. It may be that President Wilson hesitated over political consequences of taxes that would affect the average con-sumer. Despite passage of the Sixteenth Amendment, the income tax had not yet affected the average American. At the outset Repre-sentative Cordell Hull of Tennessee had proposed 1 percent on incomes over $3,000 a year, and a graduated surtax on incomes in excess of $20,000 that reached a maximum of 6 percent. By 1917 the tax had risen to 2 percent and graduated surtax of 13 percent.

The Revenue Act of 1917 reduced exemption to $1,000, thereafter 4 percent, and surtaxes to all incomes above $5,000 that went as high as 63 percent. But this wartime enactment probably did not affect the very rich, who knew how to get out of taxes, and it did not much affect the average wage earner; average annual income was still quite low—in 1913, $621; 1917, $830; 1920, $1,407. Wartime personal income tax produced $615 million in fiscal 1918. Excise taxes on beverages, tobacco, and such luxury articles as furs, together with theater admissions and club dues, yielded more than personal income tax.

Production fell immediately after the war, with 9 million workers, one-fourth of the labor force, getting out of war industry. By the Armistice the War Department had taken delivery on goods worth $2 billion, with $6 billion in contracts outstanding. It canceled $2.5 billion worth within a month, and offered no relief to such contract holders other than a month's further operation at the current rate. Industrial production slowed in the second quarter of 1919, to 12 percent above 1914, and picked up in the third quarter.

After the war the pressure on production continued. Exports were at a high level, no longer in war goods but in other items, mostly agricultural. The government paid for these postwar exports, lending $3 billion to the Allies, former enemy states, and succession states.[33] Government spending at home as well as abroad continued into 1919, despite termination of war contracts. The railroads had cost $714 million in excess of income when returned to their owners on March 1, 1920.[34] Such payments added to HCL because money went out in increased wages and dividends and not for production. For two years after the Armistice the government continued shipbuilding; the ships had no market, no economic use, and their construction increased inflation by pouring more wages and dividends into the economy.

During part of the postwar period the Treasury continued to sell bonds—the Victory Loan of the spring of 1919. During this campaign it feared to restrict credit. In 1916 Congress had amended the Federal Reserve Act to allow reserve banks to rediscount loans made on collateral of government bonds, in addition to rediscounting commercial paper provided in the original act. Insofar as bonds became collateral for bank loans, they increased the currency and HCL.

Only after the Victory Loan did the government seek to raise the income tax. Progress of a tax bill through Congress necessarily was slow. Not until June 30, 1920, did the Treasury obtain an excess of receipts over expenditures—from the tariff, excise and other special taxes, and income tax. Excess was only $831 million, black ink registering less an increase in taxes than reduction of expenditures.

Increase in postwar prices encouraged businessmen to build plants. By 1920 annual increase in new investment had reached $3 billion, more than in any war year, more than in any year between World Wars I and II. These plants took time to build, meanwhile contributing to HCL.

City and country real estate began to appreciate, with large turnovers and long profits that purchased consumer goods or went into speculation, feeding HCL.

All the while inflation inspired consumers to buy before prices went up.

When prices soared during the war, and especially just afterward when the W.I.B. took off price controls on war commodities, and when expectation of further price increases arose, new opportunities opened for speculation. The construction industry might have siphoned off mortgage money at this time, but died because money flowed into commodity speculation; construction started down in May 1920 and by year's end was at the low wartime level. Rising prices induced businessmen to stock up on inventories of materials and finished products, and here was the principal villain in the HCL of 1919–20. As measured against any year in the next decade, the increase in inventories for 1919 was four times, save only 1923, for which the 1919 increase was almost twice; 1919 inventories rose by $6 billion, two-thirds being increase in physical stocks and the rest in price.

Buyer resistance did not break the price bubble in 1920, nor the rapid rise in the Federal Reserve rediscount rate from 4¾ percent to 7 percent. The Federal Reserve System was just seven years old, and one of the lessons its bankers learned from 1919–20 was that raising the rediscount rate was not enough to check rapid inflation. They forgot the lesson in the later twenties when Federal Reserve banks again futilely resorted to raising the rate.[35]

Where trouble came in 1920, the circumstance that broke the bubble, was very probably a combination of deflationary trends that suddenly became noticeable. For a while speculative purchase of crops concealed the developing agricultural surplus, and grain

moved into storage. Then came the reckoning, and corn that in
August 1919 stood at $1.88 fell to $.42 before the end of 1921,
wheat from $2.50 or more a bushel to below $1. Agricultural prices
plunged almost to prewar. When farm prices dropped, freight and
elevator charges and taxes tended not to match the drop immediately. In Ohio, Indiana, and Wisconsin, taxes accounted for 9.8
percent of farmers' net receipts in 1919, 17 percent in 1920, 33
percent in 1921.[36] All the while businessmen surely were nervous
about high inventories. Banks were approaching the legal maximum
on loans, fixed limits for minimum reserves of currency and depos-
its, debtors turning over loans.

Before anyone realized it the bubble had burst. The index of
wholesale commodity prices fell from 227.9 in 1920 to 150.6 in
1921 (1913 equals 100), forcing 4.7 million people out of work,
450,000 farm foreclosures, 100,000 bankruptcies. On January 1,
1921, Harry S. Truman and his haberdashery partner in Kansas
City, Edward Jacobson, had a $35,000 inventory, which they be-
lieved a sound figure. They could have sold out at that figure,
testimony to its soundness. In the twinkling of an eye, value of
inventory dropped to less than $10,000. When they closed in 1922
they were hopelessly in debt. Jacobson took bankruptcy in 1925,
and Truman did not pay off his debts for a dozen years.[37]

CHAPTER 12

Civil Liberties and Civil Rights

C ONSIDERING that the American people never had taken part in a first-class foreign war prior to 1917, the nation's actions during and after World War I demonstrated remarkable maturity, and only in a single respect, attacks upon civil liberties and civil rights, was there an egregious and irreparable failure of judgment. The story of civil liberties in that era is "a dreary, disturbing, and, in some respects, shocking chapter out of the nation's past."[1] It broke Americans loose from the moorings of reason and produced emotional appeal, coercion, jailings, deportations. In the case of civil rights there was, of course, a continuing discrimination against black Americans, in the Army and in northern (as well as southern) cities, at a time when the President of the United States was speaking about making the world safe for democracy.

The reason for failure to preserve civil liberties was not far to seek. Patriotism welled up in a demonstration of loyalty to the United States and to ideals known as Americanism, sometimes 100 percent Americanism, which easily became conformity, and the other side of the coin of conformity is intolerance. By the time the United States entered the war in 1917, the crusading zeal of imperialism and Progressivism had begun to decline. The former movement had worn itself out in the conquests of 1898 and protectorates of subsequent years, the Filipino rebellion making imperial ideas unpopular. Progressivism, perhaps better described as a series of movements, had seen its principal ideas appropriated by the Theo-

dore Roosevelt, Taft, and Wilson administrations. The Preparedness movement of 1915–16 was not so much a movement as the
activity of a few Easterners camouflaged by a slogan, and it looked
to Wilson's reelection.[2] In 1917 the country's restless idealism
needed focus. The war heightened Americanism. It satisfied large
numbers of first- and second-generation immigrant parents and
sons and daughters yearning to demonstrate loyalty. It pleased native-born citizens worried about German-Americans, pacifists, and
radicals—Socialists, Communists, members of the International
Workers of the World (I.W.W.), of the Nonpartisan League in North
Dakota and Minnesota, anarchists.[3]

As for civil rights, Americanism gave an excuse to continue discrimination against black Americans, whose wartime and postwar
treatment was in accord with behavior of white Americans, north
and south, for many years. The movement of black laborers into
northern cities, seeking work, exacerbated the situation, as did entrance of blacks into the Army.

The Progressive movement had accustomed Americans to government intervention in their lives, and made interference with civil
liberties and civil rights easier to accept. It had created belief in the
power of government to change economics and society—and why
not use government to enforce intellectual conformity during a
great national crisis?[4]

A crusade for Americanism was congenial to the time and especially to the President of the United States; to lead a crusade was to
Wilson the fulfillment of a dream that went back forty years. While
a student at Johns Hopkins he had written Ellen Axson that he had
no patience for the tedious toil of what was known as research.
Rather, he possessed a passion for interpreting great thoughts to
the world, and he believed that he would be complete only if he
inspired a great movement of opinion, if he could "read the experiences of the past into the practical life of the men of today."[5] This
may have been the effusion of a young man impressing a young
woman, and the youthful Wilson had a tendency to draw his future
in large strokes, but unlike many young dreamers he determined to
succeed, to lead a crusade. In 1917 it was at hand. Everywhere
appeared signs of conformity. On the evening of April 2, 1917, the
President entered the House chamber for his fateful address and on
the floor beheld the little American flags.

It was necessary to organize the crusade, and an instrument appeared in the person of a forty-year-old journalist who had much the same messianic zeal as Wilson. George Creel proposed "a plain publicity proposition, a vast enterprise in salesmanship, the world's greatest adventure in advertising." He had written books and articles about a variety of subjects and it was easy to turn to Americanism. He believed in using truth to present America's case to people at home and abroad; the truth would set them free. His letters proposing a publicity bureau arrived when Wilson had been thinking uncertainly of censorship and of what might be necessary to restrain newspaper reporters. The idea of using truth was engaging. On April 13 a joint letter arrived from Secretaries Lansing, Baker, and Daniels recommending a Committee on Public Information to deal with "censorship and publicity." Next day Wilson issued an executive order establishing a committee with the three Cabinet members and Creel as co-chairmen. In subsequent weeks Creel clearly emerged as the leader of this committee. Lansing withdrew from active participation as he was not in favor of Creel's proposal, favoring instead the British policy of strict censorship. Baker and Daniels remained, but Baker was too busy and it was Daniels who became Creel's strongest supporter.

The journalist chairman of the C.P.I., together with the hundreds of men and women who worked for that agency, deluged America, saturated it, with information, or as Mark Sullivan wrote, with truth. Since it came from the C.P.I. bereft of unfavorable criticism it was therefore propaganda.[6] Creel organized more than twenty subcommittees or divisions, each with the purpose of spreading America's message. The C.P.I. mobilized the oratorical talent of the country, chiefly amateur, 75,000 speakers known as Four Minute Men. Every ten days the Four Minute Men received a topic, such as Universal Service by Selective Draft, Why Are We Fighting, or Maintaining Morals and Morale. Speakers talked on behalf of government departments to convince Americans to conserve food and fuel. During bond drives they sold bonds. When the war ended the Four Minute Men received the thanks of the President, who told them they might justly feel a glow of proper pride, and Creel said they had been unique in world annals, as effective in the battle at home as the onward rush of Pershing's heroes at St. Mihiel. The C.P.I. chairman totaled their effort: 7,555,190 speeches to 314,454,514 people. A motion picture division showed such films as *Pershing's Crusaders*, *America's Answer*, and *Under Four Flags*. Stills by the thousands went to newspapers.

Creel's committee used virtually every medium of communication, and undoubtedly among the most effective was the printed word. The C.P.I.'s division of civil and educational cooperation enlisted historians and other scholars to write pamphlets showing the war's meaning, including Carl L. Becker of Cornell University, who explained after the war that "we were only professors, but the world was still young, and we wanted to do something to beat the Hun and make the world safe for democracy." Guy Stanton Ford of the University of Minnesota, later executive secretary of the American Historical Association, assisted by Samuel B. Harding of Indiana University, supervised the wartime historical work. Typical was the pamphlet by Wallace Notestein, then a member of Ford's Minnesota department, who annotated the Flag Day speech of President Wilson in 1917; the address arraigned the German government, and Notestein found supporting quotations; the C.P.I. ultimately printed 6,813,340 copies. Pamphlets affirmed the ideas of America and the Allies, or analyzed the behavior of the Central Powers, including Germany's guilt in starting the war, or suggested ways for Americans to serve their country. Thirty-three million pamphlets appeared, on more than thirty topics. Grade schools and high schools received tons of literature, including the *National School Service*, which went to teachers. The C.P.I. used cartoonists to show issues, and newspapers received boilerplate that they printed as news.[7]

Abroad C.P.I. workers described America's war preparation, always circulating Wilson's speeches and photographs. The Wilson cult, Creel's agents in Spain and Denmark wrote, made astonishing progress. Italian villagers placed the President's picture in family shrines, surrounding it with candles.[8]

Salesmanship was infectious, the spirit spread, and the home front became giddy, especially during bond drives. Joseph C. Grew visited New York City during one such campaign and found Fifth Avenue a mass of flags, every taxi and almost every private automobile, van, dray, and delivery wagon carrying posters advising BUY, LEND, and BUY MORE. Traffic signals that policemen in those days turned by hand said GO, BUY BONDS or STOP, BUY BONDS. Shop windows displayed paintings of Belgian atrocities, with the inscription, "Save the world from this by buying bonds." Downtown a troop of mounted policemen carried effigies of the Emperor, Crown

Prince, and Hindenburg. Douglas Fairbanks was speaking to an enormous throng from the steps of the Subtreasury building. Grew avowed that the enthusiasm and spirit made him proud to be an American.[9] It was impossible to escape the sentiment. Eddie Rickenbacker, the racing car driver who had gone to France with Pershing as a chauffeur and learned to fly, remembered his first thought when he went up in the air and met a German pilot. His heart had started pounding, but the image of a beautiful girl with outstretched arms arose in front of him, a Liberty Bond poster labeled in black letters, FIGHT OR BUY BONDS. He recalled that he did not have much choice.[10]

The principal method of the crusade for Americanism was exhortation—written, oral, and visual—but if that failed, coercion remained. Theodore Roosevelt preached Americanism, "sternly" insisting as was his wont that "all our people practice the patriotism of service," that no one could render loyalty "in even the smallest degree divided." No longer in his prime, the Rough Rider strained his logic, filled syllogisms with more than the usual non sequiturs, but spoke effectively. He advocated measures against pacifists, whom he never had admired, and one evening in New York at the Harvard Club described them as a whole raft of sexless creatures. His friend Root spoke at the Union League and said men walked city streets that very night who ought to be taken out at sunrise and shot.[11] With such encouragement the average American easily became intolerant. A man in a Pittsburgh theater refused to stand during the national anthem, and authorities jailed him, charged him with disorderly conduct, and fined him ten dollars. A judge fined a Chicago man fifty. Patriots beat victims, doused them in horse troughs, clipped their hair, tarred and feathered, painted them yellow, drove them out of town on rails. Early war months saw much flag kissing. In Montana a man described the flag as nothing but a piece of cotton with a little paint and marks in the corner and said he would not kiss it because it might be covered with microbes. He was arrested, fined $500 and costs, and given a long prison sentence. In Canton, Ohio, home of the late President McKinley, twenty shopgirls wrapped a co-worker in an American flag, forced her to kiss it, and marched her to the bank to buy a $50 bond. Neighbors of a farmer near West Dover, Ohio, accused him of tearing down a flag on his farm. They made him kiss it and also buy $2,500 worth of bonds.[12]

German-Americans found themselves in an awkward position during the crusade for Americanism, and despite nimble moves to get out of the way of patriots they did not always succeed. They sought to demonstrate that they too were patriots. They hoped to rely on their long prominence in American life, and also their sheer numbers. But it was difficult to explain the acts of the German government in Belgium, stories of which had been dinned into American consciousness. Secretary Daniels during a White House dinner on June 18, 1917, met a Belgian general who said that when the Germans invaded Belgium a woman asked a German officer, "What shall I do? I have nine children to feed." According to the general, the officer killed five.[13] Billy Sunday offered a prayer in the House of Representatives and began: "Thou knowest, O Lord, that no nation so infamous, vile, greedy, sensuous, bloodthirsty ever disgraced the pages of history." Sunday also said that "if you turn hell upside down, you will find 'Made in Germany' stamped on the bottom." A cleric of less evangelical outlook, Lyman Abbott, described the German military as the most efficient band of brigands the world had ever known. Henry Van Dyke wrote that the predatory Potsdam gang had started the war to realize their robber dream of Pan-Germanism and that no one, anywhere, could labor or sleep so long as the Potsdam Werewolf—William II—was at large.[14] Governor James M. Cox of Ohio, Democratic presidential nominee in 1920, urged the Ohio legislature to forbid instruction in German in elementary schools, public, private, and parochial, because it was part of a German plot to gain loyalty of schoolchildren. In Lima, Ohio, the superintendent of schools, board members, and city officials attended a ceremony to burn German works. Communities allowed superintendents to apply the match, to accompaniment of band music, songs by children, speeches by elders. The school board of Columbus sold German publications to a wastepaper company for fifty cents a hundred pounds. The Cincinnati public library hid its volumes.

The crusade spread to nomenclature, and for years afterward people laughed at the stupidities—rechristening the hamburger as liberty steak, sauerkraut as liberty cabbage. The game of pinochle became Liberty, the Bismarck School of Chicago changed to the General Frederick Funston School; the Deutsches Haus of Indianapolis, the Athenaeum of Indiana; the Germania Maennerchor of Chicago, the Lincoln Club. East Germantown, Indiana, turned into Pershing. Kaiser Street became Marne Way. People changed names: Eddie Rickenbacker had happened to sign his name with a second *k* instead of *h* and his correspondent advised the wire services; papers printed stories headed EDDIE RICKENBACKER HAS TAKEN THE HUN OUT OF HIS NAME!

Music and musicians ran into problems, Fritz Kreisler was denied halls, Ernestine Schumann-Heink, who had sons in both the German and the American armies, was forced to remove German songs from her repertoire, the Swiss-born conductor of the Boston Symphony, Karl Muck, lost his post. The conductor of the Philadelphia Orchestra, Leopold Stokowski, wrote President Wilson as to whether his orchestra should play music by German and Austrian composers. He himself thought that German opera, any music by living composers of German origin, and the German language should be banned during the war, but wondered about Bach, Beethoven, Mozart, and Brahms—he felt that these great classical masters belonged to mankind and should not be considered an exclusive possession of German-speaking nations. Their music was still played in France and England. The President told Tumulty to tell the conductor to consult the taste of audiences and procedures of other orchestras.[15]

Against German aliens, of whom there were a half million, Wilson invoked the power of the federal government, the Alien Enemies Act of 1798, which gave him authority to imprison dangerous enemy aliens without trial. Government agents seized 63 immediately and arrested 1,200 during the war's first year, moderate behavior considering that the British government had interned all of its 45,000 German aliens.[16] There were undoubtedly many coercive acts against German aliens on the state and local levels, often by private individuals, and in the latter respect one case stood out, the lynching of Robert P. Prager in Collinsville, Illinois.

As German-Americans got into trouble, whether they wanted to or not, so did other groups whose loyalty patriots might impugn, such as pacifists. In the case of pacifists, however, it was officers of the U.S. Army who stood for Americanism. During the war 64,693 men claimed noncombatant service because of scruple against fighting, and local draft boards recognized 56,830 claims as sincere. Of all claimants 29,679 passed the physical examination, and the Army took 20,873. Only 4,000 maintained their position once they reached camp. In regard to treatment of pacifists the War Department was partly at fault, for at the outset it did not recognize objection to service on other than religious grounds. Moreover, to leave objectors of any sort under military control was to ask for trouble. Baker wrote the President loosely that objectors could enjoy "a wholesome outdoor life and are kept busy upon things that are worth doing," and passed particulars to his special assistant for personnel, Frederick P. Keppel, who proved ineffective. Much depended on the post commander, and Major General J. Franklin Bell at Camp Upton, New York, gave little cause for complaint. But Leonard Wood, who commanded training divisions at Fort Riley and Camp Funston, believed the administration was temporizing with objectors, and it bothered him to see Mennonites refuse not merely military duty but "ordinary work in connection with the sanitary section," which probably meant cleaning latrines. Soon he was fuming over "Mennonites, Hutterians, Holy Rollers and other noncombatant, nonresistant, spineless sects"—almost without exception, he noticed, men of German descent. Hutterites refused to change clothes or bathe, and their beards became matted and filthy. They refused exercise, and Wood sent them out in trucks at high speed over frozen, rutted roads. He had no feeling for such men, whose forebears had come out of rural Europe in protest against military service. Their zeal had brought them to small communities in the Midwest, which by ill chance became hotbeds of wartime Americanism. Threatened with a wholesome outdoor life in Wood's camps, 1,500 Mennonites and Hutterites fled to Canada. The National Civil Liberties Bureau (predecessor of the American Civil Liberties Union) defended objectors but could not prevent mistreatment and prison sentences. In November 1920, Baker ordered release of the last thirty-three conscientious objectors.[17]

Where civil liberties came apart during wartime and collapsed in 1919–20 was not in the treatment of German-Americans, nor in the Army's measures against pacifists, but in injustices meted out impartially, by individual Americans and their government, to so-called radicals. The Alien Enemies Act, together with five other statutes, served as the legal basis of an initial drive against the Socialist party. The Selective Service Act allowed the government to jail people who obstructed the draft. The Espionage Act of 1917, primarily against treason, covered such lesser disloyalty as conveying false reports or statements intended to interfere with the Army and Navy. The Trading-with-the-Enemy Act of 1917 gave the Postmaster General authority over foreign-language newspapers and other publications. The Sedition Act of 1918 forbade "uttering, printing, writing, or publishing any disloyal, profane, scurrilous, or abusive language" about the United States government, Army, or Navy. The Alien Act of 1918 permitted deportation of alien anarchists or believers in violent overthrow of the government or advocates of assassination of officials. With this legal armory it was possible to do virtually anything. Postmaster General Burleson took away mailing privileges from the *American Socialist,* New York *Call,* and Milwaukee *Leader,* their error probably being socialism. The magazine *The Masses* was mainly pacifist, but prominent Socialists wrote for it and made their points with Socialist overtones, so it too came under Burleson's ban. John Reed had written in the June 1917 issue that "Woodrow Wilson knew, or ought to have known, that the masses of America will not enlist, and that that is why conscription must be used. This is Woodrow Wilson's and Wall Street's war." Max Eastman had said Socialists were "able to stand up against the patriotic stampede."[18]

These actions arose before courts and the public had thought deeply about First Amendment liberties, before post–World War II experiences raised them in sharp form.[19] But the behavior of the Wilson administration makes uneasy reading. One has the feeling that repression of Socialist publications may have been to keep larger periodicals in line. Burleson's purposes are difficult to measure; he was a bluff man not given to analysis.[20] But his solicitor, William H. Lamar, had declared, "You know, I am not working in the dark on this censorship thing. I know exactly what I am after. I am after three things and only three things—pro-Germanism, pacifism, and 'high-browism.' " The President did not stand up to Burleson and Lamar, and wrote notes of inquiry or raised points in Cabinet and contented himself with explanations.

Individuals as well as newspapers and magazines came into conflict with prejudice and the law. A court sentenced the editor of the Milwaukee *Leader,* Victor Berger, to twenty years in prison under the Espionage Act, only to have the Supreme Court set it aside. In November 1918 Berger was elected to Congress. The House of Representatives refused to seat him, by a vote of 309 to 1; he was reelected, and again refused. He took his seat only in December 1923. Eugene V. Debs received ten years in the Atlanta penitentiary for similar charges, and the Supreme Court upheld his sentence in a majority opinion on March 10, 1919, read by Justice Oliver Wendell Holmes, Jr., though it was doubtful if the case constituted a clear and present danger as Holmes a week earlier had defined it.[21] Debs's case was the best reported of its time. An aging doctrinaire from Terre Haute, Indiana, perennial candidate for the presidency, a devout Christian, he was a threat to no one, least of all the U.S. Army, but Wilson refused to pardon him; at last the President's successor, Harding, released him at Christmas 1921 and invited him to the White House.[22]

Attacks upon Socialists produced a schism in Socialist ranks. The party expelled its radicals, whom Berger labeled a lot of anarchists, and expellees formed two groups: the Communist party of 35,000 mostly alien workers, and the Communist Labor party of 15,000 native-born. Combined figures for both Communist parties amounted to less than one-tenth of 1 percent of the country's adult population.

When Socialists met with trouble it was natural that the radical labor union, the International Workers of the World, should get into difficulty. In the summer of 1917 the sheriff and 2,000 patriotic citizens of Bisbee, Arizona, roused 1,186 I.W.W. miners out of bed and sent them by train to Hermanas, New Mexico, a desert town, where they were without adequate food, water, or shelter for two days. Their "deportation" received wide justification, having been led by a former Rough Rider and supported by Theodore Roosevelt, who said no human being in his senses doubted the men were bent on destruction and murder. Federal authorities arrested nearly 200 I.W.W. members under the Espionage Act, and trials in Chicago, Kansas City, and Sacramento resulted in long prison terms from which some obtained release only in December 1923.[23]

The Nonpartisan League of North Dakota and Minnesota came under pressure of Americanism, if for a somewhat different reason than Socialists and the I.W.W. A farmer-labor organization in a mainly rural area, founded in 1915 by a disenchanted "flax king," Arthur C. Townley, the league had dominated state government in North Dakota and threatened Republican party control of Minnesota. For a while the Wilson administration toyed with the idea of using it, for the Democratic party was weak in those states. Wilson received Townley in the White House in November 1917. But Minnesota's Republican Governor Joseph A. A. Burnquist saw the threat and moved to meet it. The league had made itself vulnerable by assailing "war profiteers" and arguing that the government should take over industry and tax large incomes and corporations. In the G.O.P. gubernatorial primary in 1918 the league endorsed Charles A. Lindbergh, Sr., father of the later famous flyer. Opponents pelted Lindbergh with rotten eggs, stones, ran him out of town, hanged him in effigy at Red Wing and Stanton, refused him permission to speak in places throughout the state, and arrested him for trying to conduct a Nonpartisan League meeting on a farm near Monterey (the charge was unlawful assembly and conspiracy to violate the law interfering with enlistments). State authorities indicted Townley for sedition. The administration in Washington backed away from the local scene, and Creel announced that "Mr. Townley is under indictment in Minnesota, and there is a very bitter fight being made on the League in that state by certain groups. With this, the government has nothing to do, refusing absolutely to take part in these local differences." Townley went free, but Lindbergh lost the primary.[24]

Such were the preliminaries to the Red Scare of 1919–20, with its fear of bolshevism in Russia. As Attorney General Palmer described the problem, "The blaze of revolution was sweeping over every American institution of law and order . . . eating its way into the homes of the American workman, its sharp tongues of revolutionary heat . . . licking at the altars of the churches, leaping into the belfry of the school bell, crawling into the sacred corners of American homes, seeking to replace marriage vows with libertine laws, burning up the foundations of society."[25] The new Soviet regime could not possibly have hurt the United States, for it was too busy establishing itself in Russia. But the Bolsheviks had imposed their rule by force and maintained it by terror, and word came out of Russia in bits and pieces, through Stockholm or Berlin, of confiscation, anarchy, and slaughter. In Petrograd an electrically operated guillotine allegedly lopped off 500 heads an hour. Cartoonists portrayed the Soviet government as a smoking gun, bomb, hangman's noose, or drew scenes of wealthy, cultivated women cleaning streets, or officers of high rank, businessmen, and professors selling newspapers while Bolsheviki rode in automobiles and dined in fashionable restaurants. Russia was the paradise of Socialists, the I.W.W., the Nonpartisan League—Socialists were about to turn the United States into another Soviet Union, the I.W.W. had Bolshevik tendencies, the Nonpartisan League was no protest of farmers but a group of Communists. Public and press shouted for deportations. Why allow so many Red dynamiters and bombers into the country but let so few out? Imports were greater than exports. For many, Socialists were Communists, Socialism was bolshevism with a shave.[26]

The Socialist-Bolshevist connection to major strikes or to bombings of the time was almost nonexistent. On February 6, 1919, a general strike in Seattle after a shipyard walkout involved 60,000 workers of whom 3,500 were members of the I.W.W.; the strike was orderly, but Mayor Ole Hanson announced a Socialist plot. The Boston police, poorly paid, struck on September 29, 1919, and the resultant hooliganism killed eight people, wounded twenty-one, and cost a third of a million dollars in property destroyed or stolen.[27] The same month the steel strike began and shortly afterward the coal strike. Meanwhile a few anarchists were at work. On May 1 a maid in the house of former Senator Thomas W. Hardwick of Georgia opened a package from Gimbel Brothers, and lost both hands. Postal authorities discovered thirty-four packages in the mail addressed to, among others, the chairman of a Senate committee investigating bolshevism, Postmaster General Burleson, Attorney General Palmer, Mayor Hanson, John D. Rockefeller. On June 2 explosions occurred within the same hour in eight cities, shattering public and private buildings, including the front of Attorney General Palmer's Washington house. Palmer's neighbor, Franklin Roosevelt, called the police, and another neighbor, Alice Roosevelt Longworth, rushed over to see grisly parts of a body, the man who set the bomb, being laid out on newspapers. More than a year later, on September 16, 1920, a huge bomb went off outside the office of J. P. Morgan in New York, killing thirty-eight people, hospitalizing fifty-seven, with damage at several million dollars.

The Red Scare led to a series of raids by federal and local authorities against anarchists and Communists. On November 7, 1919, federal agents in twelve cities seized 250 members of the Union of Russian Workers, an anarchist group with an estimated membership of 4,000. In New York City and elsewhere, local patriots regarded this raid as a signal for them to act, and as a result of the federal and local raids nearly 250 aliens were detained and adjudged deportable, most of them being members of the Union of Russian Workers. Then on January 2, 1920, federal agents and local police arrested 4,000–5,000 suspected members of the Communist party and Communist Labor party in public places and even in their houses, which the police entered without authority. From the various raids the Department of Labor's bureau of immigration determined that 3,000 aliens were deportable, and transferred them to jails in Detroit, New York, and Boston. In a review of hearings Assistant Secretary Louis F. Post, a dedicated civil libertarian, released all members of the Communist Labor party, canceling 2,200 arrest warrants. Eventually, as a result of all raids, 840 aliens went back to their native lands, including Alexander Berkman, the "red king," who had attempted to murder the steelman Henry C. Frick during the Homestead strike of 1892, for which deed he had spent fourteen years in prison, and Emma Goldman, the "red queen," also a well-known anarchist.[28]

Authorities in Massachusetts arrested two Italian aliens, anarchists Nicola Sacco and Bartolomeo Vanzetti, in May 1920, for robbery and murder of a shoe company paymaster and his guard in South Braintree, and in subsequent years their case became a cause célèbre.

Early in 1920 the 100 percenters went too far when the New York legislature expelled five Socialist party members. A legislative committee meanwhile had produced a 4,500-page account of sedition known as the Lusk Report.[29] Charles Evans Hughes enlisted the New York City bar association, and the resultant outcry did not reseat the Socialists but halted the Red Scare within the state. Its example reached out to end it elsewhere, indeed finish it off throughout the country. In Boston in Faneuil Hall young Samuel E. Morison of Harvard, of impeccable Brahmin-Puritan antecedents, talked to newly naturalized citizens and Sons of the American Revolution in the same audience, and told the former they had protection in the Constitution and warned the latter not to Palmerize the human rights part of the Constitution if they expected to keep the property rights part.[30] By autumn the zealots were in full retreat.

During the war to make the world safe for democracy, the nation's 12 million black citizens kept their places at the bottom of the economic and social scale. Along with most white Americans, President Wilson did not expect the war to raise the status of blacks. He did appoint more blacks and promoted more within the government than did his Republican predecessors Roosevelt and Taft. But it was a time of racial prejudice and the President shared the feelings of his era.[31] During the period of neutrality the President worried about the world balance of races; America did not intend to become involved in the war, he told House in January 1917, because it was the only one of the great white nations free from war and it would be a crime against civilization to go in. When he changed his mind the fear remained. After the war he told Grayson that American black soldiers returning from abroad would be the greatest medium in conveying bolshevism to America; the French had put them on an equality with white men and "It has gone to their heads." He spoke of an acquaintance who had related the experience of a lady friend desiring to employ a black laundress who offered to pay the usual wage; the black woman demanded more, because "money is as much mine as it is yours."[32]

The experience of 367,000 black Americans in the wartime Army thus differed little from experience in society. Almost all black volunteers and draftees served in the Army; the Navy took 5,328, the Marine Corps none. Drafting of blacks by the War Department was grossly unfair, for General Crowder's final report showed that of 1,078,331 registered, half were in Class I, and of 9.5 million registered whites, only one-third; a third of blacks were drafted, a fourth of whites; three-fourths of blacks passed the physical, 70 percent of whites.[33]

In cantonments black troops enjoyed few opportunities. In the South local authorities and the Army mistreated them with even-handed injustice. Y.M.C.A. workers in the South frequently refused to serve blacks, and overseas workers did it with reluctance; according to one regional secretary, about a fourth of the white secretaries served black soldiers gladly, about a fourth halfheartedly, the rest either refused or made them feel unwanted.[34] The military arranged for privately run Hostess Houses on government property, where soldiers met female visitors—"a bit of home in the camps, a place of rest and refreshment for the women folks belonging to the soldiers, a sheltering chaperonage for too-enthusiastic girls, a dainty supplement to the stern fare of the camp life of the soldiers, a clearing house for the social activities which included the men in the camps and their women visitors." Not until April 1918 did segregated Hostess Houses appear for blacks. Often black soldiers had difficulties in nearby towns and cities. Stationed near Houston, black troops got into trouble with that city's Jim Crow laws when a raid by local authorities on a dice game led to a riot that killed nineteen persons, including four policemen. Military authorities hanged thirteen soldiers in an arroyo two miles east of Camp Travis and gave life sentences to forty-one. Subsequent courts-martial meted out death sentences to sixteen more, and six were hanged, with twelve additional sentences of life imprisonment.[35]

Eventually 1,200 blacks received commissions. At the outset the Army made no effort to train black officers, although some blacks had served as Regular officers, notably Lieutenant Colonel Charles Young, a West Pointer.[36] The National Association for the Advancement of Colored People petitioned the Army, and in June 1917 an officers' training camp opened at Fort Des Moines. The Army commissioned other officers directly from civilian life—physicians, dentists, chaplains, or National Guard officers. Had blacks received their share, the Army would have had to commission 8,000.[37]

When black officers went overseas they encountered intense prejudice. Aboard the *George Washington* they received second-class quarters. Whites refused to salute blacks, and white officers barred them from officers' clubs. Policy in the AEF was to get them out of command as quickly as possible, for Pershing had served in Cuba with the black 10th Cavalry and believed that under capable white officers and with training, black soldiers "acquitted themselves creditably."[38] His colonel in charge of venereal disease, Hugh Young, was certain the average black soldier did not respect a black officer. The doctor talked to a group of black Army physicians, lieutenants and captains, about the "unsurmountable barrier" between the races, need to leave white women alone, duty to impress "these facts" upon the men.[39]

The Army desired to use all black soldiers in the AEF as labor troops, but the N.A.A.C.P. pressed the War Department to create black divisions, and Secretary Baker ordered organization of the Ninety-second and Ninety-third. The latter comprised three National Guard regiments and a regiment of draftees. It lacked headquarters or supporting troops, and Pershing brigaded its regiments with the French Army, where they fought well. A white colonel said its officers were mostly white, and had to be, but that his regiment was the best-disciplined unit he ever commanded.[40] Major General Charles C. Ballou, who had been in charge at Fort Des Moines, took over the Ninety-second Division, and Pershing's officers considered it worthless. Although one of its battalions succeeded in the Meuse-Argonne where two white battalions failed, its white commander, Major John N. Merrill, claimed he drove his charges forward at pistol point. The division's principal problem, it seems, was its newly commissioned black lieutenants, who were largely from the college-educated black middle class, in the vanguard of the civil rights movement, sensitive to discrimination, desirous of all the prerogatives of officership in billets—messing, relaxing, and avoiding danger—and insensitive to the need of the men for close leadership. They did not get along with their immediate superiors, the black officers who had been sergeants in the Regular Army and who had become company commanders. This new breed of black officer considered the old Regulars to be insufficiently militant on racial issues and too anxious to follow Army ways in relation to white officers. Animosity among the Ninety-second's officers was particularly dangerous because men of the division were rural blacks of very limited education and low self-esteem—unlike infantry regiments of the Ninety-third, trained in the Guard with roots in northern cities. Unlike white divisions and the Ninety-third, the Ninety-second never had enough good noncoms and privates to fill the leadership vacuum when officers fell or failed. Ballou might have changed this state of affairs by removing incompetents, but refused. The First Army's commander, Liggett, pulled the Ninety-second out of the Meuse-Argonne and put it to work on the roads. Returning to the front in Bullard's Second Army, it came under army command of a man whose southern principles were evident in his given name of Robert Lee. Bullard hated the Ninety-second, accused it of all variety of misbehavior including a primeval desire to rape (the division produced one certified case of rape), sacked Ballou on November 17, 1918, and sent the men home as fast as he could put them on ships.[41]

In the AEF most blacks went into the Services of Supply, where Harbord found they did not like work and were unresponsive to Pershing's promise that if they worked hard he would put them in the front lines as a reward. Tired stevedores took little or no interest in war and wanted to go one place, home. Port battalion officers pointed out that three-fourths of the men were illiterate. At one time an officer ordered all men of a company to step forward if they could neither read nor write and practically the whole company advanced. Among seventeen men, four never had heard of Abraham Lincoln, seven of Booker T. Washington; none had heard of Frederick Douglass. Many soldiers never had heard of Germany, France, Russia, Kaiser, or Tsar.[42]

Jined de army fur to git free clothes,
What we're fightin' 'bout, nobody knows.

In the war's last weeks two of Harbord's assistants arranged a competition between port battalions known as the Race to Berlin, actually a race to get home, for Harbord promised winners first place on the boats. With jazz bands inspiring the men, with their totals of accomplishment listed each day in *Stars and Stripes*, and with extra awards of time off at resort areas, men worked feverishly. Tonnage through base ports increased 20 percent, with quicker turnaround of ships, thousands of ship tons saved. The Race to Berlin ended before its appointed day because of the Armistice.[43]

Military service for blacks in the AEF did not end on November 11, 1918, for if the suggestion of the undertakers of America that Pershing establish a Purple Cross came to nothing, after the war it was necessary to gather the remains of tens of thousands of dead. Wherever the burial places, bodies had to be laid out either for shipment home or reinterment in military cemeteries in France. Black stevedores received this ghastly task. Daily truck convoys went out to search fields, forests, shell holes. Charles H. Williams, who represented the Federal Council of Churches of Christ in America and the Phelps-Stokes Fund, was appointed to observe every part of the life of the black soldier in camps and cantonments in the United States and abroad, and remembered nighttime labor at such places as Romagne in the Argonne—electric lights, sound of hammer and tread of feet, the lonely minor chord of song as stevedores drove nails into coffins.[44]

Black Americans who did not join the Army remained in the South or migrated north in pursuit of economic opportunity, and northern cities received the first of the influxes that changed them dramatically in future decades. By November 1918, 300,000 to 400,000 blacks had gone north to replace the cheap labor of white immigrants who had moved up the economic scale or entered the Army.[45] A recent student has described the exodus of the World War I era as the most important event for black America since emancipation.[46]

Like military service, the movement north to opportunity proved intensely difficult, filled with initial innocence and then keen disappointment. Migrants arrived in Chicago by train wearing overalls and house dresses, carrying sacks of belongings, some bringing chickens, goats, pigs, sugarcane. Chester Wilkins, chief redcap at the Illinois Central Station, beheld these poor people "totally unprepared" for life in a great city. Many did not know where they were going, but knew someone in Chicago. The Chicago Urban League helped 55,000 blacks find places to live and work. Olivet Baptist Church sponsored clubs to teach migrants how to adjust; its membership increased from 4,271 in 1916 to 8,430 in 1919, making it the largest Protestant congregation in the United States. The Wabash Avenue Y.M.C.A., financed by industrialists and meatpackers and the black newspaper *The Defender*, offered dos and don'ts such as do not stick your head out of the window, do not appear on the street with old dustcaps, dirty aprons, and ragged clothes, do not loaf on the corner of 35th and State streets and make insulting remarks about women, avoid raucous laughter and talking, observe "streetcar etiquette," and if possible bathe and change clothes after work and before boarding the streetcar. But to all these careful efforts white Chicagoans responded mostly with ill will, and Wentworth Avenue divided blacks and whites. To get on the white side meant trouble. The poet Langston Hughes, then a high school student, went walking during his first Sunday in Chicago in 1918 and met a group of white boys who said they "didn't allow niggers" in that neighborhood, and beat him. It was all rather dangerous for black children who had to cross over to school, and adults who had to cross to work in the Union Stockyards.

Blacks in Chicago fell victim to a race riot in the summer of 1918 resulting in the deaths of twenty-three blacks and fifteen whites and injury to five hundred Chicagoans of both races. A similar riot in East St. Louis the preceding year was nearly as bad, caused by the same problem, massive influx of blacks into a city unprepared to receive them. After the St. Louis riot 1,500 blacks marched down Fifth Avenue in New York in silent protest, with banners that Wilson might have read about in Washington: "Mr. President, Why Not Make AMERICA Safe for Democracy?" and "Patriotism and Loyalty Presuppose Protection and Liberty." A sign suppressed by police appealed to the President to "Bring Democracy to America Before You Carry It to Europe."

Mobs murdered seventy-eight black people in 1919, most of them in twenty-five urban race riots. That was fifteen people over 1918, thirty over 1917. Lynchings between 1896 and 1917 may have numbered nearly 3,000. In 1919 ten victims were veterans, several in uniform. The N.A.A.C.P. expressed shock in 1918 when mobs murdered two black men by fire; in 1919 mobs burned eleven. The Ku Klux Klan grew phenomenally in 1920, in part because of the Red Scare. The K.K.K. gave special attention to blacks.[47]

Within black society a debate went on between followers of the late Booker T. Washington of Tuskegee Institute and the Harvard-trained W. E. B. Du Bois of Atlanta University, between believers in the need for blacks to make themselves useful to white Americans through hard work and thereby receive respect, and believers in political activism. The debate hissed and sputtered, but the mass of blacks did not know of its existence, the dream of what America might be.

In conclusion one might well inquire how Woodrow Wilson's record in the presidency appeared on civil liberties and civil rights —in this dismal period in American history. Here one must say that it was considerably better than that of his countrymen. It is perhaps faint praise to say that the President did not stop the excesses of his era because he could not. At the worst of the hysteria, the time of the Palmer raids, he was ill, and it is an open question as to whether he ever knew the raids occurred. Such points nonetheless deserve to be made. Moreover, it is necessary to point out that he took positive measures to keep the country sane during the war. He killed the Chamberlain Bill for creation of military courts within the United States. He constantly sought to stem the tide of anti-German hysteria, notably in an appeal of 1918 to the American people. In prosecution of the war he refused to stir up hatred against the German people, always referring to the nation's enemies as Germany's leaders.

Everything considered, something also must be said for the country at large—namely, that despite its tarnished record on civil liberties and civil rights the United States was a civil libertarian paradise during the war, compared with the actions of Britain, France, and Germany.

20. Liberty Bond posters were everywhere, and some of them impossible to forget. Eddie Rickenbacker, the racing car driver who had gone to France with Pershing as a chauffeur and learned to fly, remembered his first thought when he went up in the air and met a German pilot. His heart had started pounding, but the image of a beautiful girl with outstretched arms arose in front of him, the above Liberty Bond poster with its message. He recalled that he did not have much choice.

21. Field Marshal Paul von Hindenburg was the nominal German commander on the Western Front, General Erich Ludendorff the actual commander, but the bulky Hindenburg made a better subject for posters.

22. In a gesture of wartime conservancy that caught national attention, President Wilson arranged for a flock of Shropshire Downs sheep to graze on the grounds in back of the White House. The sheep produced ninety-eight pounds of wool, which the Red Cross distributed among forty-eight states, Puerto Rico, Hawaii, and the Philippines, and auctioned it for $100,000.

23. In the presence of President and Mrs. Wilson the Emergency Fleet Corporation's great yard at Hog Island near Philadelphia launched its first ship, the *Quistconck* (Indian for Hog Island), on August 5, 1918. It was not delivered until December 3.

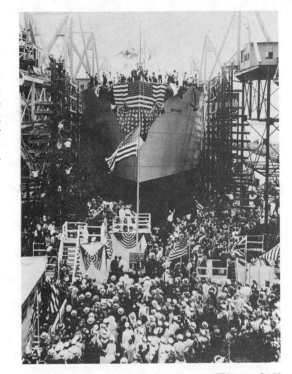

Keel Laid May 15th. Will Be Launched JUNE 1st. 4 DAYS OLD TO-DAY
SHE'S SOME BABY

24. *U.S.S. Ward* under construction at Mare Island Navy Yard, California, May 1918. Notice the small sign at right, "This destroyer is needed to sink Hun submarines." The *Ward* never sank a German submarine, but on the morning of December 7, 1941, an hour before the Japanese attacked Pearl Harbor, it sank a Japanese submarine trying to slip through the harbor defense nets. For the United States this was the opening shot of World War II.

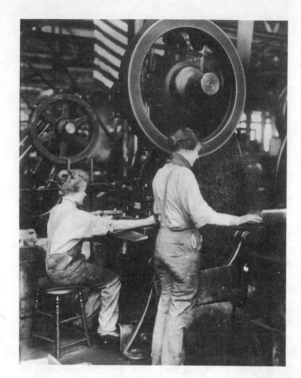

25.   In a Detroit shop.

26.   Colonel Edward M. House, adviser
of the President. Wilson broke with him
after the Paris Peace Conference.

27. The Big Four at the Paris Peace Conference, 1919. L. to r., Lloyd George, Orlando, Clemenceau, the President.

28. Paris welcomes the President, December 14, 1918.

29. Henry Cabot Lodge, chairman of the Senate Committee on Foreign Relations, 1919. Like Wilson, Lodge held a doctorate in American history, albeit from Harvard. Asked on one occasion about a Wilson speech, Lodge quipped that "It might get by at Princeton but not at Harvard."

30. The President in St. Paul, September 9, 1919. Behind Wilson, at the top of the rear platform, is his private secretary, Joseph P. Tumulty. Standing directly below the President is his personal physician, Rear Admiral Cary T. Grayson, flanked by secret servicemen, Colonel Edmund W. Starling (left) and Joseph E. Murphy. The President spoke to the state legislature in the morning, gave an address at the Minneapolis armory in the afternoon, and addressed 15,000 people in the St. Paul auditorium in the evening. He said that lowering the cost of living and bettering the relations of capital and labor awaited the restoration of a status of general peace.

31.   Parade during Western tour. Mrs. Wilson is seated beside the President.

32. The invalid on the White House grounds, winter of 1919–20. At left is Mrs. Wilson, at right the President's daughter Margaret.

33. Vice President Thomas R. Marshall. After Wilson suffered the stroke in October 1919, Marshall never saw him until the inauguration of Harding in March 1921.

34. Washington welcomes Pershing: parade up Pennsylvania Avenue, September 17, 1919. The reconstituted First Division of 24,000 men followed the same route taken by Civil War veterans in their Grand Review fifty-four years before. Photographed from an Army balloon.

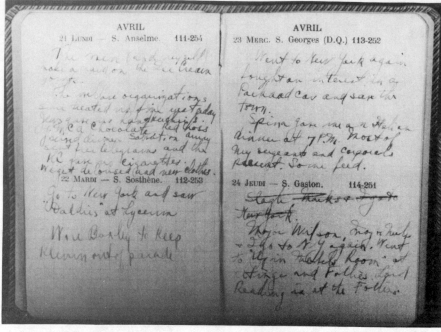

35, 36. Home from war: diary of Captain Truman, April 21-28, 1919. Truman and his men of Battery D, 129th Field Artillery Regiment, 35th Division, arrived in New York on Easter Sunday morning, April 20.

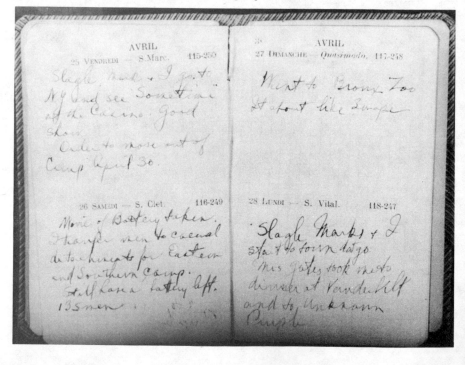

37.   Truman and Jacobson haberdashery at 104 West 12th Street, opposite the Muehlebach Hotel in Kansas City. Former Captain Truman at left.

38.   New York City office worker during influenza epidemic, October 16, 1918. Everyone wore gauze masks.

39.   Explosion at house of Attorney General A. Mitchell Palmer, Washington, June 2
1919. Explosions occurred within the same hour in eight cities, shattering public and
private buildings. Palmer's neighbor, Assistant Secretary of the Navy Roosevelt, called
the police, and another neighbor, Alice Roosevelt Longworth, daughter of former
President Theodore Roosevelt, rushed over to see grisly parts of a body, the man who
set the bomb, being laid out on newspapers.

40.   Court martial at Fort Sam Houston, Texas, of sixty-three members of 24th
Infantry, U.S. Army, for mutiny and murder of seventeen people in the city of Houston
on August 23, 1917. In early December the men were tried. Five were acquitted, four
sentenced to jail terms, forty-one to life imprisonment, thirteen to death. The latter
sentences were carried out by hanging on December 11.

41.   Franklin D. Roosevelt, Democratic nominee for Vice President, 1920.

42.   Woodrow Wilson at his last Cabinet meeting, March 3, 1921.

CHAPTER 13

The Election of 1920

T HE year 1919 had been extremely disheartening—everywhere the country's fortunes seemed on the downturn. Samuel Morison ended his diary for 1919 with a feeling of riddance: "Wilson passed the cup of hope of a new world. Dashed it from our lips, and now insists that we must assume we drank it after all." Everything had gone wrong. "And what a country we returned to! An orgy of extravagance, . . . and a rising cost of living, all . . . unselfishness gone. No leaders, the President morally and physically bankrupt. The Treaty-League attacked, but by what arguments! And what intolerance and hypocrisy. Cruelty to foreigners, shortsighted persecution of Reds, in effect, white terror!"[1]

For disillusioned young men the new year was to prove equally unattractive. The presidential election of 1920 could have brought the era's vexatious issues to decision. It did nothing of the sort, and turned everything into an argument over personality, and not that of Governor Cox or Senator Harding but President Wilson's.

As Morison wrote, there was no dearth of issues. Cox and Harding might have discussed the administration's failure to control inflation during and after the war; the economy was in straits by 1920, HCL rising at the time but about to end in a tailspin. Another issue could have been civil liberties—early in 1920 expulsion of the Socialists had turned opinion against the Red Scare, and excesses of the wartime and postwar periods needed public discussion. Civil rights should have been an issue: race riots and lynchings warranted national attention. Candidates might have discussed the administration's mismanagement of war industry. Or near mismanagement of the Army.

Bryan attempted to discover issues for the campaign, and came up with three, one of which should have been brought into the campaign and almost got there. In the way of orators, he described these issues as "reforms of the age." The first, Prohibition, however, became the law of the land in January 1920. The Eighteenth Amendment and the Volstead Act removed it from the political arena. It provided a momentary source of concern to delegates at the Democratic National Convention in San Francisco, who sang lustily, "How Dry I Am," for bootleg liquor was $9 a pint. To their rescue came the city's mayor, who provided a carload of old, mellow bourbon.

Bryan's second issue, woman suffrage, similarly had its resolution well before the election, with passage of the Nineteenth Amendment on August 26, 1920. For years men had opposed it, but it became irresistible when women took the places of men in industry and agriculture during the war and Daniels admitted women to the Navy and Marine Corps. Harding had declared in favor in 1917. A delegation of suffragettes had waited upon him and intimated "more strongly than discreetly" that it was time for a declaration if the Republican party wanted to take advantage of the situation; in reply he had said that his own personal judgment would not be determined by the political situation so much as by his conviction of justice to women.[2] President Wilson had opposed woman suffrage but changed his mind during the war; the women earned it, he told Axson, and he was only sorry it had to come through war.[3] He may have given in because of the spectacle of suffragettes before the White House, picketing for months, with a "perpetual fire" going in the park across the street, where they burned up every sentence he said about "liberty" or "democracy." Vice President Marshall supported the Nineteenth Amendment to stop the everlasting clatter of the suffragettes (so he wrote in his memoirs) in order that the government might transact business. He said he always had favored the vote for intelligent women.[4]

After passage of the suffrage amendment people spoke of what the female vote might do in 1920 and thereafter in American politics, and both parties took precautions, organizing women's divisions, putting women on national committees. At the Democratic convention delegates amused themselves by casting glances at women in their midst and breaking into song: "Oh, you beautiful doll . . ." In any event, doubling the vote made no discernible difference in the political equations.[5]

In such manner, for the most part with levity, the American people disposed of two of Bryan's reforms of the age. As for the third, peace, President Wilson envisioned it as membership in the League of Nations. This issue Wilson himself sought to inject into the presidential election of 1920.

The President at first had believed he could coerce the Senate into passing the treaty and Covenant through a special senatorial election. When the senators in November 1919 refused to consent to the treaty, Wilson had been too ill to think how to remedy the situation. In mid-December, having recovered a bit, he began to consider a solemn referendum in which he would challenge senators opposed to the League to resign and run on anti-League records. On December 18, 1919, Mrs. Wilson wrote Attorney General Palmer for information on state laws regarding senatorial vacancies. The President had in mind to challenge fifty-seven opposition senators from thirty-eight states to "take immediate steps to seek reelection." If voters reelected a majority, Wilson and Marshall would then resign after appointing a leader of the opposition party Secretary of State to succeed to the presidency. But this was a harebrained scheme. A special election would have reflected an impossible group of issues; no one, not even Wilson in his prime, with all his imperious energy, could have kept senators seeking reelection on the straight and narrow, devoting arguments to their anti-League records.[6]

In a Jackson Day message read before an assemblage in Washington on January 8, the President then made another proposal to push the treaty through: he would turn the presidential election itself into a referendum on the League. Again the idea was absurd, although perhaps not a supreme act of folly, as one historian has described it.[7] Just as Wilson could not have concentrated a special senatorial election on one topic, so he could not have forced presidential candidates to discuss a single issue. Moreover, the League issue still lay with the Senate, and not enough senators were coming up for reelection to allow passage of the League in the form Wilson desired. If every Democratic senator up for reelection won, and every Republican lost, the Democrats still would not have a two-thirds majority.[8] At the Jackson Day banquet Bryan said a treaty with reservations was better than one without, that it was silly to stick for no reservations. The audience was with him. Ambassador Davis in London, who was to be Democratic standard-bearer in 1924, wrote in his diary that "for the first time, I believe, . . . I find myself in accord with Bryan. It seems manifest to me that a compromise ratification is better than none at all, and only those who wish the defeat of the treaty entire can draw any satisfaction from the present situation."[9]

In January 1920, just after the President gave up the idea of a referendum for anti-League senators, about the time of his Jackson Day pronouncement, Grayson apparently took the courageous step of advising Wilson to resign, right then. What a pity the President did not do so! Wilson trusted the doctor more than any other human being except his wife. For Grayson to have suggested such a thing was surprising; his discretion, together with the fact that he was a fellow Virginian, had endeared him to the President. Moreover, there is only one piece of evidence, a thirdhand account. But the account is reliable, the diary of Ambassador John W. Davis. According to the diary, the ambassador had dinner with Undersecretary of State Norman Davis on September 2, 1920, after which Grayson came in and the three men talked until after midnight. "He describes the Pres. as 'amphibious' from time to time. Looks pale and has had an awful time of it. Especially interested in advice given Pres. last January to resign, his inclination, and Mrs. W's persuasion to the contrary. How different things might have been." In a diary entry for October 10, Davis cleared up what might seem an ambiguity in the above statement—that is, who advised Wilson to resign. Speaking of Wilson's inaccessibility (Davis had just come from a White House luncheon at which the President had absented himself because, Mrs. Wilson said, he had a nervous dread of seeing people), the ambassador remarked, "What could better justify Grayson's advice to him last January to resign."[10] One can only conclude that in a moment of depression the President had agreed with Grayson, but that Mrs. Wilson changed his mind because of her often expressed feeling that for him to leave the presidency would have interfered with recovery from the stroke.[11]

In any case, by the spring of 1920 the President's intimates saw that he desired a third term, and this helped bring his final League strategy into focus. Even in his crippled condition, barely able to walk with a cane, mental powers so impaired he could not hold attention on any problem, public or private, for more than a few minutes, Wilson believed he could defeat any candidate of the Republican party. The President had talked of retirement. Early in 1919 he had worked out a formula for a place to live after leaving the presidency, according to percentages for five factors—freedom, friendship, literary study, variety, and amusement.[12] As negotiation went on at Paris, and he sensed a gathering of opinion in the Senate, he may have weakened in his resolve to retire, and the weakening perhaps took the form of dislike of other candidates for the presidency. Edith Benham, secretary to Mrs. Wilson, who was accustomed to lunch with the Wilsons, sensed the President might run again. Wilson talked of the joy of being free and how nothing would induce him to run, but any mention of the name of a possible Democratic candidate inspired him to give conclusive reasons why the man should not run.[13] The same, of course, held for Republicans. John E. Nevin of the International News Service told Wilson in Paris in June that Harding was the choice of the inner circle that usually dominated the Republican machine. This surprised him, and he spoke of Harding as possessing absolutely no brains— the Republicans surely would not nominate him. Margaret Wilson asked Grayson who would be the probable Democratic candidate, and Grayson said it was still a secret, that the President "said that he did not know who the candidate would be but he felt very confident who it would not be."[14] Then one Sunday night in August 1919, sitting on the rear portico of the White House after dinner with Mrs. Wilson, Margaret, and the President, Axson heard Wilson say he did not think the two-term tradition was right and if he were younger he would be inclined to break it, just to do so; Wilson added the presidency was not itself a strong office, but what the holder made of it; neither Newton Baker nor Secretary of Agriculture Houston could be elected, although both were reflective men; and his son-in-law, McAdoo, was not reflective ("I never caught Mac reflecting"). A President, Wilson said, had to be reflective.[15]

By the spring of 1920 the presidential bug had bitten, and Wilson went to the length of writing out his acceptance speech. He did not make any open pronouncement of what he had in mind. The State Department had not "the vaguest idea" what he was going to do about the second failure of the treaty and the Covenant in March 1920.[16] The President, however, revealed his strategy to Grayson.

After the presidential election, he told Grayson, he hoped the Senate would be more amenable to an acceptable compromise. No group of Democrats had given him any assurance it wanted him as a candidate, and "In fact, everyone seems to be opposed to my running." But to withdraw would turn the party over to Bryan and diminish the prospect of making the League an issue. The convention might deadlock on candidates and need someone to lead them. Convention members might feel he was the logical leader, and he would accept "even if I thought it would cost me my life."[17]

Grayson, aghast at this prospect, went to see a Democratic publicist, Robert W. Woolley, and informed him that the President was permanently ill physically and gradually weakening mentally.[18] Wilson's friends then set to work.[19] Already the House of Representatives had cheered when a Democratic member asked for presidential withdrawal. At San Francisco, Daniels assembled Cabinet colleagues aboard a battleship, hoping to defeat the plans of Secretary of State Colby, who represented Wilson at the convention. Although the President's picture appeared prominently at San Francisco, Daniels and colleagues accomplished the behind-the-scenes work. McAdoo contended with Attorney General Palmer, who showed some strength; Wilson refused to endorse his son-in-law. Palmer's strength proved well short of enough to take the nomination, and after forty-four ballots the vote went to Cox.

Cox and the Democratic vice-presidential nominee, Franklin D. Roosevelt, did their best to produce a lively campaign. Cox traveled 22,000 miles into thirty-six states and addressed 2 million people. For a while F.D.R. stirred excitement, particularly in the West, and his friendly feeling for crowds came through. "Do you know," said the engineer on the Roosevelt train, "that lad's got a 'million vote smile' and mine's going to be one of them." His successes worried the Republicans, and the G.O.P. sent Theodore Roosevelt, Jr., to trail Franklin, with some effect, as T.R. Jr. had been in France in the Army and could claim an even better war record than Franklin, as well as being the son of the great T.R. "He is a maverick," said Ted Roosevelt in Sheridan, Wyoming. "He does not have the brand of our family." The Democratic Roosevelt then got himself into trouble by showing how the British Empire with six Dominion votes in the League Assembly was not better off than the United States, which had its client nations. "Why, I have been running Haiti or San Domingo for the past seven years," F.D.R. announced in San Francisco, speaking of his work supervising Marine occupations of the two republics. Another time he remarked that "I wrote Haiti's constitution myself and, if I do say it, I think it a pretty good constitution."[20]

But the Republicans were almost bound to win if they could produce an attractive candidate and eliminate any serious discussion of the peace issue and concentrate on Wilsonism.

The G.O.P. did not suffer from lack of candidates, even if something untoward tended to happen to most of them. Had Theodore Roosevelt lived—he died in January 1919—he might have been his party's standard-bearer. The nominee of 1916, Hughes, refused to consider renomination even though it meant election, heartbroken because of the death of a daughter from tuberculosis early in 1920. "I don't want to be President of the United States," he told a friend. Another possibility, Herbert Hoover, appeared indecisive as to party allegiance. He told Colonel House he was neither Democrat nor Republican, that he would have been a Democrat if not for the reactionary element in the South, Republican if not for the reactionary element in the East. There was talk of Pershing, who indicated he would accept; his father-in-law, Senator Warren, sensing the possibilities, wrote him that "way down underneath I must tell you that it looks very much as if *you are in for it.* . . . Best prepare for the White House!" Unfortunately Pershing entered the primary in Nebraska and lost.

The strongest Republican candidates were General Wood and Governor Frank O. Lowden of Illinois, both powerful men who might have made good Presidents. Both worked for the nomination. Wood spent $1.5 million and Lowden $414,000. Lowden money went into bank accounts of two delegates to the convention, and Senator Borah destroyed both Wood and Lowden, charging them with trying to buy the nomination.[21]

A series of meetings in the Blackstone Hotel pointed to an obvious compromise. The choice did not occur in a smoke-filled room but came out of the Wood-Lowden deadlock, the unavailability of other national figures, and Harding's own attractive qualities. He won on the tenth ballot. The decision took longer than any other in Republican history, save the choice of Garfield in 1880, and was the eleventh time a native of Ohio received the Republican nomination.[22]

The Republican convention balked over an effort by party managers to give the vice-presidential nomination to Senator Irvine L. Lenroot of Wisconsin. Two senators on the ticket seemed too much, and a small, haggard man, Wallace McCamant, stood on a chair in the Oregon section and shouted for "a man who is sterling in his Americanism and stands for all that the Republican Party holds dear." In a hotel room in Boston not long afterward Governor Coolidge put down the telephone and turned to his wife, Grace.

"Nominated for Vice President," said he.

"You aren't going to take it, are you?" said she.

"I suppose I'll have to," was the response.

Coolidge had made a national reputation during the police strike when, after doing nothing, he waited until rioting ceased and brought in the militia and declared in a telegram to Gompers, "There is no right to strike against the public safety by anybody, anywhere, any time." The public gained the impression he had saved the country in a Second Battle of Boston against the Reds instead of the Redcoats. During the campaign he assisted the ticket by thrifty remarks, affirming that rent for his half of the Massasoit Street double house in Northampton, which he rented from his mother-in-law, was $32 a month and that he was afraid she would raise it.[23]

The G.O.P.'s move back to conservatism, with the handsome standpatter Harding, caught party liberals by surprise, and they found they had nowhere else to go. It was farewell to twenty years of Theodore Roosevelt. William Allen White, who had favored Hoover, had warned the Kansas delegation against Harding, and contemplated apostasy, jumping into the fiery furnace as a martyr, but opted to "save my hide and go along on the broad way that leadeth to destruction." He had followed the Kansas banner in the convention parade for Harding, ashamed, disheveled in body and spirit, a "sad fat figure" toddling along while bands played, trumpets brayed, and the crowd howled.[24]

During the campaign that autumn Harding said little that was memorable. At the outset there was some thought he should not speak; former Senator Boies Penrose of Pennsylvania advised G.O.P. leaders to "Keep Warren at home. Don't let him make any speeches. If he goes out on a tour, somebody's sure to ask him questions, and Warren's just the sort of damn fool that'll try to answer them." The candidate remodeled the front porch of his Marion house after the Victorian style of the McKinley house in

Canton, and even brought the McKinley flagpole to Marion; flag-raising ceremonies each day lent color to the campaign. Early in August the man whom Oswald G. Villard of the *Nation* described as the Marion marionette got off the front porch and traveled to Min-neapolis, and by the end of the campaign had made 112 speeches around the country. His oratory was safe. Months before the nomi-nation he had remarked that "America's present need is not heroics but healing; not nostrums but normalcy; not revolution but restora-tion." Rarely did he rise above such pronouncements. McAdoo years later said Harding spoke in a "big, bow-wow style" of oratory and used words that had no relation to the topic at hand, "an army of pompous phrases moving over the landscape in search of an idea." Sometimes, he said, the words captured a straggling thought and bore it triumphantly, a prisoner in their midst, until it died of overwork.[25]

Harding privately characterized his speeches as "bloviation," thereby coining a word ("normalcy," also often listed as his coinage, went back far before his time), and they proved a severe test to some Republicans accustomed to something better. Senator Lodge and his Boston friends were beside themselves, for no Republican of national stature in recent years had spoken like Harding. The editor and author John T. Morse was scathing. "Why does he not get a private Secretary who can clothe for him his 'ideas' in the language customarily used by educated men?" Morse demanded. At a club dinner, conversation turned to the difficult position of a special French envoy to the United States, Viviani, who spoke no English. "Neither can Mr. Harding," Morse remarked slyly.[26]

With such a candidate, no one knew—that is, could understand —the Republican position on the League. Harding himself knew very well what he was doing—he was a lazy man, not a stupid one. His obfuscation on the League issue was deliberate, a way of keep-ing his party together on a divisive issue. In the Senate he had been a strong reservationist who had drifted in and out of the camp of the irreconcilables. In the campaign he drifted in and out of the camp of the League supporters. He championed not Wilson's League but "an association of nations, cooperating in sublime ac-cord, to attain and preserve peace through justice rather than force, determined to add security through international law, so clarified that no misconstruction can be possible without affronting world honor." Elihu Root arranged a form of words that thirty-one prominent Republicans signed to draw attention to the need to take the country into the League. Root was no believer in an unreserved League, and his formula was as obscure as Harding's. It seemed to say the issue was the Wilson League based on force versus an "Americanized" League based on law. Years later one of the signers, a protégé of Root's, Henry L. Stimson, said Harding had deceived him.[27]

In the end the campaign centered on Wilson. Harding had a few "issues" that he pushed. "America first" covered many of them, which included immigration restriction, higher tariff duties, repayment of war loans, strong merchant marine—all of these fitted in with his antipathy toward the League. But Senator Lodge had made the keynote address to the Republican convention: "Mr. Wilson and his dynasty, his heirs and assigns, or anybody that is his, anybody who with bent knee has served his purpose, must be driven from all control of the government and all influence in it."[28] The New York *Post* beheld a colossal protest against the President. The *Tribune* believed the country weary of Wilsonism in all its manifestations.

The main problem had been the President's constant summoning of the country to idealism. For eight years the nation had listened to calls for Progressivism, a New Freedom, New Diplomacy, Making the World Safe for Democracy, Preserving the Heart of the World. A secondary problem had been the President's demand for his League as he had drawn it at Paris; anyone else's League was in error. The Democrats also had grossly mismanaged reconversion of the economy. Wilson admittedly had been out of the country and then become ill during reconversion, and no President had ever done much anyway about the economy after a war; his war leadership nonetheless had accustomed people to look to him and he offered little, and when in the summer of 1920 just before the Democratic convention he made a show that his health was coming back (he gave an interview to a friendly newspaperman) it only demonstrated his incapacity.

Stephen T. Early, later press secretary to President Franklin Roosevelt, in 1920 a worker for the Democratic National Committee, wrote from Sioux Falls, South Dakota: "The bitterness toward Wilson is evident everywhere and deeply rooted. He hasn't a friend." Franklin K. Lane, who resigned as Secretary of the Interior in February 1920, wrote that things looked dark politically, the little

Wilson (as distinguished from the Great Wilson) was having his day, Cox making a manly fight on behalf of the President's League but the administration sullen, do-nothing, Cox would lose because of popular dislike of Wilson. Cox thus was beaten because Wilson was as unpopular as he had once been popular. "Oh! if he had been frank as to his illness, the people would have forgotten everything, his going to Paris, his refusal to deal with the mild Reservationists —everything would have been swept away in a great wave of sympathy. But he could not be frank, he who talked so high of faith in the people distrusted them; and they will not be mastered by mystery. So he is so much less than a hero that he bears down his party to defeat."[29]

The brush of Wilsonism tarred everything. German-Americans, independent radicals, antiwar agrarians held him responsible for their experiences; race riots antagonized blacks; unions resented inaction in the steel strike and the return of railroads to private ownership;[30] isolationists and idealists were angry over the Peace Conference; farmers were up in arms because during the war a southern President refused to put a ceiling on cotton, and in 1920 failed to stop the plunge of farm prices.

Idealism went down to defeat—and not merely did the Democrats get defeated but they found themselves caught in a landslide, an earthquake, a deluge: 9 million votes for Cox and Roosevelt, 16 million for Harding and Coolidge. Cox was the most badly beaten Democrat since Stephen A. Douglas.[31]

Right up to the day of the election, Wilson believed Cox would win. When Stockton Axson objected, the answer was: "You pessimist! You don't know the American people. They always rise to a moral occasion. Harding will be deluged."[32]

Afterward came the appraisals. Harding's victory speech on the evening of November 4 was florid but clear. "You just didn't want a surrender of the United States of America; you wanted America to go under American ideals," he shouted. "That's why you didn't care for the League, which is now deceased." Lodge in a private letter put the issue more succinctly: "We have torn up Wilsonism by the roots."[33] Senator Smoot, one of Wilson's severest critics, wrote in his diary that the American people had answered Wilson's solemn referendum, that it was a great day for America. Later he talked to Senators Gore and Reed, both Democrats, and found them much pleased by the defeat of their own party. He believed the Democrats generally did not care, for "they are all pleased to get rid of Wilson."[34]

The Senate meanwhile had begun to entertain projects for a separate peace with the defeated European nations, and gradually these projects turned into reality, a formal end to World War I.[35] In the spring of 1920, Senator Knox had offered a peace resolution, and it passed on May 20, whereupon Wilson vetoed it. The proposal went through six major revisions and finally became the basis of a joint resolution that President Harding signed on July 2, 1921, ending the technical state of war with the enemy belligerents of Europe. A treaty signed in Berlin on August 25 confirmed to the United States all rights and advantages of the Treaty of Versailles. The Harding administration signed similar treaties with Austria on August 24 and Hungary on August 29. Other treaties established diplomatic relations with the seven European succession states. In 1927 an executive agreement by Harding's successor, Coolidge, established relations with Turkey.

CHAPTER 14

Conclusion

W OODROW Wilson told a Princeton friend in 1913 that it
would be an irony of fate if his administration had to deal
chiefly with foreign affairs. The ironical became fact. The President
soon was instructing his fellow citizens that America up to that time
by choice confined and provincial henceforth would belong to the
world, its purposes tested by those of mankind and not national
ambition.

As fate changed Wilson's presidency, so it changed the lives of
Europeans. Armageddon, too, had caught them unprepared; when
hostilities opened in 1914 they believed the war could not last more
than a few months.[1]

How to understand World War I? The scale of events, the more
than four years of destruction, bore no comparison to wars of the
Victorian era. With a feeling almost akin to admiration Winston
Churchill looked back to the nineteenth century's "small wars between great nations, its earnest disputes about superficial issues, the
high, keen intellectualism of its personages, the sober, frugal, narrow limitations of their action," all of which, he said, belonged to
a vanished age. "The smooth river with its eddies and ripples along
which we then sailed, seems inconceivably remote from the cataract
down which we have been hurled and the rapids in whose turbu-
lence we are now struggling." The fire roared on, he wrote, changing the metaphor, until it burned itself out: "events passed very
largely outside the scope of conscious choice. Governments and

individuals conformed to the rhythm of the tragedy, and swayed and staggered forward in helpless violence, slaughtering and squandering on ever-increasing scales, till injuries were wrought to the structure of human society which a century will not efface, and which may conceivably prove fatal to the present civilization."[2]

War in 1914–18 became the great auditor of institutions. It pitilessly revealed British industrial decay, French economic and social obsolescence, Russian economic and social and political weakness. One of the war's surprises was its revelation of Germany's technological and military strength—far beyond what contemporaries had anticipated.[3] German military power produced a series of Sommes and Passchendaeles. All the while the leaders of each nation promised its citizens victory, maintaining control by promises; and all the while the mounting human costs required ever more rewards. The nation that succumbed to defeat would almost inevitably succumb —given the promises—to revolution.[4]

The turning point came in 1917, the year of American entry and Russian withdrawal, the turning point not only in the war but, as the future showed, in history itself. In 1917 the European frame of modern history finally collapsed. Until then, it had been possible to write the history of modern times in terms of Europe. The illusion was not merely European but American: the whole rationale of American isolation assumed a European equilibrium.[5] The illusion shattered when, at last, it was necessary to bring in the Americans.

Victory on November 11, 1918, was preeminently the victory of the U.S. Army. One might argue who won the war, but no one could deny the difference made by two million troops from the New World. Beginning in 1917, the strategy of the British and French— of Haig and Pétain—was to wait for the Americans, the strategy of Ludendorff was to break through before their arrival. The dramatic appearance of the Second Division's Marine brigade in Belleau Wood—the clouds of dust, trucks bumper to bumper full of singing Americans: here was one of the great moments of our century. A few weeks later came the stand of U. G. McAlexander's regiment and the counteroffensive at Soissons, the roll-up of the St. Mihiel salient and then of the Meuse-Argonne, when Pershing threw in hundreds of thousands of men, division after huge division. For the Germans and the Allies it was the end.

Destiny then posed a question to the people of the United States —would they accept world responsibility? Before the American people could poise their minds on the question, Wilson's stubbornness brought disaster. Lloyd George told the American Ambassador in London that the Allies had offered America leadership of the world, and the Senate threw the scepter into the sea.[6]

Americans, new to world power, could not easily understand it; thus the opportunity for dominance in international relations was lost. Just a generation earlier the country had emerged as the world's greatest industrial power. The Spanish War had raised the question of world responsibility. The territories of 1898 were imperial, and so were the protectorates in Panama, Cuba, Santo Domingo, Nicaragua, Haiti. But Americans did not view sovereignty over the Philippines or hegemony over Central America and the Caribbean as an attractive enterprise. Local populations showed little enthusiasm for American rule. The country was debating this colonial expansion when the European war broke out in 1914. Only a short time was available for the President to present his own vision of world responsibility. Wilson at first spoke cautiously. Toward the end of the war he began to organize his ideas. His countrymen concentrated on victory, for until the war's last months they "had not demonstrated, no less to Europe than to themselves, that they were capable of large and sustained military action overseas."[7] It did not take much confusion, little more than the Paris Peace Conference and the League fight, to return the country to the nineteenth-century stance of isolationism.

To write of failure to accept world political responsibility is to say nothing of economics. A few Americans sensed what was to happen after 1919–20. In a series of lectures Henry L. Stimson, who became Secretary of State in 1929, considered what the industrial revolution had wrought—a much more fragile civilization, he said, a complex of industry, communication, and markets that could collapse during a war, threatening the livelihoods of masses of Europeans.[8] The Paris statesmen of 1919 did not understand economics. Wilson had devoted most of his life to academe, Lloyd George had been a political agitator, Clemenceau a journalist. The statesmen also were busy with the Covenant, penalties against the Central Powers, national self-determination, interviews with suitors and suppliants. The important economic problems were long-range and would not come to crisis within the next year or two, and Wilson believed the League could handle them. But within a decade the economies of the industrial nations collapsed in the Great Depression. The issues of the twenties were political when they should have been economic, the thirties issues economic when they should have been political.

And yet by ensuring Allied victory in 1918 the American people had not really forced this huge change upon history. Blame for what came afterward belonged to Europe, where for decades every large nation had engaged in diplomatic error, especially the government of Prussia prior to 1870, Imperial Germany afterward. When hostilities opened in 1914 the German government fought to the end, unwilling to compromise. It created a situation (hardly comparable in scale, of course) akin to that in Cuba where in the nineties the Spanish had refused to settle with the insurgents, a hopeless situation, and where McKinley like Wilson a generation later had to send in the Army and Navy.

World War I did teach America some lessons.[9] The country learned to operate under alliance conditions. Only once, in the Revolution, had Americans fought in alliance. In World War I, Wilson pursued too independent a course, describing the country as an Associate rather than Ally, refusing military liaison, proposing peace terms without consultation, compromising awkwardly at the Peace Conference, failing with the Senate. Wilson's successors in World War II acted much better. President Roosevelt established an Anglo-American Combined Chiefs of Staff sitting in Washington, in contrast to Wilson's refusal of military liaison. Roosevelt and his successor Truman stated war aims in realizable terms. In creating another world organization they treated the Senate with respect— the U.N. Charter passed by a vote of 89 to 2, and if the second world organization later failed it was not because of domestic politics.

Whether economic mobilization during World War I taught any lesson is less easy to say. Wilson, even more than Theodore Roosevelt, had established precedents for government intervention in the economy. In organizing the New Deal, President Franklin D. Roosevelt turned for advice to several officials of the earlier era. The National Recovery Administration resembled the wartime War Industries Board in its effort to organize cooperation between government and industry during a great national emergency. The N.R.A. like the wartime Treasury Department conducted an ambitious public relations program; indeed the N.R.A. administrator, Hugh Johnson, consulted McAdoo, who recommended that he employ the organizers of the Liberty and Victory Loan drives. Curiously, however, and despite the fact that the nation had about the same time to prepare economically in 1939–41 as in 1914–17, F.D.R. moved very slowly. After Pearl Harbor, American industry produced in "miraculous" fashion, unlike World War I, enough to equip its own armed forces and the Allies. But it did not reach full production until 1944, too late to keep the Soviet Union out of Eastern Europe and save millions of Jews from extermination camps.

The U.S. Army failed to profit from its harrowing experience in 1917–18, of changing from a small garrison into a mass army. World War I veterans dominated the Army after 1918; from Pershing to George C. Marshall, every Chief of Staff had served in France. The Army tried to arouse Congress, which may have been the culprit. But on September 1, 1939, the Army was not much larger than on April 2, 1917. By Pearl Harbor it was larger but grossly inadequate for a two-front war.

During and after World War II the United States avoided claims for war debts and reparations: Roosevelt substituted "lend-lease" and Truman the Marshall Plan.

The deplorable return to laissez-faire economics after World War I was not repeated after World War II. The International Monetary Fund managed world currencies until the early seventies, the World Bank stabilized finances, and the General Agreement on Tariffs and Trade reduced trade barriers.

Failure of many World War I veterans to adjust to civil life, and contention over the Bonus Act, persuaded Congress in 1944 to pass the so-called G.I. Bill of Rights, which among other benefits offered veterans college and university educations and in many cases changed their lives.

During World War II the American government acted more sensibly over civil liberties, save the forced relocation of Japanese-Americans. The Army and Navy again segregated black Americans, and again race riots broke out in northern industrial cities. After World War II another Red Scare mindlessly repeated the errors of 1919–20.

Success and failure—such, perhaps, makes up the inevitable balance sheet in human affairs. Wonderfully prophetic were the words of Woodrow Wilson, that America by choice had been confined and provincial and henceforth belonged to the world. The leader failed in the testing time that followed. But so did leaders of later generations as they confronted the almost intractable problems of the twentieth century.

Notes

Chapter 1. April 1917

1. Ellery Sedgwick, *The Happy Profession* (Boston, 1946), pp. 184–185.
2. Arthur S. Link, *Woodrow Wilson: Revolution, War, and Peace* (Arlington Heights, Ill., 1979), p. xv. In this new edition of *Wilson the Diplomatist: A Look at His Major Foreign Policies* (Baltimore, 1957), Link writes, "If I were writing these pages now, I would give much greater emphasis than I did in the original text to Wilson's conviction that the war was in its final stages, American belligerency would have the effect of shortening, not prolonging, the war, and belligerency had the one advantage of guaranteeing him an important role in peacemaking." Author of the preceding volume in the present series, *Woodrow Wilson and the Progressive Era: 1910–1917* (New York, 1954), Link is editor of *The Papers of Woodrow Wilson* (Princeton, N.J., 1966–), forty-seven volumes published to date (1984), and author of the magisterial *Wilson* (Princeton, N.J., 1947–), of which five volumes have appeared, for 1856–1917.
3. Arthur S. Link, *Wilson: Campaigns for Progressivism and Peace, 1916–1917* (Princeton, N.J., 1965), pp. 419–431; Arthur Walworth, *Woodrow Wilson* (3d ed., 2 vols. in 1, New York, 1978), II, 97–100; Arthur S. Link et al. (eds), *The Papers of Woodrow Wilson*, vol. 41 (1983), 523, 526–527. Also John Milton Cooper, Jr., *The Warrior and the Priest: Woodrow Wilson and Theodore Roosevelt* (Cambridge, Mass., 1983), pp. 303–323.
4. *Historical Statistics of the United States: Colonial Times to 1970* (Washington, D.C., 1975), pp. 116–117.

5. John Higham, *Strangers in the Land: Patterns of American Nativism, 1860–1925* (New Brunswick, N.J., 1955), p. 200.

6. Edith Bolling Wilson, *My Memoir* (Indianapolis, 1939), p. 101.

7. *Historical Statistics of the United States,* pp. 224, 869, 903, 906. Also Charles Gilbert, *American Financing of World War I* (Westport, Conn., 1970).

8. Ship tonnage is defined four ways. Net tonnage represents the amount after deduction of space for machinery and officers' and crew's quarters, gross tonnage gives total enclosed capacity, and deadweight refers to cargo capacity on the basis of weight. Displacement indicates weight of water displaced by a loaded ship, and is the normal basis for measuring warships but is "seldom used in the merchant marine except to make a cruise ship seem larger than she really is." Ordinary ratio of net, gross, and deadweight for freighters is 3–5–8. Robert Greenhalgh Albion and Jennie Barnes Pope, *Sea Lanes in Wartime: The American Experience, 1775–1942* (New York, 1942), pp. 180–181. Unless otherwise specified, all figures in the present book are gross tonnage.

9. *Historical Statistics of the United States,* p. 168; Thomas C. Cochran and William Miller, *The Age of Enterprise: A Social History of Industrial America* (3d ed., New York, 1961), p. 309.

10. *Historical Statistics of the United States,* pp. 212–213.

11. Louis Galambos, *The Public Image of Big Business in America, 1880–1940: A Quantitative Study in Social Change* (Baltimore, 1975), pp. 185, 259–261. See also Alfred D. Chandler, *Strategy and Structure* (Cambridge, Mass., 1962); James Weinstein, *The Corporate Ideal in the Liberal State: 1900–1918* (Boston, 1968); Glenn Porter, *The Rise of Big Business: 1860–1910* (New York, 1973); and Ellis W. Hawley, *The Great War and the Search for a Modern Order: A History of the American People and Their Institutions, 1917–1933* (New York, 1979). Also George Soule, *Prosperity Decade: From War to Depression, 1917–1929* (New York, 1947); Cochran and Miller, *The Age of Enterprise;* and especially Samuel P. Hays, *The Response to Industrialism: 1885–1914* (Chicago, 1957).

12. The strange "duality" in American foreign policy appears in Calvin D. Davis, *The United States and the First Hague Peace Conference* (Ithaca, N.Y., 1962); see the same author's *The United States and the Second Hague Peace Conference: American Diplomacy and International Organization, 1899–1914* (Durham, N.C., 1975).

13. Diary of Reed Smoot, courtesy of Jan Shipps, Indiana University–Purdue University, Indianapolis.

14. The literature of American entrance into World War I is huge, and suffice to mention Link's *Woodrow Wilson and the Progressive Era,* his biographical volumes on President Wilson, the excellent study by

Ernest R. May, *The World War and American Isolation: 1914–1917* (Cambridge, Mass., 1966), Patrick Devlin, *Too Proud to Fight: Woodrow Wilson's Neutrality* (New York, 1975); and—from the German side—the landmark work by Fritz Fischer, *Griff nach der Weltmacht: Die Kriegszielpolitik des kaiserlichen Deutschland, 1914–18* (Duesseldorf, 1961) and its English edition, *Germany's Aims in the First World War* (New York, 1967), together with Reinhard R. Doerries, *Washington-Berlin: 1908–1917* (Duesseldorf, 1975), on the German Ambassador in Washington, Count Johann von Bernstorff, and the same author's "New Light on Germany's Foreign Policy and America's Entry into World War I," *Central European History*, vol. 11 (1978), 23–49, stressing Germany's ill-conceived propaganda campaign, a network of sabotage agents, refusal of mediation despite the battlefield stalemate, unrestricted submarine warfare, and the absurd alliance offer to Mexico —the so-called Zimmermann telegram.

15. Stockton Axson memoir of Woodrow Wilson, ch. entitled "Neutrality and the League of Nations Idea," pp. 1–5; typescript in the office of The Papers of Woodrow Wilson, Princeton University Library, Princeton, N.J. See also Cary T. Grayson, *Woodrow Wilson: An Intimate Memoir* (New York, 1960), p. 38.

16. Memorandum by Charles Seymour of a conversation with Whitlock, Brussels, Dec. 23, 1924, box 52, Seymour MSS, Yale University Library, New Haven, Conn. See also Sir Cecil Spring Rice to the Foreign Office, Jan. 9, 1918, in Arthur S. Link et al. (eds.), *The Papers of Woodrow Wilson*, vol. 45 (1984), 549, in which the British Ambassador related that the President always had known the United States would be drawn into the war. The country, however, was not united on intervention until the final moment. Wilson, the ambassador wrote, had studied German books in the university and always disliked German institutions.

17. Stockton Axson memoir of Wilson, ch. entitled "The Big Four," pp. 12–13; also "Woodrow Wilson's Educational Career," p. 4, insert "A"; Grayson, *Woodrow Wilson*, pp. 75–79. En route aboard the *George Washington* the President told his physician, Rear Admiral Grayson, that "at one time if it had not been for his realization that Germany was the scourge of the world, he would have been ready to have it out with England." Grayson diary, Dec. 8, 1918, office of The Papers of Woodrow Wilson.

18. Charles Seymour (ed.), *The Intimate Papers of Colonel House* (4 vols., Boston, 1926–28), II, 412.

19. Diary of Edward M. House, Aug. 25, 1922, House MSS, Yale University Library.

20. Letter of Aug. 22, 1915, Edith B. Wilson MSS, Library of Congress,

Washington, D.C. For a selection from this correspondence, see
Edwin Tribble (ed.), *A President in Love: The Courtship Letters of Woodrow
Wilson and Edith Bolling Galt* (Boston, 1981).
21. Link, *Wilson the Diplomatist*, p. 21.

Chapter 2. War

1. James G. Harbord, *The American Army in France: 1917–1919* (Boston,
   1936), p. 4. For more recent accounts of the U.S. Army and World
   War I, see Harvey A. DeWeerd, *President Wilson Fights His War: World
   War I and the American Intervention* (New York, 1968), a volume in the
   Macmillan Wars of the United States series; and Edward M. Coffman,
   *The War to End All Wars: The American Military Experience in World War
   I* (New York, 1968).
2. Michael J. Lenihan, "I Remember—I Remember," typescript remi-
   niscence, told to Mina W. Lenihan, c. 1956–57, copy in U.S. Army
   Military History Institute, Carlisle Barracks, Penn.
3. Charles D. Rhodes, Preface to "Diary Notes of a Soldier," manuscript
   in library of National Archives, Washington, D.C.
4. Henry L. Stimson and McGeorge Bundy, *On Active Service in Peace and
   War* (New York, 1948), p. 88.
5. For the draft, see David A. Lockmiller, *Enoch H. Crowder: Soldier,
   Lawyer and Statesman* (Columbia, Mo., 1955); John Garry Clifford, *The
   Citizen Soldiers: The Plattsburg Training Camp Movement, 1913–1920*
   (Lexington, Ky., 1972); David M. Kennedy, *Over Here: The First World
   War and American Society* (New York, 1980); I. B. Holley, Jr., *General
   John M. Palmer, Citizen Soldiers, and the Army of a Democracy* (Westport,
   Conn., 1982).
6. H. C. Peterson and Gilbert C. Fite, *Opponents of War: 1917–1918*
   (Madison, Wis., 1957), p. 234; Joan M. Jensen, *The Price of Vigilance*
   (Chicago, 1968), on the A.P.L.; Kennedy, *Over Here*, pp. 165–167;
   Gregory to Wilson, Sept. 9, and diary of Josephus Daniels, Sept. 10,
   in Arthur S. Link et al. (eds.), *The Papers of Woodrow Wilson*, vol. 49
   (Princeton, N.J., forthcoming); Cary T. Grayson diary, June 4, 1919,
   office of The Papers of Woodrow Wilson, Princeton University Library, Princeton, N.J. For Gregory's defense of the A.P.L. in 1917
   against objections by Secretary of the Treasury William G. McAdoo
   and by the President see *The Papers of Woodrow Wilson*, vol. 42 (1983),
   440–443, 446, 509–519.
7. An individualist, Bergdoll had failed courses at the University of
   Pennsylvania, preferring to spend his time piloting an airplane and
   racing automobiles. In the latter occupation he collected traffic tick-

ets for speeding on public roads, and served three months in jail for driving without a license. When his final draft notice arrived he vanished, but sent postcards to the government and visited his mother in Philadelphia. Government agents caught him on one of his postwar visits and turned him over to the Army. He escaped captivity under bizarre circumstances and departed for Germany; years later he came back voluntarily and served two years in prison. In 1950 his son Albert was arrested for draft evasion. For an entertaining account, see Pierce G. Fredericks, *The Great Adventure: America in the First World War* (New York, 1960), pp. 197–198.

8. Mark Sullivan, *Our Times: The United States, 1900–1925* (6 vols., New York, 1926–35), V, 310–311; George Soule, *Prosperity Decade: From War to Depression, 1917–1929* (New York, 1947), p. 38. A statistician later calculated that the Army used enough lumber in all the cantonments to build a twelve-inch-wide and one-inch-thick boardwalk to the moon and halfway back.

9. The problem of insurance logistics persuaded the War Department in February 1918 to give each soldier a serial number. By that time insurance records were getting out of hand. With each soldier's name on a card, filed vertically, records extended for three miles and contained 25,270 soldiers named Jones, 26,620 Millers, 28,140 Williamses, 29,960 Browns, 41,580 Johnsons, and 55,180 Smiths. *Infantry Journal*, vol. 19 (1921), 195. For the insurance system, see William G. McAdoo, *Crowded Years* (Boston, 1931), pp. 430–435. The Army exerted pressure on men to take out insurance, and Major General William H. Johnson wrote Baker on Feb. 12, 1918, that at Camp Travis, Texas, "I gave a holiday yesterday to all insured, and confined to quarters all others until insured. This plan proved effective . . ." He insured every officer and all but 200 men out of 28,500. Those not insured included sixty-seven Mennonites and possibly fifty conscientious objectors—really, he added, pro-Germans "whom I am investigating for trial for sedition, or discharge." He hoped to wire $250 million. Baker MSS, Library of Congress.

10. Coffman, *The War to End All Wars*, pp. 60–61; Fred Davis Baldwin, "The American Enlisted Man in World War I," Princeton University dissertation, 1964, pp. 67–79; Daniel J. Kevles, "Testing the Army's Intelligence: Psychologists and the Military in World War I," *Journal of American History*, vol. 55 (1968–69), 565–581. Alvin York, a draftee who twice appealed for deferment, was inducted Nov. 14, 1917, before the Army's testing program was in full swing, and seems not to have taken a test. For his incredible exploit during the Battle of the Meuse-Argonne see Frank E. Vandiver, "Alvin Cullum York,"

Dictionary of American Biography, Supplement Seven (New York, 1981), pp. 806–808; Tom Skeyhill (ed.), *Sergeant York: His Own Life Story and War Diary* (New York, 1928).

11. Arthur E. Barbeau and Florette Henri, *The Unknown Soldiers: Black American Troops in World War I* (Philadelphia, 1974), pp. 45–48. Brigham recanted this conclusion in 1930, describing it as pretentious and without foundation. Matthew T. Downey, *Carl Campbell Brigham: Scientist and Educator* (Princeton, N.J., 1961), pp. 26–28.

12. Colonel George C. Marshall did not object to the tests but to inability of draftees to reason well, even if they possessed high school diplomas. To the inquiry, "If a horse standing on four feet weighs twelve hundred pounds, how much does it weigh when standing on three feet," thousands of men answered nine hundred pounds. Joseph L. Collins, Jr. (ed.), George C. Marshall, *Memoirs of My Services in the World War, 1917–1918* (Boston, 1976), p. 79.

13. For prostitution near the cantonments and bases see Baldwin, "The American Enlisted Man in World War I," pp. 34–45, 111–115. Walter Camp conducted an exercise program for Washington officials, and Secretary Daniels, who detested exercise, found the result amusing. Secretary of the Interior Franklin K. Lane, Secretary McAdoo, Assistant Secretary of the Navy Franklin D. Roosevelt, and two admirals had to go to the hospital. When Camp got after Daniels for being a slacker, Daniels consulted Dr. Sterling Ruffin. "Joe," said the doctor, "you never took any exercise in your life. You never walked when you could ride. Stay away from that crowd and you'll live longer." Jonathan Daniels, *The End of Innocence* (Philadelphia, 1954), pp. 230–231. In his memoirs Daniels recalled that "Walter and his pupils have passed on, while I was strong and vigorous when I celebrated my eighty-third birthday." *The Wilson Era: Years of War and After, 1917–1923* (Chapel Hill, N.C., 1946), p. 194.

14. Hermann Hagedorn, *Leonard Wood: A Biography* (2 vols., New York, 1931), II, 240–241.

15. Peyton C. March, *The Nation at War* (Garden City, N.Y., 1932), pp. 361–362.

16. Keppel to Newton D. Baker, Apr. 17, 1919, John McA. Palmer MSS, Library of Congress.

17. William Matthews and Dixon Wecter, *Our Soldiers Speak: 1775–1918* (Boston, 1943), pp. 280–287.

18. Margaret L. Coit, *Mr. Baruch* (Boston, 1957), p. 170.

19. Baker had taken Wilson's Hopkins course on the theory of administration. His pastoral view of his office appears in Elting E. Morison, "Newton D. Baker," *Dictionary of American Biography, Supplement Two* (New York, 1958), pp. 17–19. Baker told Frederick Palmer that his

father, a Confederate soldier, many times said the Confederates did well because of the free hand that President Jefferson Davis gave Lee, compared to the meddling of Lincoln and Secretary of War Edwin M. Stanton. Frederick Palmer, *Newton D. Baker: America at War* (2 vols., New York, 1931), I, 159. C. H. Cramer, *Newton D. Baker: A Biography* (Cleveland, 1961), p. 138, writes that Baker was the head, not figurehead, of a great successful enterprise, who gave the military opportunities. But Daniel Beaver, *Newton D. Baker and the American War Effort: 1917–1919* (Lincoln, Nebr., 1966), p. 109, sees Baker as seriously deficient as late as the end of 1917: "it is impossible to escape the conclusion that he had not yet shown the qualities that characterize a great Secretary of War." James E. Hewes, Jr., agrees: "Secretary Baker had allowed the department's operations to drift until the resultant anarchy threatened to paralyze the war effort." *From Root to McNamara: Army Organization and Administration, 1900–1963* (Washington, D.C., 1975), p. 49.

20. Baker's initial difficulty was that he knew nothing about the War Department. James W. Wadsworth memoir, pp. 179ff., Oral History Collection, Columbia University, New York. For the bureau system, see James E. Hewes, Jr., "The War Department," *Dictionary of American History* (rev. ed., 7 vols., New York, 1976), VII, 229–230; and the same author's "The United States Army General Staff, 1900–1917," *Military Affairs*, vol. 38 (1974), 67–71. The Spanish American War analogue was unfair to the War Department, which had done better than was popularly believed. See David R. Trask, *The War with Spain in 1898* (New York, 1981), pp. 484–485. The embalmed beef controversy is in Graham A. Cosmas, *An Army For Empire: The United States Army in the Spanish-American War* (Columbia, Mo., 1971), pp. 287–294.

21. Hagedorn, *Leonard Wood*, II, 215.

22. Robert Lee Bullard, *Personalities and Reminiscences of the War* (Garden City, N.Y., 1925), p. 23.

23. Hewes, *From Root to McNamara*, p. 23.

24. T. Bentley Mott, *Twenty Years as Military Attaché* (New York, 1937), p. 201.

25. "General Scott was a man who knew very little about the war, and he spent most of his time asleep. . . . when Baker went to him to have me made a major, we found the General asleep in his office. One day Scott asked Colonel Robert E. Lee Mickey, a colonel who was with us, 'Mickey, everybody's talking about the Battle of the Marne. What happened at the Battle of the Marne anyway?' That's all Scott knew about war. . . . General Leonard Wood was Chief of Staff at the time of Wilson's inauguration, and Mrs. Wood told me that the first thing Wilson did after he came back from the inauguration was to ask

Wood, 'Have I the authority to make a brigadier general?' When Wood told him that he had the authority, Wilson made Scott a brigadier general." Stanley Washburn memoir, pp. 112–113, Oral History Collection, Columbia University. March retired Scott after March and Baker visited him at Dix and Scott spent forty-five minutes showing the two men an Indian headdress and pointing out the meaning of the various feathers. March to Baker, Oct. 19, 1932, Newton D. Baker MSS.

26. Bullard, *Personalities and Reminiscences of the War,* p. 22. Bullard told Colonel House that Bliss was a poor soldier—that as far as he knew the only active service Bliss ever had was parading some troops in San Diego. Edward M. House diary, Mar. 7, 1920, House MSS, Yale University Library, New Haven, Conn.

27. March, *The Nation at War,* p. 39. When March's book appeared Baker took gentle difference with him about the War Department being deserted at night, and said Crowder and Major General William Crozier of ordnance usually were there, and that he himself was there until as late as midnight, and he thought the quartermaster corps was open evenings. Baker to March, Oct. 17, 1932, Baker MSS. But he was referring to the preceding year.

28. Robert E. Wood memoir, pp. 27–28, Oral History Collection, Columbia University.

29. James E. Hewes to the author, June 22, 1977. ". . . the structure of the Supply Department of the Panama Canal Zone under the Chief Quartermaster [Wood] was the prototype for the same organization —and headed by the same two men, Goethals and Wood—as the Purchase, Storage and Traffic Division of the General Staff after August 1918. There was a distinct difference in the personalities of the two men. Goethals was exactly like [General Brehon B.] Somervell in World War II—autocratic, arrogant, and sarcastic. In those days industrial managers generally all tended to be that way. None of them believed anything could ever be accomplished by a committee, commission or board. Wood may have been an autocrat, but he was anything but arrogant and sarcastic in his dealings with subordinates. Both Goethals and Wood knew how to delegate authority, and both of them welcomed suggestions and advice coming up the line from below."

30. To George Goethals, Goethals MSS, Library of Congress. See also Daniel R. Beaver, "George W. Goethals and the Problem of Military Supply," in D. R. Beaver (ed.), *Some Pathways in Twentieth-Century History: Essays in Honor of Reginald Charles McGrane* (Detroit, 1969), pp. 95–108; Hewes, "The War Department," *Dictionary of American History,* VII, 229–230. Colonel Edwin W. Fullam in a memorandum of

Mar. 11, 1919, to the chief of the coordination branch of the General Staff, Colonel J. S. Fair, suggested that officers should study perhaps at the Harvard Business School and work at such large business enterprises as Marshall Field or Sears, Roebuck. In two memos on the same subject, Mar. 14 and Apr. 2, Lt. Col. Herbert H. Lehman wrote that neither Regular Army officers nor civilian officers of business experience had proved successful during the war, that both were "totally unacquainted with the problems which unfortunately were changed almost from day to day." He thought the Army ought to get up a reserve so that people could come in, in case of emergency; reserve officers needed not merely a course in paperwork but field operations. Lehman described the extreme confusion of the bureaus and concluded that "It is inconceivable that there should be any serious effort made to return to the old bureau system and its attendant evils. It cannot be justified on either economic, military or business lines." A young political scientist at the University of California at Berkeley, J. R. Douglas, came into the department at the end of the war and drew together suggestions of wartime officers into a remarkable memorandum of early 1919 ("The War's Lessons with Reference to the Supply System of the Army"). An undated memo, probably by Douglas, concludes that

Surely a study of the chaotic conditions in Washington during the first half of the war—the various departments and bureaus and agencies each feverishly preparing for war according to its own ideas, interfering and competing with and paralleling the work of others; the maze of commissions and committees and boards hastily appointed with powers and responsibilities ill understood; the wilderness of newly commissioned officers and war workers, eager to help but not knowing how, inefficiently controlled and directed; the captains of industry and contractors and war adventurers wandering in circles in the dazed mass, seeking information for uses patriotic or selfish—and then the gradual emergence in the latter half of the war, of the War Industries Board dominating the situation, with the War Trade Board, and efficient food and fuel control and in the War Department a General Staff potent enough to bring together and point in a common direction the divergent activities of its various components—surely a study of such a history should lead to a useful conclusion and a rational plan of operation in the vital first days of the next major war.

See Col. Fair's MSS, box 507, record group 165, National Archives. After World War I the bureaus regained independence. They lost it during World War II, only to regain it in the years thereafter.

31. To George Goethals, Apr. 14, 1918, Goethals MSS.
32. Goethals to his son George, May 10, 1918, Goethals MSS.
33. Edward M. Coffman, "Peyton C. March," *Dictionary of American Biography, Supplement Five* (New York, 1977), p. 468.
34. Goethals to George Goethals, Apr. 20, 1918, Goethals MSS.
35. Edward M. Coffman, *The Hilt of the Sword: The Career of Peyton C. March* (Madison, Wis., 1966); War Dept., *Annual Reports: 1919* (3 vols., Washington, D.C., 1920), I, 235–479 (report of the Chief of Staff). Baker was not a forceful man and needed March desperately in early 1918, and knew what he was getting. Years later, when Frederick Palmer was writing an authorized biography of Baker, he ventured to his subject that the former Chief of Staff was ruthless, daring, not always considered a jolly good fellow. In reply the Secretary made an appraisal: ". . . from my very first contact with him, he gave me the impression of driving power and determination which never flagged. I am not sure that there can be a combination of so much crude force as March has with any gentleness or sweet reasonableness, but whether there can be or not, there was not in him. Our relations were always excellent and not in a single incident do I recall the slightest difficulty on either of our parts in getting along with the other, but I had had a lot of experience as an executive and had read Macaulay's Essay on the History of the Popes and I knew something of the secret of using enthusiasm in others even when it wasn't exactly your enthusiasm." Palmer to Baker, Dec. 16, 1930, Baker to Palmer, Dec. 24, Baker MSS.

Chapter 3. Getting "Over There"

1. Jonathan Daniels, *The End of Innocence* (Philadelphia, 1954), p. 316; Joseph P. Lash, *Eleanor and Franklin* (New York, 1971), p. 201; Joseph L. Morrison, *Josephus Daniels: The Small-d Democrat* (Chapel Hill, N.C., 1966), p. 85; Leonard Wood diary, Nov. 13, 1917, Wood MSS, Library of Congress; David F. Trask, *Captains and Cabinets: Anglo-American Naval Relations, 1917–1918* (Columbia, Mo., 1972), p. 166. The latter volume is the outstanding account of U.S. Navy activities during the war.
2. Philip K. Lundeberg, "Undersea Warfare and Allied Strategy in World War I," pt. 1, *Smithsonian Journal of History*, I, no. 3 (1966–67), 6.
3. Gerald E. Wheeler, *Admiral William Veazie Pratt, U.S. Navy: A Sailor's Life* (Washington, D.C., 1974), pp. 92–94.
4. For submarine tactics and convoys, see Capt. Thomas C. Hart, lecture on submarines at the Naval War College, Dec. 20, 1920, pam-

phlet hle (mimeograph) at Naval War College, Newport, R.I.; William S. Sims, *The Victory at Sea* (Garden City, N.Y., 1920); Albert Gleaves, *A History of the Transport Service: Adventures and Experiences of United States Transports and Cruisers in the World War* (New York, 1921); Thomas G. Frothingham, *The Naval History of the World War* (3 vols., Cambridge, Mass., 1924–26), III. The Naval Institute Press has reissued Sims's book (Annapolis, Md., 1984) with an introduction by David F. Trask.

5. William Graves Sharp, *War Memoirs* (London, 1931), p. 169.

6. Holger H. Herwig and David F. Trask, "The Failure of Imperial Germany's Undersea Offensive Against World Shipping, February 1917–October 1918," *The Historian*, vol. 33 (1970–71), 613.

7. Sims, *The Victory at Sea*, p. 14. Balfour MSS, FO/800/208, passim, British Foreign Office records, Public Record Office, London.

8. Robert Greenhalgh Albion and Jennie Barnes Pope, *Sea Lanes in Wartime: The American Experience, 1775–1942* (New York, 1942), pp. 244–245, 252. Actually the Germans sank an average of 647,000 tons per month, from February through June 1917. Regular convoys were introduced in July, when the battle should have been decided. The submarine campaign, however, did not starve Britain; it was a technical success and economic miscalculation. Gerd Hardach, *The First World War* (Berkeley, Calif., 1977), p. 51.

9. Holger H. Herwig, *Politics of Frustration: The United States in German Naval Planning, 1889–1941* (Boston, 1976), p. 145.

10. Daniels diary, Mar. 6, Arthur S. Link et al. (eds.), *The Papers of Woodrow Wilson*, vol. 41 (Princeton, N.J., 1983), 346.

11. Link, *Wilson: Campaigns for Progressivism and Peace, 1916–1917* (Princeton, N.J., 1965), p. 376; Dean C. Allard, "Admiral William S. Sims and United States Naval Policy in World War I," *The American Neptune*, vol. 35 (1975), 107; Forrest C. Pogue, *George C. Marshall: Education of a General, 1880–1939* (New York, 1963), p. 144.

12. William D. Leahy diary, May 10, 1918, Leahy MSS, Library of Congress.

13. Early in the war the British Navy invented the depth charge after a cruiser, attacked by a submarine, maneuvered to avoid the torpedo and, in hope of ramming, went full speed to the spot where the submarine fired, only to discover that the sub had submerged so deeply that the cruiser passed over it. Officers and crew could see the submerged hull, in full view yet perfectly safe. The incident was reported to the Grand Fleet's commander, Sir John Jellicoe, in the presence of his second in command, Admiral Charles E. Madden, who mused about how fine it would have been if the Navy had possessed a mine to drop overboard and explode at the submarine's

depth. The depth charge proved easy to construct, a steel cylinder of TNT fitted with a simple firing device set off by water pressure, adjustable to any depth. Sims, *The Victory at Sea*, pp. 94–95.

14. Cecil to Balfour, Apr. 26, 1917, FO 800/208, p. 93.

15. Josephus Daniels, *The Wilson Era: Years of War and After, 1917–1923* (Chapel Hill, N.C., 1946), pp. 96–98. If one counted both troop transports and supply ships, convoys were mostly British—the U.S. Navy convoyed 27 per cent. Trask, *Captains and Cabinets*, p. 363.

16. Frederick A. Pottle, *Stretchers: The Story of a Hospital Unit on the Western Front* (New Haven, Conn., 1929), p. 69; Ernest H. Ferrell, Sr., *Stories I Want My Grandchildren to Know* (Columbus, Ind., 1980), pp. 37–39; Joseph Douglas Lawrence, "Fighting Soldier," pp. 29–31, copy in possession of the present writer; letter, Shipping Ministry to War Office, Oct. 1918, FO 371/3493, pp. 282–283. For a sickening description of the making of rabbit stew aboard the *Caserta*, see Pottle, *Stretchers*, pp. 72–73. See also Fred Davis Baldwin, "The American Enlisted Man in World War I," Princeton University dissertation, 1964, pp. 143–164.

17. Horace Hobbs diary, Oct. 14, 21, 1917, Hobbs MSS, U.S. Army Military History Institute, Carlisle Barracks, Penn. When a common soldier showed initiative, as in the case of Private Philip C. Jessup, he too could see a great deal. "In the danger zone I volunteered for the crow's nest watch and had a wonderful time. My first time up was 4 a.m. of a wet cold morning, when dawn was just making its appearance, and of course I was scared pink. Going up the sloped ratlines to the first platform was easy enough, but then you had to climb up a swaying ladder which ran straight up the mast. But after you reached the crow's nest and looked down 160 feet on the ship and the rest of the convoy, it was worth anything. It was a large fleet, and had some big ships, but the largest looked like a model. . . . The destroyers darted around like those little black water beetles. I made about eight trips in all, and after the first two enjoyed every second of it all." (Letter of Jessup to his father and mother, July 13, 1918, in Edward G. Duffy's manuscript of the AEF service of his father, Francis Joseph Duffy; personal possession of Mr. Duffy.) Many years later Ambassador Jessup could still recall these occasions: "I remember how irritated we were at having to wear full battle gear when going on the crow's nest watch when the holster might catch in the rigging. I remember we used to be equally irritated by the orders governing guard duty on deck at night. One had to dress in full field equipment shouldering a rifle with orders to 'shoot submarines at sight.'" Letter to the author, Jan. 2, 1985.

18. World War I Collection, 1917–19, Ohio Historical Society, Colum-

bus. Letter in extract sent to Arthur M. Schlesinger, Sr., of Ohio State University.

19. Clark to "Dear Folks," Mar. 1918, World War I Collection, 1917–19, Ohio Historical Society. Clark's parents sent the letter to Schlesinger. Charles L. Samson was on the *Tuscania* and wrote his wife Mar. 16 that he never thought of asking divine intervention until several days later when an Arkansas youth, Lt. Sutton, admitted to praying most lustily. A major, Samson said, hid in a lifeboat not assigned to him and took the place of a captain who was killed. Samson MSS, Chicago Historical Society.

20. Felecia Hyde draft biography of Pratt, Pratt MSS, Library of Congress. A German naval officer told a member of the Reichstag that submarines were on the lookout for the *Leviathan*. "It would be a tremendous coup for a naval officer," he said, "to send it to the bottom with ten thousand men . . ." Hans P. Hanssen, *Diary of a Dying Empire* (Bloomington, Ind., 1955), p. 287 (June 16, 1918).

21. Hyde draft biography, Pratt MSS.

22. The *San Diego*, originally named the *California* and once the flagship of the Pacific Fleet, was zigzagging at fifteen knots off Fire Island, late in the morning of July 19, 1918, when it struck a mine and went down in twenty minutes with the loss of six lives out of a complement of 1,189. See William Bell Clark, *When the U-Boats Came to America* (Boston, 1929), pp. 144–155. In recent years the wreck has received much attention from scuba divers. The massive, rusting hulk, 503 feet long, rests sixty-five feet below on the sandy bottom, upside down, and looks more like a reef than a ship, covered with lacy sea anemones in hues of pinks and beige. *The New York Times*, Oct. 26, 1981.

23. Shipping Ministry to Foreign Office, Aug. 20, 1918, FO 371/3493, p. 230.

24. Capt. T. C. Hart, lecture on submarines at the Naval War College, Dec. 20, 1920.

25. Trask, *Captains and Cabinets*, ch. 7, "Frustration in the Mediterranean," pp. 225–282.

26. Philip K. Lundeberg, "Undersea Warfare and Allied Strategy in World War I," pt. 2, *Smithsonian Journal of History*, I, no. 4 (1966–67), 65–67. S. W. Roskill, *The Strategy of Sea Power: Its Development and Application* (London, 1962), pp. 134–135, argues that mines of the North Sea barrage were of poor quality, that submarines still could have used Norwegian territorial waters, that the best strategy was convoys, hence the barrage demonstrated American lack of faith in convoys. See also Olav Riste, *The Neutral Ally: Norway's Relations with Belligerent Powers in the First World War* (Oslo and London, 1965).

27. Thomas A. Bailey, *The Policy of the United States toward the Neutrals:*

1917–1918 (Baltimore, 1942), pp. 343–347.
28. Letter, Spring Rice to Balfour, Dec. 7, 1917, FO 800/209. To the French government the United States seemed slow in announcing its blacklist. See letter from Premier Alexandre Ribot to Ambassador Jules Jusserand, Aug. 16, 1917, Papiers Jusserand, vol. 32, Quai d'Orsay records, Paris. Presumably the French were as happy as the British with the announcement of Dec. 1917.
29. David F. Trask, *The War with Spain in 1898* (New York, 1981), pp. 265–266.
30. Felecia Hyde draft biography of Pratt, Pratt MSS.
31. But see Edward B. Parsons, *Wilsonian Diplomacy: Allied-American Rivalries in War and Peace* (St. Louis, 1978), which contends that President Wilson held back destroyers as part of a larger policy of assisting the British and French only enough to permit victory over Germany—so as to prevent the Allies from controlling the United States after the war.
32. Elting E. Morison, *Admiral Sims and the Modern American Navy* (Cambridge, Mass., 1942), pp. 441ff. During the war Ray Stannard Baker heard Sims blow off in the lunchroom of the London embassy. "He would decapitate all the Irish, thought that Irish conscription could be enforced with 'trifling losses.' He would hang certain members of Parliament, and as for the pacifists and labor leaders, why, they should quite simply be shot. As for the war in France, let the British and American armies withdraw and fight the Germans on the sea for twenty years if necessary. The navy would do it!" *American Chronicle: The Autobiography of Ray Stannard Baker* (New York, 1945), pp. 324–325.

Chapter 4. The AEF

1. Edward M. Coffman, "American Command and Commanders in World War I," in Russell F. Weigley (ed.), *New Dimensions in Military History: An Anthology* (San Rafael, Calif., 1976), p. 186.
2. Donald Smythe, *Guerrilla Warrior: The Early Life of John J. Pershing* (New York, 1973), p. 8.
3. ". . . Deliver us from theorists and sophists and psalm singers." Ibid., pp. 206–207.
4. Roosevelt, Elihu Root, Robert Bacon, and Charles E. Hughes gathered at a restaurant during T.R.'s campaign to go to France, and the ex-President was bubbling over with fighting zeal. "You must see Wilson," he declared, turning to Root and Hughes, "and get his consent to let me go." His voice deepened with solemnity and emotion. "I must go," he said, "but I will not come back. My sons will

go too, and they will not come back." For a moment there was silence, and then Root spoke up. "Theodore, if you can make Wilson believe that you will not come back, he will let you go." David J. Danelski and Joseph S. Tulchin (eds.), *The Autobiographical Notes of Charles Evans Hughes* (Cambridge, Mass., 1973), p. 187. But the story may be apocryphal, for another version has T.R. talking with House.

Roosevelt: "All I asked of the President was an opportunity to go and get killed." House: "Did you make that clear?"

Lloyd George told the House version to Ambassador John W. Davis in London. Davis diary, Dec. 17, 1918, Davis MSS, Yale University Library, New Haven, Conn. Roosevelt asked Wilson personally for a command, and the interview went well. According to a clerk in the White House offices, Wilson was "not one bit effusive in his greeting," but that did not stop Roosevelt, who commended the President for raising an army by conscription and then proceeded to outline his plans. By the end of the twenty-five-minute interview Wilson had thawed out and was laughing and talking back. "They had a real good visit." Thomas W. Brahany diary, Apr. 10, 1917, in Arthur S. Link et al. (eds.), *The Papers of Woodrow Wilson*, vol. 42 (Princeton, N.J., 1983), 31. For the President's public statement of May 18, 1917, refusing Roosevelt a command, see ibid., pp. 324–326.

5. Joseph P. Tumulty, *Woodrow Wilson as I Know Him* (Garden City, N.Y., 1921), pp. 290–291. The President told Grayson he had come to distrust Wood, who had criticized T.R. in front of him; he thought him exceedingly able, but full of intrigue and disloyal to superiors; he believed the problem came from brain damage; the President had recommended to Baker that Wood have opportunity for service abroad, and the matter went to Pershing, who objected. Cary T. Grayson diary, May 13, 1919, office of The Papers of Woodrow Wilson, Princeton University Library, Princeton, N.J. See Hermann Hagedorn, *Leonard Wood: A Biography* (2 vols., New York, 1931); Jack C. Lane, *Armed Progressive: General Leonard Wood* (San Rafael, Calif., 1978). President Wilson in advance of his interview with Wood had written a statement, which he did not use, that set Wood's problem out dispassionately: "General Wood is a very able man and can be made serviceable to the army in many ways; but he is by temperament —and I dare say by conviction—an agitator. He boldly contests and attempts to discourage the decision of his superiors in command. Such contests can do little harm here at home: they can be taken care of by public opinion; but in the face of the enemy they would be fatal. I cannot permit them in France, where our officers must be single-minded and devote every thought to doing a single thing." "An

Unpublished Statement," c. May 28, 1918, Link et al. (eds.), *The Papers of Woodrow Wilson*, vol. 48 (forthcoming). See also diary of Josephus Daniels, May 28, 1918, ibid.; Wilson to John Franklin Shafroth, May 29, to Richard Hooker, June 5.

6. *The General: Robert L. Bullard and Officership in the United States Army, 1881–1925* (Westport, Conn., 1975), p. 305.

7. John J. Pershing, *My Experiences in the World War* (2 vols., New York, 1931), I, 319.

8. In the early thirties a battle of memoirs erupted between Pershing and March. When the AEF commander's memoirs began coming out in newspapers March rushed out a book, and because Pershing could not get back—his book was in press, and if he made changes they could be compared to the newspaper excerpts—he put his friend General Harbord up to it. Harbord nominally was to write a history of the AEF, but the feud was to occupy a prominent place and perhaps even serve as its theme. Baker liked both March and Pershing and considered himself in the middle, and the Harbord and Baker MSS in the Library of Congress contain a ten-letter exchange in 1934–35 over the form of treating the Pershing-March differences. Harbord was inclined to accentuate them if only to please Pershing. Baker worked to get Harbord to tone down the argument and ideally to eliminate it. At one point Baker told Harbord that March's post in Washington made him less likely to be remembered than Pershing in the field; it was analogous to Halleck and Grant during the Civil War: "I am a fairly well read American and at the moment I cannot remember Halleck's first name." Letter of Sept. 27, 1934, Baker MSS, Library of Congress. At Baker's advice Harbord went to Root, who told Harbord to put the problem in a footnote. The footnote was jagged, so Baker rewrote it, and by this time Pershing was in ill health and satisfied. See Donald Smythe, "Literary Salvos: James G. Harbord and the Pershing-March Controversy," *Mid-America*, vol. 57 (1975), 173–183.

Pershing pursued his Army enemies with an implacable vengeance. "The time was 1928, my father was on temporary duty at the War Department, which was then housed in the old State, War and Navy Building, which is now the Executive Office of the President—the Victorian wedding cake at the corner of 17th and Pennsylvania Avenue. As my father told the story, Pershing was no longer Chief of Staff, but had an office next to the Chief's. These offices were along the back of a very large room, where the 'Indians' worked. Pershing would enter the large room each morning, someone would shout 'Attention!' Pershing would say, 'Good morning, gentlemen. At ease.' And he would walk across the room to his office. On this particular morning, instead of giving his usual greeting, Pershing paused thoughtfully, looked around the room slowly and said, 'Gentlemen, this is a red letter day for me. I've gotten the last man who ever did anything to me in the Army.' " Roger Hilsman to the author, Dec. 6, 1983.

9. Edward M. Coffman, *The War to End All Wars: The American Military Experience in World War I* (New York, 1968), p. 227.
10. Letter of Jessup to his father and mother, May 29, 1918, in Edward G. Duffy's manuscript of the AEF service of his father, Francis Joseph Duffy; personal possession of Mr. Duffy.
11. William L. Langer, *Gas and Flame in World War I* (New York, 1965), p. 14.
12. Frederick A. Pottle, *Stretchers: The Story of a Hospital Unit on the Western Front* (New Haven, Conn., 1929), p. 87.
13. The colonel of the black 371st Infantry Regiment being organized in New York City, Chester D. Haywood, exasperated by neglect of his troops and desiring to get them overseas, asked to have the regiment made a part of the Forty-second Division, but the answer was that "black was not one of the colors of the rainbow." Arthur E. Barbeau and Florette Henri, *The Unknown Soldiers: Black American Troops in World War I* (Philadelphia, 1974), p. 72.
14. Robert Lee Bullard, *Personalities and Reminiscences of the War* (Garden City, N.Y., 1925), p. 39.
15. House diary, Dec. 3, 1917, House MSS, Yale University Library, New Haven, Conn.
16. James G. Harbord, *Leaves from a War Diary* (New York, 1925), p. 214.
17. David F. Trask, *Captains and Cabinets: Anglo-American Naval Relations, 1917–1918* (Columbia, Mo., 1973), pp. 140–141.
18. James G. Harbord, *The American Army in France: 1917–1919* (Boston, 1936), p. 150.
19. Pershing, *My Experiences in the World War*, I, 380.
20. Mar. 1, 1931, March MSS, Library of Congress.
21. Robert E. Wood memoir, pp. 24–25, Oral History Collection, Columbia University, New York. Pershing's assistant, Brigadier General George Van Horn Moseley, deserves some of the credit for the supply effort in France.
22. Harbord, *The American Army in France*, p. 152.
23. Hagood diary, Nov. 1–Dec. 1, 1917, Hagood MSS, U.S. Army Military History Institute, Carlisle Barracks, Penn.
24. Hagood diary, Apr. 14, 1918, Hagood MSS.
25. Dawes diary, Dec. 9, 1917; Jan. 6, 1918, Dawes MSS, Northwestern University Library, Evanston, Ill. Dawes deleted these sections from his published diary, *A Journal of the Great War* (2 vols., Boston, 1921).

The present writer asked to see the original in the Dawes MSS and the curator found it with difficulty, wrapped in paper and tied by string, unopened for years, probably since Dawes published from it; wrapping paper had darkened over places not covered by string. But it showed that Dawes had published almost the full diary, omitting only a few passages, mostly about his adversary in the Services of Supply, General Atterbury.

26. Dawes, *A Journal of the Great War*, I, 63–64.
27. Harvey Cushing, *From a Surgeon's Journal: 1915–1918* (Boston, 1936), p. 404.
28. George W. Crile diary, Sept. 7, 1918, Crile MSS, Western Reserve Historical Society, Cleveland, Ohio.
29. Ibid., Oct. 4.
30. Hugh Young, *A Surgeon's Autobiography* (New York, 1940), 378–379. He wanted to prefer charges but realized it could gain nothing.
31. Ibid., p. 309. See also Fred Davis Baldwin, "The American Enlisted Man in World War I," Princeton University dissertation, 1964, pp. 203–214, 230–232; Donald Smythe, "Venereal Disease: The A.E.F.'s Experience," *Prologue*, vol. 9 (1977), 65–74.
32. Coffman, *The War to End All Wars*, p. 133.
33. Joseph T. Dickman, *The Great Crusade: A Narrative of the World War* (New York, 1927), p. 247.
34. Questionnaire in U.S. Army Military History Institute.
35. Mar. 14, 1918, Harrison MSS, Newberry Library, Chicago.
36. Sherwood diary, Sept. 10, 1918, Lilly Library, Indiana University, Bloomington, Ind.

Chapter 5. Victory

1. Laszlo M. Alfoldi, "The Hutier Legend," *Parameters*, vol. 5 (1975), 69–74.
2. Clark to Pershing, May 30, 31, June 2, 1918, Pershing MSS, box 1, record group 200, National Archives.
3. Winston Churchill, *The World Crisis* (New York, 1931), pp. 806–807. Interestingly, the drivers of the French trucks that took the Second Division to its positions were Vietnamese.
4. Gibbons may have made this up, for General Harbord wrote that a Confederate captain at Gettysburg said the same thing. Diary, July 20, 1918, Harbord MSS, box 1, record group 200, National Archives. Harbord's *Leaves from a War Diary* (New York, 1925) omits this commentary. The original of the Harbord diary has disappeared, and a search in the Harbord MSS in the New-York Historical Society failed to turn it up.

5. John W. Thomason, *Fix Bayonets! And Other Stories* (New York, 1970), p. 15. A book by another participant at Belleau Wood is Thomas Boyd, *Through the Wheat* (New York, 1923).
6. John A. Lejeune, "Brief Narrative History of the Second Division, American Expeditionary Forces," p. 8, undated, Lejeune MSS, Library of Congress.
7. Joseph T. Dickman, *The Great Crusade: A Narrative of the World War* (New York, 1927), pp. 270–272.
8. Quoted in Richard Suskind, *Do You want to Live Forever!* (New York, 1964), p. 139.
9. Edward M. Coffman, *The War to End All Wars: The American Military Experience in World War I* (New York, 1968), pp. 221–222.
10. Harbord diary, July 20, 1918, in *Leaves from a War Diary*, p. 323.
11. Thomason, *Fix Bayonets!*, pp. 72–74.
12. Horatio Rogers, *World War I Through My Sights* (San Rafael, Calif., 1976), p. 182.
13. "On the 18th," he wrote, "even the most optimistic among us knew that all was lost. The history of the world was played out in three days." James G. Harbord, *The American Army in France: 1917–1919* (Boston, 1936), p. 337.
14. The story is in James L. Collins, Jr. (ed.), George C. Marshall, *Memoirs of My Services in the World War: 1917–1918* (Boston, 1976), p. 145. Erich Ludendorff, *Ludendorff's Own Story: August 1914–November 1918* (2 vols., New York, 1919), II, 361 relates that local commanders were confident they could hold an attack, and general headquarters hesitated to evacuate the salient because of the industrial centers behind it, but in view of the probability of an American offensive, headquarters ordered evacuation on September 8.
15. Hunter Liggett, *A.E.F.: Ten Years Ago in France* (New York, 1928), p. 159.
16. Hugh A. Drum diary, courtesy of Edward M. Coffman.
17. Liggett, *A.E.F.*, p. 167. Pershing at the Meuse-Argonne commanded twelve times as many troops as Grant at the Battle of the Wilderness in 1864, used ten times as many guns, a hundred times as much ammunition (weight greater than Union forces used in 1861–65), and suffered four times the casualties. Leonard P. Ayres, *The War with Germany: A Statistical Summary* (2d ed., Washington, D.C., 1919), pp. 112–113.
18. Roy V. Myers memoir, p. 39, Myers MSS, U.S. Army Military History Institute, Carlisle Barracks, Penn.
19. George W. Crile diary, Sept. 24, 1918, Crile MSS, Western Reserve Historical Society, Cleveland, Ohio.
20. Brent diary, undated, Brent MSS, Library of Congress.

256 NOTES TO PAGES 81–89

21. Letter of Sept. 28 [?], Merritt MSS, Evanston Historical Society, Evanston, Ill.
22. Elden S. Betts to family, Betts MSS, World War I Collection, Illinois State Historical Library, Springfield.
23. With green divisions Cameron was in an impossible position, and unwilling to take casualties necessary to do what Pershing wanted. (Tilford Cameron Creel, the general's grandson, to author.) Years later at Fort Benning the then Colonel Cameron told Charles L. Bolté that the First Army's chief of staff, Drum, called Cameron on the field telephone, spoke harshly, and Cameron retorted, "You can't talk to me like that; only the army commander can do that." Cameron believed this conversation sufficed for his relief. (Edward M. Coffman to author.)
24. George B. Duncan, "Reminiscences of the World War," II, 139–140, courtesy of Edward M. Coffman.
25. Donald Smythe, "A.E.F. Snafu at Sedan," *Prologue*, vol. 5 (1973), 135–149.

Chapter 6. Money and Food

1. The Secretary's critics considered him sly; one of the reasons Ambassador Spring Rice was persona non grata at the White House was for such remarks as "If the President is the shepherd of his people, then McAdoo is his crook."
2. See Robert K. Murray, *The 103rd Ballot: Democrats and the Disaster in Madison Square Garden* (New York, 1976).
3. McAdoo later wrote of war finance in *Crowded Years* (Boston, 1931), pp. 378ff. See also Charles Gilbert, *American Financing of World War I* (Westport, Conn., 1970), pp. 117–144.
4. For the Morgan overdraft see Wilton B. Fowler, *British-American Relations, 1917–1918: The Role of Sir William Wiseman* (Princeton, N.J., 1969), pp. 38–59. The best source for the Nye Committee is John Edward Wiltz, *In Search of Peace: The Senate Munitions Inquiry, 1934–36* (Baton Rouge, La., 1963). See also Warren I. Cohen, *The American Revisionists* (Chicago, 1967).
5. Cable, Balfour to Spring Rice, June 29, 1917, FO 371/3115, pp. 104–108, British Foreign Office records, Public Record Office, London.
6. "If we cannot keep up the exchange neither we nor our Allies can pay our dollar debts, we should be driven off the gold basis, and all purchases from United States would immediately cease and the Allies' credit would be shattered. These consequences which would be of incalculable gravity may be upon us on Monday next if nothing

effective is done in the meantime." Arthur S. Link et al. (eds.), *The Papers of Woodrow Wilson*, vol. 43 (Princeton, N.J., 1983), 38–39.

7. Charles Seymour (ed.), *The Intimate Papers of Colonel House* (4 vols., Boston, 1926–28), III, 97.

8. Edward M. House diary, June 30, 1917, House MSS, Yale University Library, New Haven, Conn.

9. For the resort to a Morgan syndicate to bolster the gold reserve in 1895 see Harold U. Faulkner, *Politics, Reform and Expansion: 1890–1900* (New York, 1959), pp. 147–157. For years controversy raged over how much the bankers made on a loan of $31 million (a European syndicate took the remainder of the $65 million loan). Estimates for the Morgan syndicate, with sixty-one members, ran as high as $16 million. Frederick Lewis Allen received access to Morgan records and in *The Great Pierpont Morgan* (New York, 1949), pp. 124–125, reported the syndicate made $1,534,516.72, the firm $295,652.93.

10. For the Page cable see Link et al. (eds.), *The Papers of Woodrow Wilson*, vol. 41 (1983), 336–337.

11. Robert D. Cuff, "Herbert Hoover, the Ideology of Voluntarism and War Organization during the Great War," *Journal of American History*, vol. 64 (1977–78), 360. Hoover and his opposite in the War Industries Board, Baruch, both opted for voluntary staffs, but were apostles of voluntarism for different reasons—Hoover because he believed in it, Baruch because, when he took over the W.I.B. in March 1918, he had no time to create a bureaucracy. Industrialists, Cuff has shown, later acclaimed voluntarism as the principal lesson of mobilization during World War I and a fit procedure for mobilization during World War II, which proved a much longer conflict that demanded far more of the economy. Ibid., p. 372.

12. *Woodrow Wilson and the World War* (New Haven, Conn., 1921), p. 164.

13. Maxcy Robson Dickson, *The Food Front in World War I* (Washington, D.C., 1944), pp. 17–18, 25, 33, 38. See also William C. Mullendore, *History of the United States Food Administration: 1917–1919* (Stanford, Calif., 1941).

14. Ishbel Ross, *Power with Grace: The Life Story of Mrs. Woodrow Wilson* (New York, 1975), p. 113; Arthur Walworth, *Woodrow Wilson* (3d ed., 2 vols. in 1, New York, 1978), II, 119–120; Link et al. (eds.), *The Papers of Woodrow Wilson*, vol. 48 (forthcoming), telegram, Keith Neville to Wilson, May 28, 1918; Wilson to Homer P. Snyder, July 1.

15. Dickson, *The Food Front in World War I*, p. 63.

16. Edgar E. Robinson and Paul C. Edwards (eds.), *The Memoirs of Ray Lyman Wilbur: 1875–1949* (Stanford, Calif., 1960), pp. 263–265.

17. Frank M. Surface, *The Grain Trade during the World War* (New York, 1928), pp. 18–24, 27–29, 35–63. The Food Control Act allowed

capitalization of the Grain Corporation at $50 million and a Sugar Equalization Board at $5 million. The latter purchased sugar in the United States, Cuba, the West Indies, and the Philippines. The two organizations made a profit of $60 million. Administrative expenses of the Food Administration were $7.8 million. *The Memoirs of Herbert Hoover: Years of Adventure, 1874–1920* (New York, 1951), pp. 270–271.

Chapter 7. Ships and Arms

1. *Lord Northcliffe's War Book: With Chapters on America at War* (New York, 1917), p. 13.
2. Willard Straight to Henry P. Fletcher, May 23, 1917, Fletcher MSS, Library of Congress.
3. Robert Greenhalgh Albion and Jennie Barnes Pope, *Sea Lanes in Wartime: The American Experience, 1775–1942* (New York, 1942), p. 185. Figures for national tonnage are difficult to draw conclusions from. Totals frequently included all vessels over 100 tons; so calculated, United States tonnage in 1914 amounted to 5.3 million. Including only ships above 1,600 tons, and counting Philippine but not Great Lakes shipping, it was 2.1 million. But in the latter figure were excursion boats and ferries that could never have navigated the Cape of Good Hope or the stormy North Atlantic; scores of old wooden steamers and side-wheelers would also have had to be written off. The 123 sailing vessels above 1,600 tons were far more useful. The net seagoing tonnage in 1914 actually was quite small, 1 million. And in this tonnage only 23 vessels were as large as the Liberty ships of World War II, of which more than 3,000 were built, each of 7,170 gross tons. Ibid., p. 313.
4. Goethals to his son George R. Goethals, Apr. 19, 1917, Goethals MSS, Library of Congress.
5. George Rublee carried Goethals's resignation to President Wilson's secretary, Joseph P. Tumulty; his oral history memoir is the source of Denman's comment about Goethals. Rublee memoir, pp. 155–156, Oral History Collection, Columbia University Library, New York.
6. "Hog Island," *Independent,* vol. 94 (May 4, 1918), 196.
7. The following is from a private letter of Aug. 12, 1918, in FO 371/3488, pp. 356–360; British Foreign Office records, Public Record Office, London.
8. Robert Hessen, *Steel Titan: The Life of Charles M. Schwab* (New York, 1975), p. 243. In Jan. 1921 a witness before a congressional committee accused Bethlehem Steel of attempting to get the government to pay $100,000 of Schwab's expenses during the nine months he

worked for the government; his expenses, largely for his private railway car together with telegrams and telephone calls, amounted to $269,543. It had been announced that he served without salary or expense account. Actually his salary equaled that of the champion riveter in the yards. Bethlehem had picked up the expenses and then, so the witness said, tried to get back $100,000 by billing the government for "cost of ship construction."

9. George Soule, *Prosperity Decade: From War to Depression, 1917–1929* (New York, 1947), p. 55; David F. Trask, *Captains and Cabinets: Anglo-American Naval Relations, 1917–1918* (Columbia, Mo., 1973), p. 207.

10. Albion and Pope, *Sea Lanes in Wartime*, p. 332; William Joe Webb, "The United States Wooden Steamship Program during World War I," *The American Neptune*, vol. 35 (1975), 286.

11. Memorandum probably by Lord Eustace Percy, enclosed in letter of Sir Cecil Spring Rice to Foreign Secretary Balfour, July 27, 1917, FO 371/3121, pp. 355–357.

12. Admittedly the bureaus were not responsible for the Army's division program, which rose from thirty to eighty and veered toward a hundred. But they took little interest in it, preferring to get as much of everything as they could.

13. Walker D. Hines, *War History of American Railroads* (New Haven, Conn., 1928), pp. 13–14, 16–17; K. Austin Kerr, "Decision for Federal Control: Wilson, McAdoo, and the Railroads, 1917," *Journal of American History*, vol. 54 (1967–68), 550–560; the same author's *American Railroad Politics: 1914–1920* (Pittsburgh, 1968).

14. James P. Johnson, "The Wilsonians as War Managers: Coal and the 1917–18 Winter Crisis," *Prologue*, vol. 9 (1977), 193–208.

15. House diary, undated, House MSS, Yale University Library, New Haven, Conn. See also entry of Sept. 8, 1918, in Arthur S. Link et al. (eds.), *The Papers of Woodrow Wilson*, vol. 49 (Princeton, N.J., forthcoming). Wilson listened quietly to House's proposal and said nothing other than it might break the heart of the secretary he had, Tumulty.

16. 65th Cong., 2d sess., *Hearings by the Senate Committee on Military Affairs, Investigation of the War Department* (Washington, D.C., 1918).

17. House diary, Jan. 17, 1918, in Link et al. (eds.), *The Papers of Woodrow Wilson*, vol. 46 (1984), 23–24.

18. Letter of Dec. 24, 1917, Bryce MSS, microfilm, Bodleian Library, Oxford University.

19. House diary, undated, House MSS.

20. Ibid., May 27, 1917. A few weeks earlier Baruch's name had come up in Cabinet for appointment to a munitions committee. "He is somewhat vain," said Secretary Daniels. "Did you ever see a Jew who was

not?" responded the President. Daniels diary, Apr. 9, 1917 in Link et al. (eds.), *The Papers of Woodrow Wilson*, vol. 42 (1983), 23. For Baruch see Jordan A. Schwarz, *The Speculator: Bernard M. Baruch in Washington, 1917–1965* (Chapel Hill, N.C., 1981); James Grant, *Bernard Baruch: The Adventures of a Wall Street Legend* (New York, 1983).

21. The leading scholarly account is Robert D. Cuff, *The War Industries Board: Business-Government Relations During World War I* (Baltimore, 1973).

22. Grosvenor B. Clarkson, *Industrial America in the World War: The Strategy Behind the Line, 1917–1918* (Boston, 1930), pp. 217, 221, 223.

23. Schwarz, *The Speculator*, p. 76.

24. The following is based on John K. Ohl, "Old Iron Pants: The Wartime Career of General Hugh S. Johnson, 1917–1918," University of Cincinnati dissertation, 1971, pp. 103–145.

25. General Hugh S. Johnson's files, entry 145, box 3, records of the General Staff, U.S. Army, record group 165, National Archives. This is the conclusion of Phyllis Zimmerman's dissertation on Army supply, Indiana University, forthcoming: "My view, before looking at Army supply records, was that the W.I.B. and the Army worked well and that the military was held in check rather well by a powerful W.I.B. and wily Baruch. I don't think so now. The Army never gave up its hold on supply and used the W.I.B. more than the other way around."

26. Edward M. Coffman, *The War to End All Wars: The American Military Experience in World War I* (New York, 1968), pp. 41–42. The Mar. 15, 1918, memorandum comparing the American 1902 and the French 75 is in William J. Snow, *Signposts of Experience: World War Memoirs* (Washington, D.C., 1941), pp. 197–200, by the chief of field artillery.

27. Russell F. Weigley, *History of the United States Army* (New York, 1967), pp. 391–392; S. D. Rockenbach, undated lecture on tanks at St. Mihiel and the Argonne, in Charles P. Summerall MSS, Library of Congress; Hunter Liggett, *A.E.F.: Ten Years Ago in France* (New York, 1928), p. 325; Laurence Stallings, *The Doughboys: The Story of the AEF, 1917–1918* (New York, 1963), p. 98; James G. Harbord, *The American Army in France: 1917–1919* (Boston, 1936), p. 453; James L. Collins, Jr. (ed.), George C. Marshall, *Memoirs of My Services in the World War, 1917–1918* (Boston, 1976), p. 183.

28. Alfred F. Hurley, *Billy Mitchell: Crusader for Air Power* (rev. ed., Bloomington, Ind., 1975), p. 20; Daniel R. Beaver, *Newton D. Baker and the American War Effort: 1917–1919* (Lincoln, Nebr., 1966), p. 58; Baker to Wilson, June 20, 1917, House to Wilson, June 17, in Link et al. (eds.), *The Papers of Woodrow Wilson*, vol. 42 (1983), 531, 549. See also Irving B. Holley, *Ideas and Weapons* (New Haven, Conn., 1953).

29. Benjamin D. Foulois, *From the Wright Brothers to the Astronauts* (New York, 1968), pp. 154–155.
30. Merlo J. Pusey, *Charles Evans Hughes* (2 vols., New York, 1951), I, 374–382. For the officer who released the exaggerated report, Edward A. Deeds, the Dayton, Ohio, industrialist, see Isaac F. Marcosson, *Colonel Deeds: Industrial Builder* (New York, 1947).
31. Hurley, *Billy Mitchell,* p. 37.
32. For the following see Alfred D. Chandler, Jr., and Stephen Salsbury, *Pierre S. du Pont and the Making of the Modern Corporation* (New York, 1971), pp. 359–430. Cuff, *The War Industries Board,* p. 9, remarks "the striking disparity which existed in the pace and level of bureaucratic development between the private and public sectors of American society. Big business outdistanced all others in organizational achievement. . . ." See also Stephen Skowronek, *Building a New American State: The Expansion of National Administrative Capacities, 1877–1920* (New York, 1982).

Chapter 8. The Allies

1. Notes of an interview between Sir William Wiseman and President Wilson, July 13, 1917, Arthur S. Link et al. (eds.), *The Papers of Woodrow Wilson,* vol. 43 (Princeton, N.J., 1983), 174.
2. Edith Benham diary, Jan. 10, 1919, Edith Benham Helm MSS, Library of Congress.
3. One soldier wrote home that he was billeted on the Rue de Manure. Many reported solemnly that in each village the Frenchman with the biggest manure pile automatically became mayor. Fred Davis Baldwin, "The American Enlisted Man in World War I," Princeton University dissertation, 1964, pp. 186–187. President Wilson's comment about paying rent for the trenches appears in the Benham diary, Dec. 3, 1918, Jan. 10, 1919, Helm MSS. Curiously, censorship may have been a reason for anti-French remarks in soldiers' letters—after exhausting their fund of sentiment for home and sweethearts and engaging in essays on weather and food, men had little left to say and turned to the iniquities of the French. The author's uncle, Ivan C. Meggitt of Green Springs, Ohio, a sergeant in a field hospital, wrote several dozen such letters. And perhaps the anti-French comments in letters have taken more prominence than they deserved. Baldwin points out (pp. 197–198) that most soldiers in the AEF thought only of home, that the base censor of the Twenty-sixth Division in 1919 found that of 506 letters, 24 mentioned the French, and the censor of the Twenty-ninth Division found the exact same number of comments in 509 letters. The present-day reader of soldiers' letters, of

which hundreds of thousands seem to have survived, nonetheless has the impression of a massive amount of anti-French feeling. For the general subject see André Kaspi, *Le Temps des américains: le concours américain à la France en 1917–1918* (Paris, 1976).

4. Memorandum of a conversation with Sir Horace Plunkett, by Charles Seymour, Aug. 1, 1925, Seymour MSS, Yale University Library, New Haven, Conn.

5. William Phillips, *Ventures in Diplomacy* (Boston, 1952), p. 84.

6. House diary, Dec. 11, 1917, at sea; House MSS, Yale University Library. For House's Paris mission, see David F. Trask, *The United States in the Supreme War Council: American War Aims and Inter-Allied Strategy, 1917–18* (Middletown, Conn., 1961), pp. 20–37.

7. Charles Seymour, *American Diplomacy during the World War* (Baltimore, 1934), p. 239.

8. At the outset the military advisers to the Supreme War Council were an awkward group, for the Italian government sent General Luigi Cadorna, the defeated commander at Caporetto, the French government sent Foch, who until the spring of 1918 maintained very awkward relations with the French Army's field commander, Pétain, and the British government sent Sir Henry Wilson, who until he replaced Sir William Robertson as Chief of the Imperial General Staff was Lloyd George's representative against Haig. The American adviser was the retired Chief of Staff of the U.S. Army, General Bliss. Possessing little influence on field commanders, this group was incapable of action. For military liaison in 1917–18, see Trask, *The United States in the Supreme War Council,* pp. 41–46; for unified command and the issue of amalgamation, pp. 53–99.

9. Apr. 6, 1918, in Link et al. (eds.), *The Papers of Woodrow Wilson,* vol. 47 (1984), 271.

10. John J. Pershing, *My Experiences in the World War* (2 vols., New York, 1931), I, 33, II, 28–29.

11. Johnson Hagood diary, May 20, 1918, Hagood MSS, U.S. Army Military History Institute, Carlisle Barracks, Penn.

12. FO 800/224, p. 102, British Foreign Office records. Newton Baker was much amused in later years when Lloyd George published his memoirs and devoted the first four volumes to the thesis that the British high command was inept, but in the fifth continued the argument that it should have received the extra burden of mismanaging the American Army. C. H. Cramer, *Newton D. Baker: A Biography* (Cleveland, 1961), p. 117.

13. Newspapers in the United States did not publish the secret treaties until Jan. 25–28, 1918, when Oswald G. Villard printed their texts in the New York *Post.* Only nine papers followed, and they published

excerpts. Michael Wreszin, *Oswald Garrison Villard: Pacifist at War* (Bloomington, Ind., 1965), p. 84.

14. For the remark about the President's casualness see House diary, Dec. 18, 1917, Link et al. (eds.), *The Papers of Woodrow Wilson*, vol. 45 (1984), 323. "An important decision the President and I made was to formulate the war aims of the United States. . . . I urged Lloyd George, Reading and Balfour at Paris to join me in formulating a broad declaration of war aims that would unite the world against Germany, and would not only help the Russian situation, but would knit together the best and most unselfish opinion of the world. I could not persuade them to do this, and now it will be done by the President. It would have been better if the Interallied Conference had done it . . ." Ibid., pp. 323–324. Under a heading of "Memorandum of Subjects in the President's Statement of War Aims on January 8, 1918 which are Open to Debate," Jan. 10, 1918, Lansing wrote: "The longstanding and complex situation in the Balkans cannot be cured on the basis of national aspirations; and it is doubtful if it can be justly on the principle of self-determination." Lansing diary, Lansing MSS, Library of Congress. Secretary of the Interior Lane, Secretary of Agriculture David F. Houston, and Secretary of Labor William B. Wilson knew nothing of the speech until after delivery. "I had an engagement with Secretary Lane on Tuesday at two o'clock at the White House. I asked him how he liked the President's address. He replied 'what speech do you mean, his message to Congress?' He was dumbfounded when I told him that the President had just delivered what was perhaps the most important utterance since he had been in office. Lane thought it was the limit of humiliation as far as the Cabinet was concerned." House diary, Jan. 9, 1918, *Papers of Woodrow Wilson*, vol. 45 (1984), 555. For a thorough review of the construction of the Fourteen Points speech see ibid., pp. 476ff.

15. The story of Czech troops in Russia appears in Victor M. Fic, *The Bolsheviks and the Czechoslovak Legion: Origin of Their Armed Conflict, March–May 1918* (New Delhi, 1978). Next to Prague, Chicago was the largest Czech city in the world; Cleveland by 1920 had 50,000 Czechs. By 1930 total Czechoslovak stock in the United States was nearly 1.4 million. Carl Wittke, *We Who Built America* (New York, 1939), pp. 410–411. For financial organization, see Thomas G. Masaryk, *The Making of a State: Memories and Observations, 1914–1918* (London, 1927), pp. 93–94. By 1920, 400,000 Slovaks lived in America, with 35,000 in Pittsburgh and others in such cities as Youngstown, Ohio, and Bridgeport, Connecticut. Wittke, *We Who Built America*, p. 417. Also Alfred Cobban, *National Self-determination* (Chicago, 1947 [?]), p. 23; Masaryk, *The Making of a State*, p. 209; Karel Capek,

264 NOTES TO PAGES 127–132

President Masaryk Tells His Story (New York, 1935), p. 282. Masaryk to Wilson, Sept. 7, Wilson to Masaryk, Sept. 10, in Arthur S. Link et al. (eds.), *The Papers of Woodrow Wilson*, vol. 49 (forthcoming). See Victor S. Mamatey, *The United States and East Central Europe, 1914–1918: A Study in Wilsonian Diplomacy and Propaganda* (Princeton, N.J., 1957); Dagmar Horna-Perman, *The Shaping of the Czechoslovak State: Diplomatic History of the Boundaries of Czechoslovakia, 1914–1920* (Leiden, 1962); and the same author's "The Making of a New State: Czechoslovakia and the Peace Conference, 1919," in Gerhard L. Weinberg (ed.), *Transformation of a Continent: Europe in the Twentieth Century* (Minneapolis, 1975), pp. 59–149.

16. Charles Seymour, *Geography, Justice, and Politics at the Paris Conference of 1919* (New York, 1951), p. 9.
17. Harry R. Rudin, *Armistice: 1918* (New Haven, Conn., 1944), p. 69.
18. Winston Churchill, *The World Crisis* (New York, 1931), pp. 828–829.
19. L. L. Farrar, *Divide and Conquer: German Efforts to Conclude a Separate Peace, 1914–1918* (New York, 1978), 103–104, 106–107, 114–115, 124–125. See also Klaus Epstein, *Matthias Erzberger and the Dilemma of German Democracy* (Princeton, N.J., 1959), p. 158; Charles F. Sidman, *The German Collapse in 1918* (Lawrence, Kans., 1972).
20. Farrar, *Divide and Conquer*, p. 125.
21. Rudin, *Armistice* pp. 12–13; Gerald D. Feldman, *Army, Industry and Labor in Germany: 1914–1918* (Princeton, N.J., 1966), p. 459.
22. Years later Sir Arthur Willert, who in 1917–18 was Washington correspondent of the London *Times*, speculated what the quick communications and personal contact of World War II might have done for Anglo-American relations in 1917–18, because of the incompatibility of Lloyd George and Wilson as revealed during the Peace Conference. *The Road to Safety: A Study in Anglo-American Relations* (New York, 1953), p. 141. For the pre-Armistice negotiations, see Rudin, *Armistice;* Trask, *The United States in the Supreme War Council*, pp. 151–175.
23. House diary, Aug. 22, House MSS.
24. Maurice Hankey diary, Oct. 24, 1918, in Stephen Roskill, *Hankey: Man of Secrets* (2 vols., London, 1970–72), I, 620–621. Shortly before Geddes left America, he gave a newspaper statement that President Wilson described as a piece of impertinence, and for Geddes to obtain a final interview with Wilson it was necessary for House to intervene with Mrs. Wilson. The interview seemed to go off well. "The President was exceedingly cordial and Sir Eric went away as happy as could be. He came up to our apartment later to see me for a final word before sailing. He spoke of the President in enthusiastic terms." House diary, Oct. 13, 1918, House MSS.
25. Charles Seymour (ed.), *The Intimate Papers of Colonel House* (4 vols.,

Boston, 1926–28), IV, 165. Explanation in the diary of the secretary of the British Cabinet, Sir Maurice Hankey, who was taking notes (above, pp. 140–141), is different, for he has Lloyd George answering House, "We shall be very sorry if you won't [continue in the war]—but we shall fight on." After that, "Ll. G. having made it clear we were not to be bullied, things went better, and eventually we agreed to put up a draft. Clemenceau said few specially witty things, but looked unutterable things when Col. House spoke in hushed tones of what the President thinks . . . " Diary, Oct. 29, in Roskill (ed.), *Hankey*, I, 623. House always considered this meeting an occasion: "If there was ever a fight it was in Paris at the Armistice proceedings over the Fourteen Points. We had the whip-hand then and I pushed our position to the limit. Later when the Senate had the whip-hand I counselled compromise." Letter to Stephen Bonsal, Mar. 17, 1929, Bonsal MSS, Library of Congress. For this negotiation see especially Link et al. (eds.), *The Papers of Woodrow Wilson*, vol. 51 (forthcoming).

26. Baker informed Pershing of the President's desires concerning the Armistice in a cable of Oct. 27. House cabled Pershing's proposal to the President on Oct. 31. See Link et al. (eds.), *The Papers of Woodrow Wilson*, vol. 51. Also Bullitt Lowry, "Pershing and the Armistice," *Journal of American History*, vol. 55 (1968–69), 281–291; Lloyd C. to Bronson W. Griscom, Nov. 21, 1918, Griscom MSS, Library of Congress; the Dawes diary says little about Pershing's intervention in the Armistice negotiation (*A Journal of the Great War* [2 vols., Boston, 1921]).

27. Calvin Hoover, *Memoirs of Capitalism, Communism, and Nazism* (Durham, N.C., 1965), p. 58.

28. *Rickenbacker* (Englewood Cliffs, N.J., 1967), p. 135.

29. Emily Frankenstein diary, Chicago Historical Society.

30. Edith Bolling Wilson, *My Memoir* (Indianapolis, 1939), pp. 170–171.

Chapter 9. Peace

1. Arthur James Balfour MSS, FO 800/211, pp. 95–96, British Foreign Office records. The President received the foreign correspondents on Monday afternoon, Apr. 8, 1918, and according to the stenographic record made the following remarks: "Personally, if I were in a peace conference right now, I would say, 'Gentlemen, I am here to say for the United States that I don't want anything out of this. And I am here to see that you don't get anything out of it.' " Arthur S. Link et al. (eds.), *The Papers of Woodrow Wilson*, vol. 47 (Princeton, N.J., 1984), 287.

2. Bryce to Charles W. Eliot, Mar. 2, 1920, Bryce MSS, microfilm, Bodleian Library, Oxford University.

3. John W. Davis diary, June 8, 1920, Davis MSS, Yale University Library, New Haven, Conn.
4. Stockton Axson memoir of Woodrow Wilson, ch. entitled "Why President Wilson Went to Europe," pp. 6–11, office of The Papers of Woodrow Wilson, Princeton University Library, Princeton, N.J.
5. Nov. 15, 1918, Pittman MSS, Library of Congress.
6. Charles Seymour, memorandum of a conversation with Colonel House, Mar. 17, 1922, Seymour MSS, Yale University Library; Ray Stannard Baker diary, Mar. 29, 1919, Baker MSS, Library of Congress. Paris and London probably were the only European cities with enough hotel space to accommodate the hordes of delegates and assistants. But without accommodation perhaps some of them might have remained at home.
7. In his diary for Mar. 28, 1917, House recorded the President as saying that Lansing had no imagination, no constructive ability, indeed little real ability of any kind; Apr. 26, that the Secretary of State had a wooden mind; Aug. 15, that Lansing (so the President told Polk) could not write clearly and that he, Wilson, always had to do the work; Sept. 9, the President spoke of sending Lansing on a mission to Brazil; Dec. 18, Wilson told House that Lansing should be included in a discussion so he would feel he had something to do now and then; Sept. 27, 1918, the President said Lansing was so stupid he was constantly afraid he would make a serious blunder. Link et al. (eds.), *The Papers of Woodrow Wilson*, vol. 41 (Princeton, N.J., 1983), 497; vol. 42 (1983), 142; vol. 43 (1983), 485–486; vol. 44 (1983), 176; vol. 45 (1984), 323; vol. 51 (forthcoming). Lansing was tired, for he had been working daily from nine until six and often attended social occasions in the evening. He suffered from diabetes and the new insulin treatment caused trouble, as frequently he had to abstain from eating for a day to adjust himself to medication. Burton F. Beers, *Vain Endeavor: Robert Lansing's Attempts to End the American-Japanese Rivalry* (Durham, N.C., 1962), p. 149.
8. The general wrote able memoranda and dispatches, for which see David F. Trask, *General Tasker Howard Bliss and the "Sessions of the World": 1919* (Philadelphia, 1966).
9. Diary, Dec. 22, 1918, Baker MSS.
10. Arthur Walworth, *America's Moment, 1918: American Diplomacy at the End of World War I* (New York, 1977) catches the President's exuberance. Walworth's volume is the first of his forthcoming history of the Paris Peace Conference. The Keynes quotation appears in *The Economic Consequences of the Peace* (New York, 1920), p. 35.
11. Charles Seymour, *Letters from the Paris Peace Conference* (New Haven, Conn., 1965), p. 8.

12. Wilson had contemplated thirteen points instead of fourteen for his speech of Jan. 1918. His initial draft of the League of Nations, completed in Aug., contained thirteen articles. When he went to France in Dec. he took thirteen limousines for his Paris staff. The League of Nations Commission (above, pp. 165–166) finished the Covenant on Feb. 13, and the document of peace had twenty-six articles. The President went back to the United States shortly afterward, and returned to France on Mar. 13.

13. Irwin H. Hoover diary, Dec. 13, 1918, Hoover MSS, Library of Congress.

14. Stockton Axson memoir of Wilson, ch. entitled "Hope of the World," pp. 5–6.

15. Only 191 were civilians. Letter of Jan. 25, 1919, Polk MSS, Yale University Library.

16. House diary, Mar. 24, 1919, House MSS, Yale University Library. See also Waldo H. Heinrichs, Jr., *American Ambassador: Joseph C. Grew and the Development of the United States Diplomatic Tradition* (Boston, 1966), pp. 36–41. But after return from America in Mar. the President made little use of House's staff: "The President is still lacking in any kind of organization around him. I believe I can do more work in a day than he can do in a week for the reason that I have the very highest type of advisers and secretaries about me. If he had someone in his immediate entourage that measurably compared with the force I have, a tremendous burden would be lifted from his shoulders. The people with me, directly or indirectly, can do most of the things that come up better than I can do them myself or than the President could do them. He has never learned this lesson and, I take it, never will." Diary, May 6, 1919. Lansing deeply resented House's creation of a staff, for which see Lansing to Polk, July 26, 1919, Polk MSS.

17. Cary T. Grayson diary, Jan. 2, 5, 1919, office of The Papers of Woodrow Wilson.

18. *The Autobiography of James T. Shotwell* (Indianapolis, 1961), pp. 113–114. In the course of a long talk Clemenceau spoke over his shoulder to the French foreign minister, Stephen Pichon, in a stage whisper that carried to Shotwell immediately behind: "What did you get that fellow here for anyway?" Pichon spread out his hands in impotent protest and said, "Well, I didn't know he was going to carry on this way." Halfway through, Ghanem looked around anxiously and asked if he should go on, and then went back three pages and reread them, a particularly gross section in which he said Syrians would rather be delivered to the Turks than live under the British.

19. The Department of State published Hankey's notes in *Foreign Relations of the United States: The Paris Peace Conference, 1919* (13 vols.,

Washington, 1942–1947), V–VI. Hankey never learned that Mantoux was taking notes until the latter published *Les Délibérations du conseil des quatre (24 mars–28 juin 1919)* (2 vols., Paris, 1955). The two records are confusing, for Hankey wrote notes in a matter-of-fact way, whereas Mantoux used imagination. In regard to a proposed American mandate for Armenia (above, p. 144), Hankey had Wilson saying of his country, "She will take the Armenian mandate for humanitarian reasons." Mantoux recorded Wilson differently: "It was difficult for her to take a mandate even for Armenia, where she had permanent interests of long standing, and where a good deal of money had been spent by Americans for the relief of the Armenian people." James Gidney, *Mandate for Armenia* (Kent, Ohio, 1967), p. 88. See also Seymour, *Letters from the Paris Peace Conference,* p. 155.

20. Lawrence E. Gelfand, *The Inquiry: American Preparations for Peace, 1917–1919* (New Haven, Conn., 1963), p. 103; Bonsal diary, undated (Apr. 1919), Bonsal MSS, Library of Congress. See also Robert F. Byrnes, *Awakening American Education to the World: The Role of Archibald Cary Coolidge, 1866–1928* (Notre Dame, Ind., 1982), pp. 164–179.

21. See ch. 10.

22. Cary T. Grayson diary, May 6, 1919.

23. Lloyd E. Ambrosius, "Wilson, the Republicans, and French Security after World War I," *Journal of American History,* vol. 59 (1972–73), 341–352, shows how the treaty was taken seriously in the United States, by Senator Lodge among others. As time passed and President Wilson linked the guarantee treaty to the League of Nations (article 3 of the guarantee treaty said that the treaty required approval of the League Council), its support diminished.

24. House diary, Feb. 21, 1919, Charles Seymour (ed.), *The Intimate Papers of Colonel House* (4 vols., New York, 1926–28), IV, 343–344. Also Bonsal diary, Feb. 23, 1919, Bonsal MSS: "Tom Lamont, the Banker of New York and the King Pin of our economic section, came in and, as he said, with no pride of authorship, presented the tentative reparations bill. The colonel [House] saw at a glance that it was $280 billion. 'Is there,' he asked, 'so much money in the world?' 'I doubt it,' laughed the Morgan banker, but then he had been contending with Lord Cunliffe who represented the English government and the Bank of England. 'I must tell you, regretfully, that he is the biggest ass of the Galaxy—of the many that have foregathered here.' Lamont had proposed that we should not kill the goose that might lay some golden eggs. That in anything like measurable time the Germans could not pay more than $20 billion. 'What,' shrieked Lord Cunliffe, 'they can pay that amount right over the counter—today.' "

25. Thomas W. Lamont, *Across World Frontiers* (New York, 1951), pp.

138–139. See also Jordan A. Schwarz, *The Speculator: Bernard M. Baruch in Washington, 1917–1965* (Chapel Hill, N.C., 1981), pp. 109–160; Ronald W. Pruessen, "John Foster Dulles and Reparations at the Paris Peace Conference, 1919: Early Patterns of a Life, " *Perspectives in American History*, vol. 8 (1974), 381–410.

26. "Everyone is laughing at the British Admiralty. It is all to the liking of Benson and myself who wanted the boats sunk. The French are indignant and blame the British for not being more careful. Lloyd George has asked each of the Allied Governments to give an opinion whether the English exercised due care. Admiral Knapp, who is now acting in Benson's place, thinks not." House diary, June 23, 1919, House MSS. "Morning papers report the sinking of the German ships at Scapa Flow. Good riddance to bad rubbish if the sea there is deep enough, and shows some evidence of pride on the part of the Germans which is almost welcome." John W. Davis diary, Davis MSS.

27. The mandate system provided classes, "A," "B," and "C," with mandatory powers exercising more supervision for class B mandates and virtual sovereignty over class C. They were to make annual reports to the League of Nations.

28. Charles Seymour, "Versailles in Perspective," in Herman Ausubel (ed.), *The Making of Modern Europe* (New York, 1951), II, 992–1006. For the abortive effort to try the Kaiser and other "war criminals" see James F. Willis, *Prologue to Nuremberg: The Politics and Diplomacy of Punishing War Criminals of the First World War* (Westport, Conn., 1982).

29. House in E. M. House and Charles Seymour (eds.), *What Really Happened at Paris* (New York, 1921), p. 431.

30. Robert Lansing, *The Peace Negotiations: A Personal Narrative* (Boston, 1921), pp. 97–98.

31. House diary, May 14, Sept. 22, 1917, House MSS. "If he were less naïve and childlike I would be suspicious of him . . . His statements leave me dumb with confusion." Diary, Sept. 22. Also Jan. 12, 1918. For the Polish issue, Louis L. Gerson, *Woodrow Wilson and the Rebirth of Poland* (New Haven, Conn., 1953); Piotr S. Wandycz, *France and Her Eastern Allies* (Minneapolis, 1962).

32. Kay Lundgreen-Nielsen, "Woodrow Wilson and the Rebirth of Poland," in Link (ed.), *Woodrow Wilson and a Revolutionary World: 1913–1921* (Chapel Hill, N.C., 1982), p. 109.

33. Bonsal diary, May 13, 1919, Stephen Bonsal, *Suitors and Suppliants: The Little Nations at Versailles* (New York, 1946), p. 129.

34. Mar. 14, 1919, Polk MSS.

35. Cary T. Grayson diary, Feb. 14, 1919.

36. See above, pp. 126–127.

37. Georges Clemenceau, *Grandeur and Misery of Victory* (New York, 1930),

p. 149; John Wells Gould, "Italy and the United States, 1914–1918: Background to Confrontation," pp. 117, 119, 131, 142, 174, Yale University dissertation, 1969. "The whole interest centers around Fiume. It seems quite clear that they do not care for Fiume itself or for its Italian population, but the purpose is to strangle it in order to make a greater Trieste. I am told that a majority of the Adriatic tonnage is other than Italy, and that if the Jugo-Slavs have a port of their own, Trieste is bound to suffer." House diary, Apr. 9, 1919. For the remark about New York City, see Cary T. Grayson diary, Jan. 6, 1919. See also Ivo J. Lederer, *Yugoslavia at the Paris Peace Conference: A Study in Frontier Making* (New Haven, Conn., 1963); Dragan R. Zivojinović, *America, Italy and the Birth of Yugoslavia: 1917–1919* (New York, 1972).

38. The most recent and exhaustive account of the literature is Eugene P. Trani, "Woodrow Wilson and the Decision to Intervene in Russia: A Reconsideration," *Journal of Modern History*, vol. 48 (1976), 440–461. Betty Miller Unterberger (ed.), *American Intervention in the Russian Civil War* (Lexington, Mass., 1969) sets out the several interpretations. For the first, to prevent the Japanese from occupying large parts of Siberia, see her *America's Siberian Expedition: 1918–1920* (Durham, N.C., 1956). In a later essay, "Woodrow Wilson and the Russian Revolution," in Link (ed.), *Woodrow Wilson and a Revolutionary World*, pp. 49–104, the same author is less clear, stressing the President's "impossible task" (p. 88). For the second interpretation, to rescue the Czech Legion, George F. Kennan, *Soviet-American Relations* (2 vols., Princeton, N.J., 1956–58). The antibolshevism interpretation is in William A. Williams, *American-Russian Relations: 1781–1947* (New York, 1952), and Lloyd C. Gardner, *Wilson and Revolutions: 1913–1921* (Philadelphia, 1976). Robert J. Maddox, *The Unknown War with Russia: Wilson's Siberian Intervention* (San Rafael, Calif., 1977), shares this interpretation but sees Wilson as disguising his measures, for fear of public and congressional disapproval. The German agent point of view appears in Christopher Lasch, *The American Liberals and the Russian Revolution* (New York, 1962). Link et al. (eds.), *The Papers of Woodrow Wilson*, vols. 48, 49 (forthcoming), offers many documents, especially vol. 49, in which an extract from the diary of William Phillips, July 20, 1918, shows the President attempting, through a draft announcement done on his own typewriter, to back away from the Siberian intervention. The North Russian intervention was quite different, with no confusing issue of the Japanese nor of the Czech Legion; here Wilson's desire to avoid intervention was clear, for which see John W. Long, "American Intervention in Russia: The North Russian Expedition, 1918–19," *Diplomatic History*, vol. 6 (1982), 45–67. Linda Killen, *The Russian Bureau: A Case Study in Wil-*

sonian Diplomacy (Lexington, Ky., 1983) examines the Wilson administration's organization to assist economically the Russia of the March 1917—not Bolshevik—revolution, and concludes that the President never looked closely at the issues and thought that somehow everything would come together for good, that he was unable to decide between "exercise of power or reliance on moral persuasion" (p. 165). For the Russian problem in general see Robert D. Warth, *The Allies and the Russian Revolution* (Durham, N.C., 1954); John M. Thompson, *Russia, Bolshevism, and the Versailles Peace* (Princeton, N.J., 1966); George A. Brinkley, *The Volunteer Army and Allied Intervention in South Russia, 1917–1921* (Notre Dame, Ind., 1966); Peter G. Filene, *Americans and the Soviet Experiment: 1917–1933* (Cambridge, Mass., 1967); and Beatrice Farnsworth, *William C. Bullitt and the Soviet Union* (Bloomington, Ind., 1967). The most recent account of the Russian Revolution is Lloyd C. Gardner, *Safe for Democracy: The Anglo-American Response to Revolution, 1913–1923* (New York, 1984), which also considers the Mexican and Chinese revolutions.

39. See the seminal books by Arno J. Mayer, *Political Origins of the New Diplomacy: 1917–1918* (New Haven, Conn., 1959) and *Politics and Diplomacy of Peacemaking: Containment and Counterrevolution at Versailles, 1918–1919* (New York, 1967). Also N. Gordon Levin, *Woodrow Wilson and World Politics: America's Response to War and Revolution* (New York, 1968).

40. Maddox, *The Unknown War with Russia*, p. 46; Trani, "Woodrow Wilson and the Decision to Intervene in Russia," p. 443. See memoranda by Secretary of State Lansing, June 3, 6, 1918, relating the decisions to intervene at Murmansk and Siberia; Link et al. (eds.), *The Papers of Woodrow Wilson*, vol. 48 (forthcoming). They appeared in an aidememoire of July 16; final draft of July 17 typed by the President.

41. Wiseman notes of an interview on Oct. 16, 1918, in Link et al. (eds.), *The Papers of Woodrow Wilson*, vol. 51 (forthcoming).

42. At this meeting on April 11 the League Commission had just voted to include in the Covenant a statement reserving the right of the United States to act in the Western Hemisphere under the Monroe Doctrine, and this statement had passed by majority vote. A French legal expert called the point to Wilson's attention. The President admitted the anomaly, but said there were "too serious objections on the part of some of us" to the racial-equality clause. "I am obliged," he explained, "to say that it is not accepted." Paul Gordon Lauren, "Human Rights in History: Diplomacy and Racial Equality at the Paris Peace Conference," *Diplomatic History*, vol. 2 (1978), 272–273.

43. *American Chronicle: The Autobiography of Ray Stannard Baker* (New York 1945), pp. 411–412.

44. Ray Stannard Baker diary, Apr. 25, 30, 1919, Baker MSS; Cary T.

Grayson diary, Apr. 25, 30, 1919. With extraordinary prescience the
President told Baker that if the Japanese went home there was danger
of a Japanese-Russian-German alliance and a return to the old bal-
ance-of-power system on a greater scale than ever. (Baker diary, Apr.
30.) In an unsigned agreement the Japanese representatives promised the return of Shantung, and it went back to China in 1922. For
the Chinese side see Paul S. Reinsch, *An American Diplomat in China*
(Garden City, N.Y., 1922); Tien-yi Li, *Woodrow Wilson's China Policy:
1913–1917* (New York, 1952); Russell H. Fifield, *Woodrow Wilson and
the Far East: The Diplomacy of the Shantung Question* (New York, 1952);
Roy Watson Curry, *Woodrow Wilson and Far Eastern Policy: 1913–1925*
(New York, 1957); Wunsz King, *Woodrow Wilson, Wellington Koo and the
China Question at the Paris Peace Conference* (Leyden, 1959); Jerry Israel,
Progressivism and the Open Door: America and China: 1905–1921 (Pitts-
burgh, 1971).

45. Cary T. Grayson diary, Apr. 23, May 2, 1919. "Lloyd George reminds
me very much of [Theodore] Roosevelt. He is a typical politician and
is more or less superficial. . . . He loves to play in public. I have found,
however, that very frequently he will say: 'We will decide this in this
manner but we will not say anything about it to the people.' . . . He
does not characterize as did Roosevelt every public utterance as 'My
Policies,' but the result is inevitably the same in his case." Ibid., June
15. See Seth P. Tillman, *Anglo-American Relations at the Paris Peace
Conference of 1919* (Princeton, N.J., 1961).

46. Memorandum of conversation with Colonel House, May 12, 1922,
Seymour MSS.

47. Roy Harrod, *The Life of John Maynard Keynes: A Personal Biography* (New
York, 1951), p. 260. Also George W. Curry, "Woodrow Wilson, Jan
Smuts, and the Versailles Settlement," *American Historical Review*, vol.
66 (1961), 968–986; William K. Hancock, *Smuts* (2 vols., Cambridge,
Eng., 1962–68).

48. Keynes, *The Economic Consequences of the Peace*, p. 4.

49. Harold Nicolson, *Peacemaking: 1919* (Boston, 1933), p. 6.

50. See Gerd Hardach, *The First World War: 1914–1918* (Berkeley, Calif.,
1977), especially pp. 283–294.

Chapter 10. The Senate and the Treaty

1. "I believe that Wilson would have been well advised to accept the
Lodge reservations to the Versailles Treaty. It was perfectly obvious
by December, 1919, that American ratification could not be accomplished without them, whereas with them he could have won for the
League of Nations a chance to succeed through American leader-

ship." Arthur S. Link, "World War I," in John A. Garraty, *Interpreting American History: Conversations with Historians* (2 vols., New York, 1970), II, 140.

2. See Sondra R. Herman, *Eleven Against War: Studies in American Internationalist Thought, 1898–1921* (Stanford, Calif., 1969); Charles Chatfield, *For Peace and Justice: Pacifism in America, 1914–1941* (Knoxville, Tenn., 1971); C. Roland Marchand, *The American Peace Movement and Social Reform: 1898–1918* (Princeton, N.J., 1972); Charles Chatfield (ed.), *Peace Movements in America* (New York, 1973); David S. Patterson, *Toward a Warless World: The Travail of the American Peace Movement, 1887–1914* (Bloomington, Ind., 1976); Charles DeBenedetti, *Origins of the Modern American Peace Movement: 1915–1929* (Millwood, N.Y., 1978); the same author's *The Peace Reform in American History* (Bloomington, Ind., 1980).

3. Arthur S. Link, "Woodrow Wilson: The Philosophy, Methods, and Impact of Leadership," in Arthur P. Dudden (ed.), *Woodrow Wilson and the World of Today* (Philadelphia, 1957), p. 10.

4. Illness of any public figure tends to create speculation, and newspapermen and diplomats momentarily commented about Wilson's health in Apr. 1919. Herbert Hoover was in Paris and heard the talk and took alarm; he was not a member of the President's inner circle and perhaps for that reason did not rid himself of apprehension. The later stroke confirmed his suspicion, and not long after Wilson's death in 1924 he wrote William Allen White that Wilson's failure with the League of Nations was pathological and began with the "first physical shock" in Apr. 1919, and thereafter "real history ought to end," for "petty incidents of his personal relations with myself or Colonel House or any other of the men with whom he got out of patience and refused to cooperate are in my mind not worth consideration." Letter of June 13, 1924; Francis W. O'Brien (ed.), *The Hoover-Wilson Wartime Correspondence: September 24, 1914 to November 11, 1918* (Ames, Iowa, 1974), p. 294. Hoover had written privately. In the twenties and thirties not much more was heard of this theory. After World War II, availability of more information, notably Colonel House's full diary (Charles Seymour had published portions in the twenties), led to publication of Alexander L. and Juliette L. George, *Woodrow Wilson and Colonel House: A Personality Study* (New York, 1956), a psychological interpretation, that the President's father made him feel inferior as a child, and this led to overweening behavior as an adult. Sigmund Freud and William C. Bullitt, *Thomas Woodrow Wilson* (Boston, 1967), boldly presented psychoanalytic reasoning—which Link neatly demolished in "The Case for Woodrow Wilson," *Harper's*, Apr. 1967, 85–93. Analysis then veered back toward Hoover's

explanation. A psychiatrist and neurologist at Mount Sinai School of Medicine in New York, Edwin A. Weinstein, concluded that Wilson had suffered a series of strokes and "the cerebral dysfunction which resulted from Wilson's devastating strokes prevented the ratification of the Treaty." *Woodrow Wilson: A Medical and Psychological Biography* (Princeton, N.J., 1981), p. 363. Just before the latter book appeared, and together with Link and James William Anderson, Weinstein criticized the Georges' volume of years before in "Woodrow Wilson's Political Personality: A Reappraisal," *Political Science Quarterly,* vol. 93 (1978–79), 585–598, pointing out that the President's difficulty was physical, not psychological. The Georges responded in "Woodrow Wilson and Colonel House: A Reply to Weinstein, Anderson, and Link," *PSQ,* vol. 96 (1981–82), 641–665, reasserting their psychological interpretation; they contended that Wilson acted toward the Senate no differently before than after the stroke of Oct. 1919 and that the President's basic problem was inability to compromise. They also accused Weinstein of extrapolating his stroke theory from weak evidence, related that a Harvard internist, Robert T. Monroe, had disputed Weinstein's position in 1971 shortly after the psychiatrist-neurologist had published a preliminary article ("Woodrow Wilson's Neurological Illness," *Journal of American History,* vol. 57 [1970–71], 324–351), and appended a letter from Michael F. Marmor, an ophthalmologist at Stanford University Medical School, who saw no clear evidence of strokes prior to Oct. 1919. Marmor's subsequent "Wilson, Strokes, and Zebras," *New England Journal of Medicine,* vol. 307 (Aug. 26, 1982), 528–535, explained that Wilson in 1906 may have suffered only from a burst blood vessel in his eye, not an embolic clot: "the most reasonable diagnosis for a historical figure is the most prevalent and ordinary condition. There is no better application for the old medical-school adage, 'When you hear hoofbeats, don't think of zebras!' " (p. 532) Unwilling to rest the issue in a medical journal the Georges and Marmor repeated their points in "Research Note/ Issues in Wilson Scholarship: References to Early 'Strokes' in the *Papers of Woodrow Wilson,* " in *Journal of American History,* vol. 70 (1983–84), 845–853. The editors of the Wilson Papers responded in the same journal and issue, pp. 945–955, the Georges and Marmor in turn, pp. 955–956.

5. John Milton Cooper, Jr., *The Warrior and the Priest: Woodrow Wilson and Theodore Roosevelt* (Cambridge, Mass., 1983), pp. 342–343 offers an explanation for Wilson's failure with the League that is almost as convincing as the stroke theory. The President, he writes, did not sufficiently awaken Americans to involvement in world affairs, and neglected to counter expressions of excessively militant idealism, like

those of Theodore Roosevelt, or dreams of universal peace, freedom, and justice. Cooper's volume, a landmark in Wilson literature, deserves the closest attention.

Another possible reason for the President's failure with the Senate — though it would only have been a minor one—was his notorious (there were many instances) tactlessness. Possessing a quick intelligence he easily turned it on opponents, high and low. Friends thought these ripostes clever, but they were anything but that. Consider the following account of Wilson golfing during a visit to Magnolia, Massachusetts, in mid-Aug. 1918: "On one occasion at Myopia [the name was ironic] the Club boor came up to him at the first tee, introduced himself, and offered to play a round with the President and show him the course. With the coldest look I have ever seen the President turned to him and said, 'Thank you, I have a caddy.' Out of ear-shot I asked him who his friend was, 'Oh just a Boston ass' was the President's reply." Sir William Wiseman to Arthur Murray, Aug. 30, in Link et al. (eds.), *The Papers of Woodrow Wilson*, vol. 49 (Princeton, N.J., forthcoming).

6. Lloyd E. Ambrosius, "Wilson's League of Nations," *Maryland Historical Magazine*, vol. 65 (1970), 369–393, contends that the President's ideas for the League did not break much with tradition, that Wilson carefully trimmed American responsibilities. As its author admits, this is not a widely held interpretation. See Calvin D. Davis, *The United States and the First Hague Peace Conference* (Ithaca, N.Y., 1962) and *The United States and the Second Hague Peace Conference: American Diplomacy and International Organization, 1899–1914* (Durham, N.C., 1975); Warren F. Kuehl, *Seeking World Order: The United States and International Organization to 1920* (Nashville, Tenn., 1969); Martin D. Dubin, "The Carnegie Endowment for International Peace and the Advocacy of a League of Nations, 1914–1918," *Proceedings of the American Philosophical Society*, vol. 123 (1979), 344–368; and such biographies as "John W. Foster" and "Robert Lansing" by Calvin D. Davis in Warren F. Kuehl (ed.), *Biographical Dictionary of Internationalists* (Westport, Conn., 1983).

7. Martin D. Dubin, "Toward the Concept of Collective Security: The Bryce Group's 'Proposals for the Avoidance of War,' 1914–1917," *International Organization*, vol. 24 (1970), 288–318.

8. Stockton Axson memoir of Woodrow Wilson, chs. on "Mr. Wilson in August, 1914, Sketches the League of Nations Idea," pp. 1–4, and "The Personality of Woodrow Wilson," p. 58, office of The Papers of Woodrow Wilson, Princeton University Library, Princeton, N.J. Thomas J. Knock, "Woodrow Wilson and the Origins of the League of Nations," Princeton University dissertation, 1982, pp. 66–67, be-

lieves the conversation of Aug. 1914 probably occurred in Feb. 1915. For reviews of the President's ideas, including his remarkable conversations with Axson, see Knock, op. cit., especially pp. 243ff, and Kurt Wimer, "Woodrow Wilson and World Order," in Link (ed.), *Woodrow Wilson and a Revolutionary World: 1913–1921* (Chapel Hill, N.C., 1982), pp. 146–173.

9. Wiseman to Reading, Aug. 16, Sept. 5, 1918, in Link et al. (eds.), *The Papers of Woodrow Wilson*, vol. 49 (forthcoming). House's draft constitution for a League of Nations is in ibid., vol. 48 (forthcoming): House to Wilson, July 14, 1918, enclosing a draft; House to Wilson, July 16. In a letter to Charles R. Van Hise, Aug. 13, 1918, the President again refused to have anything to do with the League to Enforce Peace. *The Papers of Woodrow Wilson*, vol. 49. He explained that he could not endorse the L.E.P.'s program but added, interestingly, that "I am a very warm advocate of a league to enforce peace." For Wilson's draft league see House diary, Aug. 15, Sept. 9; Wilson to House, Sept. 7, enclosing the draft; in ibid.

10. Seward W. Livermore, "The Sectional Issue in the 1918 Congressional Elections," *Mississippi Valley Historical Review*, vol. 35 (1948–49), 29–60 relates the deciding factor as resentment of midwestern wheat farmers; also Link, *Woodrow Wilson: A Brief Biography* (Cleveland, 1963), p. 139. But see Thomas A. Bailey, *Woodrow Wilson and the Lost Peace* (New York, 1944), pp. 54–56; John Morton Blum, *Joe Tumulty and the Wilson Era* (Boston, 1951), pp. 160–166, and the same author's *Woodrow Wilson and the Politics of Morality* (Boston, 1956), pp. 152–153; Seward W. Livermore, *Politics Is Adjourned: Woodrow Wilson and the War Congress, 1916–1918* (Middletown, Conn., 1966), pp. 217–226, 243–247. William G. McAdoo, *Crowded Years* (Boston, 1931), p. 412 notes the lateness of the Armistice. Several Republicans won Senate seats by close margins, such as Truman Newberry of Michigan, who in a contest with Henry Ford won by 2,000 votes; Newberry resigned in 1922 when it became apparent that expenditure of perhaps $700,000 in his campaign, then deemed an outrageous sum, might bring expulsion. Ford's close race however was remarkable in a state where a Democrat could have expected to lose. Two Republican senators irreconcilably against the treaty, George H. Moses of New Hampshire and Albert Fall of New Mexico, squeaked through by, respectively, 1,000 and fewer than 2,000 votes. Ralph Stone, *The Irreconcilables: The Fight Against the League of Nations* (Lexington, Ky., 1970), pp. 29–30. Livermore, *Politics Is Adjourned*, pp. 236–237, puts Moses's margin at 500, Fall's at 900. He also points out how a shift of 250 in Idaho would have lost a Democratic seat to a reactionary Republican and that extreme closeness in most states indicated Dem-

ocratic disinclination or inability to meet local issues that Wilson's appeal failed to consider. Link et al. (eds.), *The Papers of Woodrow Wilson*, vol. 51 (forthcoming) testifies to the forces and factors that persuaded Wilson to make his appeal; see especially the memorandum by Homer S. Cummings, Nov. 8 or 9, of a conversation with Wilson after the defeat, in which the President revealed his dismay over the results.

11. As to whether Lodge packed the Foreign Relations committee there is debate; see John A. Garraty, *Henry Cabot Lodge: A Biography* (New York, 1953), p. 364.

12. Colville Barclay to the Foreign Office, Dec. 19, 1918, FO 371/3493, pp. 513–514.

13. Robert Lansing, *The Peace Negotiations: A Personal Narrative* (Boston, 1921), pp. 37, 46, 167. The quotation is from the Secretary's desk diary for Dec. 11, 1918, Lansing MSS, Library of Congress.

14. Jonathan Daniels, *The End of Innocence* (Philadelphia, 1954), p. 291.

15. Cary T. Grayson diary, July 9, 1919, office of The Papers of Woodrow Wilson.

16. Letter of Dec. 18, 1884, Link et al. (eds.), *The Papers of Woodrow Wilson*, vol. 2 (1967), 553. Garraty, "Woodrow Wilson: A Study in Personality," *South Atlantic Quarterly*, vol. 56 (1957), 185, finds in this phrase the answer to the riddle of Wilson's personality. The discussions between Wilson and the Senate committee appear in 66th Cong., 1st sess., *Hearings before the Committee on Foreign Relations of the United States on the Treaty of Peace with Germany Signed at Versailles, on June 28, 1919* (Washington, D.C., 1920). For a careful account, see Arthur Walworth, *Woodrow Wilson* (3d ed., 2 vols. in 1, New York, 1978), II, 348–352. Kurt Wimer believes that during the time between Wilson's return and his decision to take the League issue to the country, he made every effort to compromise with the Senate. "Woodrow Wilson Tries Conciliation: An Effort that Failed," *The Historian*, vol. 25 (1963), 419–438.

17. Cary T. Grayson diary, Sept. 4, 5, 6, 9, 10, 13, 15, 17, 18, 1919. For the tiredness, the headaches, also Sept. 20, 23, 24.

18. Ibid., Sept. 19; also Cary T. Grayson, *Woodrow Wilson: An Intimate Memoir* (New York, 1960), p. 7. Loudspeakers revolutionized American politics. At the Democratic convention in San Francisco in 1920, "Bryan came into the convention like a roaring lion. . . . He made the best speech he ever made in his life; but for the first time amplifiers had been placed in the convention hall, and with the coming of the amplifiers Bryan's power over his fellow men died. At Baltimore [in 1912] he had been the one man always audible. At San Francisco the little, rasping voice of Carter Glass, answering him, carried just as far

as his own." Arthur F. Mullen, *Western Democrat* (New York, 1940), p. 185.

19. William Bayard Hale, *The Story of a Style* (New York, 1920), pp. 257–303 shows the tired quality of the League speeches. After the Seattle address Tumulty prepared a series of memoranda with suggestions for remaining speeches, and comparison of the memos with the speeches shows incorporation. The greatest response to the President's speeches came after he used Tumulty's suggestions. Blum, *Joe Tumulty and the Wilson Era*, pp. 210–213; Stanley J. Underdal, "Woodrow Wilson at Pueblo, Colorado, September 15, 1919," seminar paper, Indiana University, 1972, p. 31.

20. Cary T. Grayson diary, Sept. 26, 1919.

21. Irwin Hood (Ike) Hoover, *Forty-Two Years in the White House* (Boston, 1934), p. 101.

22. Ibid., pp. 103, 107–108.

23. Grayson, *Woodrow Wilson*, p. 53.

24. So Grayson told Daniels. Josephus Daniels, *The Wilson Era: Years of War and After, 1917–1923* (Chapel Hill, N.C., 1946), p. 512.

25. For the affair of Major Charles Kennedy Campbell Stuart (usually known as Crauford-Stuart), see William Phillips, *Ventures in Diplomacy* (Boston, 1952), pp. 91–92; Jonathan Daniels, *The End of Innocence*, pp. 295–296; George W. Egerton, *Great Britain and the Creation of the League of Nations: Strategy, Politics, and International Organization, 1914–1919* (Chapel Hill, N.C., 1978), p. 191; Edward M. House diary, Nov. 20, Dec. 5, 21, 22, 1919; Jan. 2, Mar. 20, 28, 1920, House MSS, Yale University Library, New Haven, Conn.; Charles Seymour, "End of a Friendship," *American Heritage*, vol. 14 (Aug. 1963), 78n; Joyce G. Williams, "The Resignation of Secretary of State Robert Lansing," *Diplomatic History*, vol. 3 (1979), 342; the same author's *Colonel House and Sir Edward Grey: A Study in Anglo-American Diplomacy* (Lanham, Md., 1984). One questionable remark seems to have been in the form of a question and answer:

Q: What did Mrs. Galt do when President Wilson proposed to her?
A: She fell out of bed.

Also Sir Arthur Willert, *The Road to Safety: A Study in Anglo-American Relations* (New York, 1953), p. 53; Shane Leslie, *Long Shadows* (London, 1966), pp. 179–180. When Grayson visited Lloyd George years later, Sept. 17, 1934, both men assumed the Campbell Stuart affair was the reason Wilson did not see Grey. Frances Stevenson, *Lloyd George: A Diary* (New York, 1971), p. 277. But behind Mrs. Wilson's wrath may have been a far more devious story. There is some evidence that Campbell Stuart was not the cause of President Wilson's refusal to see Grey—that U.S. Army intelligence was the cause. The erstwhile German Ambassador, Bernstorff, it seems, had maintained a connection with a woman who later was friendly with Baruch. The latter refused to sever the relationship, despite the fact that the woman was a German spy. The head of Army intelligence, Colonel (later Brigadier General) Marlborough Churchill, arranged through Assistant Secretary of the Navy Franklin Roosevelt for F.D.R.'s cousin, Alice Roosevelt Longworth, who knew the woman, to place hearing devices in her apartment. Michael Teague, *Mrs. L.: Conversations with Alice Roosevelt Longworth* (Garden City, N.Y., 1981), pp. 162–163. When the woman discovered the devices and informed Baruch, Colonel Churchill blamed Campbell Stuart. Furious because the devices had recorded indiscreet conversations, Baruch appears to have gone to Grayson who went to Mrs. Wilson, who went to the President. In the spring of 1918, Lord Reading heard of presidential displeasure and sent Campbell Stuart home, but the major returned with Grey, who refused to dismiss him without a hearing, which understandably never took place: Grey's assistant Sir William Tyrrell took the woman to lunch and invited her to bring suit against the British government, which she would not do. House diary, loc. cit.; Seymour, "End of a Friendship," p. 78n; James E. Hewes, Jr., to the author, Sept. 19, 1982. Secretary of War Baker possessed the dictaphone recordings and refused to give them to Baruch—and another possible result of the affair may have been the President's unwillingness to appoint Baker as Secretary of State upon Lansing's resignation. Charles Seymour memorandum of a conversation with Colonel House, May 12, 1922, Seymour MSS, Yale University Library.

26. Stockton Axson, memoir of Wilson, ch. on "The Personality of Woodrow Wilson," p. 23.

27. Seeking to discover changes in the Covenant required by the Republican leadership, House during the Peace Conference dealt with Lodge through Henry White, and overtures went to other Republicans. Lodge thought White was speaking for the President. This may well have struck Wilson as disloyalty, when he found out about it. When the President returned to the United States in July, House's enemies may have magnified the colonel's supposed surrenders at Paris in Feb. and Mar., and played on the President's egotism about his new position in world affairs. Irwin H. Hoover MSS, Library of Congress. A toned-down version of this commentary is in *Forty-Two Years in the White House.* But a few weeks before House died, he spoke on Jan. 5, 1938, to Charles Seymour, with the injunction that Seymour not reveal the account for twenty-five years, and in 1963 when Seymour was close to death the account appeared. "The main under-

lying cause was, of course," House said, "the second Mrs. Wilson
. . . He was enchanted by the second Mrs. Wilson and became constantly more dependent upon her." When she first met House in
1915 she had disliked him. At the Peace Conference, House's assistant, Stephen Bonsal, believed Mrs. Wilson was a malign influence.
"Whenever the Colonel appears on the scene Mrs. Wilson's by no
means sunny countenance looks like a thunder cloud. The newspaper
men as well as the Marines now call her 'Mrs. Sitting Bull.' According
to them our unfortunate first lady who likes to describe herself (ignoring her buxom proportions) as a 'little American girl' can only talk
about her Indian ancestry [the President's wife traced her ancestry to
Pocahontas] which they, harsh critics that they are, find quite unnecessary. 'That is revealed' they assert 'or rather proclaimed by the
cockatoo feathers invariably waving from her hats and the clashing
colors of the startling gowns she wears.' " Bonsal diary, undated
1919 (May 3?), Bonsal MSS, Library of Congress. House told Seymour that during Wilson's illness Baruch, Grayson, and Mrs. Wilson
"absolutely controlled" the President. The posthumous testimony of
House elicited posthumous testimony from Grayson, released by the
Grayson family, an essay composed by Wilson's physician after appearance of the House memoirs in the twenties. Grayson stressed
nepotism and egotism as causes of the break. He remarked the presence in Paris of the colonel's brother-in-law, Mezes, and son-in-law,
Gordon Auchincloss, who acted as House's secretary. The House
diary is full of references to the break with the President—Oct. 21,
Nov. 20, Dec. 2, 11, 13, 20, 1919; Jan. 5, 9, July 12, 1920; Oct. 14,
1921; Mar. 10, 23, 31, Apr. 10, Aug. 9, 23, 1924; Mar. 25, 1925; Mar.
28, Dec. 20, 1926. Tumulty, with whom Wilson broke after retirement from the presidency, described Grayson as "the slimy one."
House diary, Mar. 10, 1924. Grayson in turn attributed the break to
House's increased view of himself: "Too many trips to Europe, too
much association with the great folk of the world, too much delegated
responsibility, and too many adulators, spoiled the Colonel House
that I had known in the early years of the Wilson administration."
Cary T. Grayson, "The Colonel's Folly and the President's Distress,"
American Heritage, vol. 15 (Oct. 1964), 96. See also the Grayson diary,
Mar. 15, Apr. 6, 7, 19, 21, 1919. A detailed account of House's
troubles with Wilson and the resultant break is in Inga Floto, *Colonel
House in Paris* (Aarhus, Denmark, 1973; 2d ed., Princeton, N.J., 1981);
the author stresses House's disloyalty, his desire to be an independent negotiator.

28. Lansing's testimony on Shantung, and Bullitt's on the Covenant,
appears in 66th Cong., 1st sess., *Hearings before the Committee on Foreign*

Relations of the United States on the Treaty of Peace with Germany . . . , pp. 182–183, 1276–1277; Beatrice Farnsworth, *William C. Bullitt and the Soviet Union* (Bloomington, Ind., 1967), pp. 66–69; Lansing, *The Peace Negotiations.* The incapacity issue appears in Joseph P. Tumulty, *Woodrow Wilson as I Know Him* (Garden City, N.Y., 1921), p. 445: "When Lansing sought to oust me, I was upon my back. I am on my feet now and I will not have disloyalty about me." Mrs. Wilson in a draft of her book *(My Memoir* [Indianapolis, 1939]) relates that she told her husband to "expose this slimy trail across the fair page of his administration." Edith B. Wilson MSS, Library of Congress. Mrs. Wilson's private secretary, Edith Benham, dictated a memorandum on Feb. 18, 1920, not revealed for more than fifty years, relating how the President's wife hated Lansing for this reason. Joyce G. Williams, "The Resignation of Secretary of State Robert Lansing," pp. 337–343. After appearance of Grey's letter to the London *Times* on accepting ratification with reservations the Secretary also refused to make a secret service investigation of the French Ambassador, Jusserand; next day the President asked for his resignation on the ground that he had usurped executive power by calling Cabinet meetings. James E. Hewes, Jr., to the author, July 27, Sept. 10, 1979. To Secretary Daniels the reason for Lansing's dismissal was his demand upon Mexico late in 1919 for release of the imprisoned consul; Daniels thought Lansing tried to arrange a war with Mexico without consulting the President, and wrote *(The Wilson Era: Years of War and After,* pp. 521, 529–532) that one could not mention the Jenkins case in public. See also Lloyd C. Gardner, "Woodrow Wilson and the Mexican Revolution," in Link (ed.), *Woodrow Wilson and a Revolutionary World: 1913–1921* (Chapel Hill, N.C., 1982), pp. 34–36; Clifford W. Trow, "Woodrow Wilson and the Mexican Interventionist Movement of 1919," *Journal of American History,* vol. 58 (1971–72), 46–72; Mark T. Gilderhus, *Diplomacy and Revolution: U.S.-Mexican Relations under Wilson and Carranza* (Tucson, 1977), ch. 6, "The Question of Intervention," pp. 87–105.

29. Thomas A. Bailey, *Woodrow Wilson and the Great Betrayal* (New York, 1945), p. 61. Taft to Gus Karger, Feb. 22, 1919, Henry F. Pringle, *The Life and Times of William Howard Taft* (2 vols., New York, 1939), II, 943. See also Stone, *The Irreconcilables.*

30. J. Chalmers Vinson, *Referendum for Isolation: Defeat of Article Ten of the League of Nations Covenant* (Athens, Ga., 1961), pp. 16, 21–23.

31. 66th Cong., 1st sess., *Hearings before the Committee on Foreign Relations of the United States on the Treaty of Peace with Germany* . . . , p. 515.

32. Lodge to Theodore Roosevelt, May 18, 1917. Also Roosevelt to Lodge, Jan. 15, 1916 ("What a swine Wilson is!"); Lodge to Roose-

velt, Apr. 23, 1917 ("a mean soul and the fact that he delivered a good message on April 2d does not alter his character"). Lodge nonetheless was willing to work for a compromise: on the "most momentous question" and "making the treaty safe or reasonably safe," to Samuel Colcord, Feb. 27, 1919; to Charles A. Prince, Dec. 1, 1919. Lodge MSS, Massachusetts Historical Society, Boston. A convincing defense of Lodge appears in James E. Hewes, Jr., "Henry Cabot Lodge and the League of Nations," *Proceedings of the American Philosophical Society,* vol. 114 (Aug. 1970).

33. For the way the Covenant broke with tradition see Roland N. Stromberg, *Collective Security and American Foreign Policy: From the League of Nations to Nato* (New York, 1963); Vinson, *Referendum for Isolation.* Also Stromberg's "Uncertainties and Obscurities about the League of Nations," *Journal of the History of Ideas,* vol. 33 (1972), 139–154.

34. Baker MSS, Library of Congress.

35. As the months passed without word from Wilson, House mulled over his personal fall from grace as well as the treaty's collapsing fortunes in the Senate, and in his analyses may have been unfair to his former friend. Certainly the President was not as outgoing as House. For whatever reason the colonel once told Charles Seymour that he, House, had never met a congressman at the presidential dining table. The family, particularly Margaret who was a singer, always invited whatever guests were present, and House said most of hers were rather queer musicians. According to the colonel, Wilson thought that if a proposed measure was right in itself, congressmen ought to vote for it without interviews with the President. It never occurred to him to flatter people; he did not know what political tactics were. He used to say to House, "What is the use of having anything to do with this crowd in Congress?" Memoranda of Mar. 17, 1920, May 12, 1922, Seymour MSS.

36. Cary T. Grayson diary, Mar. 4, 1919.

37. Ibid., Mar. 11.

38. John W. Davis diary, May 31, 1919, Davis MSS, Yale University Library.

39. See the House diary, June 4, 1924, recording a conversation with former Senator Kellogg, then Ambassador to London, soon to be Secretary of State: "Among the things the Ambassador told me was that he himself was the author of the Lodge Reservations; that Lodge did his best to kill them, but when he found it impossible he was forced to report them out of the Committee to the Senate. They then became the Lodge Reservations although he had had practically nothing whatever to do with them. I told the Ambassador that it was a pity that this was not known at the time because I was sure that if

Wilson had known that Kellogg had written the reservations and not Lodge, he would have accepted them. Kellogg said, however, that he told Wilson that after a careful survey of the Senate he could assure him it was not possible to get anything better than these reservations as presented to him. He took them to Wilson, discussed the matter with him, and advised him not to tell him, Kellogg, whether he would accept them for the reason that he did not want to be asked by his colleagues whether the President had accepted them because, if he gave an affirmative answer, they might want to make them stronger. He advised the President to wait until the reservations were adopted by the Senate and then in the two days interval before the vote was taken and when it was impossible to alter them, to tell his Democratic friends in the Senate to accept them. If Wilson had done this another story might have been told."

40. Cable to Curzon, Dec. 6, 1919, FO 800/158, p. 120.
41. Smuts agreed with Grey about the inconsequential nature of the reservations and described them as of "minor importance and not affecting real essence of the Covenant." America, he cabled Lloyd George, "is really necessary to League and even where they are not quite reasonable we should spare no efforts to meet her points of view. Political structure of civilisation has become so unstable that danger of collapse is very great without new factor like League." Nov. 29, 1919, FO 371/4251, pp. 477–479.
42. William C. Widenor, *Henry Cabot Lodge and the Search for an American Foreign Policy* (Berkeley, Calif., 1980), pp. 316–317; Salvatore Prisco III, *John Barrett, Progressive Era Diplomat: A Study of a Commercial Expansionist, 1887–1920* (University, Ala., 1973), pp. 85–86.
43. The following is from Hewes, "Henry Cabot Lodge and the League of Nations," p. 251.
44. The wartime head of the Shipping Board, Edward N. Hurley, met with a group of the President's friends at the Chevy Chase Club in Mar. 1920, in accord with Wilson's wishes, concerning the President's part in the forthcoming political campaign, and the question arose of the Senate's reservations to the Treaty of Versailles. Present were Colby, Glass, Houston, Baruch, Secretary of Labor William B. Wilson, Burleson, Tumulty, Homer S. Cummings who was chairman of the Democratic National Committee, and others. Virtually everyone agreed that the treaty should pass with whatever reservations, the latter being far less important than passage. The question arose of who would inform the President. No one would do it. Hurley, *The Bridge to France* (Philadelphia, 1927), pp. 325–327.

As for the President's possibly vetoing the treaty, that was not an issue, for if he refused to accept the treaty as advised and consented to, he would be refusing to ratify the treaty. No override of his decision then was possible.

In regard to the expression of sympathy with Ireland, Lodge told a member of the British embassy in Washington, Colville Barclay, that adoption by the Senate of such a resolution was really an attack on the President and the Peace Conference "for meddling in affairs extraneous to peace with Germany, in fact it was an attack on the League of Nations." Other nations had meddled with the Monroe Doctrine, he said, so why not meddle in Ireland? Asked if he favored an independent Ireland he replied, "Certainly not." Barclay inquired if he, the senator, would care to send a message to London. "You can say," was the reply, "that I am not as bad as I seem. I have not changed." Cable, Barclay to the Foreign Office, June 8, 1919, FO 371/4248. Lord Curzon minuted the cable: "Party politics once more reign supreme in U.S.A." See Charles Callan Tansill, *America and the Fight for Irish Freedom: 1866–1922* (New York, 1957); John B. Duff, "The Versailles Treaty and the Irish-Americans," *Journal of American History*, vol. 55 (1968–69), 582–598; Francis M. Carroll, *American Opinion and the Irish Question, 1910–23: A Study in Opinion and Policy* (Dublin and New York, 1978). The Irish question bothered President Wilson and his advisers, during and after the war; see the many reports and comments in Link et al. (eds.), *The Papers of Woodrow Wilson*, vols. 43ff.

45. Grayson, *Woodrow Wilson: An Intimate Memoir*, p. 106.

Chapter 11. Readjustment

1. Letter of Jan. 20, 1919, Noland MSS, Harry S. Truman Library, Independence, Mo. "I want to follow a mule down a corn row all the rest of my days or be a Congressman or something where I can cuss Colonels and Generals to my heart's content." To Ethel Noland, Dec. 18, 1918. For demobilization see Burl Noggle, *Into the Twenties: The United States from Armistice to Normalcy* (Urbana, Ill., 1974).
2. Dixon Wecter, *When Johnny Comes Marching Home* (Boston, 1944), p. 304.
3. John W. Thomason, *Fix Bayonets! and Other Stories* (New York, 1970), p. 163.
4. Sidney Fine, *Frank Murphy: The Detroit Years* (Ann Arbor, Mich., 1975), p. 49.
5. Joseph T. Dickman, *The Great Crusade: A Narrative of the World War* (New York, 1927), pp. 227–228; Alfred E. Cornebise, "*Der Rhein Entlang:* The American Occupation Forces in Germany, 1918–1923, a Photo Essay," *Military History*, vol. 46 (1982), 183–189.

NOTES TO PAGES 183-188
285

6. T. Bentley Mott, *Twenty Years as Military Attaché* (New York, 1937), pp. 65–66; Calvin Hoover, *Memoirs of Capitalism, Communism, and Nazism* (Durham, N.C., 1965), p. 67; Keith L. Nelson, *Victors Divided: America and the Allies in Germany, 1918–1923* (Berkeley and Los Angeles, 1975), pp. 49–50, 212, 225–226.

7. Harold and Margaret Sprout, *Toward a New Order of Sea Power: American Naval Policy and the World Scene, 1918–1922* (2d ed., Princeton, N.J., 1943), p. 54; David F. Trask, *Captains and Cabinets: Anglo-American Naval Relations, 1917–1918* (Columbia, Mo., 1972), pp. 285–291; William R. Braisted, *The United States Navy in the Pacific: 1909–1922* (Austin, 1971).

8. Harold and Margaret Sprout, *Toward a New Order of Sea Power*, p. 112.

9. Henry H. Arnold, *Global Mission* (New York, 1949), p. 97.

10. Alfred F. Hurley, *Billy Mitchell: Crusader for Air Power* (rev. ed., Bloomington, Ind., 1975), pp. 43, 68.

11. Lewis Einstein, *A Prophecy of War* (New York, 1918), p. 90.

12. Walter Millis, *Arms and Men* (New York, 1956), p. 200.

13. Forrest C. Pogue, *George C. Marshall: Education of a General, 1880–1939* (New York, 1963), pp. 204, 206, 213; Edward M. Coffman, *The Hilt of the Sword: The Career of Peyton C. March* (Madison, Wis., 1966), p. 199; John Garry Clifford, *The Citizen Soldiers: The Plattsburg Training Camp Movement, 1913–1920* (Lexington, Ky., 1972), pp. 262–295; James E. Hewes, Jr., *From Root to McNamara: Army Organization and Administration, 1900–1963* (Washington, D.C., 1975), pp. 52–53; I. B. Holley, Jr., *General John M. Palmer, Citizen Soldiers, and the Army of a Democracy* (Westport, Conn., 1982), pp. 402–479; undated memorandum by Palmer in Palmer MSS, Library of Congress; James W. Wadsworth, Jr., to Harding, Jan. 21, 1921, Wadsworth MSS, Library of Congress. The New York senator worried about prejudice against the "so-called officer class." He thought the Army could recruit enlisted personnel in time of need but it would be difficult to get officers. Years later, in 1940, by that time a member of the House, Wadsworth became co-sponsor of the new draft law, the Burke-Wadsworth Act.

14. Hewes, *From Root to McNamara*, p. 51.

15. Mark Sullivan, *Our Times: The United States, 1900–1925* (6 vols., New York, 1926–35), V, 652, 654; Daniel Beaver, *Newton D. Baker and the American War Effort: 1917–1919* (Lincoln, Nebr., 1966), p. 199; Charles Sawyer, *Concerns of a Conservative Democrat* (Carbondale, Ill., 1968), p. 32. The *Leviathan* arrived with 514 cases of flu, 463 of pneumonia, and 68 dead. At Brest the situation was bad—1,540 cases of flu, 1,062 of pneumonia, 77 deaths, men dying every ten minutes. Johnson Hagood diary, Oct. 7, 1918, U.S. Army Military History Institute, Carlisle Barracks, Penn. Thirty-eight ships carried 130,000

men across during the epidemic, and 2,000 died. Thomas G. Frothingham, *The Naval History of the World War* (3 vols., Cambridge, Mass.,
1924–26), Ill, 263–264. See also Fred Davis Baldwin, "The American
Enlisted Man in World War I," Princeton University dissertation,
1964, pp. 160–164; A. A. Hoehling, *The Great Epidemic* (Boston,
1961). Because of the epidemic the Navy halted double berthing.

16. Diary, Oct. 10, Wood MSS, Library of Congress.
17. Charles Lanphier Patton diary, undated, Illinois State Historical Library, Springfield.
18. Claude Bowers, *My Life* (New York, 1962), p. 92. See also Marybelle
Burch, " 'Don't Know Only What We Hear': The Soldiers' View of
the 1918 Influenza Epidemic," *Indiana Medical History Quarterly*, vol.
9 (1983), 23–27.
19. Louis Brownlow, *A Passion for Anonymity* (2 vols., Chicago, 1958), II,
72.
20. Lawrence W. Levine, *Defender of the Faith: William Jennings Bryan, the
Last Decade, 1915–1925* (New York, 1965), pp. 118, 128; Paolo E.
Coletta, *William Jennings Bryan: Political Puritan, 1915–1925* (Lincoln,
Nebr., 1969), p. 59.
21. Alice Roosevelt Longworth, *Crowded Hours: Reminiscences* (New York,
1933), p. 307. Daniels diary, Mar. 5, 1918, in Arthur S. Link et al.
(eds.), *The Papers of Woodrow Wilson*, vol. 46 (Princeton, N.J., 1984),
553–554; E. David Cronon (ed.), *The Cabinet Diaries of Josephus Daniels:
1913–1921* (Lincoln, Nebr., 1963), p. 287.
22. To O. S. Rapp, Dec. 26, 1917, Harding MSS, microfilm, Ohio Historical Society, Columbus.
23. Joseph P. Tumulty, *Woodrow Wilson as I Know Him* (Garden City, N.Y.,
1921), p. 410; Virginius Dabney, *Dry Messiah: The Life of Bishop Cannon*
(New York, 1949), pp. 133–134; Coletta, *William Jennings Bryan: Political Puritan*, pp. 7–9. The leading book on Prohibition is James H.
Timberlake, *Prohibition and the Progressive Movement: 1900–1920* (Cambridge, Mass., 1963).
24. Jordan A. Schwarz, *The Speculator: Bernard M. Baruch in Washington,
1917–1965* (Chapel Hill, N.C., 1981), p. 106.
25. Carl P. Parrini, *Heir to Empire: United States Economic Diplomacy, 1916–
1923* (Pittsburgh, 1969); Joseph S. Tulchin, *The Aftermath of War:
World War I and U.S. Policy Toward Latin America* (New York, 1971);
Joan Hoff Wilson, *American Business and Foreign Policy: 1920–1932*
(Lexington, Ky., 1971); Burton I. Kaufman, *Efficiency and Expansion:
Foreign Trade Organization in the Wilson Administration, 1913–1921*
(Westport, Conn., 1974); Michael J. Hogan, *Informal Entente: The Pri-
vate Structure of Cooperation in Anglo-American Economic Diplomacy, 1918–
1928* (Columbia, Mo., 1977); Jeffrey J. Safford, *Wilsonian Maritime*

Diplomacy: 1913–1921 (New Brunswick, N.J., 1978); Ellis W. Hawley, *The Great War and the Search for a Modern Order: A History of the American People and Their Institutions, 1917–1933* (New York, 1979). Also David M. Kennedy, *Over Here: The First World War and American Society* (New York, 1980), pp. 296–347.

26. Edward N. Hurley, *The New Merchant Marine* (New York, 1919), pp. 272–273, quoted in Safford, *Wilsonian Maritime Diplomacy*, p. 252.
27. Hogan, *Informal Entente*, pp. 1–37.
28. Henry F. Pringle, *The Life and Times of William Howard Taft* (2 vols., New York, 1939), II, 915–916. See Valerie Jean Conner, *The National War Labor Board: Stability, Social Justice, and the Voluntary State in World War I* (Chapel Hill, N.C., 1983). A somewhat similarly entitled War Labor Policies Board looked into policies and guides for hours, wages, and working conditions. Arthur S. Link et al. (eds.), *The Papers of Woodrow Wilson*, vol. 49 (forthcoming) relates the attention given by the administration to hourly rates on railroads and street railways.
29. See Bernard Mandel, *Samuel Gompers: A Biography* (Yellow Springs, Ohio, 1963); Frank L. Grubbs, Jr., *The Struggle for Labor Loyalty: Gompers, the A.F. of L., and the Pacifists, 1917–1920* (Durham, N.C., 1968); Simeon Larson, *Labor and Foreign Policy: Gompers, the AFL, and the First World War, 1914–1918* (Cranbury, N.J., 1975); Harold C. Livesay, *Samuel Gompers and Organized Labor in America* (Boston, 1978).
30. It is true that World War I created 21,000 millionaires, doubling their prewar number, but this only reflected inflation.
31. David Brody, *Labor in Crisis: The Steel Strike of 1919* (Philadelphia, 1965), pp. 13–15, 112–114, 162–163, 166–174, 176, 178. For background see Melvin T. Urofsky, *Big Steel and the Wilson Administration: A Study in Business-Government Relations* (Columbus, Ohio, 1969). Labor lost collective bargaining in 1919 but in 1923 achieved the eight-hour day, largely because the strike publicized the industry's impossible working hours. At Homestead on Aug. 20, 1919, Mother Jones related: "Our Kaisers sit up and smoke seventy-five-cent cigars and have lackeys with knee pants bring them champagne while you starve, while you grow old at forty, stoking their furnaces. You pull in your belts while they banquet. They have stomachs two miles long and two miles wide and you fill them. . . . If Gary wants to work twelve hours a day let him go in the blooming mill and work. What we want is a little leisure, time for music, playgrounds, a decent home, books, and the things that make life worthwhile." Brody, *Labor in Crisis*, p. 94. Mother Jones lived to be 100; see Helen Sumner Woodbury, "Mary Harris Jones," *Dictionary of American Biography*, V, Part 2 (New York, 1932), 195–196.
32. For the following account of HCL, see George Soule, *Prosperity Dec-*

ade: From War to Depression, 1917–1929 (New York, 1947), pp. 81–106, and John D. Hicks, *Rehearsal for Disaster* (Gainesville, Fla., 1961), passim.

33. The total of American loans, wartime and immediate postwar, principal only, in millions of dollars: (Associates) Britain, 4,277; France, 3,404; Italy, 1,648; Belgium, 379; Russia, 192; Rumania, 37; Greece, 27; Cuba, 10; Nicaragua,.4; Liberia, .02; (succession states) Poland, 159; Czechoslovakia, 91; Yugoslavia, 51; Austria, 24; Estonia, 13; Armenia, 11; Finland, 8; Latvia, 5; Lithuania, 4; Hungary, 1. See Denise Artaud, *La Question des dettes interalliées et la reconstruction de l'Europe (1917–1929)* (2 vols., Paris and Lille, 1978).

34. Losses were partly because of increased cost of coal, extra maintenance, and much higher wages. In postwar months the government hesitated to raise rates. Railroads later claimed losses under government management and obtained $22,696,015. William G. McAdoo, *Crowded Years* (Boston, 1931), pp. 494, 505–508.

35. Elmus R. Wicker, *Federal Reserve Monetary Policy: 1917–1933* (New York, 1966), pp. 25–56, very interestingly shows that the system's board of governors did not help stem the inflation because they considered supervision of money supply as short-term, seasonal, in accord with the Reserve Act of 1913; and Assistant Secretary of the Treasury Russell Leffingwell, who dominated Treasury policy, mistakenly beheld inflation in terms of bank holdings of government obligations, rather than monetization of government bonds regardless of institutional or private possession. Reserve and Treasury officials raised the rediscount rate to preserve the Treasury's gold supply, fearing that too much money might bring a run on it.

36. Link, *The Higher Realism of Woodrow Wilson and Other Essays* (Nashville, Tenn., 1971), p. 333.

37. Harry S. Truman, *Memoirs: Year of Decisions* (Garden City, N.Y., 1955), p. 134; Robert H. Ferrell (ed.), *The Autobiography of Harry S. Truman* (Boulder, Colo., 1980), pp. 55–56, 130. The haberdashery's failure dogged Truman for years. Because Jacobson took bankruptcy Truman had to pay all the debts of the partnership. He got out from under them in the early thirties, only to find himself in two Senate campaigns that plunged him back into debt. In the midst of the second campaign, in 1940, the farm that had been in his mother's family for a century was foreclosed. He did not have enough money to keep it from being sold, and his sister and aged mother had to move into a little bungalow in the nearby town of Grandview. Seeking to get about in an unfamiliar house, his mother fell down the stairs and broke her hip.

Chapter 12. Civil Liberties and Civil Rights

1. Paul L. Murphy, *World War I and the Origin of Civil Liberties in the United States* (New York, 1979), p. 15.
2. John Garry Clifford, *The Citizen Soldiers: The Plattsburg Training Camp Movement, 1913–1920* (Lexington, Ky., 1972); John Patrick Finnegan, *Against the Specter of a Dragon: The Campaign for American Military Preparedness, 1914–1917* (Westport, Conn., 1974).
3. It attracted many of the country's industrialists, for it ensured a cooperative labor force during a time of economic boom. In the old days employers often welcomed immigrants, but with the coming of the war the stream of immigrant labor declined markedly. They hence urged that Americanism meant cooperation, efficiency, output, "getting the job done." John Higham, *Strangers in the Land: Patterns of American Nativism, 1860–1925* (New Brunswick, N.J., 1955), p. 244. Immigration declined from 1,218,480 in 1914 to 326,700 in 1915; 298,826 in 1916; 295,403 in 1917; 110,618 in 1918; 141,132 in 1919; and 430,001 in 1920. *Historical Statistics of the United States: Colonial Times to 1970* (Washington, D.C., 1975), p. 105.
4. Murphy, *World War I and the Origin of Civil Liberties in the United States*, p. 25.
5. Letter of Feb. 24, 1885, in Arthur S. Link et al. (eds.), *The Papers of Woodrow Wilson*, vol. 4 (Princeton, N.J., 1968), 287.
6. Mark Sullivan, *Our Times: The United States, 1900–1925* (6 vols., New York, 1926–35), V, 439. Early accounts were James R. Mock and Cedric Larson, *Words That Won the War* (Princeton, N.J., 1939) and James R. Mock, *Censorship: 1917* (Princeton, N.J., 1941). The definitive book is Stephen L. Vaughn, *Holding Fast the Inner Lines: Democracy, Nationalism, and the Committee on Public Information* (Chapel Hill, N.C., 1980).
7. Ibid., passim. For the Four Minute Men see Alfred E. Cornebise, *War as Advertised* (Philadelphia, 1984). For the historians and other scholars, George T. Blakey, *Historians on the Homefront: American Propagandists for the Great War* (Lexington, Ky., 1970); Carol Gruber, *Mars and Minerva: World War I and the Uses of the Higher Learning in America* (Baton Rouge, La., 1975).
8. Sullivan, *Our Times: The United States, 1900–1925*, V, 445. The saturation of America and Europe cost a surprisingly small amount, perhaps out of necessity, considering Creel's poor relations with Congress. Speaking in New York he had heard a member of his audience ask whether all congressmen were loyal and his answer was "I do not like slumming, so I won't explore into the hearts of Congress for you." Congress hence limited his appropriation to $1.25 million.

Wilson set aside $5.6 million from a discretionary fund, and sales of
C.P.I. literature brought in $2.8 million. With these modest amounts
Creel did the job.

9. Joseph C. Grew, *Turbulent Era: A Diplomatic Record of Forty Years, 1904–1945* (2 vols., Boston, 1952), I, 334–335.

10. Edward V. Rickenbacker, *Rickenbacker* (Englewood Cliffs, N.J., 1967), p. 104.

11. Higham, *Strangers in the Land,* p. 205; Blakey, *Historians on the Homefront,* p. 1; H. C. Peterson and Gilbert C. Fite, *Opponents of War, 1917–1918* (Madison, Wis., 1957), pp. 14, 194. The coming of war seems to have deranged Root's judgment. Colonel House met him for the first time early in 1917 for dinner at the Plaza in New York, and the talk was intemperate, Root proposing to hang Germans to lampposts upon the slightest provocation. Edward M. House diary, Mar. 23, 1917, House MSS, Yale University Library, New Haven, Conn. See also Richard W. Leopold, *Elihu Root and the Conservative Tradition* (Boston, 1954), p. 121.

12. Peterson and Fite, *Opponents of War,* pp. 14, 162, 196–197; Carl Wittke, *We Who Built America* (New York, 1939), p. 159. See William Preston, Jr., *Aliens and Dissenters: Federal Suppression of Radicals, 1903–1933* (Cambridge, Mass., 1963); Joan M. Jensen, *The Price of Vigilance* (Chicago, 1968).

13. E. David Cronon (ed.), *The Cabinet Diaries of Josephus Daniels: 1913–1921* (Lincoln, Nebr., 1963), p. 166.

14. Ray H. Abrams, *Preachers Present Arms* (New York, 1933), pp. 79, 105; Sullivan, *Our Times: The United States, 1900–1925,* V, 467–468. Van Dyke proposed to hang every man who lifted his voice against America's entering the war.

15. Wittke, *We Who Built America,* pp. 180–182, 184–186, 189; Peterson and Fite, *Opponents of War,* pp. 195–196; Rickenbacker, *Rickenbacker,* p. 115; William L. Langer, "From Isolation to Mediation," in Arthur P. Dudden (ed.), *Woodrow Wilson and the World of Today* (Philadelphia, 1957), p. 54; Link et al. (eds.), *The Papers of Woodrow Wilson,* vol. 49 (forthcoming). Earlier Wilson had taken a strong position in favor of German music and apparently was pilloried for it. For the Germans see especially Frederick C. Luebke, *Bonds of Loyalty: German-Americans and World War I* (DeKalb, Ill., 1974). The strength of anti-German sentiment in 1917–18 has no simple explanation, as Vaughn shows (*Holding Fast the Inner Lines,* pp. 62–65, 273–275). Tensions and differences between the native-born and German-Americans had been increasing for a generation and more, and came to the surface during the war.

16. Higham, *Strangers in the Land,* p. 210. Vaughn, *Holding Fast the Inner*

Lines, pp. 214–215, 327–328, touches on the general subject of foreign governments and civil liberties. For the most part those governments displayed little patience with dissent.

17. Guy F. Hershberger, *War, Peace, and Nonresistance* (Scottsdale, Penn., 1946), ch. 7, "Mennonites in the World War," pp. 113–135; Peterson and Fite, *Opponents of War,* pp. 122–123, 128, 138, 256–264, 274; Daniel Beaver, *Newton D. Baker and the American War Effort: 1917–1919* (Lincoln, Nebr., 1966), p. 233; Edward M. Coffman, *The War to End All Wars: The American Military Experience in World War I* (New York, 1968), p. 75; Charles Chatfield, *For Peace and Justice: Pacifism in America, 1914–1941* (Knoxville, Tenn., 1971), p. 68; Allan Teichroew, "World War I and the Mennonite Migration to Canada to Avoid the Draft," *Mennonite Quarterly Review,* vol. 45 (1971), 219–249; David M. Kennedy, *Over Here: The First World War and American Society* (New York, 1980), pp. 163–165; Baker to Wilson, July 22, 1918, in Link et al. (eds.), *The Papers of Woodrow Wilson,* vol. 49 (forthcoming); Wood diary, Oct. 14, 22, 1917, Wood MSS, Library of Congress.

18. A cartoon in the July issue showed Jesus in prison stripes with ball and chain around his leg and a caption, "The prisoner used language tending to discourage men from enlisting in the United States army." The magazine had a circulation of 25,000 and could have done little harm. Its editors received support from such public-spirited progressives as Amos Pinchot, the suffragist Mrs. O. H. P. Belmont, and the newspaper publisher E. W. Scripps. George Juergens, *News from the White House: The President-Press Relationship in the Progressive Era* (Chicago, 1981), p. 197.

19. This is not to say that the courts ignored First Amendment theories prior to World War I. See Alex J. Anderson, "The Formation Period of First Amendment Theory, 1870–1915," *American Journal of Legal History,* vol. 24 (1980), 56–75; David M. Rabban, "The First Amendment in Its Forgotten Years," *Yale Law Journal,* vol. 90 (1981), 516–595. I am indebted to Stephen L. Vaughn for pointing out how Zechariah Chafee, Jr.'s *Free Speech in the United States* (New York, 1920) skipped over or ignored legal cases about the First Amendment between 1798 and 1917.

20. Donald O. Johnson, "Wilson, Burleson, and Censorship in the First World War," *Journal of Southern History,* vol. 28 (1962), 46–58. See also Johnson's *The Challenge to American Freedoms: World War I and the Rise of the American Civil Liberties Union* (Lexington, Ky., 1963).

21. Holmes came around to Chafee's position, of constructing the "clear and present danger" formula in favor of civil liberties, only in *Abrams v. the U.S.,* Nov. 10, 1919. See Fred D. Ragan, "Justice Oliver Wendell Holmes, Jr., Zechariah Chafee, Jr., and the Clear and Present

Danger Test for Free Speech: The First Year, 1919," *Journal of American History*, vol. 58 (1971–72), 24–45.

22. See Sally M. Miller, *Victor Berger and the Promise of Constructive Socialism: 1910–1920* (Westport, Conn., 1973); and Frederick C. Griffin, *Six Who Protested: Radical Opposition to the First World War* (Port Washington, N.Y., 1977), with chs. on Debs, Morris Hillquit, Eastman, Reed, William D. Haywood, and Emma Goldman.

23. See Fred Thompson, *The IWW: Its First Fifty Years, 1905–1955* (Chicago, 1955), and Harvey O'Connor, *Revolution in Seattle* (New York, 1964), both recollections; together with Robert L. Tyler, *Rebels of the Woods: The IWW in the Pacific Northwest* (Eugene, Ore., 1967), and Melvyn Dubofsky, *We Shall Be All: A History of the Industrial Workers of the World* (2d ed., New York, 1975).

24. See Bruce L. Larson, *Lindbergh of Minnesota: A Political Biography* (New York, 1973), pp. 216–218, 221, 223–224, 235, 238–239, 243–244; Robert L. Morlan, *Political Prairie Fire: The Nonpartisan League, 1915–1922* (Minneapolis, 1955), p. 167; also Carl H. Chrislock, *The Progressive Era in Minnesota: 1889–1918* (St. Paul, Minn., 1971); Murphy, *World War I and the Origin of Civil Liberties in the United States*. Vaughn, *Holding Fast the Inner Lines*, pp. 216, 328–330, maintains that some of the severest repression came from patriots who often headed state and county councils of defense (local offspring of the Council of National Defense created in 1916) or state commissions on public safety, and that this is a largely unexplored area regarding civil liberties during the war.

25. Johnson, *The Challenge to American Freedoms*, p. 119. See also Stanley Coben, *A. Mitchell Palmer: Politician* (New York, 1963).

26. Robert K. Murray, *Red Scare: A Study in National Hysteria* (Minneapolis, 1955), pp. 36, 206.

27. Francis Russell, *A City in Terror: 1919, the Boston Police Strike* (New York, 1975), pp. 47–49, 170.

28. Murray, *Red Scare*, pp. 196–222, 251. See David Williams, "The Bureau of Investigation and Its Critics, 1919–1921: The Origins of Federal Political Surveillance," *Journal of American History*, vol. 68 (1981–82), 560–579, based on investigative records of the Federal Bureau of Investigation released in 1977.

29. *Revolutionary Radicalism: Its History, Purposes and Tactics* (4 vols., Albany, 1920).

30. Morison to Albert J. Beveridge, Aug. 20, 1920, Beveridge MSS, Library of Congress.

31. Wilson did not draw the color line at Princeton. His brother-in-law Stockton Axson remembered that Wilson had written each black applicant that never in his administration of the university had there

been any trouble with Negroes, that whenever one applied for admission the university administration responded that there was no constitutional or other bar, but that many of Princeton's students came from the South and hence the applicant would find himself in an unhappy and embarrassing position, that the applicant's embarrassment would embarrass the administration, and hence the suggestion that in the interest of mutual comfort the applicant should withdraw his application. No black applicant had pressed his application after that. Two or three black graduate students from the theological seminary once attended a professor's philosophy course and sat in the rear of the room. Stockton Axson to Ray Stannard Baker, Oct. 31, 1928, Baker MSS, Library of Congress.

32. Cary T. Grayson diary, Mar. 10, 1919, office of The Papers of Woodrow Wilson, Princeton University Library, Princeton, N.J. The President told the editor of the London *News*, A. G. Gardner, that a noted educator had considered the two greatest men in America, the two whose achievements were most striking, to have been Booker T. Washington and Theodore Roosevelt, but would hardly have considered it any honor to have shaken hands with Roosevelt after he invited Washington to the White House for a luncheon. Ibid., Jan. 21, 1919.

33. Charles H. Williams, *Sidelights on Negro Soldiers* (Boston, 1923), pp. 22–23. Kennedy, *Over Here*, pp. 158–163, points out that discrimination against black registrants derived in part from the effective ban on black volunteering, which left a larger pool of able-bodied men. Moreover, blacks had been historically barred from the skilled trades and could claim few deferments. And black family men were too poor to claim exemptions as husbands and fathers.

34. Of 7,850 Y.M.C.A. workers overseas, 1,350 were women. Only eighty-seven were black, nineteen of them women, and three of the latter were in France before the Armistice, despite the fact that 200,000 black Americans were in that country.

35. See Robert V. Haynes, *A Night of Violence: The Houston Riot of 1917* (Baton Rouge, La., 1976). The President's reaction at the outset was that the "Negro in uniform wants the whole sidewalk." Daniels diary, Aug. 24, 1917, Link et al. (eds.), *The Papers of Woodrow Wilson*, vol. 44 (1983), 49.

36. Young suffered from high blood pressure and the Army retired him, though a medical board said it should have put him on active duty and promoted him. After retirement he went on duty with the Ohio National Guard. "As there is no National Guard," he wrote Pershing, "I am jobless." In June 1918 he rode horseback three-fourths of the way, and walked the remainder, to Washington, 497 miles, where

Baker received him kindly and promised attention but did nothing. Young to Pershing, Sept. 9, 1918, Baker MSS.

37. John Dittmer, *Black Georgia in the Progressive Era: 1900–1920* (Urbana, Ill., 1977), p. 194.

38. John J. Pershing, *My Experiences in the World War* (2 vols., New York, 1931), II, 117.

39. Hugh Young, *A Surgeon's Autobiography* (New York, 1940), p. 362.

40. Perry L. Miles, *Fallen Leaves: Memories of an Old Soldier* (Berkeley, Calif., 1961), pp. 293–294. Miles commanded the draftee regiment, the 371st Infantry, his men from the Deep South. One of the regiments of the Ninety-third, the 369th Infantry, never lost a foot of ground nor had a single soldier captured. The French awarded the regiment the Croix de Guerre and 171 individual medals. On Apr. 6, 1982, the sixty-fifth anniversary of American entrance into the war, the French military attaché at the U.N. honored four survivors of the 369th at a ceremony in Harlem by rewarding his country's decorations. *The New York Times*, June 1, 1982.

41. Allan R. Millett, *The General: Robert L. Bullard and Officership in the United States Army, 1881–1925* (Westport, Conn., 1975), pp. 425–427, 429; Gerald W. Patton, *War and Race: The Black Officer in the American Military, 1915–1941* (Westport, Conn., 1981), pp. 83, 86, 91; Pershing, *My Experiences in the World War*, II, 228–229; Bullard diary, Nov. 7, 12, 1918, Bullard MSS, Library of Congress; Pershing MSS, box 1953, record group 200, National Archives.

42. Williams, *Sidelights on Negro Soldiers*, pp. 24–25.

43. James G. Harbord, *The American Army in France: 1917–1919* (Boston, 1936), pp. 390–392.

44. Williams, *Sidelights on Negro Soldiers*, pp. 146–147.

45. Arthur E. Barbeau and Florette Henri, *The Unknown Soldiers: Black American Troops in World War I* (Philadelphia, 1974), p. 9. Estimates of blacks leaving the South are as high as a million, probably too high, as the census of 1920 showed a net gain of 330,000 in states of the North and West. John Hope Franklin, *From Slavery to Freedom: A History of Negro Americans* (3d ed., New York, 1967), pp. 472–473. For the "great migration" see Nancy J. Weiss, *The National Urban League: 1910–1940* (New York, 1974), pp. 93–128; Florette Henri, *Black Migration: Movement North, 1900–1920* (New York, 1975).

46. Dittmer, *Black Georgia in the Progressive Era*, p. 186.

47. William M. Tuttle, Jr., *Race Riot: Chicago in the Red Summer of 1919* (New York, 1970), passim, especially pp. 10, 95, 98–103. A figure of 2,867 lynchings appears in the resolution presented to the President's secretary, Tumulty, by twenty members of the Committee of the Negro Silent Protest Parade of 1917, in Link et al. (eds.), *The*

Papers of Woodrow Wilson, vol. 43 (1983), 342–343. See also Elliott M. Rudwick, *Race Riot at East St. Louis: July 2, 1917* (Carbondale, Ill., 1964). *The Papers of Woodrow Wilson* contain eloquent letters to the President protesting wartime injustices to blacks, such as Robert R. Moton's letter of June 15, 1918, vol. 48 (forthcoming): ". . . there is more genuine restlessness, and perhaps dissatisfaction, on the part of the colored people than I have ever before known. . . . the whole question is worth your serious personal consideration."

Chapter 13. The Election of 1920

1. Diary, 1919, undated (probably Dec. 31), Morison MSS, Harvard University Archives, Cambridge, Mass. By permission of the Harvard University Archives.
2. Harding to Frank B. Willis, June 1, 1917, Willis MSS, Ohio Historical Society, Columbus.
3. Stockton Axson to Ray Stannard Baker, Oct. 31, 1928, Baker MSS, Library of Congress. Such suffragettes as Carrie Chapman Catt wrote incessantly to the President; after the 1916 presidential election the pressure was very great to support the suffrage amendment. See Arthur S. Link et al. (eds.), *The Papers of Woodrow Wilson*, vols. 40–51 (Princeton, N.J., 1982ff), passim. The President eventually went to great lengths to get the amendment through in time for the 1920 election. When Senator Ollie M. James of Kentucky died, Wilson on Aug. 30, 1918, wrote Governor Augustus O. Stanley that "The matter of woman suffrage is critically important just now, and I am going to make bold to suggest that it would be of great advantage to the party and to the country if his successor entertained views favorable to the pending constitutional amendment." *The Papers of Woodrow Wilson*, vol. 49 (forthcoming). Stanley appointed George B. Martin and duly wrote that the new senator's "profound deference for the wisdom and sagacity of the President will induce him to waive any personal preference or preconceived opinion in this matter." Letter to Wilson, Sept. 7, ibid. Eager to demonstrate his zeal, the governor sent a longer letter to Tumulty, of the same date. Arthur Krock, Princeton '08, by that time editorial manager of the Louisville *Courier-Journal* and *Times*, explained (letter to Wilson, same date) that the governor intended to run for the Senate seat in the regular election and much needed a presidential endorsement. On Sept. 30 the President went before the Senate to ask passage of the amendment as a war measure.
4. Thomas R. Marshall, *Recollections: A Hoosier Salad* (Indianapolis, 1925), p. 234.

5. See Aileen S. Kraditor, *The Ideas of the Woman Suffrage Movement: 1890–1920* (New York, 1965); Alan Grimes, *The Puritan Ethic and Woman Suffrage* (New York, 1967); Christine A. Lunardini, "From Equal Suffrage to Equal Rights: The National Woman's Party, 1913–1923," dissertation at Princeton University, 1981; Barbara J. Steinson, *American Women's Activism in World War I* (New York, 1982).

6. Kurt Wimer, "Woodrow Wilson's Plan for a Vote of Confidence," *Pennsylvania History*, vol. 28 (1961), 4–6, 8, 10–12.

7. Dexter Perkins, *The Evolution of American Foreign Policy* (New York, 1948), p. 110.

8. Alexander L. and Juliette L. George, *Woodrow Wilson and Colonel House: A Personality Study* (New York, 1956), p. 307. Also J. Chalmers Vinson, *Referendum for Isolation: Defeat of Article Ten of the League of Nations Covenant* (Athens, Ga., 1961), p. 110.

9. Davis diary, Jan. 9, 1920, Davis MSS, Yale University Library, New Haven, Conn. Kurt Wimer believes that "Wilson saw it differently during that period. He expected the liberal Republicans to have sufficient influence to secure ratification of the League with reservations—in case of a Republican victory. For this reason it was not necessary for him to compromise." Letter to the author, Mar. 11, 1983.

10. Davis diary, Sept. 2, Oct. 10, 1920, Davis MSS.

11. "Grayson was usually a truthful man and, on the face of it, there seems to be no reason to doubt his statement. On the other hand, Grayson was about the most discreet person who ever lived. Perhaps he gave his advice in response to a direct question from Wilson himself. Mrs. Wilson, in her autobiography, is notoriously unreliable, but I think that we can accept her statement that she usually fended off all suggestions of resignation on the ground that mild activity and continuance in office was essential to Wilson's recovery. As she says very frankly, her first concern was Woodrow Wilson the husband and not Woodrow Wilson the President." Arthur S. Link to the author, Oct. 4, 1982. It is unfortunate that Grayson's diary covers only 1918–19—the trip to Europe, Peace Conference, and "swing around the circle" in September—and he apparently left no personal account of the possibility of the President's resignation other than a brief passage in *Woodrow Wilson: An Intimate Memoir* (New York, 1960), p. 114: "One night he summoned me to his room, and asking the nurse to leave us, he said: 'I have been thinking over this matter of resigning and letting the Vice-President take my place. It is clear that I should do this if I have not the strength to fill the office. If I become convinced that the country is suffering any ill effects from my sickness I shall summon Congress in special session and have you arrange to

get me wheeled in my chair into the House of Representatives. I shall have my address of resignation prepared and shall try to read it myself, but if my voice is not strong enough I shall ask the Speaker of the House to read it, and at its conclusion I shall be wheeled out of the room.' " Grayson added that Wilson never broached the subject again, so this must have been the occasion of which he spoke to Ambassador Davis; but he carefully did not say what he, Grayson, said to Wilson in reply or what Mrs. Wilson later said.

12. Cary T. Grayson diary, Mar. 12, 1919, office of The Papers of Woodrow Wilson, Princeton University Library, Princeton, N.J.

13. Benham diary, May 12, 1919, Edith Benham Helm MSS, Library of Congress.

14. Cary T. Grayson diary, June 11, 1919.

15. Stockton Axson, "Essential Qualities for United States President— Reflectiveness. Notes on a Conversation one Sunday night in August, 1919," pp. 1–3, Axson memoir in office of The Papers of Woodrow Wilson. Arthur Walworth, Woodrow Wilson (3d ed., 2 vols. in 1, New York, 1978), II, 398, dates this conversation as 1918. House that year discerned third-term ambitions; see Link et al. (eds.), The Papers of Woodrow Wilson, vol. 49 (forthcoming), for House diary of Aug. 16, 18, Sept. 8. Shortly after the Nov. elections, the President asked Postmaster General Burleson, "Do you think Mac has got it in his head to run for the presidency?" "I believe he has," said Burleson. "He is not fit for it," said Wilson. So Burleson told Josephus Daniels, who reported it in The Wilson Era: Years of War and After, 1917–1923 (Chapel Hill, N.C., 1946), p. 553.

16. Frank L. Polk diary, Apr. 2, 1920, Polk MSS, Yale University Library.

17. Grayson, Woodrow Wilson: An Intimate Memoir, pp. 116–118.

18. "No matter what others may tell you," Grayson told Woolley, "no matter what you may read about the president being on the road to recovery, I tell you that he is permanently ill physically, is gradually weakening mentally and can't recover. He couldn't possibly survive the campaign. Only the urgency of the situation justifies me in coming to you and making such a statement even in confidence. At times the president, whose grit and determination are marvelous, seems to show a slight improvement, is in good spirits for several days, even a week or ten days—transacts business with Tumulty—and then suffers a relapse, or I should say becomes very morose. At such times it is distressing to be in the room with him. I repeat that he is definitely becoming more feeble. No one can possibly appreciate what Mrs. Wilson, as unselfish and devoted a wife as ever lived, and I have had to endure." Robert W. Woolley, unpublished manuscript entitled "Politics Is Hell," ch. 42; Woolley MSS, Library of Congress.

19. The following account is based on Wimer, "Woodrow Wilson and a Third Nomination," *Pennsylvania History*, vol. 29 (1962), 193, 201–204, 207, 209–210; Jonathan Daniels, *The End of Innocence* (Philadelphia, 1954), p. 315; Edward M. House diary, June 3, 1921, House MSS, Yale University Library; Gene Smith, *When the Cheering Stopped: The Last Years of Woodrow Wilson* (New York, 1964), pp. 161–162; Wesley M. Bagby, "Woodrow Wilson, A Third Term, and The Solemn Referendum," *American Historical Review*, vol. 60 (1954–55), 575; Robert K. Murray, *The Harding Era: Warren G. Harding and His Administration* (Minneapolis, 1969), p. 80.

20. Joseph P. Lash, *Eleanor and Franklin* (New York, 1971), p. 254; Frank Freidel, *Franklin D. Roosevelt: The Ordeal* (Boston, 1954), pp. 81–83. Many years later Marvin McIntyre told Jonathan Daniels that he had asked F.D.R. if he had any illusions he might be elected. "Nary an illusion," was the response. Daniels, *The End of Innocence*, pp. 320–321.

21. Merlo J. Pusey, *Charles Evans Hughes* (2 vols., New York, 1951), I, 403; House in 1919 told Pershing that the general was his favorite Republican hopeful; diary, May 21, Nov. 23, 30, 1919, House MSS. Also Frank E. Vandiver, *Black Jack: The Life and Times of John J. Pershing* (2 vols., College Station, Tex., 1977), II, 997; Pershing to Charles G. Dawes, May 26, June 2, 6, 1920, Dawes MSS, Northwestern University Library, Evanston, Ill. William T. Hutchinson, *Lowden of Illinois: The Life of Frank O. Lowden* (2 vols., Chicago, 1957), II, 383–470, almost convincingly argues a possibility first raised by the newspaperman Irving Brant in 1930, that a hostile Senate subcommittee "set up" Lowden by arranging to display the venality of two Missouri delegates to the Chicago convention.

22. For the convention, see Wesley M. Bagby, "The 'Smoke Filled Room' and the nomination of Warren G. Harding," *Mississippi Valley Historical Review*, vol. 41 (1954–55), 659–661, 663, 672–674, and the same author's *The Road to Normalcy: The Presidential Campaign and Election of 1920* (Baltimore, 1962).

23. Donald R. McCoy, *Calvin Coolidge: The Quiet President* (New York, 1967), pp. 82, 88, 92–94, 113, 120–121, 123.

24. William Allen White, *Autobiography* (New York, 1956), p. 587.

25. William G. McAdoo, *Crowded Years* (Boston, 1931), pp. 388–389.

26. John A. Garraty, *Henry Cabot Lodge: A Biography* (New York, 1953), p. 395. I am indebted to Robert K. Murray for pointing out that "many average men in the street identified with Harding's 'July 4th-style oratory'—especially in the Midwest . . . Not all Americans liked Wilson's intellectualism. Harding was more 'comfortable' to them."

27. Henry L. Stimson and McGeorge Bundy, *On Active Service in Peace and*

War (New York, 1948), p. 105; Richard W. Leopold, *Elihu Root and the Conservative Tradition* (Boston, 1954), p. 148; Garraty, *Henry Cabot Lodge*, p. 393; Vinson, *Referendum for Isolation*, pp. 115–116; Walden S. Freeman, "Will H. Hays and the League of Nations," Indiana University dissertation, 1967; Robert James Maddox, *William E. Borah and American Foreign Policy* (Baton Rouge, La., 1969), pp. 76–77.

28. The manner in which the G.O.P.'s leaders centered the campaign on Wilson, to be sure the League did not get serious discussion, reminded the Democratic publicist Robert Woolley of the story about a Washington bon vivant who was accustomed to evade his masterful mother-in-law by going to New York to get on "a real bender." On one of these trips he received a telegram that the old lady was dead and asking instructions. "Embalm her, then cremate her," was the answer. "Take no chances." "Politics Is Hell," ch. 41, Woolley MSS.

29. Murray, *The Harding Era*, p. 69; the same author's *The Politics of Normalcy: Government Theory and Practice in the Harding-Coolidge Era* (New York, 1973), pp. 2–6, 14–15; Jonathan Daniels, *The Time Between the Wars: Armistice to Pearl Harbor* (Garden City, N.Y., 1966), p. 60; Freidel, *Franklin D. Roosevelt: The Ordeal*, p. 89; Anne W. Lane and Louise H. Wall (eds.), *The Letters of Franklin K. Lane: Personal and Political* (Boston, 1922), pp. 356, 359. Also Carl Wittke, *We Who Built America* (New York, 1939), p. 209; White, *Autobiography*, p. 597; Leopold, *Elihu Root and the Conservative Tradition*, p. 149; William H. Taft to Lord Bryce, Nov. 8, 1920, Bryce MSS, microfilm, Bodleian Library, Oxford University; Link, *Woodrow Wilson: A Brief Biography* (Cleveland, 1963), p. 178. See House diary, Oct. 5, 1920: "It is not the League of Nations, it is not prohibition; it is the unreasonable and unreasoning desire for a change." House MSS, Yale University Library. Nicholas Murray Butler to Bryce, Nov. 16, 1920, Bryce MSS: "My chief error was in underestimating the widespread and deep-seated character of the revolt against President Wilson, his associates, his personality, and his policies. . . . There were no issues except President Wilson. It may be doubted whether more than 500,000 voters . . . cast their votes with reference to the League of Nations."

30. The unions were strongly in favor of nationalizing the railroads under a plan proposed by the counsel of the railroad brotherhoods, Glenn R. Plumb, for a corporation representing public, management and labor. See K. Austin Kerr, *American Railroad Politics: 1914–1920* (Pittsburgh, 1968).

31. Link, *The Higher Realism of Woodrow Wilson and Other Essays* (Nashville, Tenn., 1971), pp. 355–356; the same author's "World War I," in John A. Garraty, *Interpreting American History: Conversations with Historians* (2 vols., New York, 1970), II, 140–141.

32. Axson to Ray Stannard Baker, Aug. 29, 1928, Baker MSS, Library of Congress. After the election the President was serene: "I have not lost faith in the American people. They have merely been temporarily deceived. They will realize their error in a little while."
33. Lodge to Medill McCormick, Nov. 13, 1920, Hanna-McCormick MSS, Library of Congress.
34. Smoot diary, Nov. 2, Dec. 4, 1920, courtesy of Jan Shipps, Indiana University–Purdue University, Indianapolis.
35. K. Austin Kerr, unpublished manuscript on the separate peace with Germany, 1920–21; Kurt and Sarah Wimer, "The Harding Administration, the League of Nations, and the Separate Peace Treaty," *Review of Politics*, vol. 29 (Jan. 1967), 13–24; Peter H. Buckingham, *International Normalcy: The Open Door Peace with the Former Central Powers, 1921–29* (Wilmington, Del., 1983).

Chapter 14. Conclusion

1. The usual view of Wilson is that the President gave little attention to foreign affairs prior to August 1914. For the falseness of this claim (the President devoted much time and energy to Mexican and other Western Hemisphere problems, and some attention to Japan and China) see John Milton Cooper, Jr., " 'An Irony of Fate': Woodrow Wilson's Pre-World War I Diplomacy," *Diplomatic History*, vol. 3 (1979), 425–437. This new view rests on Arthur S. Link et al. (eds.), *The Papers of Woodrow Wilson*, vols. 27–30 (Princeton, N.J., 1978–79). For the address of Oct. 5, 1916, about America no longer confined and provincial see ibid., vol. 38 (1982), 337–338. "Now, the time has come when America, having surrounded herself with all sorts of artificial safeguards and difficulties and timidities, and having refused to play the great part in the world which was providentially cut out for her, has that part thrust upon her."
2. Winston Churchill, *The World Crisis* (New York, 1931), pp. 15, 297.
3. Correlli Barnett, *The Swordbearers: Supreme Command in the First World War* (New York, 1964), p. xvi.
4. L. L. Farrar, Jr., *Divide and Conquer: German Efforts to Conclude a Separate Peace, 1914–1918* (New York, 1978), p. 125.
5. Max Beloff, "Historians in a Revolutionary Age," *Foreign Affairs*, vol. 29 (1950–51), 251.
6. William H. Harbaugh, *Lawyer's Lawyer: The Life of John W. Davis* (New York, 1973), pp. 140–141.
7. Edward H. Buehrig, *Woodrow Wilson and the Balance of Power* (Bloomington, Ind., 1955), pp. 266–267.

8. Henry L. Stimson, *Democracy and Nationalism in Europe* (Princeton, N.J., 1934), p. 29.
9. Gerald D. Nash, "Experiments in Industrial Mobilization: WIB and NRA," *Mid-America*, vol. 45 (1963), 157–174; William E. Leuchtenburg, "The New Deal and the Analogue of War," in John Braeman et al. (eds.), *Change and Continuity in Twentieth-Century America* (Columbus, 1966); Link, "World War I," in John A. Garraty, *Interpreting American History: Conversations with Historians* (2 vols., New York, 1970), II, 142; John Milton Cooper, Jr., *The Warrior and the Priest: Woodrow Wilson and Theodore Roosevelt* (Cambridge, Mass., 1983), ch. 21, "Legacies," pp. 346–361.

Bibliography

Manuscript Sources

Archives

United States—Department of State, National Archives, Washington, D.C.; War and Navy Departments, National Archives.
Great Britain—Foreign Office, Public Record Office, London.
France—Foreign Ministry, Quai d'Orsay, Paris.
Germany—Foreign Ministry, microfilm, National Archives, Washington; Army and Navy Ministries, National Archives.

Diaries

Chandler P. Anderson, Library of Congress, Washington, D.C.; Adin Baber, Chicago Historical Society; Ray Stannard Baker, Library of Congress, courtesy of John W. Davidson[1]; Harry Hill Bandholtz, U.S. Army

[1]"The really great men of action and responsibility never keep diaries. All their energies and thoughts are involved in the thing they do. They write their lives as they go. The President is the only one of the Commissioners here who never stands aside to look at himself or consider this movement as one of historical importance—in which unless he makes the record no one will know he has a part. It is amusing, going about as I do, to discover them all more or less surreptitiously keeping diaries. Lansing writes in a small neat book in a small neat hand. House dictates, sitting on his long couch with his legs coddled in a blanket, to his stenographer and secretary Miss Denton. He speaks in a soft even voice of the celebrities he has had in conference and what he could have done with them. As he talks he brings his small hands together softly from time to time, sometimes just touching the finger tips. Some-

Military History Research Collection,[2] Carlisle Barracks, Carlisle, Penn.; John J. Barada, MHRC; Clee B. Baugher, Liberty Memorial Collection, Kansas City, Mo.; George Louis Beer, Columbia University Library, New York, courtesy of John W. Davidson; Carl E. Black, Illinois State Historical Library, Springfield, Ill.; Tasker H. Bliss, Library of Congress; Stephen Bonsal, Library of Congress; Perry L. Boyer, MHRC; Thomas W. Brahany, Franklin D. Roosevelt Library, Hyde Park, N.Y.; Charles H. Brent, Library of Congress; Karl B. Bretzfelder, MHRC; Wales Brewster, MHRC; Robert L. Bullard, Library of Congress; Garreta H. Busey, World War I Collection, Illinois State Historical Library; John J. Callahan, Missouri Historical Society, St. Louis; Robert Cecil, Bodleian Library, Oxford University, courtesy of John W. Davidson; John Dodge Clark, MHRC; Frederick W. Coleman, MHRC; James L. Collins, Sr., Center of Military History, Department of the Army, Washington, D.C., courtesy of Brigadier General James L. Collins, Jr.; George C. Cook, MHRC; William Bailey Crawford, MHRC; George W. Crile, Western Reserve Historical Society, Cleveland; Edward A. Davies, Evanston Historical Society, Evanston, Ill.; John W. Davis, Yale University Library, New Haven, Conn.; Charles G. Dawes, Northwestern University Library, Evanston, Ill.; Harold P. Doane, Liberty Memorial Collection; William J. Donovan, MHRC; Francis Joseph Duffy, courtesy of Edward G. Duffy; Henry W. Dwight, U.S. Air Force Academy Library, Colorado Springs, Colo.; Bradley A. Fiske, Library of Congress; Emily Frankenstein, Chicago Historical Society; Albert Gleaves, Library of Congress; George W. Goethals, Library of Congress; C. D. Grant, Liberty Memorial Collection; Cary T. Grayson, The Papers of Woodrow Wilson, Princeton University Library, Princeton, N.J.; William G. Haan, MHRC; Johnson Hagood II, MHRC; Charles L. Hamlin, Library of Congress; Dudley J. Hard, Western Reserve Historical Society; W. D. Haselton, MHRC; Edith Benham Helm, Library of Congress; John L. Hines, MHRC; Horace Hobbs, MHRC; Irwin H. Hoover, Library of Congress; Edward M. House, Yale University Library, courtesy of Howard Gotlieb; C. E. N. Howard, MHRC; Edward N. Hurley, University of Notre Dame Archives, South Bend, Ind.; George W. Jean, MHRC; Mark Jefferson, University Microfilms, Ann Arbor, Mich.; Emmett Kent, World War I Collection, Illinois State Historical Library; Robert Lansing, microfilm, Library of Congress; William D. Leahy, Library of Congress; Walter Lippmann, Yale University Library; Breckinridge Long, Library of Congress; Albert H. Lybyer, University of Illinois Archives, Urbana, Ill.; Orville G. Mayer, World War I Collection, Illinois State Historical Library; James E. Meehan, MHRC; Charles B. Merritt, Evanston Historical Society; Evan J. Miller, MHRC; Oscar C. Miller, Chicago Histori-

times the whole palms. General Bliss writes regularly and voluminously in long hand. . . ."—Baker diary, Apr. 28, 1919.
[2]Hereafter MHRC.

cal Society; Clarence J. Minick, Liberty Memorial Collection; Samuel Eliot Morison, Harvard University Archives, Cambridge, Mass.; George Van Horn Moseley, Library of Congress; Howard Webster Munder, Evanston Historical Society; Willard M. Newton, MHRC; Paul Ottenstein, Liberty Memorial Collection; Mason Patrick, U.S. Air Force Academy Library; Charles Lanphier Patton, Illinois State Historical Library; John J. Pershing, Library of Congress; William R. Phillips, Liberty Memorial Collection; Frank L. Polk, Yale University Library; Charles D. Rhodes, National Archives Library; Elmer W. Sherwood, Lilly Library, Indiana University, Bloomington; Reed Smoot, courtesy of Jan Shipps; Henry L. Stimson, Yale University Library; Willard T. Thompson, Liberty Memorial Collection; David Miles Thornton, Evanston Historical Society; James W. Wadsworth, Jr., Library of Congress; Jonas E. Warrell, MHRC; Charles L. White, Indiana State Library, Indianapolis; Walter S. Williams, U.S. Air Force Academy; Leonard Wood, Library of Congress; Emma Marie Zangler, MHRC.

Manuscript Collections

Raymond B. Austin, MHRC; James E. Babb, Yale University Library; Adin Baber, Chicago Historical Society; Newton D. Baker, Case-Western Reserve University Archives, Cleveland; Newton D. Baker, Library of Congress; Newton D. Baker, Western Reserve Historical Society, Cleveland; Ray Stannard Baker, Library of Congress; Arthur J. Balfour, British Foreign Office records, Public Record Office; Harry H. Bandholtz, MHRC; Louis H. Bash, Illinois State Historical Library; Reginald R. Belknap, Naval Historical Foundation Collection, Library of Congress; Edward Price Bell, Newberry Library, Chicago; Louis Berger, World War I Collection, Illinois State Historical Library; Elden Sprague Betts, World War I Collection, Illinois State Historical Library; Albert J. Beveridge, Library of Congress; Tasker H. Bliss, Library of Congress; Stephen Bonsal, Library of Congress; Mary Josephine Booth, Illinois State Historical Library; Gutzon Borglum, Library of Congress; Perry L. Boyer, MHRC; Charles H. Brent, Library of Congress; Karl B. Bretzfelder, MHRC; Mark L. Bristol, Naval Historical Foundation Collection, Library of Congress; John W. Broad, MHRC; William Carey Brown, MHRC; James Bryce, microfilm, Bodleian Library, Oxford; James Bryce, British Foreign Office records, Public Record Office; Robert J. Bulkley, Western Reserve Historical Society; Robert L. Bullard, Library of Congress; Theodore E. Burton, Western Reserve Historical Society; Robert Cecil, British Foreign Office records, Public Record Office; Chicago Peace Society, Chicago Historical Society; Bradford G. Chynoweth, MHRC; John Dodge Clark, MHRC; Paul H. Clark, Library of Congress; Powhatan H. Clarke, Missouri Historical Society; James L. Collins, Sr., Center of Military History, Department of the Army, courtesy of Brigadier General

James L. Collins, Jr.; George C. Cook, MHRC; Charles H. Corlett, MHRC; James M. Cox, Ohio Historical Society; George W. Crile, Western Reserve Historical Society; Benedict Crowell, Case-Western Reserve University; Benedict Crowell, Western Reserve Historical Society; George Curzon, British Foreign Office records, Public Record Office; Charles G. Dawes, Northwestern University Library; Frederick M. Delano, MHRC; William J. Donovan, MHRC; Norman Arthur Dunham, MHRC; Henry W. Dwight, U.S. Air Force Academy Library; Clarence Edwards, Massachusetts Historical Society, Boston; Harold B. Fiske, record group 200, National Archives; Henry P. Fletcher, Library of Congress; David R. Francis, Missouri Historical Society; Tod B. Galloway, Ohio Historical Society; Albert Gleaves, Library of Congress; Harold J. Gordon, Ohio Historical Society; George W. Goethals, Library of Congress; Lloyd C. Griscom, Library of Congress; Hermann Hagedorn, Library of Congress; James G. Harbord, Library of Congress; James G. Harbord, record group 200, National Archives; James G. Harbord, New-York Historical Society, New York; Warren G. Harding, microfilm, Ohio Historical Society; Harman Family, Western Reserve Historical Society; Carter Harrison IV, Newberry Library; W. D. Haselton, MHRC; Nelson J. Hawley, Missouri Historical Society; Ralph Hayes, Library of Congress; Charles W. Hill, MHRC; John L. Hines, MHRC; Horace Hobbs, MHRC; Courtney H. Hodges, Dwight D. Eisenhower Library, Abilene, Kans.; Holmes and Pyott, Chicago Historical Society; Irwin H. Hoover, Library of Congress; C. E. N. Howard, MHRC; Charles E. Hughes, Library of Congress; Cordell Hull, Library of Congress; Edward N. Hurley, University of Notre Dame Archives; George W. Jean, MHRC; H. H. Kohlsaat, Illinois State Historical Library; William Kraemer, Missouri Historical Society; Frank P. Lahm, U.S. Air Force Historical Research Center, Maxwell Air Force Base, Ala.; Victor F. Lawson, Newberry Library, Chicago; John A. Lejeune, Library of Congress; Henry Cabot Lodge, Massachusetts Historical Society; Quentin R. Logie, MHRC; Albert H. Lybyer, University of Illinois Archives; Samuel and Stuart Lyon, MHRC; Walter A. McCleneghan, Illinois State Historical Library; Medill McCormick, in Hanna-McCormick Family, Library of Congress; Frank Ross McCoy, Library of Congress; Harriet M. MacDonald, Western Reserve Historical Society; Charles B. McVay, Library of Congress; Peyton C. March, Library of Congress; Leslie J. Martin, MHRC; Ivan C. Meggitt, in possession of the author; Charles B. Merritt, Evanston Historical Society; Ray T. Miller, Western Reserve Historical Society; Oswald D. Moore, MHRC; Sterling Morton, Chicago Historical Society; Morton Family, Chicago Historical Society; George Van Horn Moseley, Library of Congress; Howard Webster Munder, Evanston Historical Society; Agnes Nestor, Chicago Historical Society; Harry S. New, Indiana State Library; Richard A. Newhall, courtesy of Russell H. Bostert; Mary Ethel Noland, Harry S. Truman Library; John G.

Oglesby, Illinois State Historical Library; John McA. Palmer, Library of Congress; John J. Pershing, Library of Congress; John J. Pershing, record groups 200, 407, National Archives; Key Pittman, Library of Congress; Frank L. Polk, Yale University Library; William V. Pratt, Library of Congress; William V. Pratt, Naval War College Historical Collection, Newport, R.I.; Marquess of Reading (Rufus Isaacs), British Foreign Office records, Public Record Office; Franklin D. Roosevelt, Franklin D. Roosevelt Library; Charles L. Samson, Chicago Historical Society; Francis B. Sayre, Library of Congress; Hugh L. Scott, Library of Congress; Charles Seymour, Yale University Library; Sladen Family, MHRC; Bertrand L. Smith, Sr., MHRC; Truman and Katherine Smith, MHRC; Lawrence Y. Sherman, Illinois State Historical Society; Brehon B. Somervell, MHRC; Cecil Spring Rice, British Foreign Office records, Public Record Office; Joseph Strauss, Library of Congress; Mark Sullivan, Library of Congress; Charles P. Summerall, Library of Congress; Montgomery Meigs Taylor, Library of Congress; David Miles Thornton, Evanston Historical Society; Harry S. Truman, Harry S. Truman Library; [United States] Council of National Defense, Ohio Branch, Ohio Historical Society; Monroe Van Raalte, Missouri Historical Society; James W. Wadsworth, Jr., Library of Congress; Arthur Walworth, Yale University Library; Frederic W. Wile, Library of Congress; Walter S. Williams, U.S. Air Force Academy Library; Frank B. Willis, Ohio Historical Society; Edith Bolling Wilson, Library of Congress; Woodrow Wilson, Library of Congress; Leonard Wood, Library of Congress; World War I Collection, Illinois State Historical Society; World War I Collection, Indiana State Library; World War I Collection, Ohio Historical Society.

Unpublished Reminiscences

Stockton Axson, The Papers of Woodrow Wilson; William Bloch, Jr., MHRC; Murvyn F. Burke, MHRC; Charles H. Corlett, MHRC; A. Draper Dewees, MHRC; Hugh A. Drum, courtesy of Edward M. Coffman; George B. Duncan, courtesy of Edward M. Coffman; Norman Arthur Dunham, MHRC; Frank L. Faulkner, MHRC; Georgia E. Finley, Lilly Library, Indiana University; Charles H. Gerhardt, MHRC; Gerald F. Gilbert, MHRC; Farley E. Granger, MHRC; John L. Hackley, Liberty Memorial Collection; Johnson Hagood II, MHRC; Leroy Y. Haile, MHRC; Laurence Halstead, Sr., in Halstead-Maus Family, MHRC; Harry P. R. Hansen, MHRC; Emma Boutelle Hawley, Western Reserve Historical Society; Malcolm B. Helm, MHRC; Guy V. Henry, Jr., MHRC; Edward Guy Johnston, MHRC; E. L. Kurtzeborn, Missouri Historical Society; Joseph Douglas Lawrence, MHRC; Michael J. Lenihan, MHRC; Chris C. Loehde, Illinois State Historical Library; Wilfred A. Mack, MHRC; Clarence L. Mahan, MHRC; Walter A. McCleneghan, Illinois State Historical Library; Charles B. McVay, Library of Congress; Paul Murphy, MHRC; Roy V. Myers, MHRC; William V. Pratt (with assistance of Felecia Hyde), Naval War College Historical Collection; Daniel Sargent, MHRC; Earl D. Seaton, MHRC; Truman and Katherine Smith, MHRC; Robert W. Woolley, Library of Congress.

Oral Histories[3]

Clifton B. Cates, Frederic Coudert, Perrin C. Galpin, James W. Gerard, Lloyd C. Griscom, Florence J. Harriman, Burton J. Hendrick, Herbert H. Lehman, Vere C. Leigh, Edward D. McKim, Theodore Marks, Milton A. Reckord, George Rublee, Francis B. Sayre, Gerard Swope, Harold C. Train, James W. Wadsworth, Jr., Stanley Washburn, Robert E. Wood.

Published Sources[4]

Statistics

Department of Commerce, *Historical Statistics of the United States: Colonial Times to 1970* (2d ed., Washington, 1975) is indispensable, and may be supplemented with the *Statistical Abstract of the United States* and if necessary the decennial census. For its special subject see Leonard P. Ayres, *The War with Germany: A Statistical Summary* (2d ed., Washington, 1919), which must be used with caution, as so many of the Army's statistics amounted to informed guesses. Likewise John Maurice Clark, *The Cost of the War to the American People* (New Haven, Conn., 1931), opaque figures and a speculative text.

Documents

A first resort is the *Congressional Record,* together with committee hearings and attendant documents. The Chamberlain committee published its investigation of the war effort: 65th Cong., 2d sess., *Hearings by the Senate Committee on Military Affairs, Investigation of the War Department* (Washington, 1918). After the war came hearings on Admiral Sims' allegations concerning the Navy Department, and on reorganization of the Army. For the Senate and the League see 66th Cong., 1st sess., *Hearings Before the Committee on Foreign Relations of the United States on the Treaty of Peace with Germany Signed at Versailles, on June 28, 1919* (Washington, 1919), a mine of information.

The U.S. Army published a massive series of documents, *United States Army in the World War, 1917–1919* (17 vols., Washington, 1948). See also the

[3]All of the following are from the Oral History Collection, Columbia University, except for Vere C. Leigh, Edward D. McKim, and Theodore Marks, which are from the Harry S. Truman Library, and Milton A. Reckord from MHRC.
[4]Including dissertations.

Annual Reports of the Secretary of War, especially for 1919 (3 vols., Washington, 1920). Also *American Armies and Battlefields in Europe* (Washington, 1938), by the battle monuments commission, headed by Pershing and assisted by Major Dwight D. Eisenhower.

Diplomatic records are in regular volumes of the series *Foreign Relations of the United States,* for 1917 (Washington, 1926), 1918 (1930), 1919 (2 vols., 1934), 1920 (3 vols., 1935–36), and supplements for 1917 (3 vols., 1931–32), 1918 (3 vols., 1933), Russia: 1918 (3 vols., 1931–32), Russia: 1919 (1937), the Lansing papers that came belatedly to the Library of Congress (2 vols., 1939–40), II, and papers on the Paris Peace Conference (13 vols., 1942–47). Series are in progress for other countries—Britain, France, Germany.

For the Peace Conference see also Harold W. Temperley (ed.), *A History of the Peace Conference of Paris* (6 vols., London, 1920–24); Hunter Miller, *My Diary at the Conference of Paris* (21 vols., 1924), published in a very limited edition; the diary of Sir Maurice Hankey edited by Stephen Roskill (below, p. 326); Paul J. Mantoux, *Les délibérations du conseil des quatre* (2 vols., Paris, 1955), also in English translation (Geneva, 1964); and originals or reprints of the American Inquiry handbooks (41 vols.) and British handbooks (164 vols.).

For Woodrow Wilson's life the present-day reader may now turn to the multivolume account, *The Papers of Woodrow Wilson,* edited by Arthur S. Link and staff. The initial volume in this grand series, which includes Wilson's writings but also letters sent and received, together with diary accounts surrounding Wilson's life, appeared in 1966, and by 1984 the published series had gone to volume 47 (May 12, 1918).[5]

General

The historical literature about Woodrow Wilson and World War I has reached a size that may only be described as formidable. The best place to begin is books in the present series, The New American Nation, edited by Henry Steele Commager and Richard B. Morris, especially George E. Mowry, *The Era of Theodore Roosevelt and the Birth of Modern America: 1900–1912* (New York, 1958) and Arthur S. Link, *Woodrow Wilson and the Progressive Era: 1910–1917* (New York, 1954). The aftermath appears in John D. Hicks, *Republican Ascendancy: 1921–1933* (New York, 1960). An older account, of social history, in The History of American Life series, is Preston W. Slosson, *The Great Crusade and After: 1914–1928* (New York, 1930). Other general books are William E. Leuchtenburg, *The Perils of Prosperity: 1914–32*

[5] *The Papers of Woodrow Wilson* are based on the Wilson MSS in the Library of Congress, which now are available in 540 microfilm reels together with a three-volume index.

(Chicago, 1958); Jean-Baptiste Duroselle, *From Wilson to Roosevelt: Foreign Policy of the United States, 1913–1945* (Cambridge, Mass., 1963), by the distinguished French scholar; Daniel M. Smith, *The Great Departure: The United States and the Search for a Modern Order: A History of the American People and Their Institutions, 1917–1933* (New York, 1979), a thoughtful analysis. David M. Kennedy, *Over Here: The First World War and American Society* (New York, 1980) is the most recent general treatment, written with grace and wit and attention to the extraordinary materials, manuscript and published, that now stand available to researchers.

Estimates of the President of 1913–21 appeared while Wilson was in office and shortly after his retirement, and one of the best was by Charles Seymour, *Woodrow Wilson and the World War* (New Haven, Conn., 1921), by a member of the Inquiry who later assisted Colonel House with his memoirs. Joseph P. Tumulty, *Woodrow Wilson as I Know Him* (Garden City, N.Y., 1921) drew on memory and some correspondence. The year of Wilson's death was marked by William Allen White's *Woodrow Wilson: The Man, His Times, and His Task* (Boston, 1924), critical, with the theme that the President considered that he had a first-class mind when it indeed was second-class; and two more favorable accounts, Josephus Daniels, *The Life of Woodrow Wilson: 1856–1924* (Philadelphia, 1924), by the former Secretary of the Navy, and David Lawrence, *The True Story of Woodrow Wilson* (New York, 1924), by one of Wilson's students at Princeton, the well-known newspaperman. Ray Stannard Baker, *Woodrow Wilson: Life and Letters* (8 vols., Garden City, N.Y., 1927–39), by Wilson's press secretary during the Peace Conference, used the President's papers, which weighed four tons (including the file cabinets), was uncritical to the point of defensiveness, and only reached the Armistice; Baker meanwhile (1923) published three volumes on the Peace Conference. Edith Bolling Wilson's *My Memoir* (Indianapolis, 1939) coincided with the last of the Baker books. Herbert C. F. Bell, *Woodrow Wilson and the People* (Garden City, N.Y., 1945) beheld Wilson as a great soldier of freedom who made few if any errors, fighting against benighted antagonists; its author consulted surviving Wilsonians. Then, beginning in 1947, Arthur S. Link brought out his magisterial biography, *Wilson* (Princeton, N.J.); in five volumes he has reached the beginning of Wilson's second presidential term. The Link biography represents the last word on Wilson scholarship. Meanwhile other books, including short one-volume accounts by Link, have come out: Edward H. Buehrig, *Woodrow Wilson and the Balance of Power* (Bloomington, Ind., 1955), a thoughtful analysis; John Morton Blum, *Woodrow Wilson and the Politics of Morality* (Boston, 1956), well-written and tightly argued; John A. Garraty, *Woodrow Wilson: A Great Life in Brief* (New York, 1956), admirable; Alexander L. and Juliette L. George, *Woodrow Wilson and Colonel House: A Personality Study* (New York, 1956), a psychological study; Arthur S. Link, *Wilson the Diplomatist: A Look at His Major Foreign*

Policies (Baltimore, 1957), and its revised edition, *Woodrow Wilson: Revolution, War, and Peace* (Arlington Heights, Ill., 1979); Edward H. Buehrig (ed.), *Wilson's Foreign Policy in Perspective* (Bloomington, Ind., 1957); Arthur P. Dudden (ed.), *Woodrow Wilson and The World of Today* (Philadelphia, 1957); Arthur Walworth, *Woodrow Wilson* (2 vols., Boston, 1958; 3d ed., New York, 1978), winner of the Pulitzer prize; Arthur S. Link, *Woodrow Wilson: A Brief Biography* (Cleveland, 1963); the same author's edited *Woodrow Wilson: A Profile* (New York, 1968); Arthur S. Link, *The Higher Realism of Woodrow Wilson and Other Essays* (Nashville, 1971); Klaus Schwabe, *Woodrow Wilson: Ein Staatsmann zwischen Puritanertum und Liberalismus* (Goettingen, 1971); Edwin Tribble (ed.), *A President in Love: The Courtship Letters of Woodrow Wilson and Edith Bolling Galt* (Boston, 1981); Arthur S. Link (ed.), *Woodrow Wilson and a Revolutionary World: 1913–1921* (Chapel Hill, N.C., 1982); John Milton Cooper, Jr., *The Warrior and the Priest: Woodrow Wilson and Theodore Roosevelt* (Cambridge, Mass., 1983), an extraordinary double biography.

Chapter 2. War

When war came in April 1917 the U.S. Army had to transform itself, and the sort of war that it faced is apparent to latterday students in the photographic books such as Alvin M. Josephy, Jr. (ed.), *The American Heritage History of World War I* (New York, 1964); Frank Freidel, *Over There: The Story of America's First Great Overseas Crusade* (Boston, 1964), a fine text based on soldiers' diaries and reminiscences, with pictures from the National Archives; and from the British side John Terraine, *The Great War, 1914–1918: A Pictorial History* (New York, 1965) and John Ellis, *Eye-Deep in Hell: Trench Warfare in World War I* (New York, 1976). From the point of view of American soldiers see Raymond B. Fosdick, *Keeping Our Fighters Fit* (New York, 1918), a period piece, together with Fosdick's *Chronicle of a Generation: An Autobiography* (New York, 1958); Mark Sullivan, *Our Times*, vol. 5, *Over Here: 1914–1918* (New York, 1933); William Matthews and Dixon Wecter, *Our Soldiers Speak: 1775–1918* (Boston, 1943), pp. 265–359; Matthew T. Downey, *Carl Campbell Brigham: Scientist and Educator* (Princeton, N.J., 1961) and the later article by Daniel J. Kevles, "Testing the Army's Intelligence: Psychologists and the Military in World War I," *Journal of American History*, vol. 55 (1968–69), 565–581; Fred Davis Baldwin, "The American Enlisted Man in World War I," dissertation at Princeton University, 1964; and John Garry Clifford's excellent *The Citizen Soldiers: The Plattsburg Training Camp Movement, 1913–1920* (Lexington, Ky., 1972).

War Department officials appear in Frederick Palmer, *Newton D. Baker: America at War* (2 vols., New York, 1931), an authorized biography; C. H. Cramer, *Newton D. Baker: A Biography* (Cleveland, 1961), well-done; Daniel Beaver, *Newton D. Baker and the American War Effort: 1917–1919* (Lincoln,

Nebr., 1966), admirably researched and written; Ralph Hayes, "Third Assistant Secretary of War," in Harry J. Carman et al., *Appreciations of Frederick Paul Keppel* (New York, 1951), pp. 17–37; John Douglas Forbes, *Stettinius, Sr.: Portrait of a Morgan Partner* (Charlottesville, Va., 1974).

For the generals whose task was to produce the new Army see Hugh Lennox Scott, *Some Memories of a Soldier* (New York, 1928), far more interesting for the old Army; Joseph B. Bishop and Farnham Bishop, *Goethals: Genius of the Panama Canal* (New York, 1930), an insufficient appraisal, perhaps because both authors died while the book was in preparation; Hermann Hagedorn, *Leonard Wood: A Biography* (2 vols., New York, 1931), an ardent defense, and Jack C. Lane, *Armed Progressive: General Leonard Wood* (San Rafael, Calif., 1978), a convincing case for Wood's incorrigibility; Peyton C. March, *The Nation at War* (Garden City, N.Y., 1932), more an attack on the Pershing memoirs ("the veriest blah," he wrote to Baker, Mar. 4, 1931; Baker MSS) than a careful drawing of March's great accomplishments, which appear in Edward M. Coffman, *The Hilt of the Sword: The Career of Peyton C. March* (Madison, Wisc., 1966); Hugh S. Johnson, *The Blue Eagle from Egg to Earth* (Garden City, N.Y., 1935), a forthright discussion of World War I but far from the analysis that Johnson deserved; and David A. Lockmiller, *Enoch H. Crowder: Soldier, Lawyer and Statesman* (Columbia, Mo., 1955), perhaps an overdrawing of Crowder's qualities.

Reconstruction of the War Department appears in its *Annual Reports*, especially March's pages (235–479) in the first volume for 1919; Pierce G. Fredericks, *The Great Adventure: America in the First World War* (New York, 1960), popular and very interesting; Edward M. Coffman, "The Battle Against Red Tape: Business Methods of the War Department General Staff, 1917–18," *Military Affairs*, vol. 26 (1962–63), 1–10; Russell F. Weigley, *History of the United States Army* (New York, 1967), pp. 355–394; Harvey A. DeWeerd, *President Wilson Fights His War: World War I and the American Intervention* (New York, 1968), a volume in the series Wars of the United States; Edward M. Coffman, *The War to End All Wars: The American Military Experience in World War I* (New York, 1968), definitive; Daniel R. Beaver, "George W. Goethals and the Problem of Military Supply," in Beaver (ed.), *Some Pathways in Twentieth-Century History: Essays in Honor of Reginald Charles McGrane* (Detroit, 1969); Peter Karsten, "Armed Progressives: The Military Reorganizes for the American Century," in Jerry Israel (ed.), *Building the Organizational Society: Essays on Associational Activities in Modern America* (New York, 1972), pp. 197–232; Russell F. Weigley, *The American Way of War: A History of United States Military Strategy and Policy* (New York, 1973); John Patrick Finnegan, *Against the Specter of a Dragon: The Campaign for American Military Preparedness, 1914–1917* (Westport, Conn., 1974); James E. Hewes, Jr., "The United States Army General Staff, 1900–1917," *Military Affairs*, vol. 38 (1974), 67–71, together with comments by Edward M. Coffman (pp.

71–72); Hewes's *From Root to McNamara: Army Organization and Administration, 1900–1963* (Washington, 1975), far and away the best source for its subject; Edward M. Coffman, *The Young Officer in the Old Army* (Air Force Academy, Colo., 1976), the Harmon lectures; Russell F. Weigley (ed.), *New Dimensions in Military History: An Anthology* (San Rafael, Calif., 1976), especially essays by Beaver, Coffman, and Gaddis Smith; Timothy K. Nenninger, *The Leavenworth Schools and the Old Army: Education, Professionalism, and the Officer Corps of the United States Army, 1881–1918* (Westport, Conn., 1978); James L. Abrahamson, *American Arms for a New Century: The Making of a Great Military Power* (New York, 1981); Andrew Joseph Bacevich, "American Military Diplomacy, 1898–1949: The Role of Frank Ross McCoy," dissertation at Princeton University, 1982.

Chapter 3. Getting "Over There"

General books on naval affairs during World War I are quite helpful, even one of the earliest, Thomas G. Frothingham, *The Naval History of the World War* (3 vols., Cambridge, Mass., 1924–26), for which see III (1926), *The United States in the War, 1917–1918*. Also Robert Greenhalgh Albion and Jennie Barnes Pope, *Sea Lanes in Wartime: The American Experience, 1775–1942* (New York, 1942); Harold and Margaret Sprout, *Toward a New Order of Sea Power: American Naval Policy and the World Scene, 1918–1922* (2d ed., Princeton, N.J., 1943); S. W. Roskill, *The Strategy of Sea Power: Its Development and Application* (London, 1962), pp. 99–142 on World War I, from a British Navy point of view. By far the best book on World War I is David F. Trask, *Captains and Cabinets: Anglo-American Naval Relations, 1917–1918* (Columbia, Mo., 1973).

The Navy Department's policies appear in Josephus Daniels, *The Wilson Era: Years of War and After, 1917–1923* (Chapel Hill, N.C., 1946); Jonathan Daniels, *The End of Innocence* (Philadelphia, 1954), by the Secretary's son, about the World War I era; E. David Cronon (ed.), *The Cabinet Diaries of Josephus Daniels: 1913–1921* (Lincoln, Nebr., 1963); Joseph L. Morrison, *Josephus Daniels: The Small-d Democrat* (Chapel Hill, N.C., 1966). For the Assistant Secretary see Frank Freidel, *Franklin D. Roosevelt: The Apprenticeship* (Boston, 1952) and *The Ordeal* (1954); also Joseph P. Lash, *Eleanor and Franklin* (New York, 1971).

The Navy's problems as viewed from Europe are in William S. Sims, *The Victory at Sea* (Garden City, N.Y., 1920), edited with an introduction by David F. Trask and reprinted by the Naval Institute Press (Annapolis, Md., 1984) in its Classics of Naval Literature series; and Elting E. Morison, *Admiral Sims and the Modern American Navy* (Cambridge, Mass., 1942). Also Albert Gleaves, *A History of the Transport Service: Adventures and Experiences of United States Transports and Cruisers in the World War* (New York, 1921); William F. Halsey and Joseph Bryan III, *Admiral Halsey's Story* (New York, 1947), by a destroyer commander at Queenstown. The Navy Department's Washington difficulties are thoroughly discussed in Gerald E. Wheeler, *Admiral William Veazie Pratt, U.S. Navy: A Sailor's Life* (Washington, 1974); and tangentially in Paolo E. Coletta, *Admiral Bradley A. Fiske and the American Navy* (Lawrence, Kans., 1979).

For their special subjects see William Bell Clark, *When the U-Boats Came to America* (Boston, 1929), together with James M. Merrill, "Submarine Scare, 1918," *Military Affairs*, vol. 17 (1953), 181–190; Thomas A. Bailey, *The Policy of the United States Toward the Neutrals: 1917–1918* (Baltimore, 1942); Philip K. Lundeberg, "Undersea Warfare and Allied Strategy in World War I," *Smithsonian Journal of History*, I, nos. 3, 4 (1966–67); Holger H. Herwig and David F. Trask, "The Failure of Imperial Germany's Undersea Offensive Against World Shipping, February 1917–October 1918," *Historian*, vol. 33 (1970–71), 611–636; Dean C. Allard, "Admiral William S. Sims and United States Naval Policy in World War I," *American Neptune*, vol. 35 (1975), 97–110; and the same author's "Anglo-American Naval Differences During World War I," *Military Affairs*, vol. 44 (1980), 75–81.

Chapter 4. The AEF

The U.S. Army in Europe receives much space in the pictorial accounts, mentioned earlier, and also the books by DeWeerd and Coffman. An early official history was Shipley Thomas, *The History of the A.E.F.* (New York, 1920). James G. Harbord, *The American Army in France: 1917–1919* (Boston, 1936) was of course sponsored by Pershing to challenge March, who in turn had challenged Pershing's memoirs.

The commander-in-chief of the AEF has received much recent scholarly attention, if only because of the angularities of his own book, *My Experiences in the World War* (2 vols., New York, 1931).[6] A notable biography is by Donald Smythe, *Guerrilla Warrior: The Early Life of John J. Pershing* (New York, 1973). Smythe's second volume, completing the biography, is in press. See

[6]The best criticism was by Pershing's former aide, George C. Marshall, who wrote on December 2, 1930, that "Your personal attitude is what most of my comments were directed towards." He advised the general to avoid the subjects of the War Department and the Allies and take the line that the Army's unreadiness was because of the Democratic Congress: "This attitude, the resistance to a properly coordinated War Department in favor of the money spending bureaus, the past refusals to accumulate important war stocks—guns, ammunition, powders, electrical technical equipment, airplanes—marks in my mind the reason for most of the errors committed by individuals and is a proper subject or text for lecturing the American people." Marshall advised him to remove some of the last sentences of paragraphs in which the general took swipes at opponents, domestic and foreign, military and civil. See Forrest C. Pogue, "General Marshall and the Pershing Papers," *Quarterly Journal of the Library of Congress*, vol. 21 (1964).

also his many articles: "Pershing and General J. Franklin Bell, 1917–1918," *Mid-America*, vol. 54 (1972), 34–51; "Pershing Goes 'Over There': The Baltic Trip," *American Neptune*, vol. 34 (1974), 262–277; "Literary Salvos: James G. Harbord and the Pershing–March Controversy," *Mid-America*, vol. 57 (1975), 173–183; "The Pershing–March Conflict in World War I," *Parameters*, vol. 11 (1981), 53–62. Richard Goldhurst, *Pipe Clay and Drill: John J. Pershing, the Classic American Soldier* (New York, 1977) is a popular account. See also Frank E. Vandiver, *Black Jack: The Life and Times of John J. Pershing* (2 vols., College Station, Tex., 1977), a very able biography, beautifully written.

AEF supply problems are in Charles G. Dawes, *A Journal of the Great War* (2 vols., Boston, 1921); James G. Harbord, *Leaves from a War Diary* (New York, 1925), by the last wartime commander of the S.O.S.; Johnson Hagood II, *The Services of Supply: A Memoir of the Great War* (Boston, 1927); William J. Wilgus, *Transporting the A.E.F. in Western Europe: 1917–1919* (New York, 1931).

For their subjects see C. Leroy Baldridge, *"I Was There": With the Yankees on the Western Front, 1917–1919* (New York, 1919), sketches while on duty with the *Stars and Stripes*; Henry P. Davison, *The American Red Cross in the Great War* (New York, 1920); Katherine Mayo, *"That Damn Y: A Record of Overseas Service"* (Boston, 1920), an effort to combat criticism; anon., "The Sam Browne Belt," *Infantry Journal*, vol. 20 (1922), 373–375, a humorous criticism of the AEF's special accoutrement; Frederick A. Pottle, *Stretchers: The Story of a Hospital Unit on the Western Front* (New Haven, Conn., 1929); Amy Gordon Grant, *Letters from Armageddon: A Collection Made During the World War* (Boston, 1930), interesting because of its literary quality; Harvey Cushing, *From a Surgeon's Journal: 1915–1918* (Boston, 1936), poignant, mostly diary, including service with the British Army in 1915; Hugh Young, *A Surgeon's Autobiography* (New York, 1940), pp. 264–403 on World War I, including attendance upon President Wilson during the latter's illness in 1919–20; J. M. T. Finney, *A Surgeon's Life* (New York, 1940); George Crile, *An Autobiography* (2 vols., Philadelphia, 1947), only a small publication from the wonderful diary; Emmet Crozier, *American Reporters on the Western Front, 1914–1918* (New York, 1959), by a wartime reporter in New York intrigued by stories of his privileged friends; Charles V. Genthe, *American War Narratives, 1917–1918: A Study and Bibliography* (New York, 1969), neither thoughtful in narrative (stories of bloodthirstiness) nor definitive in bibliography, but a start; Edward M. Coffman, "The American Military Generation Gap in World War I: The Leavenworth Clique in the AEF," in William Geffen (ed.), *Command and Commanders in Modern Warfare* (Colorado Springs, Colo., 1969), in which the author posits a clique of AEF officers who attended Leavenworth, and fifty generals who graduated from West Point between 1911 and 1917 are uncertain; Andrew Gray, "The American Field Service,"

American Heritage, vol. 26 (1974–75), no. 1, pp. 58–63, 88–92, on the volunteer ambulance service; Alfred E. Cornebise, *The Stars and Stripes: Doughboy Journalism in World War I* (Westport, Conn., 1984).

Chapter 5. Victory

The fighting appears in the pictorial histories, also in such general accounts as Coffman and DeWeerd, and the splendid biographies by Smythe and Vandiver. In addition consult Frederick Palmer, *America in France* (New York, 1918), by the contemporary reporter, himself a member of Pershing's staff; Hunter Liggett, *Commanding an American Army: Recollections of the World War* (Boston, 1925) and *A.E.F.: Ten Years Ago in France* (New York, 1928) by one of the two army commanders; Robert Lee Bullard, *Personalities and Reminiscences of the War* (Garden City, N.Y., 1925) and (with Earl Reeves) *American Soldiers Also Fought* (New York, 1936), together with the stunningly successful biography by Allan R. Millett, *The General: Robert L. Bullard and Officership in the United States Army, 1881–1925* (Westport, Conn., 1975), the AEF's other army commander; Dale Van Every, *The A.E.F. in Battle* (New York, 1928), by a skilled writer, analysis by battles with very little mention of commanding officers—an interesting approach; B. H. Liddell Hart, *The Real War: 1914–1918* (Boston, 1930), an account by the famous British analyst; J. F. C. Fuller, *A Military History of the Western World* (3 vols., New York, 1954–56), III, from the British point of view; Cyril Falls, *The Great War: 1914–1918* (New York, 1959), perhaps the best account of the entire war, by the official British historian, himself a participant; Hanson W. Baldwin, *World War I: An Outline History* (New York, 1962), a short book by *The New York Times* military analyst; Barrie Pitt, *1918: The Last Act* (London, 1962), cleverly written; Forrest C. Pogue, *George C. Marshall: Education of a General, 1880–1939* (New York, 1963), definitive, together with George C. Marshall, *Memoirs of My Services in the World War: 1917–1918* (Boston, 1976) —discovered in an attic, edited by James L. Collins, Jr.; Laurence Stallings, *The Doughboys: The Story of the AEF, 1917–1918* (New York, 1963), including a touching account of a postwar visit, in 1925, to Belleau Wood; Correlli Barnett, *The Swordbearers: Supreme Command in the First World War* (New York, 1964), essays on Moltke, Jellicoe, Pétain, and Ludendorff, an engrossing book; Don Congdon (ed.), *Combat: World War I* (New York, 1965), excerpts from seventeen authors, all very good; Gene Smith, *Still Quiet on the Western Front: Fifty Years Later* (New York, 1965), a haunting description of battle areas and French towns, with photographs in 1914–18 and half a century later; Jack J. Roth (ed.), *World War I: A Turning Point in Modern History* (New York, 1967), a fine theme and not very successful execution; Donald Smythe, "A.E.F. Snafu at Sedan," *Prologue*, vol. 5 (1973), 135–149; Elliott

L. Johnson, "The Military Experiences of Hugh A. Drum from 1898–1918," dissertation at the University of Wisconsin, 1975. Participant accounts often read as if events happened yesterday, and are the best way to understand the fighting in 1917–18, for which see Francis P. Duffy, *Father Duffy's Story* (New York, 1919); Theodore Roosevelt, Jr., *Average Americans* (New York, 1919) and *Rank and File: True Stories of the Great War* (New York, 1938); Elmer W. Sherwood, *Rainbow Hoosier* (Indianapolis, Ind., n.d. [1919]), narrative with a garbled diary; Kenneth Gow, *Letters of a Soldier* (New York, 1920), by a second lieutenant killed in October 1918; Hilton U. Brown, Sr. (ed.), *Hilton U. Brown, Jr.: One of Three Brothers in Artillery* (Indianapolis, Ind., 1920), collected letters after the younger Brown was killed in November in the Argonne; Hermann von Giehrl, "Battle of the Meuse-Argonne," *Infantry Journal*, vol. 19 (1921) and "The American Expeditionary Forces in Europe, 1917–1918," *Infantry Journal*, vol. 20 (1922), 140–149, 292–303, the German side; Elmer Frank Straub, *A Sergeant's Diary in the World War* (Indianapolis, Ind., 1923), remarkably good, by an artilleryman; Thomas Boyd, *Through the Wheat* (New York, 1923), thinly disguised autobiography by a Marine private at Belleau Wood, from Defiance, Ohio; John F. Richards II, *War Diary and Letters* (Kansas City, 1925), by a young Hotchkiss–Yale flier killed on the first day of the Meuse-Argonne; Joseph T. Dickman, *The Great Crusade: A Narrative of the World War* (New York, 1927), by one of the best of the AEF generals; Tom Skeyhill (ed.), *Sergeant York: His Own Life Story and War Diary* (Garden City, N.Y., 1928); Ernst Otto, "The Battles for the Possession of Belleau Woods," *U.S. Naval Institute Proceedings*, vol. 54 (1928), 940–962; Lowell Thomas, *Woodfill of the Regulars: A True Story of Adventure from the Arctic to the Argonne* (Garden City, N.Y., 1929), a great story of the heroism of a Regular Army soldier, a first lieutenant in World War I, who after the war retired to the obscurity of an Indiana farm; Charles E. Carrington [pseud., Charles Edmonds], *A Subaltern's War: Being a Memoir of the Great War . . .* (London, 1929), one of the best of the British accounts; John A. Lejeune, *The Reminiscences of a Marine* (Philadelphia, 1930), by the later commander (after Harbord) of the Second Division; Robert Alexander, *Memories of the World War: 1917–1918* (New York, 1931), a wonderfully frank and thoughtful memoir by a division commander; Henry L. Stimson and McGeorge Bundy, *On Active Service in Peace and War* (New York, 1948), pp. 82–110 for the wartime colonel and two-time Secretary of War, also Secretary of State, together with Elting E. Morison, *Turmoil and Tradition: A Study of the Life and Times of Henry L. Stimson* (Boston, 1960); Richard M. Huber, *Big All the Way Through: The Life of Van Santvoord Merle-Smith* (Princeton, N.J., 1952), gallant exploits on the front; Harry S. Truman, *Memoirs: Year of Decisions* (Garden City, N.Y., 1955); Richard Suskind, *Do You Want to Live Forever!* (New York, 1964), on Belleau Wood; Douglas MacArthur, *Reminiscences* (New York, 1964) and D. Clayton James, *The Years of MacArthur*, vol. 1, *1880–1941* (Boston, 1970), pp. 110–256; Robert B. Asprey, *At Belleau Wood* (New York, 1965), best on its subject; William L. Langer, *Gas and Flame in World War I* (New York, 1965), by the Harvard historian; Calvin Hoover, *Memoirs of Capitalism, Communism, and Nazism* (Durham, N.C., 1965), by the Duke economist; Guy Chapman, *A Passionate Prodigality: Fragments of Autobiography* (New York, 1966), reprinting of an edition of 1933; John W. Thomason, *Fix Bayonets! And Other Stories* (New York, 1970), by the Marine officer, storyteller, and illustrator; Martin Blumenson (ed.), *The Patton Papers* (2 vols., Boston, 1972), pp. 379–746; Herbert Sulzbach, *With the German Guns: Four Years on the Western Front, 1914–1918* (London, 1973), unrelenting action during World War I by a scion of the banking family who fled Germany in the thirties and served in the British Army in World War II; Sidney Fine, *Frank Murphy: The Detroit Years* (Ann Arbor, Mich., 1975), the later associate justice of the Supreme Court; Horatio Rogers, *World War I Through My Sights* (San Rafael, Calif., 1976), splendid reminiscence; John Kelly Raney, *My First Ninety Years: A Collection of Autobiographical Trivia, 1890–1980* (Bowling Green, Ohio, 1980); Elton Mackin, ". . . Suddenly We Didn't Want to Die," *American Heritage*, vol. 31 (Feb.–Mar., 1980), 49–64, posthumous account of Belleau Wood; Anthony Cave Brown, *The Last Hero: Wild Bill Donovan* (New York, 1982), pp. 30–72, details of horrendous action.

Chapter 6. Money and Food

The best sources for financing the war are the reminiscences of William G. McAdoo, *Crowded Years* (Boston, 1931), which go into detail on the bond drives, together with Dale N. Shook, "William G. McAdoo and the Development of National Economic Policy, 1913–1918," dissertation at the University of Cincinnati, 1975; and Charles Gilbert, *American Financing of World War I* (Westport, Conn., 1970). The Morgan overdraft appears in John Edward Wiltz, *In Search of Peace: The Senate Munitions Inquiry, 1934–36* (Baton Rouge, La., 1963); Warren I. Cohen, *The American Revisionists* (Chicago, 1967); and for clear analysis of what happened between the Morgan firm and the Treasury, Wilton B. Fowler, *British–American Relations, 1917–1918: The Role of Sir William Wiseman* (Princeton, N.J., 1969), pp. 38–59.

The leading figure in conservation and production, Herbert Hoover, has had much attention because of his later prominence, and Hoover himself was a prolific chronicler of his life and times. See his *America's First Crusade* (New York, 1942); *The Memoirs of Herbert Hoover: Years of Adventure, 1874–1920* (New York, 1951); Francis W. O'Brien (ed.), *The Hoover–Wilson Wartime Correspondence: September 24, 1914 to November 11, 1918* (Ames, Iowa,

1974); Lawrence E. Gelfand (ed.), *Herbert Hoover: The Great War and Its Aftermath, 1914–1923* (Iowa City, 1979). The food problem appears in detail in Frank M. Surface, *The Grain Trade During the World War: Being a History of the Food Administration Grain Corporation and the United States Grain Corporation* (New York, 1928); Frank M. Surface and Raymond L. Bland, *American Food in the World War and Reconstruction Period: Operations of the Organizations Under the Direction of Herbert Hoover, 1914 to 1924* (Stanford, Calif., 1931); William C. Mullendore, *History of the United States Food Administration: 1917–1919* (Stanford, Calif., 1941), a book actually finished in 1921; Maxcy Robson Dickson, *The Food Front in World War I* (Washington, 1944), the best book. Edgar E. Robinson and Paul C. Edwards (eds.), *The Memoirs of Ray Lyman Wilbur: 1875–1949* (Stanford, Calif., 1960) relates the wartime experiences of one of Hoover's assistants. Bruce Fraser, "Yankees at War: Social Mobilization on the Connecticut Homefront, 1917–1918," dissertation at Columbia University, 1976, reveals how an important Eastern state received and carried out Washington's suggestions.

Chapter 7. Ships and Arms

For the head of the Shipping Board see Edward N. Hurley, *The Bridge to France* (Philadelphia, 1927); the head of the Fleet Corporation appears in Robert Hessen, *Steel Titan: The Life of Charles M. Schwab* (New York, 1975). Three interesting articles are William N. Thurston, "Management-Leadership in the United States Shipping Board, 1917–1918," *American Neptune*, vol. 32 (1972), 155–170; William Joe Webb, "The United States Wooden Steamship Program During World War I," *American Neptune*, vol. 35 (1975), 275–288; and Jeffrey J. Safford, "Edward Hurley and American Shipping Policy: An Elaboration on Wilsonian Diplomacy, 1918–1919," *Historian*, vol. 35 (1973), 568–586. See also Safford's *Wilsonian Maritime Diplomacy: 1913–1921* (New Brunswick, N.J., 1978).

Production of arms received instant recognition in *Lord Northcliffe's War Book: With Chapters on America at War* (New York, 1917)—for whom see the later book by Reginald Pound and Geoffrey Harmsworth, *Northcliffe* (London, 1959)—and not long after the war in Grosvenor B. Clarkson, *Industrial America in the World War: The Strategy Behind the Line, 1917–1918* (Boston, 1923), by the director of the Council of Defense. The work of Baruch was first set out by the head of the War Industries Board in his report of March 1921, reprinted in Bernard M. Baruch, *American Industry in the War* (New York, 1941). The biographies and autobiographies followed: Margaret L. Coit, *Mr. Baruch* (Boston, 1957), quite friendly but evidently not enough so, for Baruch rushed out *My Own Story* (New York, 1957) and *The Public Years* (1960), in which the W.I.B. appears on pp. 19–89; Jordan A. Schwarz, *The Speculator: Bernard M. Baruch in Washington, 1917–1965* (Chapel Hill, N.C.,

1981) is an able full-dress biography; James Grant, *Bernard Baruch: The Adventures of a Wall Street Legend* (New York, 1983) is a wonderfully witty, irreverent appraisal by a financial expert. See also Hugh Johnson's autobiography, mentioned earlier, and John K. Ohl, "Old Iron Pants: The Wartime Career of General Hugh S. Johnson, 1917–1918," dissertation at the University of Cincinnati, 1971, a superior accounting of one of the present century's most interesting individuals and an avid admirer of Baruch.

Scholarly analysis of economic mobilization in World War I appears in books by Beaver and Hewes on Newton Baker and Army organization and administration; see also the article by Karsten. Robert D. Cuff is the acknowledged historian of the W.I.B., for which see his *The War Industries Board: Business–Government Relations During World War I* (Baltimore, 1973). Also the same author's "The Cooperative Impulse and War: The Origins of the Council of National Defense and Advisory Commission," in Jerry Israel (ed.), *Building the Organizational Society: Essays on Associational Activities in Modern America* (New York, 1972), pp. 233–246; "Herbert Hoover, the Ideology of Voluntarism and War Organization During the Great War," *Journal of American History*, vol. 64 (1977–78), 358–372. Essential for understanding mobilization is the work of economic historians and political scientists in recent years, notably Louis Galambos, *Competition and Cooperation: The Emergence of a National Trade Association* (Baltimore, 1966) and *The Public Image of Big Business in America: 1880–1940* (Baltimore, 1975); James Weinstein, *The Corporate Ideal in the Liberal State: 1900–1918* (Boston, 1968); Alfred D. Chandler, Jr., and Stephen Salsbury, *Pierre S. du Pont and the Making of the Modern Corporation* (New York, 1971), an impressive biography; Chandler's *The Visible Hand: The Managerial Revolution in American Business* (Cambridge, Mass., 1977); and Stephen Skowronek, *Building a New American State: The Expansion of National Administrative Capacities, 1877–1920* (New York, 1982), concerning the "striking disparity" in bureaucratic development between private and public sectors (to use the phrase of Cuff).

Armaments programs are in William Crozier, *Ordnance and the World War: A Contribution to the History of American Preparedness* (New York, 1920); Henry G. Sharpe, *The Quartermaster Corps in the Year 1917 in the World War* (New York, 1921); William J. Snow, *Signposts of Experience: World War Memoirs* (Washington, 1941), by the wartime chief of artillery who beheld Peyton March as "the ablest and most efficient man I ever served under"; Allan Nevins, *Herbert H. Lehman and His Era* (New York, 1963), a few pages on Colonel Lehman's wartime work on the general staff; two excellent articles, Daniel R. Beaver, "The Problem of American Military Supply, 1890–1920," in Benjamin Franklin Cooling, *War, Business, and American Society: Historical Perspectives on the Military–Industrial Complex* (Port Washington, N.Y., 1977), pp. 73–92, and James P. Johnson, "The Wilsonians as War Managers: Coal and the 1917–18 Winter Crisis," *Prologue*, vol. 9 (1977), 193–208; David A.

Armstrong, *Bullets and Bureaucrats: The Machine Gun and the United States Army, 1861–1916* (Westport, Conn., 1982); William H. McNeill, *The Pursuit of Power: Technology, Armed Force and Society since A.D. 1000* (Chicago, 1982). On the airplane program see Isaac F. Marcosson, *Colonel Deeds: Industrial Builder* (New York, 1947), a whitewash; Henry H. Arnold, *Global Mission* (New York, 1949), about desk work in Washington, pp. 48–112; I. B. Holley, Jr., *Ideas and Weapons: Exploitation of the Aerial Weapon by the United States During World War I: A Study in the Relationship of Technological Advance, Military Doctrine, and the Development of Weapons* (New Haven, Conn., 1953), by the military historian; Alfred F. Hurley, *Billy Mitchell: Crusader for Air Power* (2d ed., Bloomington, Ind., 1975), definitive; *Rickenbacker* (Englewood Cliffs, N.J., 1967) and Benjamin D. Foulois, *From the Wright Brothers to the Astronauts* (New York, 1968); Albert F. Simpson (ed.), *The World War I Diary of Col. Frank P. Lahm, Air Service, A.E.F.* (Maxwell Air Force Base, Ala., 1970).

For women in factories during World War I see Maurine W. Greenwald, *Women, War and Work* (Westport, Conn., 1980). Nancy E. Malan, " 'How 'Ya Gonna Keep 'Em Down?': Women and World War I," *Prologue*, vol. 5 (1973), 209–239 is a photographic essay.

Chapter 8. The Allies

For Great Britain see Stephen Gwynn (ed.), *The Letters and Friendships of Sir Cecil Spring Rice: A Record* (2 vols., Boston, 1929); Winston S. Churchill, *The World Crisis* (3 vols. in 1, New York, 1931), excluding *The Aftermath: 1918–1928* (New York, 1929); and *War Memoirs of David Lloyd George: 1917–1918* (Boston, 1936), together with Richard Lloyd George, *My Father, Lloyd George* (New York, 1961), revealing; and the best biography, Peter Rowland, *David Lloyd George: A Biography* (New York, 1975); Blanche E. C. Dugdale, *Arthur James Balfour: 1906–1930* (New York, 1937), by Balfour's niece, about an elusive personality; John Terraine, *Douglas Haig: The Educated Soldier* (London, 1963), another elusive personality; Paul Guinn, *British Strategy and Politics: 1914–1918* (Oxford, 1965); Llewellyn Woodward, *Great Britain and the War of 1914–1918* (London, 1967), reliable official history; H. Montgomery Hyde, *Lord Reading: The Life of Rufus Isaacs, First Marquess of Reading* (New York, 1968), an adept biography of a careful man; Stephen Roskill, *Hankey: Man of Secrets* (2 vols., London, 1970–72), detailed diary of the cabinet secretary, with much inside material; Sterling J. Kernek, *Distractions of Peace During War: The Lloyd George Government's Reactions to Woodrow Wilson, December 1916–November 1918* (Philadelphia, 1975); Edward B. Parsons, *Wilsonian Diplomacy: Allied–American Rivalries in War and Peace* (St. Louis, 1978).

The French side is in André Tardieu, *France and America: Some Experiences in Cooperation* (Boston, 1927); Georges Clemenceau, *Grandeur and Misery of Victory* (New York, 1930) and Geoffrey Bruun, *Clemenceau* (Cambridge,

Mass., 1944) and Wythe Williams, *The Tiger of France: Conversations with Clemenceau* (New York, 1949), boisterous reminiscences by an American newspaperman; Jean A. A. Jules Jusserand, *Le Sentiment américain pendant la guerre* (Paris, 1931); *Memoirs of Marshal Foch* (Garden City, N.Y., 1931); Jere Clemens King, *Generals and Politicians: Conflict Between France's High Command, Parliament and Government, 1914–1918* (Berkeley and Los Angeles, 1951); Pierre Renouvain, *Les Crises du xxe siècle de 1914–1929* (2 vols., Paris, 1957), translated as *War and Aftermath* (New York, 1968); Stephen Ryan, *Pétain the Soldier* (New York, 1969); André Kaspi, *La France et le concours américain, février 1917–november 1918* (3 vols., Lille, 1975), for which see Kaspi's *Le Temps des américains* (Paris, 1976); Walter A. McDougall, *France's Rhineland Diplomacy, 1914–1924: The Last Bid for a Balance of Power in Europe* (Princeton, N.J., 1978); Melvyn P. Leffler, *The Elusive Quest: America's Pursuit of European Stability and French Security, 1919–1933* (Chapel Hill, N.C., 1979).

On the collapse of the Austro-Hungarian monarchy see Thomas G. Masaryk, *The Making of a State: Memories and Observations, 1914–1918* (London, 1927); Henry Cord Meyer, *Mitteleuropa in German Thought and Action: 1815–1945* (The Hague, 1955); Victor S. Mamatey, *The United States and East Central Europe, 1914–1918: A Study in Wilsonian Diplomacy and Propaganda* (Princeton, N.J., 1957); Dagmar Horna-Perman, "The Making of a New State: Czechoslovakia and the Peace Conference, 1919," in Gerhard L. Weinberg (ed.), *Transformation of a Continent: Europe in the Twentieth Century* (Minneapolis, 1975), pp. 59–149; also the same author's *The Shaping of the Czechoslovak State* (Leiden, 1962); Peter Pastor, *Hungary Between Wilson and Lenin: The Hungarian Revolution of 1918–1919 and the Big Three* (New York, 1976); Robert A. Kann, Bela K. Kiraly, and Paula S. Fichtner (eds.), *The Habsburg Empire in World War I* (New York, 1977).

The German side appears in Erich Ludendorff, *Ludendorff's Own Story, August 1914–November 1918* (2 vols., New York, 1919), by a master tactician who believed the Americans tipped the balance, and that August 8 was the black day but St. Mihiel and the Meuse-Argonne were serious offensives; Prince Max of Baden, *Memoirs* (2 vols., New York, 1928); Arthur Rosenberg, *The Birth of the German Republic* (New York, 1931), old but very useful; Harry R. Rudin, *Armistice: 1918* (New Haven, Conn., 1944), best on its subject; Hans W. Gatzke, *Germany's Drive to the West: A Study of Germany's Western War Aims During the First World War* (Baltimore, 1950); Fred A. Sondermann, "The Wilson Administration's Image of Germany," dissertation at Yale University, 1953; Gordon A. Craig, *The Politics of the Prussian Army: 1640–1945* (Oxford, Eng., 1955); Hans Peter Hanssen, *Diary of a Dying Empire* (Bloomington, Ind., 1955); Klaus Epstein, *Matthias Erzberger and the Dilemma of German Democracy* (Princeton, N.J., 1959); Walter Goerlitz (ed.), *The Kaiser and His Court* (London, 1961), diaries, notebooks, and letters of Admiral Georg Alexander von Mueller, chief of the naval cabinet; Gerald D. Feldman, *Army, Industry and Labor in Germany: 1914–1918* (Princeton, N.J., 1966), an excellent book; Fritz Fischer, *Germany's Aims in the First World War* (New York, 1967), a classic, the English translation an abridgment of the original German; Juergen Moeckelmann, *Deutsch-amerikanische Beziehungen in der Krise: Studien zur amerikanischen Politik im ersten Weltkrieg* (Hamburg, 1967), in the Fischer school; Daniel Horn, *The German Naval Mutinies of World War I* (New Brunswick, N.J., 1969); Klaus Schwabe, *Deutsche Revolution und Wilson-Frieden: Die amerikanische und deutsche Friedensstrategie zwischen Ideologie und Machtpolitik, 1918/19* (Duesseldorf, 1971), the best German scholarship, and its English edition, *Woodrow Wilson, Revolutionary Germany, and Peacemaking, 1918–1919: Missionary Diplomacy and the Realities of Power* (Chapel Hill, N.C., 1985); Charles F. Sidman, *The German Collapse in 1918* (Lawrence, Kans., 1972); Kurt Riezler, *Tagebuecher, Aufsaetze, Dokumente* (Goettingen, 1972); Holger H. Herwig, *The German Naval Officer Corps: A Social and Political History, 1890–1918* (Oxford, Eng., 1973), stirringly good writing, and the same author's *Politics of Frustration: The United States in German Naval Planning, 1889–1941* (Boston, 1976); Konrad H. Jarausch, *The Enigmatic Chancellor: Bethmann Hollweg and the Hubris of Imperial Germany* (New Haven, Conn., 1973), from public papers and archives—Bethmann's papers were destroyed by the Russians during or after World War II; Willibald Gutsche, *Aufstieg und Fall eines kaiserlichen Reichskanzlers: Theobald von Bethmann Hollweg 1856–1921, Ein politisches Lebensbild* (Berlin, 1973), in the Fischer school; Leo Haupts, *Deutsche Friedenspolitik, 1918–19: Eine Alternative zur Machtpolitik des Ersten Weltkrieges?* (Duesseldorf, 1976); Eckart Kehr, *Economic Interest, Militarism, and Foreign Policy: Essays on German History* (Berkeley, Calif., 1977); David Calleo, *The German Problem Reconsidered: Germany and the World Order, 1870 to the Present* (New York, 1978); L. L. Farrar, Jr., *Divide and Conquer: German Efforts to Conclude a Separate Peace, 1914–1918* (New York, 1978), a very well-done monograph by a translator of Fischer; Alan Palmer, *The Kaiser: Warlord of the Second Reich* (New York, 1978), and John C. G. Roehl and Nicolaus Sombert (eds.), *Kaiser Wilhelm II: New Interpretations* (Cambridge, Eng., 1982), especially the initial essay by Roehl on the Kaiser's disturbed personality.

The American side is in Thomas C. Lonergan, *It Might Have Been Lost!: A Chronicle from Alien Sources of the Struggle to Preserve the National Identity of the A.E.F.* (New York, 1929); Mitchell P. Briggs, *George D. Herron and the European Settlement* (Stanford, Calif., 1931), on the breakup of the Austro-Hungarian monarchy; Charles Seymour, *American Diplomacy During the World War* (Baltimore, 1934), a classic, with testimony by participants; Lloyd C. Griscom, *Diplomatically Speaking* (New York, 1940), Pershing's representative in England; Hugh Wilson, *Diplomat Between Wars* (New York, 1941), from the legation in Switzerland; Arthur Willert, *The Road to Safety: A Study in Anglo-American Relations* (New York, 1953), the well-placed and informed Washington correspondent of the London *Times*, for whom see also his elegant memoir, *Washington and Other Memories* (Boston, 1972), wonderful for its scene-setting; David F. Trask, *The United States in the Supreme War Council: American War Aims and Inter-Allied Strategy, 1917–18* (Middletown, Conn., 1961), definitive; the book by Wilton B. Fowler, mentioned earlier; Mary R. Kihl, "A Failure of Ambassadorial Diplomacy," *Journal of American History*, vol. 57 (1969–70), 636–653, together with Ross Gregory, *Walter Hines Page: Ambassador to the Court of St. James's* (Lexington, Ky., 1970) and John Milton Cooper, Jr., *Walter Hines Page: The Southerner as American, 1855–1918* (Chapel Hill, N.C., 1977), first-rate analyses; Michael G. Fry, *Illusions of Security: North Atlantic Diplomacy, 1918–22* (Toronto, 1972); Arthur Walworth, *America's Moment, 1918: American Diplomacy at the End of World War I* (New York, 1977), a triumph of scholarship, first volume in Walworth's forthcoming history of the Peace Conference; Bullitt Lowry, "Pershing and the Armistice," *Journal of American History*, vol. 55 (1968–69), 281–291.

Chapter 9. Peace

The early reminiscences were hardly sufficient—such as Robert Lansing, *The Big Four and Others at the Peace Conference* (Boston, 1921), *The Peace Negotiations: A Personal Narrative* (Boston, 1921), and *The War Memoirs of Robert Lansing* (Indianapolis, Ind., 1935), which needed correction by such books as Burton F. Beers, *Vain Endeavor: Robert Lansing's Attempts to End the American–Japanese Rivalry* (Durham, N.C., 1962) and Thomas H. Hartig, *Robert Lansing: An Interpretive Biography* (New York, 1982). The same was true of E. M. House and Charles Seymour, *What Really Happened at Paris* (New York, 1921), which was not that at all.[7] See Charles Seymour (ed.), *The Intimate Papers of Colonel House* (4 vols., Boston, 1926–28) and especially Inga Floto, *Colonel House in Paris: A Study of American Policy at the Paris Peace Conference, 1919* (Aarhus, Den., 1973), republished by The Papers of Woodrow Wilson (Princeton, N.J., 1981). Allan Nevins, *Henry White: Thirty Years of American Diplomacy* (New York, 1930) is a civilized biography of a civilized man—White could not understand why President Wilson appointed him a delegate. Harold Nicolson, *Peacemaking: 1919* (Boston, 1933) relates the problem of confusion; Irwin Hood (Ike) Hoover, *Forty-Two Years in the White*

[7]"I have been writing fairly steadily since I last recorded in the diary, and have been reading manuscripts to be published in the forthcoming book entitled, 'What Really Happened at Paris.' My chapter will close the book and is called 'The Versailles Peace in Retrospect.' I have tried to write it with as little criticism of the President as possible, and I have had Frank Polk, David Miller, Mezes, Gordon and others read it with a view of getting their opinion as to whether it is critical of him. Polk thinks those who are uninformed will not consider it a criticism at all, but the few who know the inside facts will. For instance, a few of us know how impossible he made publicity either at Paris or here. We also know that he dropped the 'freedom of the seas.' Then, again, he was one of the several who delayed the Conference unnecessarily not knowing how to expedite work."—Diary, Feb. 22, 1921.

House (Boston, 1934); George Bernard Noble, *Policies and Opinions at Paris: 1919* (New York, 1935); James T. Shotwell, *At the Paris Peace Conference* (New York, 1937), and *The Autobiography of James T. Shotwell* (Indianapolis, Ind., 1961), also Harold Josephson, *James T. Shotwell and the Rise of Internationalism in America* (Rutherford, N.J., 1975); Stephen Bonsal, *Unfinished Business* (Garden City, N.Y., 1944), by House's assistant, and also his *Suitors and Suppliants: The Little Nations at Versailles* (New York, 1946); Thomas A. Bailey, *Woodrow Wilson and the Lost Peace* (New York, 1944); Ray Stannard Baker, *American Chronicle: The Autobiography of Ray Stannard Baker* [David Grayson] (New York, 1945), for which see also Robert C. Bannister, Jr., *Ray Stannard Baker: The Mind and Thought of a Progressive* (New Haven, Conn., 1966); Alfred Cobban, *National Self-determination* (Chicago, 1947 [?]); Max H. Fisch (ed.), *Selected Papers of Robert C. Binkley* (Cambridge, Mass., 1948), by an early student of the Peace Conference; Thomas W. Lamont, *Across World Frontiers* (New York, 1951), remarkably good; Joseph C. Grew, *Turbulent Era: A Diplomatic Record of Forty Years, 1904–1945* (2 vols., Boston, 1952) and Waldo H. Heinrichs, Jr., *American Ambassador: Joseph C. Grew and the Development of the United States Diplomatic Tradition* (Boston, 1966), an impressive biography; Lawrence E. Gelfand, *The Inquiry: American Preparations for Peace, 1917–1919* (New Haven, Conn., 1963), definitive; Harold B. Whiteman (ed.), *Charles Seymour, Letters from the Paris Peace Conference* (New Haven, Conn., 1965), poignant description; David F. Trask, *General Tasker Howard Bliss and the "Sessions of the World," 1919* (Philadelphia, 1966), like Gelfand's book the definitive account; James Gidney, *Mandate for Armenia* (Kent, Ohio, 1967), definitive; Joseph P. O'Grady (ed.), *The Immigrants' Influence on Wilson's Peace Policies* (Lexington, Ky., 1967); James D. Startt, "Wilson's Mission to Paris: The Making of a Decision," *Historian*, vol. 30 (1967–68), 599–616, and the same author's "The Uneasy Partnership: Wilson and the Press at Paris," *Mid-America*, vol. 52 (1970), 55–69, for which latter subject see also George Juergens, *News from the White House: The Presidential–Press Relationship in the Progressive Era* (Chicago, 1981); Howard Elcock, *Portrait of a Decision: The Council of Four and the Treaty of Versailles* (London[?], 1972); Ronald W. Pruessen, "John Foster Dulles and Reparations at the Paris Peace Conference, 1919: Early Patterns of a Life," *Perspectives in American History*, vol. 8 (1974), 381–410; Francis W. O'Brien (ed.), *Two Peacemakers in Paris: The Hoover–Wilson Post-Armistice Letters, 1918–1920* (College Station, Tex., 1978); Charles L. Mee., Jr., *The End of Order: Versailles, 1919* (New York, 1980), elegant description of the Paris Peace Conference; Geoffrey J. Martin, *The Life and Thought of Isaiah Bowman* (Hamden, Conn., 1980), uses the Bowman diary; Robert F. Byrnes, *Awakening American Education to the World: The Role of Archibald Cary Coolidge, 1866–1928* (Notre Dame, Ind., 1982), a remarkable biography of the virtual founder of European historical studies in the United States.

Britain at the Peace Conference is in John M. Keynes, *The Economic Conse-*

quences of the Peace (New York, 1920), which should be read with Etienne Mantoux, *The Carthaginian Peace: Or the Economic Consequences of Mr. Keynes* (New York, 1952) and R. F. Harrod, *The Life of John Maynard Keynes* (New York, 1951); Robert Cecil, *A Great Experiment: An Autobiography* (New York, 1941); Seth P. Tillman, *Anglo–American Relations at the Paris Peace Conference of 1919* (Princeton, N.J., 1961); Richard H. Ullman, *Anglo–Soviet Relations: 1917–1921* (3 vols., Princeton, N.J., 1961–72); Louis L. Gerson, *The Hyphenate in Recent American Politics and Diplomacy* (Lawrence, Kans., 1964), together with Alan J. Ward, *Ireland and Anglo–American Relations: 1899–1921* (London, 1969), and Francis M. Carroll, *American Opinion and the Irish Question, 1910–1923: A Study in Opinion and Policy* (New York, 1978); William Roger Louis, "Great Britain and the African Peace Settlement of 1919," *American Historical Review*, vol. 71 (1965–66), 867–892; Stephen Roskill, *Hankey* (2 vols., London, 1970–72); Agnes Headlam-Morley, Russell Bryant, and Anna Cienciala (eds.), *Sir James Headlam-Morley: A Memoir of the Paris Peace Conference, 1919* (London, 1972).

For Poland see above, ch. 9, notes 31, 32; Italy and Yugoslavia, note 37; the Soviet Union, note 38; the Far East, notes 42, 44; for a small power, Sally Marks, *Innocent Abroad: Belgium at the Paris Peace Conference of 1919* (Chapel Hill, N.C., 1981).

The Germans were not invited to the Peace Conference until the very end, but contacts continued, for which see Samuel G. Shartle, *Spa, Versailles, Munich: An Account of the Armistice Commission* (Philadelphia, 1941); Jere Clemens King, *Foch versus Clemenceau: France and German Dismemberment, 1918–1919* (Cambridge, Mass., 1960); Harold I. Nelson, *Land and Power: British and Allied Policy on Germany's Frontiers, 1916–1919* (London, 1963); Sally Marks and Denis Dulude, "German-American Relations, 1918–1921," *Mid-America*, vol. 53 (1971), 211–226; Lloyd E. Ambrosius, "Secret German–American Negotiations During the Paris Peace Conference," *Amerikastudien*, vol. 24 (1979), 288–309; Klaus Schwabe, "America's Contribution to the Stabilization of the Early Weimar Republic," in Hans L. Trefousse (ed.), *Germany and America: Essays on Problems of International Relations and Immigration* (New York, 1980), pp. 21–28, and Schwabe's book mentioned above.

Chapter 10. The Senate and the Treaty

In addition to diplomatic records of World War I and the Peace Conference, American and other, the League fight appears in Ruhl J. Bartlett, *The League to Enforce Peace* (Chapel Hill, N.C., 1944); Thomas A. Bailey, *Woodrow Wilson and the Great Betrayal* (New York, 1945); John M. Blum, *Joe Tumulty and the Wilson Era* (Boston, 1951); Kurt Wimer, "Woodrow Wilson's Plans to Enter the League of Nations Through an Executive Agreement," *Western*

Political Quarterly, vol. 11 (1958), 800–812, the same author's "Woodrow Wilson's Plan for a Vote of Confidence," *Pennsylvania History,* vol. 28 (1961), 2–16, and his "Woodrow Wilson Tries Conciliation: An Effort That Failed," *Historian,* vol. 25 (1963), 419–438; George Curry, "Woodrow Wilson, Jan Smuts, and the Versailles Settlement," *American Historical Review,* vol. 66 (1960–61), 968–986; J. Chalmers Vinson, *Referendum for Isolation: Defeat of Article Ten of the League of Nations Covenant* (Athens, Ga., 1961); Roland N. Stromberg, *Collective Security and American Foreign Policy: From the League of Nations to Nato* (New York, 1963); Seward W. Livermore, *Politics Is Adjourned: Woodrow Wilson and the War Congress, 1916–1918* (Middletown, Conn., 1966); John B. Duff, "The Versailles Treaty and the Irish–Americans," *Journal of American History,* vol. 55 (1968–69), 582–598, on a prime source of trouble; Leon E. Boothe," Anglo–American Pro-League Groups Lead Wilson, 1915–1918," *Mid-America,* vol. 51 (1969), 92–107; Daniel M. Smith, *Aftermath of War: Bainbridge Colby and Wilsonian Diplomacy, 1920–1921* (Philadelphia, 1970); Lloyd E. Ambrosius, "Wilson's League of Nations," *Maryland Historical Magazine,* vol. 65 (1969–70), 369–393; Lloyd E. Ambrosius, "Wilson, the Republicans, and French Security After World War I," *Journal of American History,* vol. 59 (1972–73), 341–352; George W. Egerton, *Great Britain and the Creation of the League of Nations: Strategy, Politics, and International Organization, 1914–1919* (Chapel Hill, N.C., 1978), an updating but not replacement of Henry Winkler, *The League of Nations Movement in Great Britain: 1914–1919* (New York, 1952); Joyce G. Williams, "The Resignation of Secretary of State Robert Lansing," *Diplomatic History,* vol. 3 (1979), 337–343; Kurt Wimer, "Woodrow Wilson and World Order," in Arthur S. Link (ed.), *Woodrow Wilson and a Revolutionary World: 1913–1921* (Chapel Hill, N.C., 1982), 146–173; Thomas J. Knock, "Woodrow Wilson and the Origins of the League of Nations," dissertation at Princeton University, 1982; Joyce Grigsby Williams, *Colonel House and Sir Edward Grey: A Study in Anglo–American Diplomacy* (Lanham, Md., 1984). For general works on the peace movement that preceded the League fight see above, ch. 10, notes 2 and 6, together with Allen F. Davis, *American Heroine: The Life and Legend of Jane Addams* (New York, 1973); Ernest C. Bolt, Jr., *Ballots Before Bullets: The War Referendum Approach to Peace in America, 1914–1941* (Charlottesville, Va., 1977).

Democratic opinion on the treaty appears in Anne W. Lane and Louise H. Wall (eds.), *The Letters of Franklin K. Lane: Personal and Political* (Boston, 1922), for which see also Keith W. Olson, *Biography of a Progressive: Franklin K. Lane, 1864–1920* (Westport, Conn., 1979); Thomas R. Marshall, *Recollections: A Hoosier Salad* (Indianapolis, Ind., 1925) and Charles M. Thomas, *Thomas Riley Marshall: Hoosier Statesman* (Oxford, Ohio, 1939); Warren F. Kuehl, *Hamilton Holt: Journalist, Internationalist, Educator* (Gainesville, Fla., 1960); Raymond B. Fosdick, *Letters on the League of Nations* (Princeton, N.J.,

1966); Robert Dallek, *Democrat and Diplomat: The Life of William E. Dodd* (New York, 1968); William H. Harbaugh, *Lawyer's Lawyer: The Life of John W. Davis* (New York, 1973).

Leading Republicans, outside of the Senate, included former Senator Albert J. Beveridge, for whom see Claude G. Bowers, *Beveridge and the Progressive Era* (New York, 1932) and John Braeman, *Albert J. Beveridge: American Nationalist* (Chicago, 1971); Philip C. Jessup, *Elihu Root* (2 vols., New York, 1938) and Richard W. Leopold, *Elihu Root and the Conservative Tradition* (Boston, 1954); Nicholas Murray Butler, *Across the Busy Years: Recollections and Reflections* (2 vols., New York, 1939); Henry F. Pringle, *The Life and Times of William Howard Taft* (2 vols., New York, 1939); William Henry Harbaugh, *Power and Responsibility: The Life and Times of Theodore Roosevelt* (New York, 1961) and Joseph L. Gardner, *Departing Glory: Theodore Roosevelt as Ex-President* (New York, 1973); Merlo J. Pusey, *Charles Evans Hughes* (2 vols., New York, 1950) and Betty Glad, *Charles Evans Hughes and the Illusions of Innocence* (Urbana, Ill., 1966); Walden S. Freeman, "Will H. Hays and the League of Nations," dissertation at Indiana University, 1967.

For the Senators see, first of all, Ralph Stone, *The Irreconcilables: The Fight Against the League of Nations* (Lexington, Ky., 1970), and for individuals Henry Cabot Lodge, *The Senate and the League of Nations* (New York, 1925), a posthumous apology, together with John A. Garraty, *Henry Cabot Lodge: A Biography* (New York, 1953), James E. Hewes, Jr., "Henry Cabot Lodge and the League of Nations," *Proceedings of the American Philosophical Society*, vol. 114 (1970), 245–255, and William C. Widenor, *Henry Cabot Lodge and the Search for an American Foreign Policy* (Berkeley, Calif., 1980); James E. Watson, *As I Knew Them* (Indianapolis, 1936); James Leonard Bates, "Senator Walsh of Montana, 1918–1924: A Liberal Under Pressure," dissertation at the University of North Carolina, Chapel Hill, 1952; Royal W. France, *My Native Grounds* (New York, 1957), by the brother of the irreconcilable Senator Joseph I. France; Dewey W. Grantham, Jr., *Hoke Smith and the Politics of the New South* (Baton Rouge, La., 1958); James E. Hewes, Jr., "William E. Borah and the Image of Isolation," dissertation at Yale University, 1955, together with Marian C. McKenna, *Borah* (Ann Arbor, Mich., 1961) and Robert James Maddox, *William E. Borah and American Foreign Policy* (Baton Rouge, La., 1969); Sewell Thomas, *Silhouettes of Charles S. Thomas: Colorado Governor and United States Senator* (Caldwell, Idaho, 1959), by the senator's son; Fred L. Israel, *Nevada's Key Pittman* (Lincoln, Nebr., 1963); Richard Lowitt, *George W. Norris: The Persistence of a Progressive, 1912–1922* (Urbana, Ill., 1971); Howard Arthur De Witt, "Hiram W. Johnson and American Foreign Policy: 1917–1941," dissertation at the University of Arizona, 1972; Herbert F. Margulies, *Senator Lenroot of Wisconsin: A Political Biography, 1900–1929* (Columbia, Mo., 1977); Howard W. Allen, *Poindexter of Washington: A Study in Progressive Politics* (Carbondale, Ill., 1981).

On miscellaneous topics pertaining to defeat of the Treaty—for Wilson's health see above, ch. 10, note 4; for the break with House, note 27; the break with Lansing, note 28.

Chapter 11. Readjustment

General books include Dixon Wecter, *When Johnny Comes Marching Home* (Boston, 1944), an obvious attempt to anticipate problems after World War II; James R. Mock and Evangeline Thurber, *Report on Demobilization* (Norman, Okla., 1944), with the same purpose; George Soule, *Prosperity Decade: From War to Depression, 1917–1929* (New York, 1947) and John D. Hicks, *Rehearsal for Disaster* (Gainesville, Fla., 1961), both examinations of the recession after World War I; Burl Noggle, *Into the Twenties: The United States from Armistice to Normalcy* (Urbana, Ill., 1974), a reappraisal of the domestic hiatus after World War I, a marvelously interesting time, neglected by historians of the twenties. The postwar recession appears in Elmus R. Wicker, *Federal Reserve Monetary Policy: 1917–1933* (New York, 1966); Paul P. Abrahams, "American Bankers and the Economic Tactics of Peace: 1919," *Journal of American History*, vol. 56 (1969–70), 572–583, the failure to finance European purchases; Gerd Hardach, *The First World War: 1914–1918* (Berkeley, Calif., 1977), masterful analysis, part of a projected six-volume history of the world economy in the twentieth century; W. Elliott Brownlee, *Dynamics of Ascent: A History of the American Economy* (2d ed., New York, 1979), superior economic history. For expansion of trade abroad see above, ch. 11, note 25. For the plight of American labor see Frank Stricker, "The Wages of Inflation: Workers Earnings in the World War One Era," *Mid-America*, vol. 63 (1981), 93–105, and above, ch. 11, notes 28–31.

The short-lived occupation is in Heath Twichell, Jr., *Allen: The Biography of an Army Officer, 1859–1930* (New Brunswick, N.J., 1974); Keith L. Nelson, *Victors Divided: America and the Allies in Germany, 1918–1923* (Berkeley and Los Angeles, 1975); Alfred E. Cornebise, *The Amaroc News: The Daily Newspaper of the American Forces in Germany, 1919–1923* (Carbondale, Ill., 1981); the same author's "*Der Rhein Entlang:* The American Occupation Forces in Germany, 1918–1923, a Photo Essay," *Military Affairs*, vol. 46 (1982), 183–189; and his *Typhus and Doughboys: The American Polish Typhus Relief Expedition, 1919–1921* (Newark, Del., 1982). For Army reorganization see Bernard L. Boylan, "Army Reorganization 1920: The Legislative Story," *Mid-America*, vol. 49 (1967), 115–128; Martin L. Fausold, *James W. Wadsworth, Jr.: The Gentleman from New York* (Syracuse, N.Y., 1975); I. B. Holley, Jr., *General John M. Palmer, Citizen Soldiers, and the Army of a Democracy* (Westport, Conn., 1982).

For woman suffrage see above, ch. 13, note 5; for prohibition, Virginius Dabney, *Dry Messiah: The Life of Bishop Cannon* (New York, 1949), together with James H. Timberlake, *Prohibition and the Progressive Movement: 1900–1920* (Cambridge, Mass., 1963), Lawrence W. Levine, *Defender of the Faith: William Jennings Bryan, The Last Decade, 1915–1925* (Lincoln, Nebr., 1969), Paolo E. Coletta, *William Jennings Bryan: Political Puritan, 1915–1925* (Lincoln, Nebr., 1969), Robert W. Cherny, *A Righteous Cause: The Life of William Jennings Bryan* (Boston, 1985); also David E. Kyvig, *Repealing National Prohibition* (Chicago, 1979), ch. 1; for influenza see A. A. Hoehling, *The Great Epidemic* (Boston, 1961); for general disillusion see Warren I. Cohen, *The American Revisionists: The Lessons of Intervention in World War I* (Chicago, 1967) and Stuart I. Rochester, *American Liberal Disillusionment in the Wake of World War I* (University Park, Penn., 1977); on the war debts, Denise Artaud, *La Question des dettes interalliées et la reconstruction de l'Europe (1917–1929)* (2 vols., Paris and Lille, 1978), a model study; and for its special subject, James F. Willis, *Prologue to Nuremberg: The Politics and Diplomacy of Punishing War Criminals of the First World War* (Westport, Conn., 1982).

Chapter 12. Civil Liberties and Civil Rights

The place to begin is such books as Robert K. Murray, *Red Scare: A Study in National Hysteria* (Minneapolis, Minn., 1955); H. C. Peterson and Gilbert C. Fite, *Opponents of War: 1917–1918* (Madison, Wisc., 1957); Harry N. Scheiber, *The Wilson Administration and Civil Liberties: 1917–1921* (Ithaca, N.Y., 1960); Paul L. Murphy, *The Constitution in Crisis Times: 1918–1969* (New York, 1972), a volume in the New American Nation series, and the same author's *World War I and the Origin of Civil Liberties* (New York, 1979). Stephen Vaughn, *Holding Fast the Inner Lines: Democracy, Nationalism, and the Committee on Public Information* (Chapel Hill, N.C., 1980) is definitive. For aspects large and small see Norman M. Thomas, *The Conscientious Objector in America* (New York, 1923); Frederic C. Howe, *Confessions of a Reformer* (New York, 1925) together with Neil Thorburn, "A Progressive and the First World War: Frederic C. Howe," *Mid-America*, vol. 51 (1964), 108–118; Ray H. Abrams, *Preachers Present Arms* (New York, 1933); Carl Wittke, *We Who Built America* (New York, 1939) and the same author's *German–Americans and the World War (with Special Emphasis on Ohio's German-Language Press* (Columbus, Ohio, 1936), together with Frederick C. Luebke, *Bonds of Loyalty: German–Americans and World War I* (De Kalb, Ill., 1974); Oswald Garrison Villard, *Fighting Years: Memoirs of a Liberal Editor* (New York, 1939) and Michael Wreszin, *Oswald Garrison Villard: Pacifist at War* (Bloomington, Ind., 1965); James R. Mock and Cedric Larson, *Words That Won the War: The Story of the Committee on Public Information, 1917–1919* (Princeton, N.J., 1939); James M. Read, *Atrocity Propaganda: 1914–1919* (New Haven, Conn., 1941); Guy F. Hershberger, *War, Peace, and Nonresistance* (Scottsdale, Penn., 1946); Ralph Chaplin, *Wobbly: The Rough-and-Tumble Story of an American Radical* (Chicago,

1948), a marvelous reminiscence of labor troubles in an awful era; Wayne A. Nicholas, "Crossroads Oratory: A Study of the Four-Minute Men of World War I," dissertation at Columbia University, 1954, together with Alfred E. Cornebise, *War as Advertised* (Philadelphia, 1984); John Higham, *Strangers in the Land: Patterns of American Nativism, 1860–1925* (New Brunswick, N.J., 1955), best on its interesting subject; Robert L. Morlan, *Political Prairie Fire: The Nonpartisan League, 1915–1922* (Minneapolis, Minn., 1955); Harold M. Hyman, *To Try Men's Souls: Loyalty Tests in American History* (Berkeley, Calif., 1959), pp. 267–315; Robert D. Ward, "The Origin and Activities of the National Security League, 1914–1919," *Mississippi Valley Historical Review*, vol. 47 (1960–61), 51–65; Richard Drinnon, *Rebel in Paradise: A Biography of Emma Goldman* (Chicago, 1961), a touching account of an idealist-anarchist; Charles Forcey, *The Crossroads of Liberalism: Croly, Weyl, Lippmann and the Progressive Era, 1900–1925* (New York, 1961); Warren I. Trattner, "Progressivism and World War I: A Reappraisal," *Mid-America*, vol. 44 (1962), 131–145; Donald O. Johnson, *The Challenge to American Freedoms: World War I and the Rise of the American Civil Liberties Union* (Lexington, Ky., 1963); William Preston, Jr., *Aliens and Dissenters: Federal Suppression of Radicals, 1903–1933* (Cambridge, Mass., 1963); Stanley Coben, *A. Mitchell Palmer: Politician* (New York, 1963); Charles Hirschfeld, "Nationalist Progressivism and World War I," *Mid-America*, vol. 45 (1963), 139–156; Edward L. Bernays, *Biography of an Idea* (New York, 1965), including the Committee on Public Information's effect on public relations; Joan M. Jensen, *The Price of Vigilance* (Chicago, 1968), on the American Protective League; George T. Blakey, *Historians on the Homefront: American Propagandists for the Great War* (Lexington, Ky., 1970) and Carol S. Gruber, *Mars and Minerva: World War I and the Uses of the Higher Learning in America* (Baton Rouge, La., 1975), embarrassing accounts of the subservience of scholarship to hysteria; Allan Teichroew, "World War I and the Mennonite Migration to Canada to Avoid the Draft," *Mennonite Quarterly Review*, vol. 45 (1971), 219–249; Niel M. Johnson, *Sylvester Viereck: German–American Propagandist* (Urbana, Ill., 1972); Bruce L. Larson, *Lindbergh of Minnesota: A Political Biography* (New York, 1973); Robert A. Rosenstone, *Romantic Revolutionary: A Biography of John Reed* (New York, 1975); David Williams, "The Bureau of Investigation and Its Critics, 1919–1921: The Origins of Federal Political Surveillance," *Journal of American History*, vol. 68 (1981–82), 560–579, newly released F.B.I. files.

On the life of black-Americans see Benjamin Brawley, *A Social History of the American Negro* (New York, 1921), pp. 341–371 and John Hope Franklin, *From Slavery to Freedom: A History of Negro Americans* (3d ed., New York, 1967), the best general account. For their special subjects, W. E. Burghardt Du Bois, "An Essay Toward a History of the Black Man in the Great War," *The Crisis*, vol. 18 (1919), 63–87, together with Francis L. Broderick, *W. E. B.*

Du Bois: Negro Leader in a Time of Crisis (Stanford, Calif., 1959); Emmett J. Scott, *The American Negro in the World War* (Cincinnati [?], 1919); Robert R. Moton, *Finding a Way Out: An Autobiography* (Garden City, N.Y., 1920); Charles H. Williams, *Sidelights on Negro Soldiers* (Boston, 1923), reprinted as *Negro Soldiers in World War I: The Human Side* (New York, 1970), very interesting account; Addie W. Hunton and Kathryn M. Johnson, *Two Colored Women with the American Expeditionary Forces* (Brooklyn, N.Y., n.d.); Chester D. Heywood, *Negro Combat Troops in the World War: The Story of the 371st Infantry* (Worcester, Mass., 1928); Arthur W. Little, *From Harlem to the Rhine: The Story of New York's Colored Volunteers* (New York, 1936); Perry L. Miles, *Fallen Leaves: Memories of an Old Soldier* (Berkeley, Calif., 1961), by the colonel of the 371st Infantry; Elliott M. Rudwick, *Race Riot at East St. Louis, July 2, 1917* (Carbondale, Ill., 1964); David M. Chalmers, *Hooded Americanism: The First Century of the Ku Klux Klan, 1865–1965* (Garden City, N.Y., 1965), pp. 28–38 on the Klan's revival; William M. Tuttle, Jr., *Race Riot: Chicago in the Red Summer of 1919* (New York, 1970); Arthur E. Barbeau and Florette Henri, *The Unknown Soldiers: Black American Troops in World War I* (Philadelphia, 1974), best for its subject; Nancy J. Weiss, *The National Urban League: 1910–1940* (New York, 1974), eloquent description of the wartime black migration, pp. 93–128, together with Florette Henri, *Black Migration: Movement North, 1900–1920* (New York, 1975); Theodore Kornweibel, Jr., *No Crystal Stair: Black Life and the Messenger, 1917–1928* (Westport, Conn., 1975) and the same author's "Apathy and Dissent: Black America's Negative Responses to World War I," *South Atlantic Quarterly*, vol. 80 (1981), 322–338; Robert V. Haynes, *A Night of Violence: The Houston Riot of 1917* (Baton Rouge, La., 1976); John Dittmer, *Black Georgia in the Progressive Era: 1900–1920* (Urbana, Ill., 1977); Robert L. Zangrando, *The NAACP Crusade Against Lynching: 1909–1950* (Philadelphia, 1980); Gerald W. Patton, *War and Race: The Black Officer in the American Military, 1915–1941* (Westport, Conn., 1981).

Chapter 13. The Election of 1920

General accounts of the election are Wesley M. Bagby, *The Road to Normalcy: The Presidential Campaign and Election of 1920* (Baltimore, 1962); and Donald R. McCoy, "Election of 1920," in Arthur M. Schlesinger, Jr., et al. (eds.), *History of American Presidential Elections, 1789–1968* (4 vols., New York, 1971), pp. 2349–2456. For the Republican victors see Francis Russell, *The Shadow of Blooming Grove: Warren G. Harding in His Times* (New York, 1968); Robert K. Murray, *The Harding Era: Warren G. Harding and His Administration* (Minneapolis, Minn., 1969) and the same author's *The Politics of Normalcy: Governmental Theory and Practice in the Harding–Coolidge Era* (New York, 1973); and for the Vice President, Donald R. McCoy, *Calvin Coolidge: The Quiet President* (New York, 1967).

Arthur F. Mullen, *Western Democrat* (New York, 1940) is very interesting because of its description of the San Francisco convention with its loudspeakers; William Allen White, *Autobiography* (New York, 1946) tells of a liberal's disappointments, for which see also Walter Johnson, *William Allen White's America* (New York, 1947) and Walter Johnson (ed.), *Selected Letters of William Allen White: 1899–1943* (New York, 1947); William T. Hutchinson, *Lowden of Illinois: The Life of Frank O. Lowden* (2 vols., Chicago, 1957) gives an intricate account of Lowden's failure at the convention; Kurt Wimer, "Woodrow Wilson and a Third Nomination," *Pennsylvania History*, vol. 29 (1962), 193–211, proof that Wilson desired nomination; Gene Smith, *When the Cheering Stopped: The Last Years of Woodrow Wilson* (New York, 1964), skillfully written; for Bryan the books by Levine, Coletta, and Cherny, cited earlier; Gary Dean Best, "The Hoover-for-President Boom of 1920," *Mid-America*, vol. 53 (1971), 227–244, not much of a boom. For its special subject, which ensured Coolidge's nomination, see Francis Russell, *A City in Terror: 1919, the Boston Police Strike* (New York, 1975).

The end of hostilities with the Central Powers is in Kurt Wimer and Sarah Wimer, "The Harding Administration, the League of Nations, and the Separate Peace Treaty," *Review of Politics*, vol. 29 (1967), 13–24; and Peter H. Buckingham, *International Normalcy: The Open Door Peace with the Former Central Powers, 1921–29* (Wilmington, Del., 1983).

Index

Abbott, Lyman, 205
Adjusted Compensation Act (1924), 178–179, 235
A.E.F. *See* American Expeditionary Forces
Airplanes, 110–113, 116, 184–185
Aisne-Marne, Battle of the (1918), 69, 73–77, 128, 181, 232
Alger, Russell A., 25
Alien Act (1918), 208
Alien Enemies Act (1798), 206–207
Allies, 9, 12–14, 37, 39, 52–53, 65, 86–88, 96, 102–103, 118–134, 159, 175, 179, 192, 196, 203, 235, 250; and food, 91–97. *See also* Paris Peace Conference (1919); Supreme War Council
Ambrosius, Lloyd E., 275
American Chicle Company, 93
American Civil Liberties Union, 207
American College of Surgeons, 103
American Expeditionary Forces, 15–16, 22, 25, 30, 108–117, 119, 133, 179–181, 186, 252; amalgamation with Allies, 122–124; battle, 65–83; and black Americans, 20, 214–216; organization, 48–64. *See also* Pershing, John J.; Services of Supply
American Federation of Labor, 103, 194
American Geographical Society, 141
American Historical Association, 203
Americanism. *See* Civil liberties; Civil rights
American Legion, 179
American Protective League, 18

American Revolution, 3, 234
American Socialist (newspaper), 208
American Telephone and Telegraph Company, 103
American Vanadium Company, 106
America's Answer (film), 202
Anarchism, 20, 212. *See also* Red Scare
Anti-Saloon League, 189
Arabic (ship), 11–12
Argentina, 5, 11, 91, 96
Armenia, 268
Armistice (1918), 132–134, 138, 157, 164, 183, 193, 195, 197, 216, 265. *See also* Prearmistice agreement
Artillery, 109–110, 116
Asquith, Herbert, 152, 165
Associates. *See* Allies
Athenaeum of Indiana. *See* Deutsches Haus of Indianapolis
Atlanta University, 218
Atlantic Monthly (magazine), 1
Attack in Position Warfare (manual), 68
Atterbury, William W., 60
Auchincloss, Gordon, 280
Australia, 5, 11, 91, 96, 150
Austria, 230
Austria-Hungary, 7–8, 43, 125–126, 146–147. *See also* Austria; Central Powers; Czechoslovakia
Axson, Stockton, 9, 136, 162, 171, 220, 223, 229, 292–293

Bach, Johann Sebastian, 206
Bacon, Robert, 250
Baker, Newton D., 16–17, 22, 26–27, 29, 31, 51, 53, 57, 104–106,

Smoot, Reed, 8, 229–230
Smuts, Jan C., 142–143, 153, 165, 283
Socialism, 130–131, 201, 208–211, 219
Soissons, Battle of (1918). See
Aisne-Marne
Somervell, Brehon B., 244
Somme, Battle of the (1916), 13–14,
68, 232
Sonnino, Sidney, 146–147
Sons of the American Revolution, 212
Sorbonne, University of the, 165
Sousa, John Philip, 32
South Africa, Union of, 143
Soviet Russia. See Russia
Spain, 61, 187, 203
Spanish-American War (1898), 14,
24–25, 32, 49–50, 61, 102–103, 136,
183, 200, 214, 233–234. See
McKinley, William; Rough Riders;
Santiago
Springfield Model 1903 rifle, 108–109
Spring Rice, Cecil, 46, 57, 122, 239,
256
Stallings, Lawrence, 110
Stanford University, 95
Stanley, Augustus O., 295
Stanton, C. E., 179
Stars and Stripes (newspaper), 133, 216
Steel strike (1919), 195–196, 229, 287
Stengel, Alfred, 161
Stettinius, Edward R., 108
Stimson, Henry L., 15, 25, 228, 233
Stokowski, Leopold, 206
Storyville (New Orleans), 21
Strong, Benjamin, 90
Sugar Equalization Board, 257–258
Sullivan, Mark, 85, 202
Summerall, Charles P., 83
Sunday, Billy, 32, 190, 205
Supreme Court, 1–2, 171, 181,
208–209
Supreme War Council, 27, 121–122,
126, 131–132, 262
Switzerland, 29, 66, 130, 137
Sykes-Picot Agreement (1916),
143–144
Syria, 140, 143–144, 267

Taft, William H., 7, 25, 133, 136–138,
162, 172–173, 194, 200–201, 212
Tank, 110, 116
Tardieu, André, 121
Taylor, Zachary, 171
Terman, Lewis M., 20
Third Division, 72
Thrity-fifth Division, 179–180
Thomason, John W., 181
Thompson, Charles T., 170
Thompson-Starrett Company, 115–116
Thorne, Robert J., 28–29

Thrift stamps, 86
Ticonderoga (ship), 40–41
Titanic (ship), 40
Townley, Arthur C., 209–210
Trading-with-the-Enemy Act (1917),
207–208
Trans-Siberian Railroad, 126
Transylvania. See Hungary; Rumania
Trianon, Treaty of (1920). See Paris
Peace Conference
Trieste, 147, 270
Trinity Episcopal Church
(Independence, Mo.), 180
Truman, Bess W. (Mrs. Harry S.),
180
Truman, Harry S., 179–180, 188, 199,
234–235, 288
Truman, Martha Ellen, 288
Truman, Mary Jane, 288
Tumulty, Joseph P., 51, 125–136, 169,
171, 206, 258, 278, 283, 294–295,
297
Turkey, 91, 141, 143–144, 230, 267.
See also Central Powers
Tuscania (ship), 40–41
Tuskegee Institute, 218
Twenty-eigthth Division, 122
Twenty-ninth Division, 261
Twenty-sixth Division, 56, 261. See also
Edwards, Clarence R.
Tyrrell, William, 279

Under Four Flags (film), 202
Underwood-Simmons Tariff (1914),
191
Union League (New York), 204
Union of Russian Workers, 211–212
Union Railroad, 195–196
United Nations Charter, 157, 166, 234
United States Steel Corporation,
194–195
Urban League (Chicago), 217
U.S. Army, 1, 11, 93, 101, 104–108,
119, 138, 196–197, 200, 206–209,
220, 232, 234–235, 241–242, 245,
260, 262, 278–279, 285–286; arms,
102–117; black Americans, 213–216,
293–294; demobilization, 178–181;
occupation of Germany, 181–183;
postwar reorganization, 183,
185–187; preparation for war,
13–30. See also Aisne-Marne;
American Expeditionary Forces;
armies, corps, divisions (numbered);
Baker, Newton D.; Belleau Wood;
Cantigny; Château-Thierry; March,
Peyton C.; Meuse-Argonne;
Oise-Aisne campaign; Pershing, John
J.; St. Mihiel; Vaux
U.S. Employment Service, 178

PHOTO CREDITS